THE
HISTORY OF
THE BALTIC STATES

THE
HISTORY OF
THE BALTIC STATES

Second Edition

Kevin C. O'Connor

The Greenwood Histories of the Modern Nations
Frank W. Thackeray and John E. Findling, Series Editors

 GREENWOOD™

An Imprint of ABC-CLIO, LLC
Santa Barbara, California • Denver, Colorado

Library of Congress Cataloging-in-Publication Data

O'Connor, Kevin, 1967–
    The history of the Baltic States / Kevin C. O'Connor. — Second edition.
        pages cm. — (The Greenwood histories of the modern nations)
    Includes bibliographical references and index.
    ISBN 978-1-61069-915-0 (acid-free paper) — ISBN 978-1-61069-916-7 (electronic)
1. Baltic States—History.   I. Title.
    DK502.7.O2   2015
    947.9—dc23   2014048417

ISBN: 978-1-61069-915-0
EISBN: 978-1-61069-916-7

19 18 17 16 15   1 2 3 4 5

This book is also available on the World Wide Web as an eBook.
Visit www.abc-clio.com for details.

Greenwood
An Imprint of ABC-CLIO, LLC

ABC-CLIO, LLC
130 Cremona Drive, P.O. Box 1911
Santa Barbara, California 93116-1911

This book is printed on acid-free paper ∞

Manufactured in the United States of America

Contents

Series Foreword

The Greenwood Histories of the Modern Nations series is intended to provide students and interested laypeople with up-to-date, concise, and analytical histories of many of the nations of the contemporary world. Not since the 1960s has there been a systematic attempt to publish a series of national histories, and as series editors, we believe that this series will prove to be a valuable contribution to our understanding of other countries in our increasingly interdependent world.

At the end of the 1960s, the Cold War was an accepted reality of global politics. The process of decolonization was still in progress, the idea of a unified Europe with a single currency was unheard of, the United States was mired in a war in Vietnam, and the economic boom in Asia was still years in the future. Richard Nixon was president of the United States, Mao Tse-tung (not yet Mao Zedong) ruled China, Leonid Brezhnev guided the Soviet Union, and Harold Wilson was prime minister of the United Kingdom. Authoritarian dictators still controlled most of Latin America, the Middle East was reeling in the wake of the Six-Day War, and Shah Mohammad Reza Pahlavi was at the height of his power in Iran.

Since then, the Cold War has ended, the Soviet Union has vanished, leaving 15 independent republics in its wake, the advent of the computer age has radically transformed global communications, the rising demand for oil makes the Middle East still a dangerous flashpoint, and the rise of new economic powers like the People's Republic of China and India threatens to bring about a new world order. All of these developments have had a dramatic impact on the recent history of every nation of the world.

For this series, which was launched in 1998, we first selected nations whose political, economic, and sociocultural affairs marked them as among the most important of our time. For each nation, we found an author who was recognized as a specialist in the history of that nation. These authors worked cooperatively with us and with Greenwood Press to produce volumes that reflected current research on their nations and that are interesting and informative to their readers. In the first decade of the series, close to 50 volumes were published, and some have now moved into second editions.

The success of the series has encouraged us to broaden our scope to include additional nations, whose histories have had significant effects on their regions, if not on the entire world. In addition, geopolitical changes have elevated other nations into positions of greater importance in world affairs and, so, we have chosen to include them in this series as well. The importance of a series such as this cannot be underestimated. As a superpower whose influence is felt all over the world, the United States can claim a "special" relationship with almost every other nation. Yet many Americans know very little about the histories of nations with which the United States relates. How did these nations get to be the way they are? What kind of political systems have evolved there? What kind of influence do they have on their own regions? What are the dominant political, religious, and cultural forces that move their leaders? These and many other questions are answered in the volumes of this series.

The authors who contribute to this series write comprehensive histories of their nations, dating back, in some instances, to prehistoric times. Each of them, however, has devoted a significant portion of their book to events of the past 40 years because the modern era has contributed the most to contemporary issues that have an impact on U.S. policy. Authors make every effort to be as up-to-date as possible so that readers can benefit from discussion and analysis of recent events.

In addition to the historical narrative, each volume contains an introductory chapter giving an overview of that country's geography, political institutions, economic structure, and cultural attributes. This is meant to give readers a snapshot of the nation as it exists in the contemporary world. Each history also includes supplementary information following the narrative, which may include a timeline that represents a succinct chronology of the nation's historical evolution, biographical sketches of the nation's most important historical figures, and a glossary of important terms or concepts that are usually expressed in a foreign language. Finally, each author prepares a comprehensive bibliography for readers who wish to pursue the subject further.

Readers of these volumes will find them fascinating and well written. More importantly, they will come away with a better understanding of the contemporary world and the nations that comprise it. As series editors, we hope that this series will contribute to a heightened sense of global understanding as we move through the early years of the 21st century.

Frank W. Thackeray and John E. Findling
Indiana University Southeast

Preface

As it is not unusual for scholars to nurture a deep interest in the history and traditions of their ancestral homelands, many of the people who have written about the Baltic states were either born in the region or enjoy some sort of family connection with it. My only personal links to these fascinating little countries are the ones I have made since I first visited the area in the summer of 2002, not long after completing a doctorate in Russian/Soviet history. As anomalous as it may seem in a field that is populated by individuals with recognizably Lithuanian, Latvian, and Estonian names, this book was written not by someone whose formal training was in the area of Baltic history, but by an historian of Russia with a conspicuously Irish name who is interested in the concept of national identity and, in that context, in the relationship between Russia and the peoples living in or near its western borderlands.

This book, however, is not about Russia, although Russia is surely present throughout. Its subjects are the three Baltic countries and the many peoples who have lived in the region over the past millennium. More specifically, it portrays the struggles of three tiny nations in a remote corner of northeastern Europe to create distinctive identities for themselves and to secure and maintain their national independence from the wars and revolutions of the 20th century through recent times. I have attempted to consider these developments not through the lens of St. Petersburg or Moscow, nor from the vantage point of Vilnius, Tallinn, or Riga (even if Riga is very much at the heart both of the region and of this book), but rather from the perspective of a U.S. academic writing primarily for a general audience. Readers will note that I do not shy from discussing controversial topics surrounding the Holocaust, the Soviet occupation, and the challenges facing the Russian-speaking communities in Estonia and Latvia today, even where doing so may offend nationalist sensibilities. While making full disclosure of my admiration for the Baltic states' courage in their struggles against foreign oppression, I intend to provide the readers of this book with a balanced, truthful, and hopefully illuminating portrayal of the eastern Baltic region's remarkable journey from medieval times to the 21st century. Whether I have done so fairly and accurately I leave to the reader to judge.

I wish to thank the many people who have helped in ways great and small in the preparation of the first two editions of this book manuscript. I am grateful first of all to those scholars, many of whose names are mentioned in the narrative that follows, whose erudition informs all aspects of the present volume. A very personal thank you to Ted Weeks and Māris Goldmanis, fine historians in their own right, who took the time to read and comment on early drafts of some of the chapters that comprise the second edition. Any errors that remain are my own responsibility.

Finally, a note on names and spellings. For Latvian and Lithuanian words I have retained all diacritical marks: thus *Sąjūdis* rather than *Sajudis,* and so on. One exception is the city of Rīga, which appears here as Riga. Cities and towns are usually rendered by the modern local designation (e.g., Tartu), with alternate names following in parentheses (Ger. *Dorpat*). When romanizing most Russian words and names I have used the Library of Congress transliteration system, although I have chosen to use more familiar forms where appropriate (e.g., Yeltsin instead of Iel'tsin). In most cases I have provided the English version of familiar names (e.g., Alexander rather than Aleksandr).

Timeline of Historical Events

ca. 3000–2000 BCE	Finno-Ugric and proto-Baltic tribes settle on the Baltic shores.
8th–12th centuries	Baltic peoples trade and battle with Scandinavian Vikings and later with Slavic tribes.
1180s	Efforts by the German priest Meinhard to convert the Livonians.
1198	Pope Innocent III sanctions a Baltic crusade that soon results in the Christianization of the Latvian and Estonian tribes.
13th century	Latvia and southern Estonia are conquered by Germans, who become the region's nobility. Danes conquer northern Estonia.
1201	Albert von Buxhoevden, the third bishop of Livonia, founds the city of Riga.
1227	Danes complete the conquest of Estonia.
1253	Mindaugas is crowned the first and only king of Lithuania.
14th century	Lithuanian territory is extended southward to the Black Sea.

1316–1341	Grand Duke Gediminas rules Lithuania; encourages traders and merchants, including Jews, to settle in the region.
1343–1345	Estonian peasant uprising forces Danes to surrender control of northern Estonia to Germans.
1386	The Lithuanian grand duke Jogaila marries into the Polish royal family, thus establishing a nominal union between Lithuania and Poland. Lithuania, Europe's last pagan kingdom, accepts Christianity.
1410	Lithuania's victory over the Teutonic Knights prevents further German expansion eastward.
1418	Founding of the Livonian Confederation.
1520s	The Protestant Reformation reaches the Baltic region.
1558–1583	Russian tsar Ivan IV attempts to conquer Livonia, but is checked by Sweden and Poland. The Livonian Confederation is dissolved and most of Livonia is incorporated into Poland-Lithuania.
1561	Sweden acquires Tallinn and surrounding region. Riga is awarded the status of free city until 1581, when it is acquired by Poland.
1569	The Lithuanian and Polish crowns formally unite to form the Polish-Lithuanian Commonwealth.
1579	Vilnius (Wilno) University is established.
1584	Sweden annexes northern Estonia, creating the Duchy of Estland.
1629	Poland cedes Livonia (Livland) to Sweden.
1632	Swedes found Tartu (Dorpat) University in the Duchy of Estland.
1699	Dissolution of the Hanseatic League.
1710	Russian tsar Peter I seizes the Swedish provinces of Estland and Livland during the Great Northern War.
1772–1795	Prussia, Austria, and Russia partition Poland. Lithuania and Courland (western Latvia) come under Russian rule.
1816–1819	Following the Russian defeat of Napoleon, serfdom is formally abolished in Estland and Livland.

1820s	Newspapers begin to be published in the Estonian and Latvian languages.
1857–1861	Publication of the Estonian national epic *Kalevipoeg*.
1860s	The "Young Latvians" movement spurs the Latvian national awakening.
1861	Lithuanian peasants are freed along with the remainder of Russia's serfs.
1863–1864	Polish insurrection, aided by Lithuanian peasants.
1867–1868	A famine is followed by the massive emigration of Lithuanians.
June 1869	The first Estonian song festival is held at Tartu.
1880s–1890s	Russification policies are implemented in the Baltic territories.
1888	Publication of the Latvian folk epic *Lāčplēsis*.
1905–1907	Revolution in St. Petersburg gives rise to unrest in the Baltic provinces; thousands of suspected rebels are punished.
1915	German soldiers occupy Lithuania and the western part of Latvia during World War I.
March 1917	Russian tsar Nicholas II abdicates the throne as the tsarist regime collapses; nationalist forces become active in the Lithuanian and Baltic provinces.
November 1917	Bolsheviks seize power in Russia.
1918	Lithuania (February 16), Estonia (February 21), and Latvia (November 18) declare their independence.
March 1918	Treaty of Brest-Litovsk ends Russia's war with Germany and compels it to surrender its western borderlands.
1918–1920	Baltic states fight the Bolsheviks, White Russian armies, and German and Polish forces to defend their independence.
1919–1922	The new Baltic governments carry out land reform and introduce democratic constitutions.
January 1923	Lithuania annexes the Klaipėda (Memel) region, formerly under international control.
1926–1929	Antanas Smetona establishes dictatorship in Lithuania.

1934	Konstantin Päts (March) and Kārlis Ulmanis (May) establish dictatorships in Estonia and Latvia.
Aug.–Sept. 1939	Nazi-Soviet nonaggression pact; secret protocols award the Baltic states to Stalin's USSR.
Winter 1939–1940	Baltic Germans are evacuated to German-held territory.
Summer 1940	Baltic states are occupied by Soviet troops, then annexed to USSR. The "Year of Terror" begins.
June 1941	Massive deportations of Baltic peoples to Soviet Russia.
1941–1944	Nazi occupation of the Baltic states. Nearly the entire Jewish populations of these countries are murdered.
1944	Soviet forces reoccupy Baltic states. Westward flight of thousands of Balts continues through 1945.
1944–1948	"Forest brothers" resist Soviet occupation. A few bands continue to resist into the mid-1950s.
1944–1952	Mass deportation of Estonians, Latvians, and Lithuanians to other Soviet republics. This is accompanied by industrialization and the first waves of Russian and other Slavic immigrants.
1947–1952	Collectivization of agriculture is carried out in the Baltic republics.
1949–1951	Bloody purge of "bourgeois nationalists" from the Communist Party of Estonia.
1955–1964	Khrushchev's "thaw" loosens ideological restrictions throughout the USSR. Cultural life begins to recover in the Baltic republics.
1959–1961	Nonlethal purge of the Communist Party of Latvia.
1960s–1970s	Years of economic growth and political stability. Dissident movements appear in the Baltic republics.
1987–1991	The "Singing Revolution" draws the world's attention to the plight of the Baltic republics.
April–June 1988	Popular Fronts are formed in Estonia and Latvia. *Sąjūdis* is formed in Lithuania.
August 23, 1989	"Baltic Way" demonstration unites up to two million Balts in protest against the Nazi-Soviet pact of August 1939.

March 1990	Elections to Baltic parliaments. Lithuania is the first of the Baltic republics to declare its secession from the USSR.
April–June 1990	Soviet embargo is imposed on Lithuania.
January 1991	Soviet paratroopers and KGB units attack the Vilnius television tower; confrontations also take place in Riga.
February–March 1991	Baltic republics hold referenda in which citizens vote overwhelmingly in favor of independence.
August 19–21, 1991	An attempt to depose Gorbachev while he is vacationing fails. Gorbachev subsequently dissolves the Communist Party.
September 6, 1991	The USSR formally recognizes the independence of the Baltic states.
December 31, 1991	Commonwealth of Independent States is created to replace the USSR. Baltic states opt not to join.
1992–1993	Baltic economies hit bottom: high inflation and unemployment, declining production. New constitutions are adopted and elections are held. Peak of Russian emigration from Baltic states.
August 1994	Russian troop withdrawal from the Baltics is completed.
September 28, 1994	A passenger ferry, the *Estonia*, sinks to the bottom of the Baltic Sea, killing 852 people.
May 1995	Collapse of Baltija Bank sets off banking crisis in Latvia.
August 1998	Russian economic crisis temporarily interrupts economic recovery of Baltic states.
July 1999	Latvia elects first woman president of east central Europe, Vaira Vīķe-Freiberga.
2000–2007	Baltic states enjoy the highest economic growth rates in Europe.
March 29, 2004	Baltic states are admitted to the European Union.
May 1, 2004	Baltic states join NATO.
April 2007	A riot breaks out in Tallinn as the government attempts to relocate a Soviet war memorial.

2008–2010	Global economic crisis devastates the Baltic states.
January 2009	Antigovernment protests in Riga and Vilnius.
January 2011	Estonia joins the euro zone. Latvia follows in 2014 and Lithuania in 2015.
September 2011	Pro-Russian party Harmony Centre wins Latvia's parliamentary elections but fails to enter the governing coalition.
March 2014	Russia's seizure of Crimea and the appearance of a separatist movement in eastern Ukraine alarms citizens of the Baltic states.

The Baltic Provinces of the Russian Empire c. 1850. Courtesy of Cartographica.

Expansion of Lithuania to 1430. Courtesy of Cartographica.

Legend:
- Medieval Livonia c. 1500
- Livonian Order
- Bishopric of Kurland
- Archbishopric of Riga
- Bishopric of Saare–Lääne
- Bishopric of Tartu

Medieval Livonia c. 1500. Courtesy of Cartographica.

The Baltic Region before and after World War II. Courtesy of Cartographica.

1

Unknown Europe

GEOGRAPHY, CLIMATE, AND POPULATION

The subjects of this book are three small and little-known countries in northeastern Europe: from north to south, they are Estonia, Latvia, and Lithuania. Because of their location along the eastern coast of the Baltic Sea—an immense inland lake that was first called *Mare Balticum* by German chroniclers in the 11th century—and the intertwined history they have shared in recent times, they are usually called the Baltic states, or simply "the Baltics." Estonia, the smallest of the three in size, is roughly comparable to Vermont and New Hampshire combined. Lithuania is only slightly bigger than Latvia, and each is about the same size as West Virginia. The geographical location of the Baltic states, across the sea from Scandinavia and between central Europe and Russia, has exerted a profound influence on their cultural and economic development and continues to affect their identities and their sense of security.

The region's topography has few outstanding features apart from 2,750 miles of coast and over 1,000 Estonian islands. The terrain is low and flat, the highest points barely reaching 1,000 feet. While Lithuania, despite its numerous lakes and swamps, has the most arable land and is the most reliant on agriculture, Estonia and Latvia are more heavily forested, with timber and wood products historically being among their most important commodity exports.

The climate of the eastern Baltic is temperate. Throughout the region winters are moderate and the temperature on summer days range from cool to warm (but rarely hot), but whatever the season the Baltic states are often wet. Even on uncommonly sunny summer days a brief shower may be in the offing. While the sun sets early during the dark Baltic winters, in mid-summer Estonians enjoy 19 hours of sunlight a day. As in the Nordic countries, the Baltic growing season is short, resulting in difficult agricultural conditions and often poor production prior to the 19th century.

In 1989, the Baltic countries, then republics of the Soviet Union, were together home to just under eight million people, a figure comparable to the populations of present-day Switzerland or Israel. Unfavorable demographic trends since the end of the Soviet era, however, have contributed to an alarming decline in the populations of all three states, which by the year 2014 had dropped below 6.3 million—a loss of about 20 percent. Part of this decline has been due to emigration, a phenomenon that has affected Latvia and Lithuania far more than Estonia. An initial exodus after the Soviet collapse saw tens of thousands of Russian speakers depart for Russia—in effect, a reversal of the migratory trends of the postwar decades—while a second wave of emigration occurred after the Baltic states' entry into the European Union in 2004. Mostly young and male, these migrants seek employment opportunities and wages that they often cannot find in their places of birth. A decline in life expectancy in the early 1990s also contributed to the contraction of the Baltic populations, but this was corrected by the end of the millennium. Nevertheless, the fertility rate of women has continued to decline in the Baltic states, where urban dwellings are small, divorces are almost as common as marriages, and large families are atypical.

PEOPLES OF THE BALTIC REGION

The Baltic countries remain unfamiliar terrain to most Westerners, who often confuse them with the equally unfamiliar Balkans. There are understandable reasons for the error. Aside from the obvious fact that the words "Baltic" and "Balkan" sound somewhat alike to the Anglophone ear, both the Balkans and the Baltics lie at a European crossroad, and as such each region has been both a transmitter of culture and a victim of the aspirations of larger and more powerful neighbors. Furthermore, the peoples of northeastern Europe, like those of southeastern Europe, have historically been ethnically and religiously diverse, and as a result all continue to struggle with questions concerning national and state identity.

A significant difference in their historical experiences, however, distinguishes the peoples of these poorly understood regions: while the peoples of the Balkans have frequently fought among themselves during the past century and a half, the native peoples of the territories that now comprise the Baltic states—that is, the Lithuanians, Latvians, and Estonians—enjoy amicable relations with each other. Indeed, while the nations that once constituted Yugoslavia plunged into war in the 1990s, the Baltic states have enjoyed a period of peace, if not exactly universal prosperity, since the end of Soviet rule. Having "returned to Europe" after half a century of foreign domination, the Baltic states remain committed to preserving the spirit of cooperation and solidarity that emerged during the struggle to regain their independence a quarter century ago.

The term "Baltic states" dates to the end of World War I, when Lithuania, Latvia, Estonia, and Finland (which at the time was often grouped with them) secured their independence from the Russian Empire. As a geographical descriptor, the appellation is problematic, for Sweden and Denmark surely have an equally legitimate claim (one that has not been exercised) to being "Baltic states." Moreover, from the beginning, the term "Baltic states" (sometimes rendered as Baltic States with a capital "S," a spelling that suggests, incorrectly, that the three states are politically joined) was understood as an outsiders' construct that blurred the distinctions between countries that are each unique in their own right. Nevertheless, the term "Baltic states" stuck and was cemented during the era of Soviet rule, during which Estonia, Latvia, and Lithuania (but not Finland) were welded together into a region that the Russians called *Sovetskaia Pribaltika*. It should be noted, however, that unlike the Latvians and Lithuanians, Estonians are not, strictly speaking, a "Baltic" people in the ethno-linguistic sense (see below). However, it is customary to refer Estonia as a "Baltic state" in the political and geographical senses.

Still more troubling is the concept of a "Baltic identity," a concept imposed by outsiders for the sake of convenience but one that is foreign to the peoples of the region. "There is little tangible Baltic identity on the ground in Estonia, Latvia or Lithuania; the number of people that would exclusively identify themselves as Baltic is infinitesimally small," Aldis Purs, a Latvian scholar, wryly observes. Nevertheless, these states "are forced to live with the Baltic concept because others insist on using it."[1]

Attempts by outsiders to impose their power, languages, and ideas are nothing new in the Baltics. Indeed, one of the region's defining features, one that was particularly apparent during the Soviet era, is the influx of foreigners whose arrival was typically preceded by bloody conquest. Having established themselves in northeastern Europe by sword in the early 13th century, the Baltic Germans, who by the 19th century had begun to identify themselves as *Deutschbalten, Baltendeutsche,* or simply *Balten,* constituted the region's elite for 700 years and profoundly influenced the cultures of Latvia and Estonia. By 1940, however, the German presence had all but vanished, and the Soviet conquest that followed was accompanied by the extensive immigration to the Sovietized Baltic republics of Russian-speakers— a term that refers to peoples hailing from Russia, Ukraine, and Belarus. Jews were once very prominent in the cultural and economic life of Lithuania and Latvia, but nearly all were killed during World War II. Sweden, which ruled Estonia and much of Latvia for a century, and Poland, to which Lithuania was adjoined for much of its history, have also shaped the region's history.

Of the three Baltic countries, only Lithuania can make the claim of having enjoyed a period of national sovereignty before the 20th century. It remains a point of pride for Lithuanians that at the end of the Middle Ages the state created by their ancestors was Europe's largest. By the 16th century, however, its history was tied closely to that of Poland, and by the end of the 18th century the Polish-Lithuanian Commonwealth (Pol. *Rzeczpospolita*) had disappeared from the map, with most of the Lithuanian areas (and most of Poland proper) being absorbed by the Russian Empire. Latvia and Estonia, on the other hand, are relative newcomers to the community of independent European states. Before creating their own states at the end of World War I, Latvians and Estonians had spent five centuries under the rule of German barons, followed by nearly 300 years of Russian domination. From 1918 to 1940, during a brief period of German and Russian weakness, all three Baltic countries were independent, and since 1991, when the Soviet Union suddenly imploded, they have enjoyed their independence once again.

Through it all, Estonians, Latvians, and Lithuanians, whether they live at home or abroad, have maintained an attachment to their ancestral homelands and are proud guardians of their national cultures. Although they have shared, to some extent, a common historical experience during the past century, each of the Baltic peoples is unique. As noted, Lithuanians and Latvians are the only remaining "Baltic" peoples in the linguistic sense. They alone speak languages that are properly classified as "Baltic," a term that acquired a philological and linguistic meaning only in the early 19th century when German scholars designated it a branch of the Indo-European family of languages. Whereas Lithuanians have been ethnically distinct since at least the 13th century, the Latvian people (*Letten,* as they were called by their German rulers) formed during the Middle Ages from the convergence of several Baltic tribes. Linguistically and culturally related to the Lithuanian and Latvian tribes were the ancient Prussians, who were also once speakers of a "Baltic" tongue, but following the Germanic conquest they were largely assimilated and disappeared as a distinct nationality.

As a Finno-Ugric language, Estonian is completely unrelated to the languages spoken by the Latvians and Lithuanians, but it is closely related to Finnish and is more distantly related to Hungarian. The Estonians' linguistic cousins also include the Livonians (or Livs), who once lived in northern Latvia but gradually assimilated into the neighboring Latvian tribes. While hundreds of Latvians claim Livonian ancestry, the last communities to use the Livonian language in everyday speech died out in the 19th century. A few elderly people living in tiny communities on the Kurzeme (Courland) coast have tried to maintain Livonian traditions, but they are the last.

Religious affiliation in the Baltic countries is almost as diverse as ethnicity. Estonians and western Latvians tend to be Lutheran, while most Latgallians, a group in southeastern Latvia that speaks a distinct dialect of Latvian (some argue that Latgallian is in fact a distinct language), and nearly all Lithuanians are Catholic. The Russians of all three Baltic states usually identify as Orthodox. Judaism all but disappeared in the region during World War II; in more recent decades much of Lithuania's residual community emigrated to Israel, leaving only a small number of Jews in Latvia (10,000) and Lithuania (5,000) today, most of whom arrived during the Soviet era. If during the Middle Ages the religiously tolerant Grand Duchy of Lithuania was home to thriving communities of Muslims, the presence of Islam was barely detectable in the Soviet Baltic republics. While even today Islam has not become a major presence in Baltic capitals in the way it has in Paris, Amsterdam, and London, Muslim populations are growing in all three Baltic states despite their vastly underreported official numbers. Hare Krishnas and other sects, completely unknown during Soviet times, can occasionally be found singing and dancing in larger cities such as Tallinn and Riga. The amplification systems they often carry with them ensure that their joyful chants can be heard from a considerable distance.

CHANGE AND PROSPECTS

The spectacle of exotica such as dancing and singing Hare Krishnas testifies to the profound changes that have swept over the region since the early 1990s. Long gone are the bronze figures of Lenin and local communist leaders, all of which were toppled as the Soviet Union collapsed. Such tributes to Soviet power have been replaced by statues of Baltic national heroes—mostly writers, artists, and musicians of the 19th and early 20th centuries—and monuments commemorating the Baltic states' struggle for freedom from foreign oppressors. The historic sections of Vilnius, Lithuania (pop. 580,000), Riga, Latvia (796,000), and Tallinn, Estonia (408,000) have each undergone a stunning transformation: cathedrals and other historic buildings have been restored while dozens of new and refurbished hotels, restaurants, bars, and clubs cater to tourists hailing from Finland, Scandinavia, western Europe, North America, Russia, and elsewhere. The changes, however, are far deeper than a mere fresh coat of paint: since 1991 democracy has been restored to the region, and with that the people's freedom to choose.

From the bell tower of Tallinn's Council Hall, which provides the visitor with a panoramic view of this charming, brightly colored Hanseatic town, one sees a healthy and prosperous "European" city—one that has benefited not only from the optimism of Scandinavian investors and the credit cards of thousands of vacationing Finns, but also from the foresight of its political leaders. The prosperity of Estonia's largest city, however, stands in stark contrast to the stagnation of southeastern Estonia or the abject poverty of Latvia's Latgale (Latgallia) region, which suffers from high unemployment and a dearth of entrepreneurial initiative. Indeed, throughout the Baltic region thousands of young people are abandoning the countryside for the opportunities they hope to find in the cities (or in western Europe). Behind them they sometimes leave those who have been less able to adapt to the changed circumstances, including the old and infirm—as well as tens of thousands of acres of deserted farmland. But even life in the cities, despite their tidy public spaces and well-stocked stores, has its drawbacks. Unlike during Soviet times, gainful employment is far from guaranteed, as one generation discovered in the early 1990s and another learned in the wake of the global financial crash of 2008. Meanwhile, millions still live in decaying Soviet-era housing developments and nearly as many live quiet lives in rural poverty.

Despite these negative factors, in the past quarter century the Baltic states managed to overhaul their centralized economies, set up durable, democratic political systems, and opened their societies to the outside world. Estonians arguably possess the best-developed sense of national identity among the Baltic peoples, and in embarking upon the massive project of transforming their country's economic profile (and its prospects for admission to Western institutions) it is Estonia that acted most decisively and has advanced most rapidly. Estonians were the first to close their unprofitable factories and privatize the remainder; they set their gaze westward and cut most of their economic ties with Russia. As one of the "Baltic tigers" that experienced an economic boom in the early years of the 21st century, in 2014 Estonia (33rd) was ranked slightly higher than its southern neighbors (Lithuania is 35th and Latvia 48th) on the United Nations' Human Development Index. Estonia also has one of Europe's tech-savviest governments and is a world leader in digital openness.

Political stability has also been one of Estonia's great blessings over the past decade. Although dozens of parties have contended for seats in the Estonian parliament, called the *Riigikogu*, and numerous prime ministers have come and gone, a sense of continuity has been provided by the Estonian presidency, the office of which was occupied by Lennart Meri for nearly the entirety of the first post-Soviet decade and later by Toomas Hendrik Ilves, a polyglot former diplomat who has been in office since 2006.

Lithuania, the boldest of the Baltic republics in its struggle with Moscow in 1990–1991, entered the post-Soviet era at a somewhat lower level of economic development than Latvia or Estonia, its public sector continuing to dominate the Lithuanian economy well into the 1990s. By the dawn of the 21st century, however, Lithuania's economy had made decisive moves toward privatizing public assets and had recovered from a series of setbacks—including a banking crisis in 1995 and fallout from Russia's economic shock of 1998. While the Lithuanian economy has attained a rough parity with that of Latvia, both the Lithuanian and Latvian economies have struggled to keep pace with that of Estonia. All three countries experienced grave economic and social challenges following the global financial crash of 2008—not least of them being a devastating decline in GDP and skyrocketing unemployment; yet each also enjoyed some of the most impressive economic growth rates in Europe after 2010.

The relationships *between* the Baltic states have been marked by cooperation in the economic, cultural, and diplomatic spheres. However, *within* the Baltic states, and particularly in Latvia and Estonia, tensions

among the national groups have sometimes been inflamed over issues concerning rights, economic opportunities, language, and history. Lithuanians are often noted for the fervor with which they have
sometimes expressed their patriotism, yet nationalist tendencies are
restrained by the fact that among the Baltic nations they have felt least
threatened by the country's ethnic minorities. Whereas Estonia and
Latvia have sizable Russian-speaking populations who are not completely reconciled to the states in which they live, Lithuania is the most
ethnically homogenous of the Baltic countries, with approximately
84 percent of the population currently identifying itself as Lithuanian.
Feeling more secure than the natives of Estonia or Latvia, from the
beginning the Lithuanians took active measures to integrate their
Russian-speaking community and to develop a positive relationship
with Russia. Relations between Moscow and the other Baltic states
have been more troubled in large measure due to the perception that
the Russian-speaking peoples who live in these countries suffer from
systematic discrimination.

Latvia is the most diverse of the Baltic countries. A relatively prosperous Riga gives the illusion of national affluence, but the standard
of living in some Latvian regions is more comparable to country life
in Russia or Ukraine. Latvia is also a divided country: in 2013 about
63 percent of its people were identified as Latvians (up from 52 percent
at the end of the Soviet period), while most of the rest are Russian-
speakers. The country's capital city is home to the region's most sizable Russian-speaking population, yet in Riga, as in the cities of the
other Baltic states, one finds no street signs in the Russian language.
Yet there is no shortage of Russian-language television, radio, or print
media in Riga or elsewhere in Latvia. This is often a source of con-
sternation to those Latvians who wonder when or if the Russians will
ever fully integrate into Latvian society. The fact that about 60 percent
of Latvia's minorities now claim fluency in the Latvian language suggests this is in fact already happening.

Despite the tensions that have sometimes arisen in the Baltic states
between the dominant nationalities and their ethnic minorities, relations between the Estonians, Latvians, and Lithuanians are generally
constructive, as their countries participate in a variety of institutions
that link them to western Europe (all three countries joined NATO and
the European Union in 2004), to the Scandinavian states (the Northern
Baltic Eight, or NB8), and directly to each other (the Baltic Assembly
and the Baltic Council of Ministers). Nevertheless, one of the most
surprising features of life in the Baltic region is how poorly the Balts

Towers of the Dom Cathedral, St. Peter's Church, and St. Saviour's Anglican Church in Riga, Latvia. These beautiful and varied steeples have long been among the most architecturally compelling features of Riga's distinctive skyline. (EPA Photo/AFI/Normunds Mezins)

know each other. For Latvians, the common stereotype of their Estonian neighbors used to be that of slow-witted but harmless bumpkins, but this has changed as Estonia forged ahead to become a more fully European country. Indeed, the Estonian people regard themselves as kin of the Finns to the north, with whom they share a certain cultural and linguistic connection, and Estonians do not underestimate the importance of their links to the other Scandinavian countries that have played such an important part in their country's history.

Lithuanians are little more familiar to Latvians than Latvians are to Estonians. Whereas Lithuanians are oriented culturally toward Poland and view themselves as belonging to the club of central European nations, Latvian and Estonian culture developed largely under German and Scandinavian tutelage. Moreover, although the Latvian and Lithuanian languages share similar origins, they are mutually unintelligible. Under Soviet rule, their common language of communication was in fact Russian, the *lingua franca* of the 15 union republics. Indeed, a common claim among older Balts and other ex-Soviet peoples is that in a room of ten people, if there is even only one Russian present then the entire group will speak Russian. Although this may be a slight exaggeration, there is an underlying truth behind this claim: during Soviet times Balts and other non-Russians were expected to learn Russian, and few Russians living in the Baltic republics mastered the local language.

This situation changed rapidly after the fall of the Soviet Union in 1991. While Russian recedes as a second language for today's Baltic students, English has taken its place. Knowledge of English is now quite common in Estonian towns, and one has no difficulty finding natives who speak English in Latvian and Lithuanian cities as well. Indeed, the Russian-speaking world of an older generation—one that was once governed from Moscow—is disappearing, and a new world—one that requires knowledge of English for advancement—has largely taken its place. This is underlined by the fact that the curricula of many of the region's business colleges and university programs frequently require fluency in English.

Of course, this is not to suggest that in the course of globalization Estonians, Latvians, and Lithuanians will hurry to abandon their national languages and cultures for English and alien Western traditions. Far from it: the efforts to preserve their languages and secure the right to use them were too arduous to surrender them. It is now the Russians and other minorities of the Baltic countries who must learn to speak the official language and integrate into the broader society. Thus it is unsurprising that many Russian speakers residing in the Baltics regard Baltic language and citizenship policies, especially in Latvia and Estonia, as discriminatory.

Times have certainly changed. At the height of Soviet power in the 1970s, it was not unusual for academicians to consign the Estonians and Latvians, and to a lesser extent the Lithuanians, to the fate of other assimilated and disappeared nations like the Livonians or ancient Prussians. Yet unlike those former Soviet republics that experienced civil war (Georgia, Tajikistan, Azerbaijan), dictatorship (Belarus and most of the Central Asian states), and widespread poverty in the 1990s and early 2000s, the Baltic states quickly became peaceful, democratic, and relatively prosperous, and they have remained so despite the many political, economic, and social challenges they have faced since regaining their independence. Given their turbulent history and well-traversed geographic location, it is in some ways amazing that these three tiny states exist at all.

NOTE

1. Aldis Purs, *Baltic Facades: Estonia, Latvia and Lithuania since 1945* (New York: Reaktion Books, 2012), 11–12.

2

Early History

PREHISTORY

During the last Ice Age an enormous glacier covered Scandinavia, the lowlands of north central Europe, and northern Russia. Its gradual retreat and melting, beginning around 14,000 years ago, left behind an enormous inland lake that came to be known as the Baltic Sea. The first humans to settle the sea's eastern littoral, the territory of contemporary Estonia, Latvia, and Lithuania, arrived probably around 9000 BCE.

To understand the prehistory of the region and its peoples from this time until around 1000 CE, when written records concerning the region and its peoples began to appear, we must rely primarily on archaeological evidence. Based on the unearthing of ancient shards of pottery and clues concerning the inhabitants' ancient burial customs, scholars have concluded that the peoples living in this region prior to the arrival of the ancestors of today's Estonians, Latvians, and Lithuanians were not in any sense a single identifiable people, but rather were broadly differentiated linguistically and ethnically. Eventually, as further migrations brought further waves of people to the region, two main linguistic groups became predominant in the lands that now comprise the three Baltic states. The first to appear were the Finno-Ugric peoples, hunter–fisher tribes likely arriving from the Urals or the Volga region of Russia. Exactly, or even approximately, when these ancestors of modern-day Estonians, Finns, Setus, Ingrians, and Karelians arrived to the Baltic region no one can say with any certainty.

Another group, arriving at the eastern shores of the Baltic Sea around 2000 BCE, consisted of speakers of an archaic Indo-European language. These were the Balts, the ancestors of the Lithuanian, Latvian, and Prussian tribes. On the basis of water names, scholars have concluded that Baltic peoples (in the linguistic sense) lived in today's Latvia, Lithuania, Belarus, the northwestern parts of Ukraine, and the western parts of Russia. Indeed, the area inhabited by the Baltic peoples in prehistoric times, before the arrival of Germans and Slavs, was perhaps six times as great as present-day Lithuania and Latvia, although it is hard to know whether they occupied the entire area at once or had migrated from one region to another.[1] Slavic expansion into the eastern Baltic region from the southeast, which began before the fifth century CE, combined with pressure from migrating Germanic tribes to push the Baltic and Finno-Ugric peoples into the geographical locations in which they live today.

Like other early Europeans, the peoples living along the eastern shores of the Baltic Sea did not yet exist as "nations." Two millennia ago the ancestors of today's Estonians were divided into clans speaking different Finno-Ugric languages, which later merged to form the basis of modern Estonian. A common proto-Baltic language may have existed at some time, but after 500 CE it evolved into groups of West Baltic languages, primarily Old Prussian, which disappeared in the centuries after German conquest, and the East Baltic tongues spoken by the Lithuanian and Latvian tribes. Linguists believe that the Latvian and Lithuanian languages began to differentiate sometime after 800 CE, with transitional dialects continuing to be used as late as the 17th century.

The geographical divide between the peoples who spoke Finno-Ugric and Baltic languages broadly conforms to the present-day Estonian-Latvian border. Livonians (or Livs) were an exception in that they were a Finno-Ugric people who had settlements in various parts of what is today northern Latvia. During the Middle Ages they were absorbed by those tribes that eventually assimilated into the Latvian nation. Thus when German conquerors established a city in 1201 in Riga, the inhabitants of the Livonian villages that were already located on that site eventually melded into the city's numerically superior Lettish (a word that is derived from the tribes of Latgale in eastern Latvia) population. Such assimilatory patterns were repeated elsewhere, and not only by the Livonian and Latvian tribes.

The ancestors of today's Latvians also included the Couronians (Latv. *kurši*), Semigallians (*zemgaļi*), Latgallians (*latgaļi*), and Selonians (*sēļi*), each of whom had marked out territories for themselves by the end of the ninth century.[2] While it is true that the present-day borders of Latvia and Lithuania generally correspond to the ethnic and political divisions that existed at the time of the Germans' arrival in the 12th century, the ethnic boundaries between "Lithuanians" and "Latvians" were at that time still porous: while Couronians (Kurs) living in German-dominated regions eventually assimilated into the Latvian nation, other Couronians fled from German control during the 13th century and eventually melded into the Lithuanian nation.

The Lithuanian tribes inhabited areas south of the Latvian lands, with the Žemaitians (Lowlanders) or Samogitians living near the mouth of the Nemunas River and the Aukštaitians (Highlanders) located further upstream. That the Lithuanian tribes were never conquered by crusading armies has much to do with the protection that the remote forests and swamps of the Nemunas River basin afforded them. The Lithuanians were particularly well known at the time for sending their raiding parties through this difficult terrain, into which they could once again disappear after their expeditions in the north.

West of the Lithuanians, in the territory of present-day Kaliningrad and northeastern Poland, lived several other Baltic tribes, including the Prussians, who were protected by the sea to the north and the lakes, streams, and swamps that partially isolated them from the outside world. But the Prussian tribes were also closest to Germany by land. Unlike the Lithuanians, who successfully resisted the German crusaders, the Prussians lost the struggle by the end of the 13th century and eventually disappeared as a distinct people—some succumbing to the ravages of war and disease, others assimilated by conquering Germans and neighboring Lithuanians. Jatvings (or Sudovians), who also spoke a West Baltic language, lived just east of the Prussian tribes, but they too capitulated to the invaders and were eventually assimilated by neighboring German, Latvian, and Slavic populations. The appearance and disappearance of numerous tribes through the ages reflects an important historical reality about this region of which the modern-day Baltic peoples are keenly aware.

In the absence of any kind of literary culture among the ancient Baltic peoples, our early written sources were penned by alien observers. An early reference to one of these tribes is found in *The Germania* by the Roman historian Tacitus. Writing in the late first century CE, Tacitus referred to one of the tribes as "Aesti," by which he likely meant the ancient Prussians rather than the Estonians as has sometimes been assumed; but there is no evidence that any of the region's inhabitants identified themselves by that name.

Mediterranean civilization's hazy familiarity with the Baltic region had much to do with the rich deposits of amber that washed up on the southern Baltic coast, especially Prussia. A hard yellowish fossil resin that was prized in ancient times for its magnetic qualities, for its alleged medicinal value, and most of all for its ornamental uses, amber made its way to the Roman Empire via the Vistula River trade route. The discovery of Arabic coins in the Baltic region can be taken as evidence of indirect contact with Constantinople and the Near East. To the German tribes the Baltic peoples dealt furs, which were easily accessible in the northern forest zone occupied by the Finno-Ugric peoples and later by the Rus' (East Slavs who formed the ethnic basis of the Russian, Belarusian, and Ukrainian peoples). While the Baltic peoples acted as mediators in the north European fur trade, they also traded amber, bear skins, horses, cattle, wax, and slaves with their neighbors.

Yet the ancient Baltic tribes, like their Slavic neighbors, were mostly farmers: they grew wheat, rye, flax, and millet while raising cattle and horses as well as goats, sheep, and chickens. They also wove linen and tended bees. Unlike the Slavs, who tended to create more communal rural dwellings, Estonians and most Balts lived on independent farms, much like early west Europeans. While an earthen hill fort might have offered protection to hundreds of people at the first sign of an impending raid, when the Germans began settling in the region at the dawn of the 13th century there were no large population centers in the lands inhabited by the Estonian and Baltic tribes—certainly nothing that what we might in any meaningful sense call a city.

Nor did the peoples of the Baltic littoral know the Christian god or anything resembling monotheism before the appearance of missionaries in the 11th and 12th centuries, when Catholics made a series of minor and unsustained efforts to introduce Christianity in Lithuania, Courland, and western Estonia. Orthodox Christian clergymen were active in eastern Estonia and Latgale, but the Rus' were more interested in tribute than conversion. Thus the people the German monks, priests, and traders later encountered in the place they called "Livonia" (Ger. *Livland, Liefland*) were, like the Balts and the Estonians, among Europe's last pagans, observing not the Christian god but the spirits of the forests, mountains, fields, and water. Medieval sources suggest that these pagan practices were likely suffused with animism (the belief that living things contain a spiritual force) and that the natives continued to practice their rituals well beyond the 13th century.

Although there may have been some diversity of religious practice among the Latvian and Lithuanian tribes, they shared in common a particular reverence for the earth—the giver of life and sustenance—as well as a number of deities and spirits. These included the sky god (Latv. *Dievs*, Lith. *Dievas*), whose position was possibly akin to that of the Greek god Zeus, and the thunder god (Latv. *Pērkons*, Lith. *Perkūnas*). Experts in Baltic mythology have also tried to demonstrate the importance of goddess such as an Earth Mother (Lith. *Žemyna*, Latv. *Zemes māte*), who was considered the giver and sustainer of life, and Laima, the winged goddess of fate or happiness.[3] Other gods have been attributed to the Balts, but the matter of what constitutes a god in the world of Baltic paganism is the subject some speculation; it is likely that these deities are the inventions of later mythologists who transformed the Baltic idols and spirits mentioned in their folk songs into gods.[4] Although a lone Estonian "god," Tharapita (or Taara), was mentioned in the Christian chronicles of the Middle Ages, the early Estonians appear to have lacked anything like the pantheons invented by 19th-century nationalists.

Nor did the Estonian tribes have anything like a king in the sense of one man ruling over a defined territory. Indeed, a fateful feature of the Baltic tribes of the early Middle Ages was their lack of political unity or organization. Only Lithuanians managed to create a united kingdom—just as the Germans began to overrun their neighbors—while the Estonians, lacking any centralized authority, lived as free peasants loosely organized into parishes and districts. Ancestors of the Latvians lived in a number of small, independent districts whose rulers could hardly be called kings; indeed, Christian chronicles themselves were often unsure as to what to call the local chieftains.

Lacking monarchs at the top of their political hierarchies, unlike the case in feudal western Europe, the settled agricultural peoples of the eastern Baltic littoral accepted the leadership of warlords who could equip themselves with horses and weapons. In return for protection they supported the warrior aristocracy with taxes on their agricultural produce and their trade. Rulers were apparently little concerned with gaining territory or subjugating populations, and relations with neighboring tribes focused on raiding for food, animals, and other valuables—and protecting one's people from deadly raids. That the region was dotted by hundreds of earthen hill forts, which provided refuge in times of conflict for hundreds or even thousands of people (and which in many cases later became the sites of castles), suggests the frequency of conflict among neighboring tribes.

It is difficult to know with any certainty how densely populated these lands were: historian Andrejs Plakans estimates the 10th-century population of the region as having stood at about 10 percent of the present-day populations of Estonia, Latvia, and Lithuania.[5] Partially isolated from the world—a fortuitous set of circumstances that facilitated the preservation of some of Europe's oldest languages—these regions were surrounded by territories that were settled by people who were more populous and better organized politically and militarily. Several of these neighbors later proceeded to build powerful states such as Sweden, Poland, and Muscovy, and all had an interest in the lands of the eastern Baltic littoral.

Occasional Scandinavian incursions into the eastern Baltic coast from the north began in the seventh century and lasted until the end of the Viking Age in the 11th century. Indeed, some of the earliest accounts of the Baltic peoples come from the Viking sagas, which mention the Couronian pirates who occasionally raided the coasts of Denmark and Sweden. Estonians were also proficient at organizing military and looting raids on the Baltic coasts. The "pagans from the eastern sea" who in 1187 destroyed Sigutna, at the time Sweden's largest city, are thought to have been Estonians.

The Rus' began to penetrate the eastern lands of the Baltic littoral (around Lake Peipsi and Latgale) in the 11th century—a development that is not unconnected to the fact that the most important trade routes of the eastern Slavs flowed through this region, connecting northern Russia to the Black Sea and Constantinople via the Neva, Narva, Daugava (Rus. *Dvina*), and Dniepr rivers. The pagans of the Baltic, however, did not control this trade, which fell instead to the more powerful Vikings and their Rurikid descendants who ruled the Rus' principalities.[6] In exchange for security, some chieftains in the eastern parts of Latvia and Estonia even paid tribute to the western Rus' principalities Novgorod and Pskov. During the second half of the 12th century, however, the lands of the eastern Baltic had also begun to attract visitors from the west on an increasingly regular basis. Among them were German merchants seeking to profit from the trade in forest products from the Russian interior; others were priests and monks of the Catholic Church, who brought with them God's word, soon backed by the Pope's armies.

THE NORTHERN CRUSADES

Christianity's arrival in the Baltic Sea region began with Charlemagne's (r. 768–814) brutal conversion of the Saxon Germans, whom he absorbed into his growing Frankish Empire. By the 10th century Christianity had gained a foothold in Poland and the Scandinavian countries, whose crowned monarchs not only accepted the Roman faith but also demonstrated an eagerness to convert others. The German archbishoprics of Bremen and Magdeburg were particularly active in northern Europe and tried to convert the neighboring West Slavs by peaceful means. However, a papal bull issued in 1147 authorized a more forceful effort to expand the boundaries of Christendom. The goal of the resulting Wendish Crusade was to convert the pagans (whom ethnologists refer to as Wends, Sorbs, or Polabian Slavs) living in the borderlands of the Holy Roman Empire. Coinciding with the Second Crusade to the Holy Land, the Wendish Crusade failed to achieve the immediate conversion of the Wends, but it did begin the process of opening up the Baltic region to increased German influence.

German colonization of the western shores of the Baltic began with the official founding of Lübeck in 1159. Around the same time the old Norse town of Visby on the island of Gotland was transformed into a significant trading center; each of these towns in turn became a base for expansion to the east. By the 1180s German merchants were making regular stops in east Baltic ports, where they traded with visiting Scandinavian and Rus'ian traders as well as with the locals. On one of these visits up the Daugava River, probably in 1184, a German merchant ship carried an Augustinian monk named Meinhard, who set up his mission near a small trading post. Promising the Livonians he encountered protection from the Lithuanian raiders who frequently threatened them, Meinhard built a church and a stone castle at Ikšķile (Ger. *Üxküll*), which was located 20 miles upstream from the spot where the more defensible Riga would later be founded. Named the first bishop of Livonia in 1186, the monk failed to make many lasting converts among the Livonians and died while holed up in his modest church-castle, whose ruins can still be seen on an islet that was created by the construction of a hydroelectric dam on the Daugava in the 1960s.

The overlap of spiritual, political, and commercial ambitions in the eastern Baltic is demonstrated in the chain of events that followed Pope Innocent III's (r. 1198–1216) authorization of a Holy War on the northeast in 1198. The crusade against the remaining pagans of the Baltic was undertaken with the same objectives as earlier crusades to the Near East: to defend Christian communities and to save souls—and to create new sources of papal revenue to meet the Church's growing commitments and ambitions. Of particular concern to the German missionaries was the possibility that the Rus' might convert the Baltic pagans to Orthodoxy.

Like those who had marched to Jerusalem fifty years earlier, the Northern crusaders, principally Germans, but also including Danes, Swedes, and others, were driven by their fidelity to the papacy and to the Roman Christian faith, as well as by the knowledge that for their services they would obtain remission of their sins. The promise of eternity in heaven justified any misdeeds performed in the cause of spreading the faith. Whether or not they received their final reward, the crusaders in the northeast enjoyed success in battle, conquering and converting most of the Latvian and Estonian heathen in the first decades of 13th century.

The conquest began with the arrival to Ikšķile of the Cistercian monk Berthold of Hanover in the summer of 1198. Consecrated the second bishop of Livonia the previous year, Berthold was backed by a small and victorious army of mostly Saxon warriors, but he nevertheless lost his life in a battle with the Livonians, after whom the Germans named the territory they soon began to conquer. Berthold's successor was longer-lived and far more successful. This was Albert von Buxhoevden (1165–1229), a nephew of the powerful archbishop of Bremen and a person of exceptional talent and considerable ambition. It was the arrival of this young priest to Livonia in the summer of 1200, backed by a flotilla of 23 ships from Lübeck and soon afterward by the creation of a permanent military force known as the Livonian Brothers of the Sword (*Fratres militiæ Christi Livoniæ*), that accelerated and systematized the process of conquest and conversion.

The Order of Swordbrothers, whose members were attired in white robes emblazoned with a red cross, was created in 1202 by Albert's able troubleshooter Theodoric, a Cistercian monk who had earlier secured permission from the papacy to launch a crusade, to defend the new Christian outposts from the pagans. Appointed the first bishop of Riga, the city he founded in 1201 near the spot where his predecessor was killed in battle, and enjoying princely power in Livonia after 1207, Albert von Buxhoevden expected that he would be able to maintain total power over the Order. But in fact the Order was responsible only to the papacy, which couldn't control it either. Hungry for land and disdainful of competing authorities, the Swordbrothers were a particular irritant to the autonomy-seeking citizens of Riga, a city that, thanks to Albert's interventions, soon acquired monopoly trading privileges on the Daugava and began to attract settlers both from Germany and the Latvian interior. Riga was also home to one of the Order's castles, initially located on the bank of a rivulet—then known as the Riga and later called the Rīdzene, whose remnants now flow under the city's cobblestone streets—next to the castle Albert built for himself.[7] While much of Albert's time was spent in Germany, where he preached crusade and recruited "pilgrims" for the annual summer campaigns, it can fairly be said that no single individual left a greater historical footprint on Livonia than Albert von Buxhoevden.

First the Livonians and then the Selonians, the weakest of the indigenous tribes, were quickly either conquered or won over as allies as the Daugava was secured for German traders all the way up to the Rus' principality of Polotsk. Albert shared the conquered territories of *Marienland*—the Land of Mary, a phrase that notionally placed participation in crusades to Livonia and Jerusalem on nearly equal footing—with the Swordbrothers, who demanded one-third of all conquests. While the Order erected castles along the Daugava and Gauja rivers as launching points for further expansion, Albert parceled out some lands as fiefs both to German-born noblemen and to accommodating

This statue of Albert von Buxhoevden, the first bishop of Riga and the city's founder (1201), is located on the exterior of the Dom Cathedral. No single individual left a bigger imprint on the city of Riga than this German prince-priest. (Artifex)

local chieftains. The native populations were then baptized and subjected to an occupying elite of priests and landlords. In order to take the struggle north to the Estonian lands, in 1208, the Swordbrothers made an alliance with the Latgallians—a typical partnership of Germans and tribesmen whereby each could benefit from the other's help in pursuit of their own objectives.

The southern Estonians were conquered by 1217 and their lands were placed under the direct control of Rome. The conquest of northern Estonia was led by the Danish king Valdemar II (r. 1202–1241), whose forces took Tallinn (called *Reval* until 1917) in 1219 and Tartu (Ger. *Dorpat*) five years later. The subjugation of the island of Saaremaa (*Ösel*) in 1227 completed the Christian conquest of northern Estonia, but quarrels soon broke out among the Danes, Albert, and the Swordbrothers as to how to divide the lands under their control.

Much of this story is recounted by the monk Henry (Heinricus), whose fascinating chronicle is the most informative source that scholars have for understanding the clash of cultures that took place on the eastern shores of Baltic Sea during the crusading era. The Livonians, Henry lamented, were "the most perfidious, and everyone stole what his neighbor had." But now that they had been baptized through the efforts of bishops Meinhard, Berthold, and Albert, their habits of "theft, violence, rapine, and similar things," Henry remarked, "were [now] forbidden."[8] Yet if Albert, upon his death in 1229, had succeeded in bringing the Christian faith to the Baltic pagans, he had failed to create a religiously and politically unified state.

The subjugation of the Prussians, whose lands were closer to Germany and more accessible by land, began at the end of the 1220s and was left to another band of crusading monks known as the Order of Teutonic Knights, founded in Palestine in 1190 but relocated to Europe after a defeat. Establishing a base at the mouth of the Vistula River (in present-day Poland), the Order was responsible only to the Pope and quickly established a reputation for brutality. More numerous and better led than the Livonians, the Prussians were better able to resist the Teutonic Knights, at least for a while. In the end they too were defeated after more than half a century of battle and uprisings. It was in the wake of the "Great Prussian Uprising" of the 1260s–1270s that the knights established a fortress at Marienberg (Pol. *Malbork*), which in the 15th century became Europe's largest brick castle. As in Latvia and Estonia, the majority of the conquered Prussians converted to Christianity and were subjected to military and labor service, while their new rulers granted privileges to a favored elite.

The first major setback for the crusaders occurred in 1236 when they were defeated by the better-organized Lithuanians (allied with

Semigallians) and most of their leaders were killed. Consequently the Order of Swordbrothers collapsed and its surviving monk-warriors were merged into the Teutonic Order, becoming its northern branch. Now known as the Livonian Order, the knights continued to rule a separate Livonian state, comprised of much of modern-day Latvia and southern Estonia. Beginning with the Germans' control of the Daugava and Gauja river basins, their holdings expanded in stages, with Courland capitulating in 1267 and the Semigallians finally succumbing in 1290. Counterbalancing the Order was the archbishop of Riga (established in 1255), under whose authority several smaller states, including the bishopric of Courland and the bishoprics of Tartu and Saare-Lääne (both in modern Estonia), banded together.

Meanwhile, Denmark's hold on northern Estonia was confirmed in 1238 by an agreement with the Livonian Order that also outlined a military alliance. The need for such an arrangement, and the difficulty he had in controlling his own local vassals, demonstrated the weak position that Danish king had in Estonia. Eventually it became more desirable to sell the Estonian lands at a good price rather than continue to govern a faraway land from across the sea. However, just as an agreement was being concluded with the Livonian Order a rebellion began on April 23, 1343—a day in the Estonian folk calendar that symbolized the beginning of spring fieldwork. While some have called the violence that spread throughout northern Estonia a peasant revolt, Estonian historians have portrayed the St. George's Day Uprising (1343–1345) as a fight for the freedom of the Estonian people. For a time the uprising freed some of the Estonians from their oppressors, but by early 1345 the Livonian Order managed to subjugate the natives and took control of the purchased territories.

Thus from the 13th century onward the Livonian, Latvian, and Estonian tribes were assimilated into a Christian world that was overseen by the Holy Roman Emperor and the Pope and whose military arm in the region was the Livonian Order. Only the Lithuanian tribes living in the forested and swampy lands southwest of the conquered areas managed, despite continuing raids by the knights of the Livonian Order, to remain free of foreign rule—and, for the time being, of Christianity. For unlike the Estonians and Latvians, the Lithuanian tribes had united to form a state under King Mindaugas.

THE LIVONIAN CONFEDERATION

The Livonian Confederation was created in 1418 from the five Baltic bishopric principalities of the Holy Roman Empire. Within its boundaries, which included the lands inhabited by the Livonian, Latvian, and

Estonian (but not Lithuanian) tribes, the knights became the new nobility in a feudal system of social relationships imported from Germany, and their numbers grew as more noblemen were invited to settle in the region, bringing with them the Low German dialect spoken by Baltic Germans into the 20th century. Yet the apex of the feudal pyramid was missing: Livonia had no kings, and there were no political authorities higher than the local nobility. Local bishops were subordinate to the Pope, whose intervention was sometimes required to check the abuses that often accompanied the attempts to convert the natives and to mediate disputes between temporal and spiritual authorities.

While the surviving indigenous leaders were effectively Germanized, as were many of the region's urban dwellers, the languages and customs of the indigenous peoples were preserved, to varying degrees, by the peasants. For nearly six centuries these two groups, a foreign upper crust (mostly Germans or *Deutsche*, initially consisting of two or three hundred knights, along with clergymen, merchants, and German noblemen who were invited to settle the colonies) and a subjugated native peasantry (*Undeutsche*, or "non-Germans," a term that is local in nature and does not encompass non-German peoples from western Europe or Scandinavia), coexisted with each other in what was essentially a colonial relationship.

As the indigenous peoples descended into powerlessness, the main focus of conflict shifted from battles between Christians and pagans to clashes among the region's new power holders, namely the Livonian Order and the archbishopric of Riga, each of which sought territorial control, and the cities (namely Riga), which sought to maintain their corporate independence from the knights and the Church. Although alliances frequently shifted, it was generally the case that the Order was the greatest irritant (and threat) to everyone else, for its thirst for land and power often seemed unquenchable.

With the lapse of the original formula for dividing new territories, which called for one-third to go to the Livonian Order and two-thirds to the Church, more territory came under the Order's control. The Order simultaneously sought to extend its power over cities like Riga, a particularly valuable prize for which the knights were willing to start a war in 1297. Only in 1330, after a long struggle that ended with the city's capitulation, did Riga acknowledge the suzerainty of the Order. It was partly due to the Order's ambitions that in 1422 the archbishop of Riga convened the first Livonian Diet (Ger. *Landtag*), which included representatives from the clergy, the Order, land-holding knights, and the city populations in an effort to regulate affairs and prevent open conflict. The Church, meanwhile, continued to control many of the institutions of Livonian life, such as parishes, congregations, clergy, and houses of worship.

Merchants from Germany (and Scandinavia) constituted the other elements of the ruling elite in Baltic cities. They were organized into their own guilds and brotherhoods from which "non-Germans" were typically excluded. As merchants rushed into the Baltic region following the Livonian conquest, the partnerships they created with merchants in other cities coalesced into the Hanseatic League, a confederation of trading towns and outposts throughout the North Sea and Baltic Sea regions. These included Riga (which joined in 1282), the area's first and largest commercial center, Gdańsk (Ger. *Danzig*), which rivaled Riga in importance, Tallinn, which German merchants shared with Danish and Swedish colonists, as well as Tartu, Königsberg in Prussia and Novgorod in Russia, where Germans had their own trading quarters. As self-governing polities, the nearly 200 city-states of the Hanseatic League (at its 15th-century peak) operated independently of the surrounding principalities and kingdoms and for more than three centuries enjoyed peaceful relations with each other.

The demise of the Hanseatic League began when industrious Dutch traders began to take over the region's commerce in the 16th century. Until that time, traders who were not German faced severe restrictions in the Baltic. Thus Germans dominated not only the religious and political life of the Baltic, but also controlled the region's economy, which supplied the prosperous cities of western Europe with grain, wax, furs, flax, and timber that were obtained from Russia and the Baltic hinterland. Imports included cloth, metal goods, weapons, salt, and various luxury items. By playing such a vital role in the west–east trade, the eastern Baltic region was incorporated into the economic life of the continent and became dependent on western Europe's demands for its agricultural products and natural resources.

Although Baltic towns were predominantly populated by German colonists who developed Tallinn and Tartu into two of northeastern Europe's most beautiful cities, they became attractive destinations for indebted (and fleeing) peasants who were otherwise largely isolated from the institutions and structures introduced by their German overlords. Riga, the region's largest city, with a 16th-century population of 12,000 living in narrow brick and stone houses (building with wood was forbidden after a great fire in 1293), is a case in point, for the ancient Latvian proverb "All roads lead to Riga" rang no less true for the area's non-German natives than did the Hanseatic League's motto, "City air makes one free," for its German merchants. Indeed, the flight of *Undeutsche* to the towns was a source of particular concern to the

The old town of Tallinn, Estonia, features a medieval city wall and a breathtaking architectural ensemble that dates to the eras of Danish, German, and Swedish rule. In the background is St. Olaf's Church, which was originally built in the 13th century and was once one of the tallest buildings in the world. (Maigi/Dreamstime.com)

largely German landowners, since the peasants formed the foundation of an economic system that by the 16th century was largely based on serfdom, under which peasants cultivated the land for the profit of the landowners.

Yet Germans were not the only landowners in the wake of the conquest, for the leaders of the conquered Baltic tribes often became vassals of the German elites. Gradually they became Germanized, adopting the languages and customs of the region's conquerors and receiving small portions of land in exchange for military service. Some of the indigenous peasants had small amounts of land, but the majority were landless, renting or owning small farms on the land of the larger manors in exchange for labor and rent (in the form of money or agricultural produce) requirements. However, by the 15th century the increasing tax burden on the small peasant farms resulted in their being swallowed up by the surrounding estates. For most peasants, accumulated debt and hereditary serfdom were the results; others moved to the cities to work as artisans and craftsmen.

As the German landowners lived on manors that were separate from the native rural communities, indigenous peoples lived a world apart from the German-speaking elite, speaking their own languages and paying their landowners rent, increasingly in the form of physical labor. This remained the case in Estonia and Livonia until the early 19th century, when serfdom was outlawed in Russia's Baltic provinces, even while it remained in place in the empire's Lithuanian provinces for several more decades. In Lithuania, this elite was mostly Polish after the 14th century, but the social, political, and economic nature of the relationship was similar.

As noted earlier, in the 14th and 15th centuries the main sources of conflict within Livonia were those between the Livonian Order, the burghers of the larger cities (Riga in particular), and the Church (namely the archbishop of Riga). However, by the end of this period the Livonian Confederation was forced to confront a major foreign threat—the Grand Principality of Muscovy, which had been active in the Baltic region since the annexation of Novgorod and its territories by Tsar Ivan III in 1477. In 1492, the Muscovites built a fortress, appropriately named Ivangorod, directly across the river from the Order fortress of Narva. The conflict produced one of the great heroes of the age, Wolter (Walter) von Plettenberg. Born in Germany around 1450 but raised in Narva, Plettenberg joined the Livonian Order at age 15 and was its master from 1494, when he defeated the city of Riga, until his death in 1535. In 1501, he assembled the largest army in the history of medieval Livonia to face Muscovy, and while the Russians agreed to an armistice in 1503, they never abandoned their ambition to control the eastern Baltic coast.

THE GRAND DUCHY OF LITHUANIA

Unlike the fragmented Livonian, Latvian, Estonian, and Prussian tribes who submitted to German rule, under threat of attack the Lithuanians managed to unite under the leadership of a ruthless tribal king named Mindaugas around 1230. Mindaugas successfully fended off the Germans by concluding an alliance with them, but the price for preventing a Lithuanian crusade was his formal acceptance of Latin Christianity. In 1253, Mindaugas was awarded the Lithuanian throne with the approval of Pope Innocent IV—and the disapproval of the archbishop of Riga, who expected to wield authority over the new see. The coexistence with the Teutonic Knights alienated some of Mindaugas's nobles, who after ten years killed their king and reverted to paganism. Despite this setback for Christian expansion, the Lithuanian state, a small territory that was home to perhaps 300,000 subjects in Mindaugas's day, continued to grow as it absorbed the lands of other Baltic tribes and of nearby eastern Slavs.

Having rejected the Catholic West, for the next century Lithuania's rulers chose to pursue ties, partly through political marriages, with the Slavic and Orthodox east. By this time the Kievan Rus', smashed by the Mongols during the 13th-century invasions and reduced to a series of Mongol tributary states, had lost their influence over neighboring Slavic principalities and a number of them subsequently drifted into the Lithuanian orbit. In fact, by the middle decades of the 14th century the vastly enlarged Lithuanian state of Grand Duke Gediminas (r. 1316–1341) was Muscovy's main rival for control over the lands of the Rus'. A favored method used by the grand duke was to marry his children into the Rus'ian ruling families of eastern Europe; some towns and lands, however, were conquered by military means.[9] Lithuanian expansion continued under Gediminas's son Algirdas (r. 1345–1377), who added most of Ukraine to the duchy, including Kiev. By the early 14th century Lithuania's rulers had also added the Rus' principalities of Polotsk and Smolensk to their domains.

The growing military might of the Lithuanian state was also a threat to the Teutonic Order that ruled neighboring Prussia. Dismayed by the Lithuanians' reversion to paganism after Mindaugas's death in 1263, the Knights still hoped to convert Europe's last remaining heathen and raided Lithuanian territory at least once a year. Their immensely destructive wars against Lithuania lasted more than a century, during which Poland too was blocked from expanding northward to the Baltic.

Despite his collaboration with the princes of the Orthodox east, the unusually tolerant (or perhaps practical-minded) Gediminas and his successors did not reject the political and material benefits of ties with the Catholic west, as they often enjoyed excellent commercial relations with German merchants in the Baltic Sea area. The Lithuanians even had a garrison stationed in Riga in the years 1298–1313 to help protect the city against the Livonian Order. Moreover, the Gediminids encouraged western traders, artisans, and landowners to settle in his realm—an important consequence of which was the emergence of a large Jewish community in Vilnius (Pol. *Wilno,* Rus. *Vilna*), which became the Lithuanian capital in 1323. Still, urban development was much slower in Lithuania than in the Hanseatic towns of the Baltic coast, and most townspeople were not foreigners but Lithuanians, supplemented by smaller numbers of German and Russian colonists, as well as Poles and Jews.

Although the nobles upon whom they relied for support were firmly opposed to Christianity, the Gediminids provided protection for both the Catholic and Orthodox clergy who resided in Lithuania while continuing to allow all people to worship their own gods. Gediminas himself contemplated converting to Catholicism in order to ward off future incursions by the Teutonic Knights, but he nevertheless remained a pagan until his death in 1341. It was not until 1386 that a Lithuanian ruler, Jogaila (1348–1434), converted to Christianity in its Catholic form. By this time the country, whose formerly pagan Lithuanian elite ruled over a majority Orthodox and East Slavic population (called Ruthenians), was the largest kingdom in Europe. Stretching from the Baltic to the Black Sea, the Lithuanian state—its proper title was the Grand Duchy of Lithuania, Rus', and Samogitia—occupied a sprawling territory, much of it thinly populated, that included modern Belarus and much of modern Ukraine. While Latin and other western languages were used in correspondence with outsiders, the official language used for record keeping was not Lithuanian but a version of the East Slavic language (Chancery Slavonic) spoken by the Orthodox subjects of the Lithuanian state.

The massive size of the Grand Duchy—it is often overlooked how much bigger eastern Europe is than western Europe—and its position at the crossroad of several powerful states and all the great western monotheistic faiths also made it harder to defend against the ambitions of its neighbors, which included not only the Teutonic Knights (who were committed to expanding Catholicism) and the Muscovite east (which would later pose as the protector of Orthodoxy), but also the Ottoman state in the south whose power was expanding during the 14th century through much of the Balkan peninsula, to which it brought the Islamic faith. Such were the circumstances faced by Grand Duke Jogaila (Pol. *Jagiełło*), a grandson of Gediminas, who in addition to a dangerous international climate had to contend with his own scheming relatives in what amounted to a Lithuanian war of succession in the 1380s. Despite his uncle Kęstutis's preference for an eastern orientation for the Lithuanian state (Jogaila had him incarcerated and murdered), Jogaila rejected an offer to marry the daughter of the Muscovite prince Dmitri Donskoi and instead chose to cast Lithuania's fate with the Catholic west. One can only speculate what a dynastic union with Orthodox Russia would have meant for the future of Lithuania.

Making an alliance with Muscovy's Tatar overlords, whose state was known as the Golden Horde, and concluding a territorial pact with the Teutonic Knights in 1382, Jogaila then cemented his ties with the Catholic world by arranging his betrothal to Jadwiga (Ger. *Hedwig*), the 11-year-old queen of Poland in 1385. The following year the grand duke was baptized and crowned Władysław II, King of Poland, thus initiating a dynasty (the Jagiellionian) that lasted two centuries. The

Christianization of the country—one might say its Europeanization as well—soon followed, and with it was laid the foundation for the Catholic Church's superior position in Lithuania, as it received considerable land concessions in addition to legal protection. While Polish and German clergymen were recruited to administer the churches, mass was conducted in Latin, a language as incomprehensible to Lithuanian parishioners as it was to Estonian and Latvian peasants.

Despite his earlier triumph, Jogaila's struggle with Lithuania's great nobles (and with the Germans) continued, and in 1392 he was forced to concede his title as grand duke of Lithuania to his cousin Vytautas (1350–1430), a son of Kęstutis and a rival in the succession struggles of the 1380s, while Jogaila himself remained king of Poland. Later, in 1410, Jogaila and Vytautas together headed a combined force of Lithuanians, Poles, and Czechs that defeated the Teutonic Knights in the Battle of Tannenberg (Ger. *Grünwald*; Lith. *Žalgaris*) and thereby prevented the further eastward expansion of the Germans. It was under Vytautas Magnus that the Grand Duchy reached the height of its territorial expansion and influence, concluding a lasting peace with the Teutonic Order in 1422.

Claims that this union of the Polish and Lithuanian crowns retarded the development of the Lithuanian state and of Lithuanian culture are well-founded. Because Lithuania's social structure was not as firmly established as that of Poland—perhaps in part because of Lithuania's failure to adopt Christianity earlier—during the period of the Lithuanian-Polish union the Lithuanian elites were essentially Polonized as they absorbed the language and culture being disseminated by the Polish church and nobility. As historian Timothy Snyder has noted, in the Grand Duchy "A nobleman could be "Lithuanian" by origin, "Polish" in politics, and "Russian" (or "Greek") by religion."[10] Lithuania's rulers are a case in point: Jogaila's grandson Casimir (r. 1447–1492) was not only the first Lithuanian monarch to be baptized at birth, he was probably also the last to speak Lithuanian. Meanwhile, the bulk of the Grand Duchy's subjects—mostly Ruthenian peasants—became enserfed, tied to the estates of the great landowners, whose independence from Lithuania's grand dukes grew along with their power. Serfdom was finally codified in the Lithuanian Statute, the Grand Duchy's separate legal code, in 1588.

To the east of Lithuania lay an expansionist Muscovy, which completely liberated itself from the domination of the Golden Horde during the 15th century and now for the first time began to pose a serious threat to Lithuania (and to Livonia), not least because the Grand Duchy was in possession of vast territories that Muscovite rulers were now bent on "gathering" under a single tsar. Already in 1494 Lithuania suffered its first territorial losses to Muscovy, whose growing power caused Lithuania and Poland to draw closer together. In 1569, they agreed to create the Union of Lublin, which abolished the Polish-Lithuanian state's confederate structure and replaced it with the Polish-Lithuanian Commonwealth (Pol. *Rzeczpospolita*, the "Republic of Both Nations"). According to an edict of King Sigismund II Augustus (r. 1548–1571), the Polish kingdom and the Grand Duchy of Lithuania henceforth constituted a single indivisible state with a king jointly elected by the country's leading magnates. Following the union, for two centuries the *Rzeczpospolita* was one of Europe's largest states, with each side maintaining its own territory, army, and treasury.

Although under the terms of the treaty the Grand Duchy retained its statehood within the Commonwealth, the reality was that Lithuania had an unequal position. One of the union's conditions, for example was that Lithuania's Ukrainian lands be transferred to Poland—a transaction that reduced the Grand Duchy's territory by half. Over time Vilnius, Lithuania's historic capital, lost its significance as the Commonwealth crowned its kings in Polish Cracow, where they also ruled. Meanwhile, the Polish aristocracy gained the upper hand over the Lithuanian aristocracy as it acquired lands and positions in Lithuania and dominated the *Sejm*, Poland's assembly of notables. By the end of the 17th century the Polonization of the Lithuanian upper classes was so complete that Polish was installed as the state language of the Grand Duchy; henceforth Lithuanian remained a peasant language until it was revived as a literary language in the 19th century.

The Grand Duchy's weakness was also reflected in the struggles by neighboring powers to place their own candidates on the throne—a situation that was made possible in large measure by the Commonwealth's joint elected monarchy. As a result, Lithuania was usually ruled by kings from other countries, including France, Sweden (the Vasa dynasty, 1587–1668), and Saxony (the Wettin dynasty, 1696–1763). The sad fact is that in the predatory international climate of 17th- and 18th-century Europe, the weak and decentralized Polish-Lithuanian Commonwealth was unable to compete with its aggressive and more centralized neighbors.

A particularly ferocious period was 1654 to 1667—a time that Poles remember as "The Deluge," the beginning of the end of Poland as a great power—when Swedish and Russian forces swept into Lithuanian territory. For the first time in its history, Vilnius, then a city of some 20,000 inhabitants, came under foreign occupation as the Russian troops headed by Tsar Aleksei (r. 1645–1676), who claimed to be defending Orthodox populations from Catholic persecution, seized the most important centers of the Grand Duchy. As a result of these battles eastern Ukraine was ceded to the Muscovite ruler, who wished to add "Grand Duke of Lithuania" to his collection of regal titles. Most of the western Ukrainian lands remained under Polish dominion for another century.

Because of constant warring, famine, and epidemics, Lithuanian areas became increasingly barbarous and depopulated, with the population of the Grand Duchy declining by nearly one-half between 1648 and 1697. The region was further damaged in the course of the calamitous war fought by the armies of Tsar Peter the Great and the Swedish king Charles XII, known as the Great Northern War (1700–1721), which is discussed in greater detail later. The impact of this war on the local populations was exacerbated by the arrival of a plague that swept through the eastern Baltic region that killed half of Lithuania's remaining population. More Lithuanians died in the following years as starving peasants from the countryside took refuge behind the city walls.[11] The plague also killed off the majority of the population of Lithuania Minor, a region that was under Prussian/German rule. In subsequent years the Prussian government began to establish colonies of German peasants in Lithuania Minor, thereby significantly altering the ethnic composition of a region where Lithuanian culture had developed somewhat more dynamically than in the Grand Duchy itself.

LITHUANIAN JEWS

The history of Jews in Lithuania dates back to Grand Duke Gediminas's invitation to merchants and craftsmen to settle in the area in the 14th century. In the early 15th century, Gediminas's grandson Vytautas granted Jews privileges, including religious freedom and protection of both person and property. During his reign the number of Jews in Lithuania grew into the thousands. Following the expulsion of Jews from Spain and the continued persecution of Jews in western Europe, by the 16th century Poland-Lithuania had become the new cultural center of Jewish life in Europe. At first concentrated in the Zamut region (including Vilnius and areas north and west of it), Lithuania's Jews, called Litvaks, eventually established communities throughout the western part of the Grand Duchy. Also moving into Lithuania during this period were Muslim Tatars and Karaim, a Turkic people who practice a form of Judaism that rejects the oral tradition of the Talmud.

During the period of the Commonwealth Jews enjoyed considerable autonomy, even apportioning and collecting the Jewish poll tax, whose

level was set by the *Sejm*. While the support of the Lithuanian nobility benefited a handful of wealthy Jews, who could even own estates
and serfs, the vast majority of Lithuanian Jews endured difficult conditions, earning their living from petty trade and the occupation that
was reserved for Jews by royal decree: money-lending. Although medieval Europe needed a banking system, the Catholic Church forbade
Christians to lend at interest; hence Jews were to provide this service
for the rest of society, and especially for Europe's royalty. While this
meant that many Jews felt safe and protected within their defined area
of residence, they nevertheless felt the brunt of an anti-Polish revolt of
Cossack forces led by Bogdan Khmelnitsky in 1648, in which Jewish
communities were singled out for destruction. Tens of thousands of
the Commonwealth's Jews were murdered, maimed, or raped.

Despite the pogroms of the previous century, by 1765 there were at
least 120,000 Jews living in ethnic Lithuania and nearly 750,000 Jews
in the Commonwealth as a whole. They formed up to 30 percent of
the population in the larger cities, including Vilnius, and more than
70 percent in some of the smaller towns. However, under Russian
rule, to which nearly all of Lithuania was subject by the end of the
18th century, Jews' legal and socioeconomic status deteriorated. The
Russian Empire's western border, including Lithuania, was made part
of the "Jewish Pale of Settlement." Jews living there were forbidden
from settling in the Russian interior, and restrictions on Jewish life
tightened throughout the first half of the 19th century.

THE REFORMATION

A sweeping religious movement known as the Reformation ensured
the permanent western orientation of Latvians and Estonians. It officially began with Martin Luther's (1483–1546) challenge to the papacy
and the Roman Catholic Church in 1517, when the German friar argued
against the Church's practice of selling indulgences (that is, the selling of one's pardon, and hence one's salvation) to parishioners. Luther
also challenged the Church's authority on numerous theological issues,
but his rebellion unintentionally turned political as the Catholic world
quickly split into warring camps. By the mid-1520s the ideas of the
Reformation had entered the Livonian Confederation via Riga, with
the result that Lutheranism soon became the prevailing religion in the
urban areas of Latvia and Estonia. Throughout the affected areas of Europe the ramifications of Luther's revolt were economic and political as
well, for the Reformation offered citizens an opportunity to free themselves of the domination of the Livonian Order and the archbishop.

In Prussia the last grand master of the Teutonic Order, Albert of Brandenburg, converted to Lutheranism and in 1525 became the duke of a secularized state. The Livonian Order's master at this time, Wolter von Plettenberg, chose not to follow Albert's lead: instead of converting and secularizing his state he chose to become a vassal of Holy Roman Emperor Charles V, who was loyal to the Church and viscerally opposed Luther and his revolution. For Riga and for the Confederation as a whole, the Reformation was a time of when loyalties were conflicted (Plettenberg supported the Lutherans against Riga's archbishop but never converted), scores were settled, and freedom from feudal overlords seemed possible.

To the peasants of Germany, Livonia, and other affected regions, the main message of the Reformation was that all men were equal before God. This was a serious challenge indeed to the hierarchical structure of feudal Europe, and rural unrest was the result. Of course, Livonia's peasants had little choice concerning which form of Christianity they would observe; that decision was left to the region's German-speaking nobility, many of whom initially fought against the reforms. Although by the 1530s the majority of the gentry had converted to Protestantism, Catholic bishops, the Livonian Order, and most cloisters remained active for several more decades.

The transition to Protestantism in the eastern Baltic was facilitated by the Reformation's campaign to translate the Bible into indigenous languages, thus making Protestant Christianity more accessible to the congregations of the littoral. Indeed, the intellectual and cultural impact of the Reformation on the eastern Baltic region was no less significant than its religious impact: former clerical and monastery libraries were now made public; new secular schools and medical institutions were created; even the region's musical cultures and its art and architecture were stimulated by Luther's revolution. The era also marked the beginning of the development of Estonian and Latvian as literary languages. In this respect, some of the most notable achievements of the Reformation include the Lutheran hymn book published in Riga by the pastor Andreas Knopken in 1530 and Lutheran catechisms published in the Estonian language in 1535 and in Lithuanian in 1547. Centuries would pass, however, before full translations of the Bible or original works of literature appeared in these languages.

While at last some Estonian and Latvian peasants could hear sermons delivered in their mother tongues, few could read the new hymn books or catechisms, as the peasantry remained illiterate in every vernacular. Moreover, for much of the local peasantry, Christianity, whether in its Roman Catholic or Lutheran form, was not a matter of religious conviction but was something imposed from the outside. Thus despite their outward obeisance to established religious authority many peasants were only nominally Christian, dismaying the Lutheran clergy by maintaining their residual pagan practices.

Within the Lithuanian territories the Reformation's impact would prove to be less consequential than in Livonia. Where Protestantism did manage to take root in Lithuania, it was often in its Calvinist variant, which by the mid-16th century had become popular among the Lithuanian nobility. Just as quickly as it arrived, however, Calvinism began to wane, and Catholicism began its recovery with the arrival in 1569 of Jesuits at the invitation of the bishop of Vilnius. Known for its dedication to foreign missions and education, this new Roman Catholic order, the Society of Jesus, set up missions and schools throughout Lithuania, including Vilnius (Wilno) University (1579), then the easternmost university in Europe. While the Jesuits enjoyed great success in their efforts to win people back to the Church (and were active as far north as Estonia), this may have been aided by the likelihood that many of the Lithuanians who had earlier converted to Calvinism had not done so with any great conviction. In the end the Catholic faith won out in Lithuania, where it still remains strong today.

THE LIVONIAN WAR

German domination of the eastern Baltic collapsed in the 16th century due to a variety of factors, not least the lack of unity between the Church and the Order and the declining power of the Hanseatic League, which was unable to maintain the Germans' trade monopoly. After centuries of internal conflict, which intensified as the Reformation wept through the region, the Baltic Sea's great powers exploited an evident power vacuum, for in an age of centralizing authority the fragmented Livonian Confederation was an anachronism whose time had passed. In the wake of the Livonian War (1558–1583), the centers of power were no longer the Livonian Order, the Teutonic Knights, and cities like Riga and Gdańsk. Now those who would shape the destinies of the peoples of the Baltic littoral were the great states that surrounded it—Poland, Sweden, and Muscovy/Russia.

Lithuanian grand dukes, who in addition to these other powers also had to contend with the Ottoman Empire in the south, were left at a disadvantage when it came to dealing with such threats, not least because they lacked the absolute authority enjoyed by Muscovite grand princes like Ivan III, whose long reign (1462–1505) was devoted to bringing the neighboring Slavic principalities—some of which had come under Lithuanian suzerainty—into Muscovy's fold. Instead of becoming powerful monarchs like the ones who were emerging in Muscovy and France, the grand dukes of Lithuania, like their Polish counterparts, gradually turned into elected constitutional monarchs who heeded the counsel of a gentry elite (*szlachta*) to whom they granted unprecedented rights and privileges.

Thus as Lithuanian grand dukes grew weaker the power of the Muscovite autocracy reached a new peak under Ivan IV ("the Dread" or "the Terrible"), Russia's first true tsar. It was Tsar Ivan IV (r. 1553–1584) who launched Russia's bid for dominance in the Baltic, but only after he defeated the khanates on Russia's southern and eastern frontiers. Victory over Kazan in 1552 was merely the first step in Russia's expansion beyond traditionally "Russian" lands. In the east, the road was now open to unknown Siberia; in the northwest, however, Ivan IV waged war against the Livonian Confederation.

With its small hold on the coastline at the mouth of the Narva River, Russia enjoyed only limited access to the Baltic, and in 1539 it was further hindered by the Livonian Confederation's decision to bar Russians from trading directly with the foreign merchants visiting its towns. Ivan IV sought to remedy these conditions by launching a war in 1558 on the flimsy pretext that Tartu was once under the suzerainty of the Russian city of Pskov, to which it then paid regular tribute. Initial Russian successes resulted in the disbandment of the Livonian Confederation in 1561 (much of its territory fell to Poland-Lithuania and Sweden), but the war dragged on for 25 years with few gains by the Russian state.

Amidst the chaos of war the Baltic peasants fended for themselves. A peasant uprising in the far north, one of the largest in Estonian history, began in the autumn of 1560 but was crushed the following year. While most peasants continued to farm, others abandoned agriculture to join mercenary armies or to loot (or both). Widespread famine was the result. These events are vividly portrayed in Balthasar Russow's chronicle (1578), an intimate first-person account of these challenging and confusing times. A minister in Tallinn who wrote in Low German but who was possibly an Estonian, Russow was convinced that the tribulations of the mid-16th century were God's punishment for the sins committed by arrogant mortals. Accusing the nobility of all manner of vices while demonstrating sympathy for the suffering common people, his account emphasizes the feelings of helplessness shared by many as the region sank into chaos.[12]

Badly outnumbered by the Muscovites and fearing a Russian takeover, Gotthard Kettler (1517–1587), the Livonian Order's last grand master, belatedly followed the lead of Albert of Brandenburg, the first Duke of Prussia, and took the decisions to convert to Lutheranism and secularize the lands of the Livonian Order. On March 5, 1562, the knights disbanded. With the breakup of medieval Livonia, Kettler became a vassal of the Polish king (rather than the Holy Roman Emperor), receiving as a fief Courland and Semigallia (Latv. *Zemgale*). Riga, however, refused to swear an oath of allegiance to the Polish king and instead became an Imperial Free City of the Holy Roman Empire—a position it enjoyed for 20 years until the city's absorption in 1582 by Poland's King Stephen Bathory (r. 1575–1586), who installed a garrison and demanded the citizens' eternal loyalty.

With the formal dissolution of the Livonian Confederation in 1567, much of the remainder of Livonia north and east of the Daugava River, including the southern half of Estonia, was directly incorporated into the Catholic Poland of King Sigismund II Augustus. The Latvian areas of Livonia, or Polish Livonia (Latgale today, but known as Inflanty during the period of Polish-Lithuanian rule), were mostly but not entirely Catholicized; however, many of the region's inhabitants managed to retain their newly acquired Lutheran religious identity—as well as elements of their old pagan traditions. While most of Livonia fell into Polish-Lithuanian hands and remained there for nearly seven decades (1561–1629), parts of Courland and the island of Saaremaa were ceded to Denmark, while northern Estonia came under the control of Sweden, a Lutheran country.

In the long run, Ivan IV's attempts to expand into the Baltic were catastrophic not only for the local peasants but for Russia itself. After 1569, it faced a united Poland and Lithuania as well as a growing Sweden, each of which was concerned less with the fate of Livonia than with checking Muscovite expansion. Moreover, Russia's northern war diverted men and resources from the Tatar threat in the south and east. Shortly before his death in 1584, Ivan IV signed treaties with both Poland and Sweden renouncing all that Russia had gained in the first part of the war. A century later Russia's rulers would again set their sight on the Baltic, but in the meantime the slow development of the Estonian, Latvian, and Lithuanian peoples continued under western—which is to say German, Swedish, and Polish—political and cultural influence.

SWEDISH AND POLISH RULE

For a century and a half, from the moment Ivan IV launched his Livonian War in 1558 until Peter I's victory over Sweden in the Great Northern War in 1721, northeastern Europe was an object of contention between Poland-Lithuania, the Muscovite/Russian state, Sweden, and Denmark. The frequency and intensity of war in the eastern Baltic mirrored the heightened religious and political tensions in Europe that culminated in the Thirty Years' War (1618–1648) and the protracted conflict between the Swedish and Polish states during the first three decades of the 17th century.

Sweden, which during this period embraced the absolutist model and had trained one of Europe's most powerful armies, ended up the winner of the struggle, and in the process brought a considerable amount of land under the ownership of the state, acquiring them from the Order and from fleeing nobles. The settlement between Poland and Sweden was recognized in the Treaty of Altmark of 1629, according to which Sweden acquired all territories north of the Daugava River from Poland. This meant that Riga, parts of Latvia, and most of Estonia—that is, the provinces of Livland and Estland—now came under Swedish rule, while Inflanty and the Duchy of Courland remained under Polish suzerainty. Later, in 1645, Sweden also acquired the islands of Saaremaa and Kuresaare, thereby bringing all of Estonian territory under one authority.

With Sweden also controlling the most important cities in the eastern Baltic littoral—Tallinn, Riga, and Narva—from this point onward Polish power in the Baltic was in retreat. But the Swedish crown acquired territories that had been devastated by decades of war. Intended to be important sources of grain and revenue, swathes of the newly acquired territories were in fact nearly depopulated and their fields went untilled for decades. During the Polish-Swedish war the Estonian population fell from more than 250,000 to as little as 100,000; some regions suffered the loss of as much as 75 percent of their population.[13] As was usually the case in these times, most of the deaths came from famine and disease. Newcomers helped make up for the losses after the return of peace: Russians, especially Old Believers escaping tsarist persecution, settled on the shores of Lake Peipsi, while Finns were settled in Estonia by the Swedish authorities.[14]

The Muscovite invasion of Swedish Livland in 1656, combined with a plague and a famine in 1657–1658, further devastated local populations. While a Swedish-Muscovite treaty ended the fighting in Livonia in 1661 with Russia abandoning its conquests in Estland and Livland, the Commonwealth managed to oust the Muscovites from Lithuania. By 1670 the population of the Grand Duchy was half what it had been a mere 20 years earlier.[15] Sweden, on the other hand, was at the pinnacle of its power.

Despite these catastrophes, Estonians and Latvians of later eras romantically tend to view the era of Swedish rule as, if not exactly a golden age, at least a time of reform and relative liberalism sandwiched between the lengthier and more repressive periods of German and Russian rule. Although Germans, with their privileges intact, remained the main landowning element in Sweden's new Baltic provinces, some Swedish officials and generals received land, while Swedes were placed in local administrative positions and in the *Landtage*. Meanwhile, Roman Catholicism and Russian Orthodoxy, favored respectively by Livonia's former Polish rulers and the Muscovites, were in retreat as the Lutheran faith now enjoyed the protection of the Swedish monarchs.

But a main reason for Sweden's colonial domination of Livonia was food, which the latter eventually exported to the former in quantities sufficient to feed Sweden's growing population and still faster-growing military forces. One historian claims that during the final years of the reign of Gustavus II Adolphus (r. 1611–1632), the king who laid the foundations of the modern Swedish state and transformed it into a European great power, as much as 400,000 bushels of grain made their way from Riga to Sweden each year.[16] Timber, used principally for ship construction, was probably the region's second most important export product.

It is worth noting that the bulk of this trade was no longer in the hands of German merchants, as the Hanseatic League was in decline (it was dissolved in 1699) and the Danes had opened up the Baltic to international shipping. This allowed the Dutch, who were rapidly building their own commercial empire during the 17th century, and to a lesser extent the English, to dominate commerce in the southern Baltic. The Baltic Sea, once closed to competition and plagued by piracy, now became one of the safest regions for long-distance shipping anywhere in Europe.[17]

While the port city of Tallinn and Narva, a manufacturing center near the Russian border, were among those towns that prospered under Swedish rule, no city was transformed by Swedish rule more than Riga, whose fortification system was extensively renovated and equipped with pentagon-shaped bastions in an effort to turn the city into a modern military stronghold.[18] The largest commercial center in the eastern Baltic region, Riga also became the biggest city in the Swedish realm with a population of 12,000 to 15,000 (more or less the same as in 1500) in the mid-17th century. That nearly half its population consisted of Latvians, who outnumbered the city's German, Polish, and Swedish populations, demonstrates the diverse nature of this important metropolis.[19]

King Charles XI (r. 1672–1697) is usually regarded as the most reform-minded of the Baltic region's Swedish rulers and even as a defender of the interests of the Baltic peasants. Like other absolutist monarchs of his day, he was bent on centralizing power in his realm, which meant tightening his control over the powerful Baltic nobility. A related goal was the improvement of tax collection in his Baltic territories, necessary for the defense of Sweden's expansive empire. Thus in 1681 the king launched a policy of massive land expropriation, called "reductions." These cost the nobles in Estland one-third of their land while their counterparts in Livland surrendered five-sixths. Whether this policy did much to improve the conditions of the Livonian and Estonian peasantry is debatable, for the institution of serfdom was actually strengthened under Swedish rule, even if it was absent in Sweden itself. On the other hand, it may be argued that Swedish policies, by increasing state control over the reduced manors, awarding peasants the right to present petitions to state offices, and mitigating some of the worst abuses on the manors (such as corporal punishment), to some degree liberated the peasants who worked on them. Whatever the conditions of their peasants, most of the barons, including the Baltic Germans, remained loyal to the Swedish crown for a century and continued to exert a profound impact on all aspects of life in the region.

While Livland and Estland developed under Swedish rule for most of the 17th century, the Duchy of Courland and Semigallia, whose peasants were mostly Latvian, was under loose Polish control. Unlike most other Polish territories, Courland and Semigallia had Lutheran populations, having followed the lead of the last Livonian Grand Master, Gotthard Kettler, who converted in the mid-16th century. Since his day Courland nobles had enjoyed virtually unlimited control over their properties and the peasants who lived on them. Unlike the case in the Swedish-controlled territories of Livland and Estland, where many peasants came under the protection of the crown (which nominally owned many of the estates), the rulers of Courland never considered undertaking any reforms to mitigate the worst aspects of serfdom.

It was during the time of Gotthard's grandson Jacob Kettler (r. 1642–1682) that the duchy reached its peak and acquired colonies in distant Gambia and Tobago. While it seems unlikely that these colonies, which exported sugar, coffee, tobacco, cotton, and other goods to Europe, did much to enrich the duchy, they did suggest the scale of Kettler's ambitions at a time when Courland, despite its modest population of only 200,000, had one of Europe's larger merchant fleets and significant ports at Liepāja (Ger. *Libau*) and Ventspils (Ger. *Windau*). After Kettler's death in 1682, however, Courland lost its political and economic influence in the region, giving rise to a long period of instability in the duchy that served only to benefit Russia, whose role in the duchy's affairs increased over the course of the following century.

LITERATURE AND EDUCATION

That Estonian and Latvian continued their development as literary languages during the era of Swedish rule owes much to the efforts of Lutheran clergymen who attempted to reach their parishioners in their own vernacular. Although dozens of books, mostly theological tracts and hymnals, were published in Estonian and Latvian during the 17th century, the emergence of Estonian as a standardized literary language was hindered by the fact that two highly distinct Estonian dialects, northern and southern, had developed by this time. Not only was there a lack of an agreed-upon system of spelling, but the earliest grammar books, composed by Germans, simply adapted the Estonian language to the rules of German. These circumstances may help to explain why an Estonian-language Bible was not published until 1739, when the region was under Russian rule.

Among the pioneers of Latvian-language publishing was Georg Mancelius (1593–1654), a Lutheran clergyman and professor of theology at the University of Tartu. Born in Livland to German-speaking parents, he recognized the importance of being able to communicate his sermons to the Latvian peasants and learned their language. Mancelius published not only his hymn collections but also a work called *Lettus* (1638) which contained a Latvian-German dictionary that remained in use for more than a century. Also noteworthy was Ernst Glück's translations of the New and Old Testaments into Latvian in 1688–1694. While such writers made great contributions to the development of literary Latvian, for the overwhelming majority of Latvian, Lithuanian, and Estonian peasants, exceedingly few of whom could read any language, it was the oral tradition of folk songs, stories, and other spoken expression that remained the main means of transmitting local culture from one generation to the next until the late 19th century.

Until that time and with relatively few exceptions, education, which was practically inseparable from the Catholic Church throughout the Middle Ages, was limited to the children of the Baltic German elite as well as to Swedes and Finns. Cathedral and monastic schools were active throughout the region's urban areas: Riga's Dom school opened its doors in 1211, only a decade after the city's founding, and within a few decades such schools were also active in Tartu, Tallinn, and

Haapsalu in Estonia. While cathedral schools groomed future canons for the church, by the 15th century individuals who aspired to higher positions in the church were required to have a university education, which at that time was obtainable only outside the Baltic littoral. Thus the young men of Livonia who sought an education had little choice but to attend a university in Europe.

The first university in Estonia, the Academia Gustaviana, was established in 1632 in Tartu, where German and Latin were the languages of instruction. Accepting Swedish and German boys as young as 14 years of age, the University of Tartu supplied the region with future pastors, doctors, schoolteachers, and state officials. The university's first century reflected the turbulence of the age: closed in 1656 because of the Swedish-Russian War, it was reopened in 1690 before poor conditions in Tartu forced its relocation to Pärnu nine years later. In 1710, its activities came to a halt when the city surrendered to Russia. There were no institutions of higher education in the Latvian territories until the Riga Technical University was founded in 1862.

Lower-level education also improved under Swedish rule. While the Reformation dramatically reduced the number of cloister schools, most basic education was now provided by town schools and, for those who could afford private tutors, home schooling. Elementary education for a small number of peasants began in the 1680s with the founding of parish schools, located mostly in southern Estonia and in Latvia's Vidzeme region. In nearly all these cases, however, the language of instruction was German—a condition that did not change substantially until the 19th century under Russian rule.

THE GREAT NORTHERN WAR

The end of Swedish rule in Livland and Estland was a direct consequence of Muscovy's reemergence as a contender for power in the region during the reign of Peter Alekseevich Romanov (r. 1689–1725), known to history as Peter the Great. Crowned Peter I in 1689, the physically imposing tsar, who as a boy delighted in war games and dreamed of building a great navy, set his gaze to the Baltic Sea, which at this time remained a Swedish lake. For two decades the Swedish Empire was ruled by Peter's adversary Charles XII (r. 1697–1718), who ascended the throne at age 15 and quickly made a reputation for himself as a military commander of genius. As the 18th century dawned these soldier-kings found themselves locked in a struggle for mastery over the Baltic provinces known as the Great Northern War. While Peter's claim that Swedish authorities in Riga had insulted him during his visit to the city in 1697 by not allowing him to inspect the city's defensive system was Russia's justification for war, the reality was that he needed ports on the Baltic to realize his imperial ambitions. The fact that the rulers of Denmark and Poland-Lithuania also found Sweden's hegemony over the Baltic Sea worrisome resulted in an alliance in 1699 and war the following year.

Once again, the Baltic area was the scene of great devastation, with Peter's scorched-earth policy, famine, and plague being responsible for what can only modestly be described as a catastrophic loss of human life. The experience of Riga illustrates this fatal combination: first it was, like all of northeastern Europe, a victim of the great famine of 1695–1697 that preceded the onset of the Great Northern War.[20] In 1700, the city was twice besieged by Polish-Saxon forces who also burned its suburbs—a frequent occurrence in Riga's storied history. Never far from the fighting, the exhausted city hardly had time to recover before it was inundated by a flood in the spring of 1709, followed by a Russian siege in November, each of which in turn contributed to a poor harvest and more starvation. Bubonic plague made its first appearance in Riga the following May, devastating the entire region from Tallinn to Lithuania. As much as 40 percent of the population in Latvian lands perished and perhaps 60 percent in Estonia during the quarter century that ended with the conclusion of the Great Northern War.[21] So extensive was the damage to the lands and cities of the Baltic littoral that the recovery took decades rather than years.

In 1721, three years after the death of Charles XII, a peace treaty was finally signed whose provisions certified Russia's acquisition of Estland, Livland, and other territories in the region (but not Courland, which came under Russian rule at the end of the century), along with perhaps 300,000 new subjects. From Sweden, Peter the Great, now a European emperor, also acquired some swampy land on the bank of the Neva River upon which he built his new capital city, St. Petersburg, which became Russia's "window on Europe." With its Baltic conquests Russia had formally become a European power, and its new acquisitions in Livland and Estland were now counted among its provinces— later known as the Russian *Pribaltika*.

Despite the devastation of the Great Northern War, the Baltic German ruling class emerged stronger than ever thanks to the extremely favorable terms of surrender offered by the Russian tsar. To the landowners, whose support the tsar would need to maintain lasting supremacy in the Baltic provinces, Peter I returned the land expropriated by the Swedish crown in the last decades of the 17th century. The tsar also confirmed the rights of the Lutheran Church and German as the language of administration and the courts. Corporate bodies known as *Rittershaften*, formed in the 16th century by the Baltic German nobility, retained their privileges, and Germans maintained their control over the provincial *Landtage* of Estland and Livland.

With its privileges confirmed by subsequent Russian tsars and tsarinas, thereby perpetuating for a time a system of self-rule in Estland and Livland that helped isolate these provinces from the Russian interior, the nobility was able to strengthen its political hold over the region. Maritime commerce and the economic life of the cities continued to be controlled by German, Dutch, Scandinavian, and British merchants. Maintaining the privileges of the Baltic landed elite, however, also meant upholding the serf status of much of the Baltic peasantry during the first century of Russian rule in the region, a subject to which we shall return in the next chapter.

DECLINE OF THE POLISH LITHUANIAN COMMONWEALTH

While Russia's acquisition of the "Baltic provinces" of Estland and Livland occurred as a result of Sweden's defeat in the Great Northern War, the territories inhabited by Lithuanians remained mostly under the administration of the Polish-Lithuanian Commonwealth until nearly the end of the 18th century, when Russia acquired them during the Polish partitions.

In an age of absolutist government that was characterized by the opulence of King Louis XIV's court at Versailles, the aggressive strengthening of royal power by Sweden's Charles XI, and Peter the Great's monumental efforts to bring the accoutrements, if not the substance, of Western civilization to the Muscovite realm, the *Rzeczpospolita* was an anomaly in that it had a weak monarchy that was elected by the country's leading magnates. With about 5 percent of the Polish population (and an even higher percentage in Lithuania) enjoying noble status, one of the highest proportions in Europe, most of the Commonwealth's noblemen were not in fact wealthy and some lacked land altogether. Nevertheless, the nobility made its influence felt in the *Sejm*, where it enjoyed the *liberum veto*, an unusual parliamentary rule whose distinctive feature was the obstruction of the body's proceedings by the objection of a single member.

The internal divisions engendered by such a system gave Poland's centralizing, absolutist neighbors—Russia in particular—plenty of opportunities to intervene in the Commonwealth's internal affairs. It was during this period of growing weakness, from the "Deluge" of the mid-17th century to the end of the 18th century, that Russian influence over Poland-Lithuania, typically justified by its moral duty to protect the Commonwealth's numerically dominant Orthodox subjects, grew precipitously.

Meanwhile, the Lithuanian part of the Commonwealth gradually lost its distinctive identity, as the numerically weaker Lithuanians lost influence to the great Polish magnates who owned most of the land and dominated the *Sejm*. As Lithuanian noblemen educated their sons at Polish universities and married into Polish noble families, Lithuanian society continued its drift into the cultural orbit of the Poles, who like the Baltic Germans were considered the bearers of a "high" culture. By the middle of the 18th century, the separateness (and greatness) of the medieval Grand Duchy of Lithuania had become little more than a memory. As the lines separating Poland and Lithuania became ever blurrier, outsiders came to see the Polish-Lithuanian Commonwealth simply as Poland, with Lithuanian as just one of many tongues spoken by the kingdom's peasants.

The fortune of the Polish-Lithuanian state reached its lowest point during the final decades of the 18th century as the Commonwealth found itself in the path of the ambitious monarchs who ruled Austria, Prussia, and Russia. Together they conspired to divide the country in three successive partitions. By the terms of the first partition (1772), Russia's Empress Catherine II obtained much of the area that comprises modern Belarus along with the Latgale (Polish Inflanty). In the second partition (1793), Russia incorporated the rest of Belarus, western Ukraine, and much of Lithuania proper. In the partition of 1795 Russia acquired the remainder of Ukraine and Lithuania, where the majority of ethnic Lithuanians lived, as well as the Duchy of Courland. While this final partition brought an end to the Polish-Lithuanian Commonwealth, it succeeded in uniting under Russian rule the Latvian populations of Courland and Latgale with those of Livland, which had been in Russia's possession since the Great Northern War. It is likely, however, that the fact of this "unification" was lost on the Latvian peasantry, who were still scattered across several provinces and who as of yet possessed little in the way of a national identity.

While the 17th and 18th centuries witnessed the decline and ultimately the disappearance of the Grand Duchy of Lithuania, it ushered into Lithuania's cities the vibrant new architectural impulses of the Baroque era. Influenced by the ornate architectural styles characteristic of Italian Baroque, a distinctive style appeared in Vilnius, spreading northward in part by the church-building efforts of the Jesuits during the Counter Reformation. For example, Vilnius's Church of St. Casimir (1618) was inspired by Il Gesù church in Rome, the Jesuits' mother church.[22] No less exquisite is the Church of St. Peter and St. Paul (1668–1676), whose construction in a Vilnius suburb was supervised by Polish and Italian architects. Despite the precipitous political circumstances of the time, Vilnius Baroque reached its full flowering after 1750: ever more elaborate churches were commissioned and built in the city at the behest of wealthy Lithuanian magnates, so that by the end of the century there were no fewer than 32 Catholic churches with 15 monasteries (as well as a handful of Uniate, Russian Orthodox, Lutheran, and Calvinist churches) in this city of 40,000 inhabitants.[23] Acquired by the Russian Empire during the Polish partitions, it was Vilnius's fate during the 19th century to become a neglected provincial town populated mostly by Poles and Jews, its Lithuanian heritage all but forgotten.

NOTES

1. Endre Bojtár, *Foreword to the Past: A Cultural History of the Baltic People* (Budapest and New York: Central European Press, 1999), 44–54.

2. The names of the proto-Latvian tribes may also be rendered Kurlanders (or Kurs), Zemgals, Latgals (or Lettigallians), Sels.

3. Marija Gimbutas, *The Living Goddesses* (Berkeley: University of California Press, 2001), 197–213.

4. Bojtár, 307–317.

5. Andrejs Plakans, *A Concise History of the Baltic States* (New York: Cambridge University Press, 2011), 14.

6. The Viking Rurik was the founder of the earliest Rus'ian state, centered in Novgorod and later in Kiev, in the ninth century.

7. Later the Order moved its headquarters from Riga to Cēsis (Ger. *Wenden*), located in the center of Livonia. After 1330 its castle in Riga was rebuilt in the opposite corner of the city after it was destroyed in a war.

8. James A. Brundage, ed. and trans., *The Chronicle of Henry of Livonia* (New York: Columbia University Press, 1961), 67.

9. See S. C. Rowell in his *Lithuania Ascending: A Pagan Empire within East-Central Europe, 1295–1345* (New York: Cambridge University Press, 1994).

10. Timothy Snyder, *The Reconstruction of Nations: Poland, Ukraine, Lithuania, Belarus, 1569–1999* (New Haven and London: Yale University Press, 2003), 24.

11. Karl-Erik Frandsen, *The Last Plague in the Baltic Region, 1709–1713* (Copenhagen: Museum Tusculanum Press, 2010), 20.

12. *The Chronicle of Balthasar Russow,* trans. Jeremy C. Smith (Madison, WI: Baltic Studies Center, 1988).

13. Toivo U. Raun, *Estonia and the Estonians*, 2nd ed. (Stanford, CA: Hoover Institution Press, 2001), 28.

14. Old Believers were schismatics who rejected as heretical the reforms to the Orthodox rites and liturgy undertaken in the 17th century.

15. Andres Kasekamp, *A History of the Baltic States* (New York: Palgrave Macmillan, 2010), 50.

16. Arnolds Spekke, *History of Latvia: An Outline* (Stockholm: M. Goppers, 1957), 231.

17. Jan Glete, *Swedish Naval Administration 1521–1721* (Leiden, The Netherlands, and Boston: Brill, 2010), 35.

18. Irēna Bākule and Arnis Siksna, *Riga beyond the Walls: The City's Planned Growth and Transformation from the 17th Century to the First World War* (Riga: Neptuns, 2009), 26–65.

19. Plakans (2011), 81, 105.

20. As the granaries of the Swedish state, Estland and Livland continued to export large quantities of grain even as tens of thousands of Estonians starved.

21. While estimates vary for the loss of life during this period, all agree that by the early 1700s the populations of this region had been reduced to their lowest levels in centuries. Kasekamp estimates that the number of people in Estonian areas plummeted to 175,000, in Latvian areas to 225,000, and in the Grand Duchy of Lithuania to 1.85 million. Kasekamp (2010), 55.

22. Under Russian rule it functioned as an Orthodox church. In the 20th century the Soviets repurposed it as a vodka warehouse and then a Museum of Atheism. Tomas Venclova, *Vilnius: A Personal History* (Riverdale-on-Hudson, NY: The Sheep Meadow Press, 2009), 69–70.

23. See Tomas Venclova's exceptionally well-illustrated *Vilnius: City Guide* (Vilnius: R. Paknio leidykla, 2003) and Laimonas Briedis, *Vilnius: City of Strangers* (New York: Central European University Press, 2009), 55–61.

3

Russian Rule, 1710–1905

Sweden's century as the dominant power in the Baltic Sea ended in 1710 with the capitulation of the provinces of Livland (northern Latvia and southern Estonia) and Estland (northern Estonia). The new reality in the region was the Russian Empire, whose possession of a Baltic coastline significantly improved the country's strategic position in northeastern Europe. The rest of the area comprising the present-day Baltic states, except for Prussian-ruled Lithuania Minor, remained under Polish control until the *Rzeczpospolita* was partitioned by its neighbors in 1772, 1793, and 1795.

Because Livland and Estland came under Russian control many decades earlier and were governed by a ruling class of Baltic Germans, here they are treated separately from the Lithuanian territories, whose landowning class consisted mainly of Poles. Indeed, Russian state policy distinguished between the "Baltic provinces" (which also included Courland after its acquisition in 1795) and the Polish-Lithuanian provinces (which did not even touch the Baltic Sea), confirming the privileges of the loyal Baltic German elite in the former, while looking upon the elites of the Polish provinces with great suspicion, especially after the Polish uprising of 1830. In each case, however, the Russian government attempted to integrate these borderland territories into the administrative and legal framework of the Russian Empire by encouraging the use of the Russian language in administration and, to some extent, education.

BALTIC GERMANS AND THE RUSSIAN STATE

Baltic Germans constituted the bulk of the ruling class in the Estonian and Latvian lands until the early decades of the 20th century. In contrast to western Europe (except Ireland), the division between elite and peasantry in the Baltic lands generally had an ethnic basis: German nobles owned most of the land, German priests constituted the religious authorities, and German merchants dominated urban commerce. The indigenous populations, speaking their own languages and maintaining their own separate cultures, supported the German-speaking elite with their labors. This division became even more pronounced in the 16th and 17th centuries when much of the native peasantry became enserfed.

Although the medieval crusaders were Roman Catholic, Germans were also responsible for bringing the ideas of Martin Luther to the region in the 16th century and likewise for converting much of the native peasantry to Protestantism. Thus in the matter of religion, Baltic Germans and the surrounding peasants shared something in common—although how much is hard to say, given the peasantry's continued attachment to their pagan customs and rituals. In almost every other respect, however, the relationship was colonial. This was reflected in the Baltic Germans' generally condescending attitude toward the natives and their reputedly harsh treatment of Latvian and Estonian peasants. While the labor of these "non-Germans" was essential—Latvians, for example, had their own crafts in Riga and other cities—until the end of the 19th century the *Undeutsche* were barred from entering the urban professions and faced other restrictions. Yet it should also be remembered that in the eastern Baltic, as in other parts of Europe colonized by Germans, one's identity as a "German" was not entirely rooted in ethnicity, for people who were born Estonians or Latvians could assume a German identity through education and residence in a largely German city like Riga or Tallinn. As one historian observed: "If someone was born a peasant, speaking a peasant tongue, but managed to raise himself to a different social order and speak German, he was no longer a peasant, but German."[1] Among the heroes of the Estonian and Latvian national awakenings of the 19th century, more than a few had a biography of this type.

Even if not all the people considered "German" in the eastern Baltic were nobles, or were even German by birth, what is clear is that Germans of noble lineage enjoyed an enviable status during the 18th century, a time that may be considered the apogee of the nobility in Russia and elsewhere in Europe. Because the Baltic German aristocrats were a trusted and even admired elite, Russian tsars allowed them an unusual degree of autonomy in running the Baltic territories and recognized their almost unlimited rights vis-à-vis the peasants, who were now almost universally enserfed and tied to the lands of their masters. As the empire's most westernized provinces, their local governments and courts were to serve as models for the rest of Russia, which Peter I sought to reform along European lines. Not only were Baltic Germans, equipped with the necessary technical and political expertise, allowed to administer local government in the Baltic provinces with minimal intervention by tsarist authorities, they also served in St. Petersburg as diplomats and administrators, filling the ranks of the country's swelling bureaucracy—and often replacing the German-speaking foreigners upon whom the state had earlier relied.

Above all, Baltic Germans were well represented in the officer corps of the Russian army, as Peter I and his successors valued their education, experience, and familiarity with Western technology and warfare. As in state service, they replaced the foreigners—men of Scots, French, German, Polish, and Swedish origin—upon whom the Russian armed forces had relied since the 17th century. Of the entire officer corps of the Russian army in the 1730s, a decade during which the Baltic Germans enjoyed particular favor under Empress Anna (r. 1730–1740), perhaps as many as one-quarter were Germans. By the 1870s, Germans constituted more than half the higher officers, three-quarters of the army's generals, and were heavily represented in the Ministry of War.[2]

The service of educated Germans like Anna's lover, the noblemen Ernst Johann Biron (1690–1772), whose sprawling Baroque palaces in Jelgava (Ger. *Mitau*) and Rundāle were among the most magnificent in the empire, was also necessary for the Russian state to achieve its diplomatic and economic goals in Europe. Russian ambassadors to Britain were almost always Baltic Germans, and since German was the *lingua franca* of the Baltic region and central Europe, nobles from Livland (which they called *Lettland*) and Estland played a vital role in furthering Russia's foreign policy and commercial objectives in Europe.

The accession to the Russian throne of Catherine II (r. 1762–1796), a German-born princess who took power during a palace coup against her husband Peter III, heralded some changes in the status of the Baltic

Germans and the provinces they governed. A product of the Enlightenment, Catherine the Great strove to achieve a higher degree of uniformity, rationality, and centralization in the empire's law and government, while retaining the absolutist basis of her rule. Enacting reforms that reorganized the empire into *gubernii* (provinces) and *uezdy* (districts), the empress made clear her intention to subordinate the empire's peripheral regions to absolute Russian rule. After the Polish partition of 1795 the region that today embraces the modern countries of Estonia, Latvia, and most of Lithuania were administered as the provinces of Estland, Livland, Courland, Kaunas (Rus. *Kovno*), and Vilnius (Rus. *Vilna*, Pol. *Wilno*).[3] Another western province, Vitebsk, included the Latgale region of present-day Latvia as well as much of modern Belarus.

While in the Ukrainian and Belarusian lands Catherine and her successors implemented what might loosely be termed "Russification" measures designed to integrate the newly annexed regions into the legal and political framework of the empire, in Estland and Livland Russia's rulers proceeded with a lighter touch. In part this caution was a reflection of the Romanovs' admiration for the institutions of the local nobility, but it also reflected the government's concern that the Baltic Germans, having been allowed to maintain the diets (*Landtage*) and noble corporations (*Ritterschaften*) that they had earlier developed in earlier times, might form an organized resistance to St. Petersburg. If the privileges of the Baltic nobility diminished during the reign of Catherine the Great, some of them were restored during the reign of her son Paul I (r. 1796–1801), who required in return that Baltic landowners provide recruits from among their serfs for the Russian army. The Baltic German nobility maintained their autonomy until the accession in 1881 of Tsar Alexander III (r. 1881–1894), a devout supporter of autocracy and Russification, who abolished the nobility's special rights.

Apart from their political and economic dominance, Baltic Germans made significant contributions to the social and cultural life of the region from the medieval era through the period of Swedish rule and under the two centuries of Russian domination. Unfortunately this record of achievement has been somewhat obscured by the efforts of Estonians and Latvians during the past century to create their own pantheons of modern cultural heroes. As a result many of the earlier contributions of the Baltic Germans—as well as those of individual Russians, Poles, and others—have sometimes been overlooked.

Perhaps the most important contributions of the Baltic Germans to the region's culture were institutional, for German educational, cultural, civic, and religious institutions preceded those of the Estonians and Latvians by hundreds of years and directly influenced them. Among the most prominent Baltic German educational institutions was the University of Tartu (Dorpat), originally founded in 1632. Closed during the Great Northern War, it was reopened in 1802 and for the remainder of the century continued to be one of the leading universities in the Russian Empire—the "Heidelberg of the North"— as it attracted leading academicians from Germany. The Academia Petrina founded in Jelgava in 1775 by Peter von Biron aspired to university status, but after Russia's acquisition of Courland it was turned into a high school. The only other institution of higher education in the areas that now comprise the Baltic states was the University of Vilnius (Wilno), which Russian authorities shut down after the rebellion of 1830–1831.

While secondary schools had existed in the towns of Latvia and Estonia since the 13th and 14th centuries, the number of schools and students grew considerably during the 19th century. The educational system of the Baltic provinces was the best in the region, unequalled elsewhere in the empire or in Poland and based on German traditions: the languages of instruction were German and Latin, and German teachers provided instruction to the children of affluent Germans in the towns and to a small number of Estonians and Latvians. Although the central authorities, lacking their own resources, encouraged the local Germans to take a leading role in providing a basic education to provincial youth, by the mid-19th century some Russian officials began to recognize the dangers inherent in an educational system that threatened to lure Latvian and Estonians toward German rather than Russian culture.

While the Baltic Germans dominated the economic, political, and social life of the provinces in which they lived, numerically they remained a small portion of the overall population. Germans always constituted less than 10 percent of the population of the Baltic provinces, and by the end of the 19th century they were probably less than 6 percent of the overall population of modern-day Latvia and Estonia. Yet while the fact that the region's pastors, doctors, lawyers, teachers, and intellectuals were overwhelmingly Germans is indisputable, it is sometimes overlooked that many of them hailed from Germany proper. Unlike those Baltic Germans who possessed estates in the countryside, transplants like the composer Richard Wagner, who directed an opera house in Riga in the late 1830s, lived almost exclusively in the cities, where they found the German urban environment hospitable. Of less interest to them was the countryside, where

Baltic Germans resided on isolated manors in a sea of Estonian and Latvian peasants. Many landlords were of the absentee variety, owning scattered estates that they left in the hands of overseers while they enjoyed life in the empire's more vibrant cities.

Although Baltic Germans had begun to nurture a distinctive geographic–ethnic identity as *Baltendeutsche,* they were divided across three provinces and were physically and politically separated from the German lands. Thus they were not a unified group and entertained no "national" aspirations. While Baltic Germans guarded their historic rights and privileges (including the privilege of not having to learn Russian—although one suspects that most of the German nobles could communicate with their Russian counterparts in French), they were loyal servants of the tsar, whose government provided the German minority with the political support necessary for maintaining their rule in the Baltic provinces.[4] Likewise, most Russian rulers regarded the Baltic Germans as honest and particularly useful subjects.

ESTONIAN AND LATVIAN PEASANTS

Estonians were the predominant ethnic group of Estland and northern Livland. In the early 18th century, after the famine of 1695–1697 and the disasters of the Great Northern War, there were perhaps only 100,000 persons living in Estonian lands. After this time, however, the Estonian population recovered rapidly and by 1782 the population of the ethnographically Estonian territories had reached close to half a million. By 1858 perhaps as many as 750,000 people—mostly Estonians, but also Russians, Swedes, Latvians, Setus, and others—lived in Estland and northern Livland.[5]

Ethnic Latvians lived in southern Livland, Courland, and Latgale (which was incorporated into Russia's Vitebsk province). In the early 18th century the number of people living in Latvian-speaking areas was perhaps 465,000, rising to 873,000 at the end of the century.[6] The western areas were the least ethnically mixed, containing mainly Latvian-speaking peasants and German landowners and town-dwellers. The eastern parts of what is now Latvia were considerably more heterogeneous: in the Latgale region Latvians, Russians, Poles, Jews, and Belarusians comprised the bulk of the population.

In contrast to the relatively simple case of the Estonians, who emerged as an identifiable ethno-linguistic group before the German conquests of the 13th century, the question of when Latvians became "Latvians" is complex. As noted in chapter 2, the ancestors of modern Latvians were Latgallians, Couronians, Semigallians, Livonians, and Selonians. While it is likely that tribal identities gradually withered under the impact of the German conquest, it is also possible that the presence of uninvited, aggressive foreigners facilitated their cultural unity and hence their emergence as Latvians. Whatever the case, by around 1500, the old group identities had been submerged into a broader, although not necessarily very deep, Latvian identity. Like the Estonians to the north, these Latvians, who the Germans had begun to call *Letten* by the 1500s, were overwhelmingly peasants and remained subordinated to the local German elites.

This remained the case throughout the centuries of Swedish rule and Russian rule. Following the disasters of the Great Northern War, conditions for Latvian and Estonian peasants stabilized during the unusually long peace that came with Russian rule, and their status as serfs underwent little change for more than a century. Under Russian rule as under the Swedes, the peasants belonged to the manor, but the manor belonged to men upon which the government relied. Rarely consisting of more than two or three hundred peasant households, Baltic estates were not as large as those in other parts of the Russian Empire, and certainly not as large as those in Poland, Ukraine, and Lithuania. However large or small, each noble landholding was divided into two areas for cultivation: the noble's estate, which consisted of a single consolidated unit, and the "peasant" land, which was held in scattered strips for periodic redivision by Latvian and Estonian peasants. Peasants worked "peasant" land in exchange for dues payable to the landowners; this sometimes involved money payments but usually meant providing labor (*corvée*) for the estate land.

In the eyes of the peasants and of the educated critics of serfdom it was an exploitive system that landowners, who by the end of the 18th century possessed an estimated 4,700 estates of widely varying sizes in the Estonian, Latvian, and Lithuanian lands, used to extract an increasing amount of labor from the peasants who could not leave.[7] Indeed, under the control of the Baltic barons serfdom was intensified for the purpose of expanding grain production for export to western Europe. Meanwhile, the Russian interior became the main market for the grain- and potato-based spirits that were distilled on Baltic manors from the 1730s onward. It is likely that the resulting rise in the amount of obligatory peasant labor on the estates was in large measure responsible for the peasant unrest that stirred the Baltic provinces during the final decades of the 18th century.

EMANCIPATION AND ITS CONSEQUENCES

Emancipation for the serfs of Estonia and most of Latvia preceded that for serfs in other parts of the Russian Empire by nearly half a century and was a major impetus behind the transformation of both the region's economy and its inhabitants' social and cultural lives. Despite the occasional peasant disturbances that accompanied the intensification of rural production, it cannot be said that emancipation was the result of the organized efforts of Estonian and Latvian peasants; nor was it an initiative undertaken by the Baltic German nobility, most of whom seemed to have felt that there was little need for change. Exceptions did exist, however, such as the clergyman Johann George Eisen von Schwarzenberg (1717–1779), who argued that it was necessary to abolish serfdom and replace the feudal manor economy with a system that favored money rent.[8] However, it was far more common for German landowners to criticize such reform efforts rather than to make earnest attempts to implement them.

Instead of being a German initiative, the process of emancipation arose out of the Russian government's concern for the condition of the peasantry—and its potential for producing tax revenues for St. Petersburg—during the reign of Catherine the Great. Visiting the region in 1764, Catherine was appalled by Baltic landlords' "despotic and cruel" treatment of their serfs and urged the landlords to reform lest change be imposed upon them by the imperial government. The empress directed the Livland *Landtag* to assure peasant rights to movable property and to provide other protective measures, but little came of it. However, Catherine's grandson Alexander I (r. 1801–1825), an enthusiastic reformer during the early years of his reign, acted more resolutely to improve the peasantry's condition not only in the Baltic provinces, but throughout the empire. The more advanced and efficient Baltic regions were to serve as test cases and the Baltic German nobility were expected to take the initiative in working out the details.

The results were the peasant laws grudgingly created by the *Landtage* of Estland in 1802 and Livland in 1804. While each focused mostly on the peasants' heredity rights, the latter went a step further by providing for the creation of peasant judicial institutions and placing limitations on the landlords' rights over the lives of peasants on their estates. But it was not until 1816, a decade after serf emancipation had begun in the areas defeated by Napoleon's armies, that genuine emancipation came to Estland, followed by Courland in 1817 and Livland in 1819. Latgallian and Lithuanian peasants were emancipated only in 1861 along with the remainder of the empire's serfs.

The emancipation laws of 1817/1819, whose terms were worked out by committees representing the local nobility, were implemented incrementally in order to minimize disorder during the transition period, which took about 14 years. In the end, nearly one million peasants were granted personal freedom; however, they were denied land, which was retained by the lords, and until 1874 they were also subject to conscription into the Russian army. Politically, the Estonian and Latvian peasants (except in Latgale) remained under the control of the German nobility, who retained judicial and police powers, including the right to administer corporal punishment.

While the landowners retained their traditional control over the peasants, emancipation meant that they gave up their traditional obligation to look out for their well-being. Indeed, some historians view the post-emancipation decades until around 1850 as a period of protracted rural crisis, during which low-level unrest among the landless and destitute peasantry was regularly in evidence. Although no longer considered property, the landless peasants made due by renting land from the nobles, paying them rent in the form of either labor or, less commonly, money. Many landowners continued to rely on the distilling of alcohol as the surest means of increasing their income—an overwhelming majority of Livland's estates were involved in distilling—but even the market for alcohol was unreliable. For peasants, the worst period was the winter of 1845–1846, when bad harvests resulted in famine. Desperate to escape hunger and rising labor rents, tens of thousands of peasants converted to Orthodoxy and begged to be allowed to move to the Russian interior.

Although significant restraints on the peasantry's freedom of movement remained in place until the 1860s, emancipation laid the groundwork for the great changes that took place in the region after mid-century. In particular, peasants enjoyed more freedom to move to the towns, which were just beginning to become centers of industry, and to join other occupations. For the time being, however, most of the region's peasants remained agricultural laborers who worked on the manors of the German landlords. Access to land improved during the 1860s following the introduction of legislation designed to boost local self-government and increased pressure by St. Petersburg on the German nobility to abolish labor rent and make more land available to peasants. Money rents began replacing labor rent in much of the region as rural properties increasingly came under peasant ownership. By 1877 peasants owned more than 40 percent of agricultural land in Livland, although in Estland the process was slower. Despite the improving conditions enjoyed by many of the region's rural families, tens of thousands of whom now became the owners of the land they worked, the peasant problem was not entirely solved, for many remained burdened by financial obligations to both the government and the landowners up to the end of the century. Moreover, hundreds of thousands of Estonian and Latvian peasants continued to suffer from landlessness (caused in part by a swelling population that drove up in absolute terms the number of landless peasants), debt, and foreclosures. Many drifted to the interior of Russia to find land and work in factories. While Riga offered a new life for many thousands of Latvian peasants, few Estonians migrated to the burgeoning metropolis on the Daugava.

Accompanying the process of emancipation was the introduction of surnames. Until then Latvian and Estonian peasants were usually known only by their Christian names and the names of their manors and fathers. Since the new surnames were usually given by the German landowners, many emancipated peasants received German or German-sounding names, usually the name of the farmstead on which the peasant was living. Many of these names stuck until the early 20th century when surnames were nativized.

If emancipation inaugurated real and lasting change in the lives of the region's rural inhabitants, the introduction of the potato was quietly momentous, as it helped to alleviate the age-old problem of hunger. Peasants in Courland had begun growing potatoes in the 17th century, but attempts to force other Baltic peasants to grow the crop failed. Only at the beginning of the 19th century was a breakthrough achieved, and soon the potato became the most important field crop in many areas. Because of its profitability, flax also gained popularity in Lithuania, Latgale, and southern Estonia. Throughout the region the raising of dairy cattle and pigs was common as Estonian and Latvian peasants increasingly became masters of their own lands.

RELIGIOUS LIFE IN LATVIA AND ESTONIA

While Lithuanian peasants remained in the orbit of the Catholic Church, the lives of Latvian and Estonian peasants, like those of their German landlords, were closely tied to the Lutheran Church, which in addition to regulating the spiritual lives of the Baltic population provided much of what little education existed before emancipation. In the 1730s and 1740s, however, a branch of Pietism known as Moravianism made inroads in the Baltic region, especially in Estonia. With its emphasis on humility, morality, equality, and self-education, Pietism played an important role in increasing the peasantry's self-consciousness; indeed, its emphasis on reading the Bible is probably one of the reasons that Estonians and Latvians later emerged from serfdom as some of the Russian Empire's most literate peoples. Since the Baltic nobility and clergy were unable to keep the movement under control, it was prohibited by the Russian state from 1743 to 1764. Nevertheless, a new wave of Moravianism, with its renewed emphasis on civil rights, spread through the Estonian lands in the early 19th century. By 1839 membership in the Moravian Brethren (*Herrnhuttern*) in the Baltic exceeded 66,000. By the 1860s, however, the dominant Lutheran Church, under the general supervision of St. Petersburg since the establishment of the General Consistory for the Evangelical-Lutheran Church in 1832, had nearly managed to eradicate the movement.

Although the Russian state upheld the privileged position that Lutheranism had enjoyed since the Reformation, the laws of the empire nevertheless favored Russian Orthodoxy, which had originally been introduced in eastern Estonia in the 11th century but whose influence on the Estonian and Latvian populations had remained quite limited until modern times. Despite the establishment of an Orthodox bishopric in Riga in 1836, the Russian government made little attempt to encourage the Baltic population to convert to Russian Orthodoxy until the late 19th century. Mostly it was concerned with meeting the needs of the small existing Orthodox community in the Baltic provinces, a community that grew substantially with the arrival of Old Believers to Lithuania and the eastern borders of Livland at the end of the 18th century. Nevertheless, the offspring of mixed marriages in the Baltic provinces were expected to be baptized and raised as Orthodox Christians, and Lutheran pastors were prohibited from proselytizing among the tsar's Orthodox subjects.

Yet the fact is that with the arrival of more Russians to the Estonian and Latvian lands during the 19th century Orthodoxy's influence was on the rise, so much so that by the 1930s, a decade after Estonia achieved its independence, more than half of the registered members of the autocephalous Estonian Apostolic Orthodox Church (EAOC) were ethnic Estonians. While Orthodoxy offered little appeal to Latvians— and practically none to Lithuanians—this did not stop tsarist authorities from authorizing the construction in Riga's city center of the imposing Nativity Cathedral, which was completed in 1883. Similarly grand Orthodox churches of the neo-Byzantine style—undeniable symbols of Russian imperialism—were completed in Tallinn in 1900 and in Vilnius in 1903.

ORIGINS OF THE NATIONAL AWAKENINGS

The imperial government's efforts to Russify its Baltic provinces paralleled efforts by local activists to assert their own national distinctiveness. It was only in the last decades of the 18th century, the Age of Enlightenment, that modern ideas about nationhood, hitherto associated exclusively with the nobility, began to take shape. Intellectuals in the German lands, for example, emphasized the *Volk* ("people"), with its oral traditions of legends, fables and songs, as the key to understanding the essence of Germanness. It wasn't long before learned Germans in the Baltic also began to "discover" the local peasantry, identifying them too as Völker possessing their own characteristics and traditions.

This scientific approach to the Baltic peasantry was taken most famously by Johann Gottfried Herder (1744–1803), a German pastor who lived in the Baltic area for some time and taught in Riga in the late 1760s. Considered the intellectual father of the German nation, Herder was also fascinated by the language and folklore of the local peasantry and included several Estonian folksongs in his *Stimmen der Völker in Liedern* (The Peoples' Voices in Song), published in 1787. Herder's great contribution to Latvian and Estonian nationhood was to stimulate interest in peoples who up to this point in history lacked their own literary culture, which was first developed by curious Baltic Germans who learned the local peasant tongues. For example, it was during this period that Gotthard Stender (1714–1796), a deeply learned man who probably exercised greater influence on the development of literary Latvian than any other individual, began to publish his folk tales for Latvian peasants as well as a Latvian grammar, dictionary, and scientific encyclopedia.

The local languages and folklore were of particular interest to such scholars, who in 1824 founded the Society of Friends of Latvians. The Estonian Learned Society, founded in 1838 by a group of Estonophiles— Baltic Germans who had an interest in Estonia—was created for much the same purposes. Likewise, it was the Baltic Germans who published the first newspapers in the local languages, although Estonians or Latvians often contributed articles. Such periodicals included the weekly *Latviešu avīzes* (The Latvian Newspaper) and the Estonian-language *Marahwa Näddala-Leht* (Countryfolk Weekly), each of which began to appear in the 1820s, shortly after peasant emancipation.

It was hardly coincidental that this era saw quickly rising literacy rates among the Protestant peoples of the littoral. By the first decades of the 19th century the majority of Latvian youth in Livland were literate.[9] And even if the Estonian peasants were further behind, by mid-century the literacy rate for Estonians over the age of 10 approached 90 percent.[10] By contrast, the literacy rate for Russian adults was around 30 percent at the end of the century. With the emergence of the

Latvian and Estonian intelligentsia, the growth of a significant reading public, and the development of Latvian and Estonian as literary
languages, by the middle of the 19th century the preconditions existed
for the "national awakenings" of the Baltic peoples.

In most areas of national development, the Lithuanians were behind
the Estonians and Latvians. Lithuanians were territorially divided,
residing on each side of a border that separated the Russian Empire
from Prussia/Germany. But a still greater impediment to the development of a sense of Lithuanian national consciousness was the fact that
over the course of the 400-year Polish-Lithuanian union the Lithuanian
elites had largely assimilated into Polish culture. Although a separate
if weakly developed Lithuanian literary language had been in existence since Lutheran clergymen began publishing religious literature in
Lithuanian in the 16th century, the Lithuanian national idea remained
dormant until the 1860s.

THE LATVIAN AWAKENING

The awakenings of Baltic nations should be seen in the context of
the popular yearnings for national unity that were developing in other
parts of Europe. While Giuseppe Mazzini worked tirelessly in the
1830s and 1840s to forge an Italian nation out of the Italian-speaking
peoples of a politically divided peninsula, in the multinational Austrian Empire a Czech national movement had been developing for
decades before the revolutionary explosions of 1848, when the historian František Palacký, now regarded as a father of the Czech nation,
led a push for Czech autonomy within the empire. This occurred just
as the Hungarians, who like the Czechs could look back to a time
when they had their own kingdom, demanded political equality with
Austria's dominant nation, the Germans. While these efforts failed
politically—the Habsburg Empire's "Springtime of Nations" ended
with the restoration of the *status quo ante*—their long-term result
was the legitimization in Europe of the nation-state as an organizing
principle.

Yet the growth of national consciousness among the Latvian and
Estonian peoples was not spurred by a desire for self-government,
for their status as subjects of the tsar appeared be a perfectly natural
and permanent feature of the existing order, but by the perceived unfairness of their continued subservience to an alien German nobility.
The Baltic German writer Garlieb Merkel (1769–1850) was among the
first to draw attention to these issues. His polemic *The Latvians*, published in Germany in 1796, lamented the ethnic and national divide

in Livonia, the inhumanity of serfdom, and the abuses committed by Baltic German landlords. While his scathing arguments, in particular his call for intervention by the Russian government, angered many of the local landowners, the book was translated into numerous languages and has cemented his reputation as a pioneer of the idea of a free Latvian nation.[11]

Yet Latvians could not fully take control of their own cultural development until they had developed a native intellectual class that willingly embraced its Latvianness. The turning point was the 1860s, the Era of Great Reforms in Russia as well as the age of Italian and German unification (and a Polish rebellion). By the end of the decade native Latvian speakers were the authors of more than half of all Latvian-language texts, most of which were stories and poems. More political concerns were often on the minds of the publishers of the weekly newspaper *Pēterburgas avīzes* (St. Petersburg Newspaper, 1862–1865), who used this organ to ridicule the Baltic Germans' pretensions to cultural and political superiority. Latvians, they were now convinced, needed to be "awakened" to the fact of their membership in the nation (*tauta*).

Yet the goal of the Latvian activists of this era was not independence or even autonomy, but the right to cultural development and the recognition of the dignity of the Latvian nation and its equality with other peoples. The *jaunlatviesi* (Young Latvians) movement of the 1860s, inspired by Mazzini's "Young Italy" and similar national movements that had sprung up elsewhere, wanted Latvians to be recognized as more than just a peasant people; the Young Latvians wished for Latvians to assume a cultural and economic presence that reflected their greater numbers in the provinces in which they resided.

A significant problem that the nascent Latvian nation faced was its territorial disunity: Latvian-speaking peoples lived in the *gubernii* of Livland, Courland, and Vitebsk, and tended to think in local terms. Another impediment to unity was that upwardly mobile Latvians tended to assimilate into one of the dominant cultures—German or Russian. For the Latvian intellectuals, the key to overcoming these difficulties then was to foster the idea that all Latvians were one people sharing a collective identity, a shared historical experience, and a common destiny. This was to be achieved by educating the Latvian peasantry and developing the Latvian language from a peasant tongue into a language of culture on a par with other literary languages. Such were the views of Krišjānis Valdemārs (1825–1891), who was one of the first educated Latvians to flout convention and regard himself as a Latvian rather than as a German. A leader of the Young Latvians and an editor for *Pēterburgas avīzes*, Valdemārs urged Latvians to increase their distance from the culturally and economically dominant Baltic Germans, suggesting instead that the Latvian nation would benefit from drawing closer to the politically powerful Russian government. From this perspective, St. Petersburg's efforts to Russify the Baltic provinces actually meant *more* freedom for the development of Latvian (and Estonian) culture.

Although often resented by the thin but growing Latvian intelligentsia, Germans were not always perceived as malevolent, as Latvian activists recognized that there were many liberal-minded Baltic Germans, such as Garlieb Merkel, who were sympathetic to the awakening of the Baltic peoples. Nevertheless, anti-German feeling was typical of many Latvian activists, and most Latvians had little reason to question the permanence of their status as subjects of the Russian Empire, to which some Latvian awakeners like Valdemārs looked to mitigate further Germanization.

During the second half of the 19th century Latvians formed numerous organizations whose goals and character, they assured tsarist authorities, were nonpolitical. The largest and wealthiest of these was the Riga Latvian Association (RLA), founded in 1868 ostensibly as a relief organization to aid victims of famine. In reality the RLA was actively involved in cultural development, and even had its own newspaper, *Baltijas vēstnesis* (Baltic Journal), an advocate for Latvian causes and ideas. Latvians also created agricultural and self-help associations. Although women, whose lives were still centered on the home, generally were little involved in the most important activities associated with the national awakening, there were nevertheless some opportunities for women to engage in public affairs. In 1818, for example, the Riga Association of Women was established for the purpose of providing aid to the needy. Fifty years later the Riga Latvian Charity Association was formed, and women played a prominent role in its leadership and activities.

The awakening continued through the period of Russification as Latvian scholars looked to the countryside to define the essence of "Latvianness." Fricis Brīvzemnieks (1846–1907), a school inspector and protégé of Valdemārs, collected Latvian folklore in the 1870s and 1880s in the belief that a widespread familiarity with it would increase the Latvian people's sense of national belonging. Jānis Cimze (1814–1881), a composer and music teacher, helped lay the groundwork for this activity by organizing the systematic collection of Latvian folk music. His work was continued by Andrejs Jurjāns (1856–1922), who became the most important name in Latvian music folk study in the early 20th century, and Krišjānis Barons (1835–1923), who remains the most celebrated of Latvia's awakeners. Taking over the folkloric materials earlier assembled by Brīvzemnieks, the meticulous Barons is reputed to have collected around 35,000 *dainas*—the traditional four-line Latvian folk songs—in about 217,996 variations.

It was also during this general period that Andrejs Pumpurs (1841–1902) published *Lāčplēsis* (The Bear-Slayer), which soon became recognized as a Latvian classic. Since Latvia had no epics comparable to those of the Scandinavian sagas, Pumpurs constructed his own folk epic out of fragments of Latvian folklore. The poem's publication in 1888 helped shape a nation's consciousness concerning the historic and ongoing struggle between Latvians and Germans, and influenced later writers and politicians who continued the national struggle against foreign oppressors.

While the Latvians of southern Livland and Courland experienced a national awakening from mid-century onward, until the 1890s Latgallians were largely isolated from these intellectual and popular currents. Because Latgale had spent more than a century under Polish rule and then was governed as part of the Russian province Vitebsk, the region's history had diverged from that of the other Latvian lands. As serf emancipation came to Latgale more than four decades later (1861) after it liberated the peasants of the Baltic provinces, the region's socioeconomic development lagged behind. Moreover, the elites of Latgale tended to be Polish and Russian rather than Baltic German. Because of this isolation and the ethnic heterogeneity of the province in which they lived, national identity among the largely Catholic Latgallians lagged behind that of the Lutheran regions of Livland and Courland. Until the 20th century the Latgallians' cultural ties to the western Latvians were minimal; only during the revolutionary tumult of 1905 can it be said that Latgale was brought into the fold of the nascent Latvian *tauta*.

THE ESTONIAN AWAKENING

Like the Latvians, Estonian intellectuals who guided the creation of Estonian nationhood had to steer a course between the economically and culturally dominant Baltic Germans on one side, and the Russian political authorities on the other. Two of the leading first-generation Estonian "awakeners" were the physicians Friedrich Reinhold Kreutzwald (1803–1882) and Friedrich Robert Faehlmann (1798–1850), each of whom attended German schools and thus may be considered Germanized Estonian intellectuals. Born the son of serfs, Kreutzwald had an especially profound impact on the Estonian national awakening as the compiler of the Estonian national epic, *Kalevipoeg* (Son of Kalev, 1857–1861). Based on both Estonian folk tradition and the Finnish epic *Kalevala* (1835), Kreutzwald's epic promised that its mythological hero, the ancient ruler of Estonia, would one day return "To bring his children happiness / and build Estonia's life anew." Thus the allegorical *Kalevipoeg* was a reflection of Kreutzwald's belief that the Estonians of his own time were perfectly capable of overcoming their socioeconomic conditions and that through education they could achieve and preserve Estonian nationhood. Faehlmann, who played a role in outlining the story, was less optimistic: unconvinced that that Estonians were likely to develop as an independent nationality, he believed that their fate was to be assimilated into German culture.

Concerned that the Baltic Germans would over time fully Germanize the Latvian and Estonian peasantry, Tsar Alexander II's government began to pay more attention to developments in the empire's Baltic region. Here there was a coincidence of interests with the local peasantry, some of whom sought protection against the power of the Baltic German establishment. Sharing a disposition similar to that of the Russian (and all) peasants, many peasants looked for the "good tsar" to rescue them from the "wicked nobility" whose economic, administrative, and cultural dominance they wished to mitigate through the actions of imperial authorities. As the impetus for reform in the Baltic region in earlier periods had come from St. Petersburg, it made perfect sense for Estonian peasants to send delegations to the capital in the 1860s to petition for the extension to the Baltic of Russia's reforms, including some administrative Russification, judicial reforms, and the introduction of institutions for local government (*zemstva*). The peasant delegations added that they would also welcome the substitution of Russian for German as the major foreign language in Estonian schools—a reform they believed would not only reduce German cultural influence on Estonian students, but that would have the added benefit of offering those who learned Russian opportunities for career advancement in the empire.

Intellectuals such as Carl Robert Jakobson (1841–1882) and Johann Köler (1826–1899) shared the Russophile perspective of these peasant petitioners. As leaders of Estonian society they even headed a delegation that in 1881 presented a memorandum to the new tsar Alexander III requesting the introduction of land, legal, and educational reforms that favored Russification. In the view of Jakobson, a schoolteacher and writer, only the benevolence of the Russian tsar could break the Germans' hold on the Estonians. Likewise, Köler, a professor at the St. Petersburg Academy of Fine Arts, saw the tsarist government as a positive force for the development of Estonian national life.

Other Estonian intellectuals who emerged in the 1860s and 1870s questioned this gravitation toward political power and were more inclined to accept the leadership of the German community, as Robert Faehlmann had done in earlier decades. Johann Voldemar Jannsen (1819–1890), a schoolteacher, journalist, and editor of the Estonian newspapers *Perno Postimees* (The Pärnu Courier, 1857–1864) and *Eesti Postimees* (The Estonian Courier, 1864–1880), believed that the Estonians should continue to work within the existing system, as they were not yet sufficiently developed as a nation to take any important initiatives on their own. Likewise, Jakob Hurt (1839–1907), a theologist, collector of folk songs, and perhaps the greatest ideologist of Estonia's national awakening, urged a conciliatory relationship between Estonians and Germans in which the former accepted the political leadership of the latter. Yet Hurt, who insisted that Estonia's high officials learn the native language, also believed in the basic goodwill of the Russian government, and saw little prospect of cultural Russification in the region. Estonians, he insisted, should focus on their spiritual and cultural mission, leaving matters of politics and power to the larger nationalities.

Still others such as Lydia Koidula (1843–1886), Jannsen's daughter, rejected both the Germanophile and Russophile perspectives, fearing that allying with one or the other could result only in the Estonians' denationalization. Estonians, she suggested, should look to Finland as a model for national development and remove themselves from the growing Russian-German confrontation. All Estonian intellectuals, however, whatever their disposition toward those who exercised power, believed that as much education as possible should be in Estonian and that Estonian should have at least equal rights with Russian as the language of administration.

Among the most inspirational manifestations of the Estonian national awakening was the national song festival, another Baltic tradition that was imported from Germany. With the transformation of timeless folk songs (which in the Herderian tradition were thought to be the authentic voice of the nation) into choral songs performed by hundreds or even thousands, the song festival tradition became an important part of Estonian and Latvian, and (much later) Lithuanian ethnic identity. The first Estonian festival, at which musicians and singers were joined by thousands of other participants summoned from all over Estonia, was held in Tartu on June 18–20, 1869. As in Latvia, which held its first major song festival four years later in Riga, where they have almost always been held ever since, the event symbolized the reawakening and unity of the new nation. By the end of the century such festivals featured choirs consisting of thousands of singers whose songs were enjoyed by audiences of tens of thousands. The tradition of song festivals continued into the 20th century and played an important role in the Balts' struggle for independence from Soviet rule in 1987–1991.

Despite the growth of educational opportunities for Estonians and the appearance during the second half of the 19th century of publishing houses and an Estonian periodical press, the organization of Estonian civic life lagged behind that of the Latvians, in part because urbanization and modernization came to the region somewhat later. As late as 1881 more than 90 percent of Estonians lived in the countryside, leaving Baltic Germans to continue their direction over much of Estonian cultural and social life in the cities. Although Estonians did organize their own local societies and clubs as well as song festivals, German cultural influence remained strong. Even Estonian intellectuals tended

More than 21,000 singers and dancers participated in the Estonian Song Festival that was held in Tallinn on July 4, 2004. Song festivals have been a feature of cultural life in the Baltic region since the first such event was organized in Tartu, Estonia, in 1869. (RAUNO VOLMAR/AFP/Getty Images)

to communicate with each other in German until the turn of the century. The development of Estonian civil society really flourished only in the two decades preceding the 1917 revolution, during which time the Estonian cities emerged as among the most modernized and urbanized in the empire, and Estonians themselves became more urban and wealthy. However, until this development took place, the Estonians remained essentially a colonial people under the tutelage of a foreign elite.

RUSSIFICATION

One of the most distinctive features of the Baltic region under Russian imperial rule was its diversity: for such a small amount of territory with such tiny populations, the Estonian, Latvian, and Lithuanian provinces were host to an impressive array of peoples whose religious practices were nearly as varied as their languages and customs. To overcome the difficulties inherent in ruling such a heterogeneous population, here and elsewhere in Russia's relentlessly expansionist empire, the imperial authorities resorted more and more to the policies and practices of Russification.

Despite the undeniably chauvinistic elements of Russification, its centrality to the imperial government is often exaggerated, for it was less a policy of transforming non-Russians into Russians than it was an instrument through which St. Petersburg attempted to further the centralization and modernization of the Russian state. An early example is the 1867 decree that required official documents in the Baltic *gubernii* to be in Russian. As noted earlier, many ordinary Estonians and Latvians welcomed the introduction of Russian administrative measures in the Baltic provinces, for one of the most important effects of Russification there was the undermining of some of the authority of the German landowning class who were now compelled to cooperate on the matter of land reform and to abstain from the use of corporal punishment on the peasants.

Indeed, to some extent Russification came to the Latvian and Estonian lands by invitation. Just as Estonian peasants had petitioned Tsar Alexander II for the extension of Russian reforms to the Baltic region (mostly in order to curb the influence of the Germans), in 1882 Latvian peasants, encouraged by the RLA, presented their grievances in the form of thousands of petitions addressed to Russian officials in Riga. While some requested the reform of the judicial system and local government along Russian lines, a few called for the administrative reorganization of the three Baltic provinces (Estland, Livland, and Courland) along ethnic lines in a manner that would recognize the predominance of the two main populations, Estonians and Latvians. Petitioners also requested the right to use Latvian and Estonian as the language of instruction in rural schools.

The assassination of Tsar Alexander II in 1881 and his replacement by his reactionary son Alexander III strengthened the hand of advocates of Russification, and over the next 20 years the process only intensified. The appointment in 1885 of new governors for Estland and Livland, men who were less pro-German than their predecessors, appeared to herald a more complete assimilation of the Baltic provinces into the Russian Empire. Everywhere, and especially in the Polish-Lithuanian provinces, Russians with little knowledge of local ways or the local languages were appointed in place of the previous administrators who in Estland, Livland, and Courland had mostly been Germans. In the same year all primary schools in the Baltic provinces came under the control of the Ministry of Education in St. Petersburg and in 1887 Russian was made the language of instruction except in the lower classes of primary schools.

The University of Tartu (*Universität Dorpat*) likewise became an object of creeping Russification: while German and Latin had traditionally been the languages of instruction, competency in Russian became a requirement in the 1840s and in the early 1890s Russian became the language of instruction at the institution that was now called Iur'ev University. The German professors who were forced to leave the university were replaced with Russians while an influx of Russian-speaking students filled the seats vacated by German and Polish (and some Estonian) students who opted to pursue university studies elsewhere.

Russian was also made the language of communication between Baltic government offices and higher authorities in St. Petersburg, and by 1889 linguistic Russification was extended to Baltic municipal governments, in which a small number of Estonians and Latvians were at last granted the right to participate. The *Ritterschaften* and provincial *Landtage*, along with peasant communal organizations, however, remained exempt from linguistic Russification. That the Baltic provincial administrations were never touched by these reforms suggests that Russification was neither systematic nor thorough. Nor did it involve a mass Russian colonization of the region, although the number of Russians living in the Baltic provinces did increase with the arrival of more Russian administrators and a greater number of Russian industrial workers.

Russificatory policies also affected the judicial systems of the Baltic provinces. Russia's judicial reform of 1864 had transformed the country's legal system into one of the most liberal in Europe; in comparison, the judicial systems of the Baltic provinces now seemed antiquated. With the introduction of the Russian judicial system in 1889, the region's courts were subordinated to the St. Petersburg Court Chamber and Russian was made their official language, although the jury system was not introduced as it had been in Russia proper. It appears that imperial authorities pondered the introduction of *zemstvo* institutions of local self-government into the Baltic provinces, ostensibly to undermine German authority, but never followed through on the matter; nor were the *zemstva* introduced to the Lithuanian regions.

Increased official support for Russian Orthodoxy in the western borderlands, especially in Ukrainian and Polish areas, also played a role in the Russification policies of the 1880s and 1890s. With the introduction of new religious regulations, the Russian state attempted to create conditions in the Baltic region more conducive to the future spread of Orthodoxy while simultaneously weakening the Lutheran Church. After 1885 no Protestant church could be built without permission from the Holy Synod in St. Petersburg, and Lutheran partners in mixed marriages were expected to convert to Orthodoxy while their children were to be raised as Orthodox Christians. Lutheran pastors who defied the religious laws of the Russian Empire—by, for example, baptizing children of mixed marriages as Lutherans—were subject to punishment. Because of these measures, or perhaps despite them, the Orthodox Church managed to attract thousands of new converts during this period. Yet at no time under tsarist rule did Orthodox believers comprise more than 10 percent of the total population of these provinces.

Despite the new cultural thrust of Russification, it is doubtful that the tsarist government had any serious plans to turn Latvians or Estonians into Russians. The government did, however, hope to diminish the threat to Russia's hold on this vulnerable region that Germanization appeared to pose, especially given the fact of Germany's political unification in 1871. In recent decades scholars have been careful to point out that the Russification policy in the Baltic had been overrated, that it was implemented only half-heartedly, and that the Russian state had lost its resolve to Russify by the mid-1890s.[12] Only in education did the Russian government continue to pursue a Russificatory policy after 1895, although a decade later concessions were made to local languages in Baltic elementary schools.

It seems clear that the Russian government was more concerned with the cultural pull exerted by a dynamic Germany on the empire's westernmost provinces than it was with the "national awakenings" of the Latvian and Estonian peoples. However, officials in St. Petersburg were disappointed that rather than being attracted to Russian culture, the locals were more concerned with their own national cultures. Indeed, the official policies likely only intensified their sense of their own "Estonianness" or "Latvianness." Whatever the government's real intentions, the development of the Estonian and Latvian nations was already too far advanced by the 1880s for any kind of mass cultural assimilation to take place—including continued assimilation into the German nation. With educated Estonians and Latvians eschewing the cultural tutelage of the Baltic Germans and increasingly writing and speaking to each other in their own languages, the local intelligentsia greeted the new century with unprecedented self-confidence.

LITHUANIA AND ITS AWAKENING

Acquired by Russia during the Polish partitions of the late 18th century, the Lithuanian territories, primarily the *gubernii* of Kaunas and Vilnius, were never subjected to the sort of experiments that were attempted in Estland and Livland in the early 19th century; thus Lithuanian peasants remained serfs into the 1860s. Nor in contrast to the privileges and autonomy the Russian government granted to the Baltic Germans were the elites of the incorporated Polish-Lithuanian areas granted their own autonomy or comparable rights and privileges. Like the Baltic Germans, however, the elites of Lithuania, mostly Poles and Polonized Lithuanians, were far removed from the cultural life of the peasants who worked their land. Indeed, most of the educated class could not even speak the Lithuanian language, which was used almost exclusively by Lithuanian peasants.

The noble class in the Polish-Lithuanian lands was always larger than the number of confirmed Russian nobles in Russia proper, despite the fact that the overall population of Russia was obviously many times larger than that of Poland-Lithuania. To a far greater extent than their Russian counterparts, however, many of the Polish-Lithuanian nobles were in fact poor and landless. In the empire they found that their opportunities were rather limited: although Polish-Lithuanian noblemen could serve in the tsar's army, the more important civil service posts in Lithuania tended to go to Russian officials.

Thus from the moment Russia acquire the Lithuanian-inhabited territories, incorporated into a new administrative region called Northwestern Territory, the local nobility found tsarist rule uncongenial to say the least. It was not long after the partitions and the accompanying

Russian occupation that Lithuanian nobles who had estates were forced to endured the exodus of thousands of Lithuanian peasants who sought to avoid induction into the tsar's army. The neighboring Grand Duchy of Warsaw (constituting the Polish lands not under Russian control), a nominally independent but short-lived state created in 1807 by the French emperor Napoleon Bonaparte (r. 1804–1814), attracted yet more fleeing Lithuanians.

Not satisfied with his conquest of much of the rest of Europe, in the spring of 1812 the Corsican general, who for the preceding five years had enjoyed a peaceful if mutually suspicious arrangement with Tsar Alexander I, attempted to conquer Russia as well, using the Duchy of Warsaw as a launching pad. Failing to achieve its military objectives before the onset of the Russian winter, Napoleon's army retreated and rapidly disintegrated. Returning westward, thousands of soldiers swept across Lithuanian territory, bringing with them arson, famine, and epidemics (mostly typhus). Vilnius, where these soldiers hoped to find food, was the graveyard of about 40,000 of these frost-bitten and overwhelmingly teenaged soldiers. Mass graves unearthed in 2002, originally presumed to contain the remains of victims of the Soviet secret police, revealed another factor that contributed to Napoleon's defeat: the lice that were consuming the flesh of his soldiers.[13] The extent of the human losses resulting from the war with Napoleon and Russian reoccupation was revealed by a census taken in 1817, which showed that Lithuania had lost one-third of its population since 1811.

After France's defeat in 1814–1815 Russia became Europe's leading hegemon, and the Polish-Lithuanian territories were reincorporated into the empire along with lands that had formerly been under Prussian and Austrian rule. Although the slogans of the French soldiers—"liberty, fraternity, equality"—had gained currency among many Lithuanians and Poles during the wars, Russia's ruler was in anything but a revolutionary mood. Nevertheless, as a concession to his Polish subjects Tsar Alexander I set up the Kingdom of Poland, with himself as sovereign, in 1815. Provided with Europe's most liberal constitution and a parliament, Poland was to act as a model for future Russian reforms. However, the kingdom, often referred to as Congress Poland, was not a restoration of Poland-Lithuania, for it included only a small portion of its population and land, centered around Warsaw. While the resurrection of a Polish state within Russia provided some Poles and Lithuanians with hope for the future, most were never reconciled to union with Russia and resented the limits the tsar imposed on Poland's sovereignty.

In late November 1830, five years into the decades-long reign of Alexander's martinet brother Nicholas I (r. 1825–1855), an uprising began in Poland, and by March of the following year the unrest spread to Lithuania. If before the insurrection imperial authorities had been relatively tolerant of Polish (and within that, Lithuanian) autonomy, with the rebellion's defeat the tsar made the Poles and Lithuanians feel the full weight of his displeasure: the Polish constitution was abolished, the University of Vilnius (Wilno) was closed, and the entire region was brought into closer association with Russia proper as the Lithuanian Statute was abolished. Russians filled the state administration in the Kaunas and Vilnius *gubernii,* which were ruled as part of Russia proper. If Vilnius had been a major city in the Russian Empire before the insurrection, the neglect it suffered afterward turned it into little more than a provincial dump—a fate that contrasts sharply with that of Riga, which underwent an urban renewal in the mid-19th century that transformed it into one of the most beautiful and vibrant cities in the empire. Following the trials of the Polish insurrectionists, many estates belonging to the nobility and the Catholic Church were confiscated and subsequently transferred to Russian landlords. Several million practitioners of the Uniate faith were affected by the anti-Catholic campaign, for after 1839 they were forcefully assimilated into the Russian Orthodox Church.[14]

Such efforts to centralize the institutions of the Russian Empire and to repress Polish political and cultural life were underway for three decades before another ill-fated Polish insurrection occurred in 1863. This second failure—the insurrectionists were severely outnumbered, lacked outside support, and failed to win any important victories— invited further Russian repression and Russification measures under the brief supervision of Governor General Mikhail "The Hangman" Murav'ev (1796–1866). Indeed, it was in the wake of the 1863 rebellion that Russification truly became imperial policy, even if it was imposed only selectively and inconsistently. A number of Catholic monasteries and churches, viewed by tsarist officials as hotbeds of treasonous activity, were shut down throughout the Polish and Lithuanian provinces, and Russian became the official language of all *guberniia* and *uezd* offices. Henceforth court proceedings were conducted in Russian, although one could testify in Polish, and the Russian language became obligatory in Polish and Lithuanian elementary schools.

Freed from serfdom in 1861 and disappointed at the result, Lithuanian peasants, armed mostly with scythes, also participated in the January Uprising of 1863. Following the rebellion's suppression the tsarist government attempted to solve the "Polish question" in part by splitting the Lithuanians from the Poles, the idea being to recognize Lithuanian as a separate culture in the hopes that educated Lithuanians would be assimilated into the Russian nation rather than the Polish one. To ease the anticipated transition from Lithuanian to Russian, authorities tried to convert the Lithuanians to the use of the Cyrillic alphabet. From 1864, until the ban was lifted 40 years later, it remained forbidden to print Lithuanian language books in Latin letters.

Yet Lithuanian-language printing continued in East Prussia (Lithuania Minor, a mostly Lutheran area in imperial Germany), from where they were smuggled into Russian Lithuania. Beginning in the 1890s, books printed by Lithuanian émigré presses in the United States (see page 77) also made their way into the empire, where officials confiscated hundreds of thousands of illegal books. Although this Lithuanian cultural revival at first had little to do with politics—the writers and books smugglers of this era were more concerned with improving the moral and intellectual condition of the Lithuanian people—it provided a vital link between the Lithuanians of Russia and Prussia and helped galvanize the national idea. In later decades the book smugglers would be celebrated as Lithuanian national heroes.

Having begun later than the awakenings in Latvia and Estonia, the Lithuanian national awakening was complicated by the ambiguous matter of identity in the Polish-Lithuanian lands, for one could simultaneously speak Polish as one's mother tongue, be a subject of the Russian tsar, and feel a powerful attachment to the Lithuanian soil. Such were the circumstances of the great Romantic poet Adam Mickiewicz (1798–1855), whose works have been read by generations of Poles and Lithuanians. To this day every Lithuanian and Polish schoolchild knows the beginning of his masterpiece *Pan Tadeusz* (subtitled *The Last Foray in Lithuania*), an epic poem set in provincial Lithuania during the Napoleonic era: "Lithuania! My fatherland! You are like health! Only he who has lost you may know your true worth." That Mickiewicz penned these words in Polish while living in Paris, hundreds of miles from his Lithuanian homeland, is only fitting for someone whose work expressed such an intense yearning for his native land. Yet if Mickiewicz could not imagine a Lithuania separate from Poland, the same could not be said of his contemporary Simon Daukantas (1793–1864), an ethnic Lithuanian (unlike Mickiewicz) and the author of the first histories of Lithuania and Samogitia in the Lithuanian/Samogitian language. Composing his works in a national Romantic style that was typical of its time, Daukantas presented an idealized version of Lithuanian history that lamented Lithuania's earlier submission to Polish influence.

In contrast to the public and largely secular nature of the awakenings in Latvia and Estonia, the activities of Lithuania's awakeners were clandestine and closely connected to Catholicism, the region's dominant faith. While the Lutheran pastors of Estonia and Latvia were usually German, in Lithuania the Church recruited its priests from the peasantry, which in turn helped to cement the bond between the Church and the nascent Lithuanian nation. Such was the background of Motiejus Valančius (1801–1875). A writer of largely nonpolitical religious works, history, and fiction, Valančius emerged from the peasantry to become one of the most significant figures in the earliest stages of Lithuania's national awakening. In 1849, appointed bishop of Samogitia, the westernmost and least Polonized part of Lithuania, Valančius established discipline among the clergy and rapidly increased the number of seminarians until the crackdown that followed the insurrection of 1863. Confronting the scourge of alcoholism, which was tacitly encouraged by a tsarist regime that depended on the proceeds from the sale of spirits, he urged Lithuania's peasants and priests to embrace the virtues of temperance. His success on this score reduced state revenues and did little to earn him favor with the authorities in St. Petersburg, against whose Russification policies he actively encouraged popular resistance. In his last years—he did not begin to write secular works until age 63—the bishop also promoted historical research and writing by his clergy and had their works, written in Lithuanian, illegally smuggled into Russian Lithuania from East Prussia.[15]

Perhaps nobody occupies a more prominent position in the pantheon of Lithuania's awakeners than Dr. Jonas Basanavičius (1851–1927), who many Lithuanians consider the patriarch of the nation he helped guide to independence in 1918. A physician by training, Basanavičius turned to activism in the 1880s with the creation of *Aušra* (The Dawn). One of the first Lithuanian newspapers, its name suggested the image, common in east central European nations whose medieval glory had been squelched by their submission to larger neighbors during the early modern era, of a nation awakening from darkness. Printed in Prussia due to tsarist restrictions and smuggled into Russian Lithuania, *Aušra* (1883–1886) acted as the intellectual center of the Lithuanian national movement, collecting and publishing information on the history of Lithuania and the Lithuanian people with the goal of evoking Lithuanian national consciousness. For Basanavičius and for many other Lithuanian intellectuals, Lithuania's place in the Russian Empire was beyond question; the main danger to the Lithuanian people was the pull of Polish language and culture, for Lithuanians who moved into the cities, where they had little choice but to speak Polish and adopt Polish customs and manners, were inevitably assimilated into an urban society that was fundamentally Polish (when it was not Jewish).

While Basanavičius would later play a decisive role in the creation of a Lithuanian state, few thought in terms of an independent Lithuania before World War I. Only with the emergence of a new democratic intelligentsia, mostly of peasant origin, and its assertion of a secular Lithuanian national culture in the public sphere at the end of the century did the idea of restoring an independent Lithuanian state—free from Russian rule and separate from Poland—begin to attract any kind of support.[16] Meanwhile, tight internal controls meant that much of the impetus behind the Lithuanian awakening came from outside Russian Lithuania. Indeed, in the last decades of the 19th century Lithuanian national consciousness was probably stronger among those Lithuanians living in the United States or East Prussia than it was among the Lithuanians of the Russian Empire.

The number of Lithuanians living outside the northwestern parts of the Russian Empire increased dramatically at the end of the 1860s, owing to the abolition of serfdom, the lack of work for the newly liberated peasants, a crackdown in the wake of the January Uprising, and the imposition of more extensive Russification measures. Perhaps the greatest impetus to emigration was the famine of 1867–1868, whose effects were exacerbated by an outbreak of cholera. While tens of thousands of Lithuanians drifted to other parts of the empire—including Siberia, Latvia, and Ukraine—others went abroad. The greatest number of Lithuanian emigrants, about 300,000, went to the United States, where they were concentrated in east coast cities such as New York, Baltimore, and Boston, as well as inland industrial cities such as Chicago and the coal-mining areas of Pennsylvania. Lithuanians immigrants were mostly attracted to the industrial centers; few took up agricultural work. By 1900 more than 10,000 Lithuanians were arriving in U.S. cities each year, a number that increased to more than 20,000 per annum by 1907. Such emigration patterns stood in stark contrast to those of migrating Latvians and Estonians who were far more likely either to migrate to nearby cities like Riga or St. Petersburg, whose growing industries had a need for workers, or to seek greener pastures (most migrants were farmers) within the Russian Empire.

Enjoying considerably greater freedom to be Lithuanians while residing outside the empire, Lithuanian communities in North America enjoyed a robust cultural life during the last decades of the 19th century.

The first Lithuanian-language newspaper in the United States, *Gazieta Lietuviška* (The Lithuanian Newspaper) appeared four years before Dr. Basanavičius's *Aušra*. Lithuanian Americans were also attracted to theater, music, and other cultural activities, which flourished in the United States but developed more slowly in Russian Lithuania. It was only in 1901 that Russia's Lithuanians were at last granted their own church, St. Michael's Church in Vilnius, which in turn immediately became a center of Lithuanian nationalist activity. Around the same time, Lithuanians in Vilnius were able to create the Lithuanian Scientific Society, found a publishing house, and start a new newspaper, *Vilniaus Žinios* (Vilnius News).

By the time a revolution broke out in Russia in 1905 the decrees against the use of the Lithuanian language had been revoked and the Lithuanian press and literature had grown more vigorous. Economically, however, the Lithuanians remained far behind other peoples in the western parts of the empire. According to the Russian census of 1897, some 93 percent of all Lithuanians in Lithuanian-majority areas were peasants; just a handful claimed to be merchants, and only a very small percentage of town-dwellers in Lithuanian areas were ethnic Lithuanians. The others were mostly Jews, Poles, and Russians. The plain fact of the matter was that the Lithuanian nation, if such a thing can be said to have existed before the end of the 19th century, had stagnated during its long association with the Polish state and then under more than a century of Russian rule.

THE LITVAKS

Like Jews everywhere in the empire, the Jews of Lithuania both flourished and suffered during the 19th century. Confined by Empress Catherine II to the Pale of Jewish Settlement, an entity that roughly coincided with the historical lands of the old Commonwealth, Jews faced restrictions on movement and property as the tsarist government attempted to isolate its Jewish populations and to prevent them from living in imperial cities like Moscow and St. Petersburg. Yet Jews too were subject to the logic of Russificatory imperial policy. It was during the 30-year reign of Tsar Nicholas I (1825–1855) that the Russian-language schools for Jewish children were introduced in the Pale, even if few attended them, and the *Kahal,* the local governing body that administered religious, legal, and communal affairs, was abolished.

Yet the large concentration of Jews in the Pale fostered an unprecedented blossoming of Jewish cultural, social, and religious life. Vilnius (Yid. *Vilna, Vilne*), home to thousands of Ashkenazi Jews, became known as the Jerusalem of Lithuania and was a major center for Jewish learning. By 1897 Jews constituted approximately 40 percent of Vilnius's population, the remainder mostly consisting of Poles and Russians. The ethnic makeup of Kaunas (Yid. *Kovna, Kovne*), Lithuania's largest city after Vilnius, was quite similar with a population that was about 35 percent Jewish. Forming a majority in many of the small towns of Lithuania, Litvaks typically engaged in traditional vocations such as trading, banking, and innkeeping; others established themselves as traders, grocers, barbers, doctors, goldsmiths, tinsmiths, and furriers.[17]

The Litvaks' migration to the towns and cities was partly due to the measures taken by Tsar Alexander II, who having liberated Russia's serfs in 1861 also removed some of the restrictions on Jews. Now allowed access to higher education, some Jews were able to settle outside the Pale, enter the professions, and take civil service positions. While Lithuanian town life had enjoyed a significant continuous Jewish presence since the 15th century, during the 19th century Jews began to make their way to Riga as well: by 1867, more than 5,000 Jewish entrepreneurs, traders, and craftsmen made their home on the outskirts of what was turning into a thriving industrial city—one that was also becoming a magnet to Latvian peasants seeking seasonal, and increasingly year-round, work.

While many of Riga's Germans saw the Jews as undesirable competitors, tsarist suspicions of the empire's Jewish communities remained intact despite the briefly more liberal political climate created by Alexander II, whose assassination in 1881 sparked a wave of violence against Jews throughout the empire's western borderlands. The more intensive Russification policies that accompanied the accession to the throne of his son Alexander III were coupled with some anti-Jewish measures designed to limit Jewish influence on the countryside. The most notorious of these were the ones known as the May Laws of 1882, which, among other things, placed new restrictions on the business practices of Jews in Russia and called for the creation of a virtual Pale within the Pale of Settlement.[18]

Many Jews began to leave the empire: some fled to neighboring Prussia, often on their way to western Europe or America; others went to southern Russia. Those who remained behind often made their living as tailors, shoemakers, industrial workers, and traders. Although by the end of the 19th century Jewish traders had become an essential link in the distribution of agricultural products, few Jews made their living from farming. In Kaunas province, for example, just 1 percent of Jews were agricultural laborers.

Just as ethnic Lithuanians began to experience a cultural renaissance in the last decades of the 19th century, Litvaks enjoyed a Jewish enlightenment movement, demonstrated by an increased interest in the Hebrew language, which hitherto had been almost exclusively the language of religious study. Some Lithuanian Jews also began to show interest in the Zionist movement, which aimed to establish a Jewish national home in Palestine. Many Jews enthusiastically contributed to and collected funds for this cause, and a few began emigrating to the Holy Land. Others who were more interested in improving the working conditions and economic situation of the Jewish proletariat gravitated toward the socialist camp. In 1897, Jewish socialists founded the General Jewish Workers' Union (*Bund*) of Lithuania, an organization that demanded both improved conditions for workers and civil rights and cultural autonomy for Jews. The strongest socialist movement in the Lithuanian lands prior to World War I, the *Bund*'s influence peaked around the time of the Revolution of 1905, the moment when the politics of class and nationality found violent expression in the northwestern regions of the Russian Empire.

Yet the notion that at the dawn of the 20th century the Lithuanian, Latvian, and Estonian peoples were poised to assume control over their own destinies as rulers of their own nation-states is mistaken. Almost nobody at that time thought in terms of independence and fewer still believed such a prospect was achievable even under the most favorable circumstances. Only Lithuania had a history of premodern statehood, and its national awakening was only just beginning to mature at a time when rural Estonians and Latvians were migrating in droves to the region's heretofore largely German cities, helping to transform them into important centers of industry in an increasingly prosperous, unwieldy, and divided Russian Empire. Few would have been able to foresee the outbreaks of violence that would consume the region in 1905–1907. A cataclysmic world war that would sweep away the Romanov, Habsburg, and Hohenzollern dynasties would have been nearly unthinkable.

NOTES

1. Aldis Purs, *Baltic Facades: Estonia, Latvia and Lithuania since 1945* (New York: Reaktion Books, 2012), 154.

2. Tadeušs Puisāns, *The Emerging Nation: The Path of Agonizing Development from Baltic Tribalism to Latvian Nationhood* (Riga: Centre of Baltic-Nordic History and Political Studies, 1995), 31–32.

3. The *gubernii* of Vilnius/Vilna and Kaunas/Kovno comprised the bulk of modern Lithuania. As a result of the Napoleonic wars, new

Lithuanian territory (hitherto under the control of Prussia) was added to the Russian Empire. Following the Congress of Vienna in 1815 this area became established as the *guberniia* of Suvalki.

4. See Anders Hendriksson's *The Tsar's Loyal Germans* (Boulder, CO: Eastern European Monographs, 1883), which focuses on the Germans of Riga.

5. Toivo U. Raun, *Estonia and the Estonians,* 2nd ed. (Stanford, CA: Hoover Institution Press, 2001), 49–50.

6. Andrejs Plakans, *The Latvians: A Short History* (Stanford, CA: Hoover Institution Press, 1995), 87–88.

7. Andrejs Plakans, *A Concise History of the Baltic States* (New York: Cambridge University Press, 2011), 177–82.

8. See Andrew James Blumbergs, *The Nationalization of Latvians and the Issue of Serfdom: The Baltic German Literary Contribution in the 1780s and 1790s* (Amherst, NY: Cambria Press, 2008), 87–91.

9. Plakans (1995), 68.

10. Raun (2001), 55.

11. Blumbergs, 170–75.

12. See Theodore R. Weeks, *Nation and State in Late Imperial Russia: Nationalism and Russification on the Western Frontier, 1863–1914* (DeKalb, IL: Northern Illinois University Press, 1996). Also Edward C. Thaden, ed., *Russification in the Baltic Provinces and Finland, 1855–1914* (Princeton, NJ: Princeton University Press, 1981).

13. Stephan Talty, *The Illustrious Dead: The Terrifying Story of How Typhus Killed Napoleon's Greatest Army* (New York: Crown, 2009).

14. Uniates are Christians who maintain Orthodox liturgy and rituals while acknowledging the supremacy of Rome in matters of faith. The Uniate Church, also called the Greek Catholic Church, was first established in the Polish-Lithuanian Commonwealth in 1596.

15. Saulius A. Girnius, "Bishop Motiejus Valančius: A Man for All Seasons," *Lituanus* 22, no. 2 (Summer 1976), http://www.lituanus.org/1976/76_2_01.htm (accessed June 13, 2014).

16. Tomas Balkelis, *The Making of Modern Lithuania* (New York: Routledge, 2009).

17. Dov Levin, *The Litvaks: A Short History of the Jews in Lithuania* (Jerusalem: Vad Yashem, 2000), 77–90.

18. See Eugene M. Avrutin, *Jews and the Imperial State: Identification Politics in Tsarist Russia* (Ithaca, NY: Cornell University Press, 2010).

4

The Revolutionary Era, 1905–1920

At the dawn of the 20th century the Estonian and Latvian territories were among the most industrialized and urbanized regions of the Russian Empire. As the beneficiaries of rising living standards and a promising demographic situation, Latvian and Estonian families—town-dwellers as well as the vast majority who continued to derive their living from the land—had never before enjoyed greater prosperity than they did during the decades that preceded World War I. Literate, politically awakened, and yet increasingly integrated into the institutions of the German and Russian elites, the peoples of Russia's Baltic provinces had every reason to look forward to enjoying still future prosperity as subjects of the tsar in a modernizing, multinational empire.

At the same time, a widespread mistrust of the imperial authorities, coupled with the resentment felt by many Estonians, Latvians, and Lithuanians toward their German, Polish, and Russian landlords, divided the peoples of the Baltic region. The early decades of the 20th century, shaped by war, revolution, and massive dislocation, would prove to be among the most turbulent in the region's history.

Old loyalties based on privilege and service were tested, and new bonds based on language, nationhood, and class were forged during a cataclysmic war that in four horrific years tore asunder the mighty empires that for centuries had dominated central and eastern Europe. The opening years of the century turned out to be the twilight of German power in the eastern Baltic, for what followed was the dawn of self-government for the Estonian, Latvian, and Lithuanian peoples amidst the rubble of empire.

URBANIZATION AND INDUSTRIALIZATION

The census carried out by imperial authorities in 1897 revealed that approximately 125 million people lived in a Russian Empire that sprawled across two continents from the Baltic Sea to the Pacific Ocean. As important as the cities, ports, and farms of the Baltic littoral were for the empire's economic development, the populations of the provinces inhabited by the Estonian, Latvian, and Lithuanian peoples constituted only a tiny fraction of the empire's human resources. Russia's Latvian territories, including southern Livland, Courland, and part of the Vitebsk province, were home to about 1.9 million people, of whom about two-thirds were of Latvian nationality.[1] Russians, Germans, Jews, Poles, and Lithuanians constituted the bulk of the remaining population of ethnographic Latvia. While most Latvians remained simple but overwhelmingly literate peasants—a reality that shaped the way that Latvia's awakeners conceptualized the nation—this was changing rapidly as the new century dawned: whereas in 1897 only about 28 percent of Latvia's population lived in urban centers, by 1913 this number exceeded 40 percent.

The most important by far of Latvia's urban center was Riga. Swelling from 102,000 inhabitants to 282,000 in the space of only 30 years (1867–1897), Riga's population would nearly double again before reaching its prewar peak of 517,000, making it one of the largest cities in the Russian Empire. With the demolition of its medieval walls in the 1860s and the urban renewal that followed, not only did Riga become a more open, more beautiful, and more modern city, it also became more heavily Latvianized as the proportion of Latvians residing in the city rose from 23.5 percent in 1867 to 41.6 percent in 1897.

The city's industrial workforce quadrupled during the same period. A port whose industry was based largely on the processing of import and export commodities—by 1913 Riga had become the most significant timber exporting harbor on the continent—the city on the Daugava needed this largely Latvian working class for its growing textile, wood-processing, and machine-building industries. Despite having only 1.5 percent of the empire's total population, during the early years of the 20th century the Latvian lands alone provided 5.5 percent of Russia's industrial production, with the majority of this activity taking place in Riga, followed by Liepāja, Jelgava, and Daugavpils.[2]

The Germans' share of the city's population declined as steeply as the proportion of Latvians and Jews rose. Even if there were twice as many Germans (14 percent) as Jews (8 percent) living in Riga in 1913, this was still a far cry from the situation in 1867, when 43 percent of Riga's population was German and Riga could still be regarded as a "German" city. In part the relative decline in the German population can be attributed to the growing tendency of Germanized Latvians to identify as Latvians, but the main factor was the influx of non-Germans, especially peasants who following the introduction of the passport system in 1864 became free to seek employment in Russia's cities.

Russians (20 percent), Poles (9.5 percent), and Lithuanians (6.9 percent) were the other leading ethnic groups who populated Riga on the eve of the Great War. Given Riga's geographical proximity to Estonia, it is easy to imagine the city being a natural magnet for Estonian peasants as well. At no time, however, did the number of Estonians in Riga exceed 10,000. Indeed, the number of other foreigners living in Riga at any time vastly exceeded the number of Estonians. In 1881, as much as 6.7 percent of the city's population consisted of foreign Germans—citizens of the German Empire who were ethnic Germans but not, strictly speaking, Baltic Germans. However, the stricter Russification policies imposed after 1881 made Riga and other urban centers of the littoral less attractive to foreign Germans—as well as to many *Baltendeutsche*, who now began to perceive, although not actively resist, the new challenges to their traditional power and influence.

The Estonian regions experienced demographic trends similar to those of ethnographic Latvia. Between 1881 and 1897 the population of Estland and northern Livland increased from 881,455 to 986,000, of whom more than 90 percent were ethnic Estonians. The relatively unimpressive growth rate of the Estonian regions is partially explained by rising Estonian emigration to other parts of the empire, including St. Petersburg, the Volga River region, and the Caucasus. However, this was offset by the migration of Russians from the interior to the growing Estonian cities. By 1897 the urban share of the Estonian population rose to nearly 20 percent, with the two largest Estonian cities being Tallinn (64,572), now an important center for the machine and metals industries and a major base for the imperial navy, and Tartu (42,308), which housed the region's only university and was the center of Estonian cultural life. These cities were followed in size by Narva, whose largest industrial establishment, the Krenholm cotton factory, underlined the importance of textiles, and Pärnu, from which grain, flax, and timber from Estonia were shipped to west European markets.

As in Riga, the proportion of Germans in Estonian cities began to decline during this period: in 1897, only 16 percent of the urban population in the Estonian territories was German, while Estonians made up 68 percent of Estonia's city-dwellers and Russians 11 percent.[3] Given the rising number of Estonians and Latvians in the littoral's urban areas, their growing economic power, and the long history of the region's colonial status, it is not difficult to understand why many Estonians and Latvians came to regard Germans and Russians (and Jews) as alien presences in their cities.

In the Lithuanian territories, still divided between Russia and Germany, the situation was quite different. Although the total population of ethnographic Lithuania had reached 2.7 million by the turn of the century, most of this growth was in the countryside. Moreover, the few cities that there were in the region did not even enjoy a Lithuanian character: in 1897, Lithuanians comprised only 2 percent of the population in Vilnius (154,000) and 6 percent of the population of Kaunas (86,500). Lithuanians, even more than the Latvians and Estonians, remained an overwhelmingly rural and agricultural people, while Poles, Russians, and Jews comprised the bulk of the urban inhabitants of the three Lithuanian *gubernii* of Vilnius, Kaunas, and Suvalki. The city of Vilnius, whose population in 1897 was 40 percent Jewish and 31 percent Polish, was the center of Jewish cultural life in northeastern Europe.

Partly because serfdom was not abolished in the Lithuanian provinces until 1861, and consequently few Lithuanian peasants were literate or mobile, industrialization arrived late in the region and remained below Estonian and Latvian levels throughout the period of Russian rule. Thus, although towns of Lithuania enjoyed great ethnic and cultural diversity, unlike the cities in ethnographic Latvia and Estonia they were neglected by St. Petersburg and experienced little development under tsarist rule.

A more intensive economic development in the Estonian and Latvian areas underlined the importance of these relatively highly industrialized provinces to the Russian Empire. Among the most important growth areas were cloth manufacturing and alcohol distillation, along with food processing and the tobacco, leather, metal, and timber industries. The paper mills of Estonia provided more than 70 percent of the empire's paper products, while the construction of three large shipyards in Tallinn in the years immediately prior to World War I demonstrated the region's military importance to the empire. While Germans continued to play a leading role in industry and finance in the urban centers of Estonia and Latvia, many factories, and more than half in Estonia, were owned by Russian business magnates. Among the most noteworthy of these enterprises was Riga's Kuznetsov Porcelain Factory (now Latelektrokeramika), which satisfied the needs of the affluent for intricately decorated tableware.

By the end of the 19th century the cities of the eastern Baltic were linked to the interior of Russia by railroad and together handled 30 percent of Russia's foreign trade. The region's first railway, constructed in 1861, connected Riga to Daugavpils (Rus. *Dvinsk*), a fortress town whose ethnic diversity mirrored that of the Latgale region as a whole: in 1897, nearly half of Daugavpils's rapidly growing population of 69,700 was Jewish, with Russians and Poles comprising most of the remainder. The opening of the Liepāja (Ger. *Libau*) to Kaunas line in 1871 ensured that Russian goods would flow through the ports of Courland, as did the opening of a line that connected Moscow directly to Ventspils (Ger. *Windau*) in the 1890s. Revived as a shipbuilding center with the added attraction of being an ice-free port, Ventspils's population quadrupled to 29,000 between 1897 and 1913.

But the unchallenged center of industry and trade in the littoral was Riga, which enjoyed rail links not only with the larger towns in the Latvian lands (Daugavpils, Jelvaga, Liepāja), but also with the empire's greatest cities, including Moscow, Warsaw, and St. Petersburg. After 1870 the imperial capital was also connected to Tallinn, which fostered that city's growing metal works and allowed the farmers of northern Estonia to ship their goods to the Russian interior. By the end of the century, nearly all the towns of Estonia and Latvia and a growing number of Lithuanian towns had a railway connection.

These developments did not take place in isolation, for the economic development of the Baltic provinces was part of a larger plan to modernize the Russian Empire, with the state playing a leading role in building the railroads that connected the Russian interior to its Baltic ports and in attracting foreign investment. Nevertheless, despite the rapid modernization of the northernmost provinces of Estland and Livland, certain things did not change. Among the continuities was the fundamentally rural and agricultural nature of the region, as the majority of the region's inhabitants continued to make a living from the land and agricultural exports remained the largest segment of the economy. Yet the traditional German domination of the rural economy was in rapid decline. By 1900 the Latvian and Estonian countryside was socially differentiated, with new classes of landowners consolidating control over small, medium, and even some large landholdings. While this came mostly at the expense of the heavily indebted nobility, Baltic Germans nevertheless continued to own nearly half the arable land.

In the cities, Latvians and Estonians had developed both a bourgeoisie and a working class. What they lacked, however, was political influence that corresponded with their numbers and their growing economic clout. While the reforms to city governance that were introduced in the late 1870s enfranchised more non-Germans in Riga and other cities, the reality was that political power in the Baltic provinces remained in large measure in the hands of the German elite and the Russian government.

POLITICAL MOVEMENTS

The first political party in the territories that presently comprise the contemporary Baltic states, the Lithuanian Social Democratic Party (LSDP), was born in Vilnius in 1896. Given the almost total absence of an urban proletariat in Lithuania, the party's existence was perhaps anomalous. In principle, the LSDP, consisting largely of Poles rather than Lithuanians, stood for solidarity with the empire's Polish and Russian working class, but it was not long before one of its principal aims became Lithuanian statehood. Its 1904 program contained the demand for an "autonomous, democratic republic, composed of Lithuanian Poland and other countries on the basis of a loose federation."[4]

If creating a truly independent Lithuanian state remained at this stage impractical, and to most people nearly unthinkable, more perplexing still would have been the problem of defining a Lithuanian state in national terms given the large numbers of Jews and Poles whose towns dotted a rural Lithuanian landscape. Other Lithuanian parties, such as the Lithuanian Democratic Party (formed 1902) and the League of Lithuanian Christian Democrats (1905), faced the question as well, but none went any further than demanding autonomy for an ethnographic Lithuania within a democratic Russia. The General Jewish Workers' Union, better known as the *Bund*, was one of the region's most influential political organizations, but its leadership gave little thought to Lithuanian statehood.

As the main vehicles for Marxism, social democratic organizations exerted greater appeal in Riga, where rapid industrialization was producing a sizable working class, than in Lithuania's cities, where a proletariat developed far more slowly. Since 1891 Marxist ideas had appeared in print in Latvia on the pages of *Dienas Lapa* (Daily Paper), a newspaper that was closely associated with New Current (*jaunā strāva*), the collective name for the broadly leftist Latvian intelligentsia of the 1890s and early 1900s. In 1897, two years after a series of strikes in Riga and Liepāja, the newspaper's staff, along with some left-wing student groups, were arrested and jailed; some were temporarily expelled from the Baltic provinces. Consequently, large numbers of Latvian intellectuals and activists became disillusioned with a government upon which they had earlier relied for protection against the Baltic German landlords.

In none of the Baltic states did Marxism have a greater impact than in Latvia. By 1904, the Latvian Social Democratic Workers' Party, founded as an expatriate group in Zürich the previous year, were prepared to publish their demands:

> We demand that each nationality which is a member of the Russian Empire should have the right to determine its own fate; that each nationality should have the right to maintain its own culture and to develop its spiritual strengths; and that the language of each nationality should have the right to be used in schools, local administrative institutions, and local courts.[5]

Although not all Social Democrats agreed with this position, the manifesto suggests that by the time the 1905 revolution broke out the nationality question in Latvia had assumed a position of prominence not only as a cultural issue but as a political issue as well.

In Estonia the main issue was the Russified educational system, opposed by nearly all Estonian activists, who instead demanded that Estonian be the language of instruction in all elementary schools and secondary schools. Still, for most Estonians, loyalty to the tsarist regime was not in question. Among the most influential of the Estonian nationalists was Jaan Tõnisson (1868–ca. 1941). Editor since 1896 of the first Estonian daily newspaper, *Postimees* (The Courier) and later one of the founders of the Estonian Republic, Tõnisson advocated loyalty to the tsarist regime (although he opposed Russification) and collaboration between Estonians and Germans (even if he resented their privileges) in order to advance their common goal of regional development. Nevertheless, calls for more radical economic and social change, emanating from intellectuals who represented the Estonian working classes, began to be heard in the newspapers *Uudised* (The News), which first appeared in Tartu, and *Teataja* (The Herald), which was founded and edited by future Estonian president Konstantin Päts (1874–1956) and published in Tallinn between 1901 and 1905.

Some workers and radical intellectuals in Estonia's bigger towns sympathized with the Russian Social Democratic Workers' Party (RSDWP), a Marxist and internationalist party founded by Russian radicals in 1898. Tallinn, for example, became an important Menshevik center, although Bolsheviks, who comprised the party's more militant elements, also enjoyed a presence there. The fact that the RSDWP operated illegally, organizing secret meetings and distributing illegal pamphlets and books, was perhaps one of the reasons that Estonian workers became attracted to it. Even if Estonians activists and intellectuals lacked a common vision, both nationalist and socialist ideals resonated among the Estonian people more powerfully than ever by the time a revolution broke out in St. Petersburg in 1905.

THE 1905 REVOLUTION

Often seen as a warm-up act for the more momentous revolutions of 1917, the Revolution of 1905 was partly a consequence of Russia's humiliating loss to Japan in a war over spheres of influence in the Far East. Disastrous as it was for the Russian military—the war is the setting for Sergei Eisenstein's propaganda film *Battleship Potemkin* (1925), which dramatizes a sailors' mutiny on a doomed warship—Russia's defeat at the hands of an Asian power highlighted the weaknesses of the absolutist system of Tsar Nicholas II (r. 1894–1917), whose refusal to introduce constitutional reforms confounded the empire's growing classes of bourgeois professionals and liberal intellectuals. Such people, who sought a solution in liberalism under a constitutional monarchy, became the main base of support for the Constitutional Democratic Party (Kadets) that was formed in October 1905 as the government in St. Petersburg struggled for its very survival.

However, the event that triggered the upheaval that nearly cost the tsar his throne was the confrontation between striking workers and the St. Petersburg police, who on January 22 (January 9 according to the old Russian calendar) fired on a demonstration and killed hundreds of peaceful protesters. Known as Bloody Sunday, the massacre placed a sea of blood between the tsar and his people and galvanized popular support for the revolutionary movement.

By this time the Marxist RSDWP had become the main organization for the empire's urban proletariat, while the Socialist Revolutionaries (SRs) believed the answer was peasant socialism based on Russian traditions. Thus when revolution broke out in early 1905, Russia was already in a state of unrest that revealed itself in the form of labor strikes (workers typically labored for 12 or more hours a day six days each week and enjoyed few government protections), student protests, peasant disturbances in the countryside, and an SR terrorist campaign that targeted government officials in the hopes of emboldening the masses and intimidating the government into making concessions.

While the Revolution of 1905 was very much a *Russian* affair, its spread to the empire's borderlands revealed the extent of discontent in the Baltic provinces.[6] Shortly after the tragedy in St. Petersburg sympathy strikes broke out in Tallinn, Narva, Pärnu, and other cities. In Riga authorities fired on a large crowd of demonstrators on January 26 (January 13, old style) as they marched from a working-class suburb toward the city center, killing dozens and injuring many more. While the conflict never reached the point of an armed uprising, strikes in the cities and towns, largely coordinated by the Latvian Social Democrats, continued through the spring and summer, by which time the focus had shifted to the countryside, where peasants directed their rage at the German landlords. By the time these spasms of uncoordinated violence subsided, hundreds of Baltic manor houses had been burned down and 82 of their owners and defenders (as well as clergymen) killed in the Baltic provinces.

Taking the side of the Baltic Germans, who formed their own militias and often took matters into their own hands, imperial forces vigorously suppressed the rebellions of the countryside and towns. On October 29 (October 16, old style), tsarist forces fired into a peaceful crowd in Tallinn, killing 94 people and wounding 200 more. Soon afterward martial law, in effect until 1908, was declared in Livland, Courland, and Estland as the regime began to regain control and bring the suspects to justice.[7] Yet it was the pressure of the revolutionary movement that forced a very reluctant tsar to sign the October Manifesto, which promised civil liberties, including the right to organize political parties, and a representative assembly.

Although these concessions satisfied few, activists in the Baltic provinces took advantage of the new opportunities as representative bodies convened to discuss the fate of the Estonian, Latvian, and Lithuanian peoples. In late November 1905 an All-Estonian Congress met in Tartu. At roughly the same time Latvian leader conducted meetings to discuss the fate of the Latvian nation. Whatever the disposition of Estonian and Latvian activists prior to the events of 1905—some were moderates and others more radical—the subsequent punishment of thousands of their countrymen tested the goodwill of even the tsar's most loyal subjects.

In the Lithuanian *gubernii,* where the proletariat was considerably smaller and less radical than in the Baltic provinces to the north, the 1905 revolution was more peaceful—although there too the official reaction was severe: hundreds, if not thousands, of Lithuanians were arrested in its wake, while many others fled. Since the Lithuanians' concerns were more national than social, unrest in the countryside was directed less at Russo-Polish landlords than at the Russian state. In early December 1905, the Vilnius Diet, chaired by Dr. Jonas Basanavičius and attended by 2,000 representatives, met to debate the future of Lithuania. Its demands were the most radical yet of any nationality within the Russian Empire, for the Lithuanians wanted nothing less than national autonomy within ethnic Lithuanian boundaries along with a democratically elected parliament. The Diet also called for the use of the Lithuanian language in schools and in local government.

Attempting to recover from the shock of revolution, the Russian government found that it had little choice but to make limited concessions to the national minorities inhabiting its western provinces, including the granting of permission to use the Estonian, Latvian, and Lithuanian languages in the schools. However, the regime coupled its compromises with muscular displays of its authority, in particular the proclamation of martial law and the repression of local activists. Among those imprisoned, sent to Siberian exile, or expelled from their homelands were two future presidents: Konstantin Päts was sentenced to death, but continued his journalistic activities in Finland before returning to Estonia in 1909, while the Latvian activist Kārlis Ulmanis (1877–1942) fled to the United States, where he studied agriculture at the University of Nebraska before returning to Latvia in 1913.

Meanwhile, the revolution found the Baltic Germans in a quandary. While administrative Russification in the decades before 1905 had eroded much of their power and strained their relationship with the imperial authorities, an alliance with the Latvians and Estonians against St. Petersburg was unthinkable for all concerned, so great was the mutual suspicion and mistrust. If most Baltic Germans cast their lot with the Russian state in the hope that the tsar would uphold their traditional position in Baltic society, a smaller number rejected the tsarist government and emigrated to Germany. (Their numbers were more than offset by the settlement in Latvia of some 13,000 Germans from the Volga region after 1908.) Caught between the hammer and the anvil, for many Baltic Germans there could be no reconciliation with either the tsar or the local nationalists.

After the Revolution of 1905 subsided the tone of politics in the Baltic provinces became more restrained. The periodical press expanded rapidly, and with the abolition of preliminary censorship in 1906 it enjoyed considerable freedom of expression, including the liberty to discuss Russification issues. However, censorship was not completely abolished and radical newspapers were shut down.

During these twilight years of the Russian Empire it was also possible for Estonians, Latvians, and Lithuanians, as it was for Russians, Germans, and others, to voice their concerns through the State Duma. With the creation of this imperial parliament, an advisory body more than a legislative one, the Baltic provinces enjoyed political representation for the first time in their history. While left-leaning Estonians, Latvians, and Lithuanians were dispatched to St. Petersburg for the first and second Dumas, following the dissolution of the latter in June 1907 changes were made to the electoral laws whose purpose was to return more conservative candidates. As a result of the modifications, in the third (1907–1912) and fourth (1912–1917) Dumas the Baltic and Lithuanian provinces were represented mostly by wealthy Germans, Russians, and Poles.

Although the peoples of the Baltic and Lithuanian provinces now enjoyed unprecedented opportunities to engage with the tsarist system, challenges to St. Petersburg's authority continued to be met with repression. Future president of Latvia Jānis Čakste (1859–1927), for example, was elected to the first Duma as a member of the moderate Constitutional Democratic Party; however, his signature on the Vyborg Manifesto (July 1906), which called for passive resistance to the regime following its dissolution of the Duma, earned him three months in a tsarist prison.

Nevertheless, even if the outcome of the Revolution of 1905 was disappointing to the recently awakened peoples of the eastern Baltic, the subsequent decade of parliamentary politics helped to furnish them with the leadership skills and the experience necessary to cope with the challenges that would soon be presented by the Great War.

WORLD WAR I AND GERMAN OCCUPATION

On June 28, 1914, little more than four weeks after a Serbian terrorist assassinated the Austrian archduke, Europe was plunged into a world war that drew in all the major powers and caused untold suffering. At the conclusion of four years of fighting between the countries of the Entente (led by Britain, France, and Russia) and the Central Powers (principally Germany and Austria-Hungary), the map of Europe was transformed, as were the political arrangements that governed most of its states. Gone were the great multinational empires of eastern, central, and southern Europe, replaced by a number of smaller, weaker, and initially democratic successor states. Following two revolutions and a civil war between 1917 and 1921, tsarist Russia, minus its western borderlands, was reinvented as a one-party socialist state, later to be called the Soviet Union.

When Germany's Kaiser Wilhelm II declared war on the Russia of his cousin Nicholas II in the summer of 1914, national self-determination seemed a remote prospect to even the most ambitious activists. Some contemporary observers concluded that a German victory would mean incorporation of Russia's Baltic provinces into the Reich. A Russian triumph, on the other hand, would likely reinforce the existing relationship between St. Petersburg and the provinces and therefore would bring few benefits to the tsar's subject nationalities.

Despite staunch opposition to the war among the empire's socialists, for the most part the populations of the Baltic provinces initially supported Nicholas II and tens of thousands of Latvians and Estonians fought in his army. Lithuanians were also drafted into the Russian army, but their leaders' demand for the unification of Lithuanian territories went unanswered. For many Baltic Germans, the choice between Kaiser and Tsar was agonizing. For the war's first six months they tried to convince the suspicious authorities in St. Petersburg of their unswerving loyalty, but Russia's military failures and the advance of German forces into Lithuania and Courland caused more than a few Baltic Germans to reconsider their allegiance to the tsar.

By autumn 1915 the littoral was cut in half at the Daugava River as the Russian army, along with endless streams of refugees, evacuated the occupied and nearby territories. Among the displaced were about 760,000 people from the Latvian lands, including most of the inhabitants of Courland and the bulk of Riga's industrial workforce. As part of a larger effort to prevent the region's industries and peoples from falling into the hands of the advancing Germans, Latvia's industries were evacuated to neighboring territories. During the war more than 2.6 million refugees from Polish, Lithuanian, and Latvian regions left to find safety in Russia proper. This included the majority of Lithuania's Jewish population, whom St. Petersburg suspected of disloyalty and compelled to leave their homes and move east in what amounted to a population "cleansing"—even if the overwhelming majority of refugees consisted of frightened women, children, and elderly people who could hardly have posed a threat to anyone.[8]

The vastness of the material and economic damage caused by the war nearly matched this human catastrophe. While advancing into Lithuania the Kaiser's army destroyed many farms, while the retreating Russian troops were observed emptying Lithuanian factories and burning their bridges. Although Estonia and northeastern Latvia managed to avoid German occupation until September 1917, when Riga and the larger Estonian islands (Saaremaa, Muhu, Hiiumaa) were seized, the peoples residing in the unoccupied territories suffered from shortages, unemployment, and the runaway inflation that resulted from Russia's attempt to finance the war effort by printing more money.

Military administration in the occupied territories, called the *Land Oberost*, was headed by Field Marshal Paul von Hindenburg, chief of the German High Command, and his second-in-command, General Erich Ludendorff.[9] Although German military leaders had long been convinced that it was necessary to weaken Russia permanently by setting up a ring of dependent barrier states on her western border, at the outset of the war Germany's goals in the Baltic were undefined. One possibility was the annexation of Lithuania and Courland. Another alternative, endorsed by some Baltic German émigrés, was German colonization of the entire Baltic region. In any case, in a speech to the Reichstag in April 1916 Chancellor Bethmann-Hollweg made it clear that Germany would not be returning the Polish, Lithuanian, or Latvian territories to the Russian Empire.

Whatever the ultimate fate of the *Land Oberost*, for the moment the territory was an indivisible administrative unit run exclusively by Reich Germans. Not only did the region provide the occupying army with food and raw materials, it also sent agricultural and industrial products to the Reich. Besides having to submit to requisitions, the inhabitants of the *Land Oberost* faced restrictions on their freedom of movement and in communications. Moreover, a German policy of divide and conquer, aiming to pit the national groups against one another (such as Lithuanians against Poles, Poles and Lithuanians against Jews), was coupled with the goal of bringing German *Kultur* to Lithuania and Courland—a particular concern of Ludendorff's. Perhaps the most enduring consequence of the German occupation was the way the encounters between soldiers and civilians in the *Land Oberost* shaped the policies and atrocities of the later Nazi occupation.[10]

THE FEBRUARY REVOLUTION

With the war going badly for Russia and hunger threatening its cities, demonstrations against the government broke out in early 1917. The largest protests occurred in Petrograd, as the German-sounding St. Petersburg was renamed in 1914, where 50,000 workers, led by the employees of the Putilov munitions plant, went on strike on March 7 (February 22, old style). As the protests in Petrograd mounted, Tsar Nicholas II ordered that the disturbances be suppressed. His popularity across Russian society, never impressive to begin with, was now fatally undermined by Russia's military failures (the tsar took personal command of the armies at the front), his inability to control events in the capital (where his "German" wife Alexandra was left in charge), and the shortages in the shops. Thus on March 8 the tsar accepted the advice of his closest advisors and abdicated the throne. Sixteen months later he and his entire family were murdered by the Bolsheviks, who played no part in the first of the two revolutions of 1917.

As the February Revolution swept away the 300-year-old Romanov dynasty it opened up Russia's political arena to an array of political activists, with the parties of the left reaping the greatest rewards. Immediately a series of "soviets," patterned on the spontaneously organized workers' and soldiers' councils that first formed during the 1905 revolution, acquired immense authority in the empire's cities, especially in Petrograd. Meanwhile, a Provisional Government was formed on the basis of the State Duma, the elected assembly that had been created in the wake of the Revolution of 1905. However, this bourgeois–democratic body, which continued to pursue Russia's losing war against Germany, was countered by the Petrograd Soviet, a socialist-dominated institution that embodied the popular forces that had overthrown the old government. This political arrangement was known as "dual power," a phrase that appropriately symbolized the country's political paralysis and ambiguous future. For the empire's non-Russian nationalities, the fall of the tsarist government represented an opportunity to pursue their dreams of political autonomy, as the new Provisional Government would have little choice but to recognize the growing authority of the Baltic provinces' national leaders and establish partnerships with them.

While some sort of autonomy became a realistic goal for the peoples of Russia's western borderlands, the situation was far from ideal. Consider the circumstances in Lithuania, where aside from the debilitating inconvenience of German occupation, a main obstacle was the Polish leadership, who regarded Lithuanian independence of any kind as undesirable and even threatening to their own plans to reconstitute a Polish state. Nevertheless, while Germany consented to the creation of the Kingdom of Poland in November 1916, Lithuanian leaders worked to secure German recognition for a Lithuanian state. Suspicious of German intentions and fed up with the deportations, compulsory work, requisitions, and personal maltreatment to which their co-nationals were subjected, other national-minded Lithuanians placed their hopes in a Russian victory to achieve their goals. Yet the prospect of a Russian triumph all but disappeared with the February Revolution.

Nevertheless, the revolution created the conditions for the spontaneous growth of national movements espousing the principle of self-determination. In May 1917, some 320 elected representatives of Lithuania's political parties met in Russia's capital to discuss the future of Lithuania. The congress was split: while Lithuanian parties on the political left called for an autonomous Lithuania within a democratic Russian federation, the majority was able to squeeze through a resolution calling for complete independence. Still, the Russian Provisional Government would not provide specific assurances of national autonomy for the Lithuanians, as had been promised the Poles at the beginning of the war.

While the government in Petrograd was reluctant to address the nationality problem, the Germans understood how the slogan of "self-determination," a phrase that was associated with President Woodrow Wilson, who brought the United States into war on the side of the Entente in April 1917, could be applied to advance their own goal of attaching the Baltic territories to the Reich—or at least of detaching them from Russia. With German permission, in September 1917, Lithuanians in Vilnius organized a 20-member State Council of Lithuanian (*Lietuvos Valstybės Taryba*), mainly representing the Lithuanian bourgeoisie, which unanimously voted for the establishment of "an independent state of Lithuania." In return, the *Taryba,* chaired by future Lithuanian president Antanas Smetona (1874–1944), vaguely agreed that the future Lithuanian state would enter into close military, economic, and political relations with the Reich. The effect of this arrangement was to bring closer to fruition the German High Command's goal of turning the entire Baltic region into a German dependency.

While Lithuanian politicians tried to gain advantages from the German occupation, the situation in the Latvian territories was less promising, as they, with the exception of German-occupied Courland, remained under Russian control with seemingly little prospect of independence in the early years of the war. However, circumstances changed after the February Revolution, which presented the Latvians with new opportunities to advance their autonomist goals. As in Petrograd and Moscow, soviets immediately appeared in Riga and other unoccupied Latvian cities, where they appealed to workers and soldiers with their promises of radical social and political change. Meanwhile, Kārlis Ulmanis and Miķelis Valters formed a new political party, the Farmers' Union, to appeal to the interests of Latvian farmers.

Competing visions of an independent Latvia, one that would include southern Livland, Courland, and Latgale, were debated throughout the Latvian provinces. Some Latvian activists called for the right of national self-determination for the Latvian people within their ethnic borders. Such were the demands of the Latvian representatives who met in Riga on July 30, whose declaration proposed an autonomous Latvia within a democratic Russia. Others went even further and called for Latvia's complete independence from Russia, but until the Bolshevik seizure of power such maximalist demands seemed unrealistic as the Provisional Government in Petrograd refused to recognize an autonomous or united Latvia. Yet another obstacle to Latvian autonomy was internal disunity among the Latvians, as many peasants and workers—the latter were increasingly drawn toward Bolshevism—were more concerned with the class struggle than the national one.

Like the Latvians, the Estonians had also entered the war as more or less loyal subjects of the tsar, but many eventually began to understand that Russia's weakness provided an opportunity for them to achieve their own national ambitions. With the fall of the imperial government in March 1917, Estonians saw little reason to continue defending the old order and were the first to take advantage of the new conditions. Immediately Jaan Tõnisson called for Estonian autonomy and began to pressure the Provisional Government to agree to the reorganization of self-government in the north Baltic region. With the establishment of an Estonian representative assembly (*Maapäev*) at the end of March, the old Baltic German- and Russian-controlled institutions of local government were abolished. Perhaps most importantly, Petrograd agreed to the administrative unification of the ethnographically Estonian territories. The imperial government's recognition of the existence of "Estonia" was a concession granted to neither the Latvians nor the Lithuanians.

Estonian political parties quickly emerged to fill the seats in the *Maapäev*, for which elections were held in May and June 1917. Rather than urging outright separation from Russia, most deputies agreed that Estonia should become part of a democratic Russian federation. However, during the summer of 1917 real power lay not with the *Maapäev*, but with the socialist-dominated soviets in which the empire's sailors, soldiers, and workers were predominant. Bolsheviks fared well in local elections in August and, as a rising force in Estonian politics, challenged the authority of the *Maapäev* to speak for all

Estonia. But with the Germans advancing and capturing Riga in mid-August, it looked as if nearby Estonia too would become an extension of the Reich.

THE BOLSHEVIKS AND THE BALTIC

By the time the Bolsheviks seized power in Petrograd in the autumn of 1917, the Lithuanian, Latvian, and Estonian peoples had already taken decisive steps in the direction of national autonomy. But just as Russia's brief experiment with liberalism ended with the Bolshevik *coup d'état* of November 6–7 (October 24–25, old style), so ended any prospect of a federal arrangement between Russia and the nascent Baltic countries.

Support for the Bolsheviks had been growing in the urban areas of Latvian and Estonia well before their leader Vladimir Lenin (1870–1924) declared Soviet power in Petrograd. By the summer of 1917, the Bolshevik faction of the Latvian Social Democratic Workers' Party, which already controlled the party's Central Committee, had even achieved majorities in some Latvian soviets. In August the Latvian Bolsheviks, supported by Riga's radicalized workers, managed to form an indigenous Executive Committee of the Soviet of Workers, Soldiers, and the Landless in Latvia (*Iskolat*) in the unoccupied eastern regions parts of Latvia; in December 1917 it formally declared itself to be Latvia's Soviet government. Headed by the Latvian Bolshevik Fricis Roziņš (1870–1919) and run by ethnic Latvians, the short-lived *Iskolat* is thought by historians to have been a significant stage in the development of Latvian statehood, as Latvian was introduced as the language of administration and the Latgale region was annexed from Russia's Vitebsk province. Yet the *Iskolat*'s main objective was not nationalist but rather to carry out Lenin's class-based revolution in Latvia.[11] Already divided geographically, as hundreds of thousands of Latvians had been evacuated to the Russian interior in 1915, the Latvian people were divided politically as well.

Assisting the Bolshevik cause in Latvia was the battalion of Latvian Riflemen, the only national fighting force to emerge in the region. Formed in August 1915 as part of the imperial army to fight the Germans and regain Courland, the Riflemen (*strēlnieki*) earned a reputation for their reliability and determination, holding a German offensive in check while suffering their most serious losses during the Christmas Battles (*Ziemassvētku kaujas*) of 1916–1917. In the wake of the February Revolution the Riflemen came under the influence of the political left and switched their allegiance to the Bolsheviks, who offered immediate and radical solutions to Russia's (and Latvia's) problems—the most pressing of which was the war, which the Bolsheviks proposed to end immediately and without reparations and annexations.[12]

The *Iskolat*'s main political competition during its short life, from December 1917 to February 1918, was the Latvian Provisional National Council (LPNC), which brought together representatives of nearly all of Latvia's most important associations and political parties at its first meeting in late November 1917—just as the Bolsheviks began to create a dictatorship in Russia. Gathering in the unoccupied city of Valka, the LPNC declared "Latvia"—including Livland, Courland, and Latgale—to be an autonomous unit within Russia. Some Latvian writers regard this as nothing less than a declaration of independence.[13] When the Bolshevik *Iskolat* that ruled the unoccupied parts of Latvia declared the LNPC's activities illegal, the latter relocated to Petrograd, where in January 1918 it adopted an unambiguous declaration of Latvian independence and began to seek international recognition for a Latvian state.

While the Germans and the Bolsheviks began the negotiations that would lead in March 1918 to the Treaty of Brest-Litovsk, popular assemblies in Lithuania and Estonia also took steps to secure their independence from a weakened Russia. On December 11, 1917, a Lithuanian government was proclaimed by the *Taryba*, which declared that Vilnius, also claimed by Poland, would be its capital city; but it was not until February 16 that the *Taryba*, meeting in Vilnius, signed an act of independence that explicitly repudiated Lithuania's ties with any foreign powers. Having received the necessary assurances from the *Taryba*, now temporarily chaired by Jonas Basanavičius, of its future close collaboration with Germany, on March 23, 1918, Kaiser Wilhelm decided to recognize a nominally independent Lithuanian state, which was to be bound in perpetuity to the Reich.

The first of the Baltic peoples to demand self-government, the Estonians were the last to declare their outright independence, for the nationalist aims being pursued by the bourgeoisie, who were represented in the *Maapäev*, carried little weight with Estonia's councils of workers and soldiers, who were increasingly embracing the Bolshevik view in the summer of 1917. The autumn of 1917 was marked by turbulence and uncertainty in the Estonian lands, for German troops had swiftly occupied the larger islands as the Russian workers and industries were evacuated to the interior and the Bolsheviks planned their coup. But the Bolsheviks failed to consolidate power in Estonia and their defenses fell apart in February 1918 as German troops advanced toward the future Estonian capital. Realizing that a German occupation could threaten the prospect of Estonian independence, Estonian leaders worked to garner national and international support for the Estonian cause. Meanwhile, as the Bolsheviks and the German High Command negotiated the terms of what would become the Treaty of Brest-Litovsk, an Estonian Committee of Elders, acting on behalf of the dispersed *Maapäev,* declared the country's independence on February 24 and simultaneously created a new Provisional Government headed by Konstantin Päts. But detachment from Russia was still a far cry from full independence, for on the next day German troops, now openly supported by much of the Baltic nobility, moved into Tallinn, where they stayed until November 1918.

As the Germans completed their occupation of the entire Baltic region, members of Latvia's *Iskolat* fled to Moscow, thereby bringing to a conclusion the first socialist experiment in Latvia. (As discussed later, Soviet power would return to Estonia and Latvia with the Red Army at the end of the year.) Desperately needing to end the war with Germany, the Bolsheviks had by this time decided to surrender the western borderlands in an effort to strengthen their hold over the Russian heartland. Under the terms of the Treaty of Brest-Litovsk, signed by Bolshevik and German representatives on March 3, 1918, the German-Russian war was declared over and the Bolsheviks were compelled to surrender vast stretches of border territory from the Baltic to the Black Sea. While in principle the fate of these territories was to be determined "in agreement with their populations," the reality was that the Germans didn't know what to do with them; the main thing now was to redouble their efforts on the western front.

If reformers in the German Reichstag pressed for national self-determination for the Baltic peoples, the German High Command continued to manipulate the situation in the region in the hopes of, at minimum, permanently depriving Russia of her western borderlands, and maximally, attaching them to the Reich. The most effective way to do achieve the latter was to rely on the traditional lords of the region, the Baltic Germans, to express a popular desire for unification with Germany. The prototype for this plan was created in German-occupied Courland, where a representative assembly, the *Landesrat,* composed of Baltic Germans and seeking the closest ties to Germany, on March 8, 1918, offered the crown of the Duchy of Courland to Kaiser Wilhelm II. The expectation was that similar experiments would be repeated in Livland and Estonia, and thus the entire *Baltikum* would fall into the hands of the Reich. Indeed, many among the Baltic German elite rejoiced at the prospect of the entire region becoming Germanized; the nobles of Livland and Estland were even prepared to offer land to

German colonists from the Reich. However, Germany's recent good fortune in war was not to last much longer and Latvian and Estonian resistance, combined with objections from the Reichstag, effectively ruined the Kaiser's plan.

Lithuania's situation differed from that of Latvia and Estonia in that its lack of a German elite meant that were no Baltic German assemblies for the Reich to use to achieve its foreign policy goals in the region. Nevertheless, in the summer of 1918, the *Taryba* controversially toyed with the idea of placing on the Lithuanian throne Duke Wilhelm von Urach, a German aristocrat who was to be known as Mindaugas II. But Wilhelm, a Roman Catholic whose appointment earned the Vatican's approval, never got to visit his adopted homeland much less assume the throne, for after the German military collapse in the autumn Lithuania no longer needed this ploy. On November 2 the *Taryba* declared Lithuania a republic with a three-member presidium that included Augustinas Voldemaras as prime minister. After the adoption of a constitution in April 1919, Antanas Smetona became Lithuania's first president.

To some extent, the fate of the provinces inhabited by the Lithuanian, Latvian, and Estonian peoples lay in the hands not of the Germans but of the Entente powers—Britain, France, and the United States, an "associate power" that joined the war in 1917. But during this period the Entente's main concern in the region, apart from reopening the eastern front and winning the war against Germany, was to maintain the territorial integrity of the Russian state, whose Bolshevik leaders many in the West believed would quickly pass from the scene. Reluctant to acknowledge the full independence of the Baltic states, the Entente nonetheless encouraged them to resist the Germans while delaying any discussion of their final status until the peace conference.

But first the war against Germany needed to be brought to a successful conclusion. Reinvigorated by a fresh infusion of U.S. forces on the western front, the Entente powers were able to turn the tide during the summer of 1918 and by October they were threatening to invade Germany, prompting General Ludendorff to seek an armistice. In quick succession a revolution in Berlin on November 9 deposed the Kaiser, a German Provisional Government was installed, an armistice was signed, and Soviet Russia repudiated the Treaty of Brest-Litovsk. Once again the Baltic region fell into chaos as the new German government acknowledged the right of Latvians and Estonians to self-determination and the Bolsheviks advanced into the Baltic region. However, the absence of any external legal authority during the transition gave Estonian and Latvian politicians an opportunity to influence the course of events in their countries.

On November 18, 1918, a day that would later be celebrated as Latvian Independence Day, representatives formed a national council in Riga that declared the existence of a Republic of Latvia and a Provisional Government headed by Kārlis Ulmanis. Immediately it was recognized by the new German government, whose leaders believed independent Baltic states to be preferable to Russian rule for the maintenance of Germany's interests in the region. However, the state of disarray in Russia's western borderlands provided the Bolsheviks, who were counting on a German evacuation and possibly a socialist uprising in Germany, with an opportunity to spread the revolution westward. In December, the Latvian Bolsheviks returned to those Latvian areas not occupied by the Germans and set up a Soviet government headed by Pēteris Stučka (1865–1932) while the Ulmanis-led Latvian Provisional Government (1918–1920) was forced to flee to German-occupied Courland, where for the time being it enjoyed German protection.

Politically close to Lenin, Stučka, like the other Latvian Bolsheviks, envisioned a socialist Latvian republic as having the "closest possible links" with Bolshevik Russia.[14] The establishment of a "dictatorship of the proletariat" was immediately followed by a wave of terror, with the Bolsheviks imprisoning and executing more than 1,000 (some sources claim that there were upward of 5,000 victims) of their aristocratic and bourgeois enemies, mostly Baltic Germans. An entry from the diary of 24-year-old Angelika von Korff describes the experience of Bolshevik rule in Riga in the spring of 1919 from the point of view of a Baltic German baroness:

> Here things are getting worse and worse. On the street one is constantly being asked for documents and often people are led off. The most anger is directed against the nobility. [Stučka] recently wrote, "We show no compromise with the nobility. They can go hide in the forest, but we will find them and get rid of them." We are totally without rights, anybody who wants to can just shoot us. Pastors and businessmen are also high on their list and the prisons are overcrowded. . . . In the empty houses, Bolsheviks move in, the maidservants, the butlers. Now they are all gone, the Engelhardts, Oelsens, Panders, Reckes, Brüggens, Roennes, Bistrams, Drude Korff, Jenny Grandidier, ach, almost all of them.[15]

The Latvian Soviet Republic also antagonized the peasants with agrarian policies that anticipated the collectivization campaign ordered by Joseph Stalin three decades later. The return of German armed forces in May 1919 (discussed below) brought an end to the Red Terror in Riga, but the Latvian Bolsheviks held onto parts of eastern Latvia until the end of the year.

Estonia, which had been occupied by the Germans since February, was also threatened by the Bolsheviks, whose invasion began on November 22, 1918, only three days after a defeated Germany had recognized *de facto* the Estonian Provisional Government headed by Konstantin Päts. While Estonia's leaders devoted their efforts to creating a national army, headed by the capable Lieutenant Colonel Johan Laidoner (1884–1953), Baltic German communities simultaneously formed their own volunteer units. At first, the Estonian defense was a failure: within a week, Bolshevik forces conquered Narva and proclaimed the Estonian Workers' Commune, headed by Jaan Anvelt (1884–1937), as an autonomous part of Soviet Russia. As other Estonian towns fell one after another, the Bolsheviks instituted a Red Terror that claimed more than 500 lives. A "White terror" would follow in both Estonia and Latvia the following year when the tables were turned and the Bolsheviks and their accomplices became the objects of revenge.

WARS OF INDEPENDENCE

What followed in the wake of the Armistice and the Bolshevik advance into the Baltic was a curious postscript to World War I in which German military forces, having been defeated on the western front, were given a green light to continue the struggle in the east. Concerned that the Bolsheviks might succeed in igniting revolutions in the areas "liberated" by the Red Army, leaders of the Entente invoked Article XII of the Armistice Agreement, which required that Germany withdraw its armed forces from the east *only* when the Entente governments thought it desirable. Although the new democratic government in Berlin, installed after the Kaiser's flight in November, hoped to build friendly relations with the Baltic countries for the purpose of securing Germany's long-term influence in the region, it nevertheless concluded that Germany would receive better peace terms from the Allies if it participated in the Baltic counteroffensive against the Bolsheviks.

Little more than two months after the proclamations of Soviet republics in Estonia, Latvia, and Lithuania in late 1918, the Iron Division entered Latvia. A unit of the German *Freikorps* (Free Corps), the Iron Division was assigned to General Rüdiger von der Goltz (1865–1946), whose recent intervention in Finland had helped its new government to defeat the combined Finnish "Red" and Soviet Russian armies.

In Latvia, von der Goltz's forces combined with Baltic German units, organized as the *Baltische Landeswehr* (Baltic Territorial Army), as well as Latvian soldiers loyal to the Provisional Government of Kārlis Ulmanis—an embryonic Latvian national army—to continue the fight against the Bolsheviks. Thus while the terms of the peace were being negotiated at Versailles, the armed struggle continued in the east, with Baltic Germans fighting to maintain their privileged position in the region and Reich Germans—ordinary soldiers with limited prospects in Germany—lured to Latvia by false promises of land.

If Latvian soldiers fought for a Latvia free of both Russian and German domination (such a Latvian state, the Ulmanis government promised, would also provide Latvian veterans with farmland), the same could not be said of von der Goltz, whose goal was to build a Baltic bridge that would connect Germany to what he hoped would be a restored "White" (nonsocialist) Russia. "[W]hy could not an economic and political sphere be created next to Russia? Russia's own intelligentsia was ruined and her land was hungering for German technicians, merchants and leaders. Her devastated and depopulated border provinces required German settlers to cultivate their fertile soil. I had in mind especially the discharged soldiers . . . Russia was no longer in a position to object."[16]

That the German forces had no authority to intervene in local political affairs did little to stop the *Freikorps* from pursuing their own goals in the Baltic. On April 16, the Germans deposed the government in Liepāja as Ulmanis and most of his ministers found sanctuary on the SS *Saratov* under the protection of the British navy, which had been delivering weapons to the Latvian Provisional Government. Five weeks later, on May 22, 1919, the combined units (Latvian forces, the *Landeswehr,* and *Freikorps*) managed to liberate Riga from the exhausted Bolsheviks. With von der Goltz's cooperation, the *Landeswehr* took over the administration and set up a rival government that was headed by the pastor Andrievs Niedra (1871–1942), a Latvian reactionary who would be reliant upon his German masters.

Since the *Freikorps* and *Landeswehr* were believed to have killed hundreds and possibly thousands of alleged communist collaborators, overwhelmingly Latvians, during their occupation of Riga, Latvian nationalists turned against their former allies. Meanwhile, native Estonian forces, having pushed the Red Army out of southern Estonia into Latgale, now advanced into Latvia, where they combined with Latvian units to capture the town of Cēsis from the Germans in June 1919.

Victory at the Battle of Cēsis (*Võnnu* in Estonian) was a decisive moment in both the Estonian and Latvian wars of independence.

In Estonia it is now celebrated as Victory Day (*Võidupüha*), a national holiday that is observed every June 23. On July 3, the combatants signed the armistice of Strazdumuiža, which forced the Germans to leave Riga while the *Landeswehr* was redeployed to fight the Red Army. As the German-backed Niedra government slipped into irrelevance, Kārlis Ulmanis reclaimed the legitimacy of his Provisional Government as Latvian units took control of the capital.[17] Concluding that it would be better to replace the German anti-Bolshevik forces with native troops, the Entente ordered the Germans to leave the region as quickly as possible. His plans in tatters, a defiant von der Goltz returned to Germany in October (five months after his recall) as volunteers flooded into the Estonian and Latvian armies and Allied aid flowed into the Latvian and Estonian governments.

Nevertheless, remnants of the *Freikorps* continued the crusade in the Baltic for months afterward. Thousands were transferred to the West Russian Volunteer Army of Pavel Bermondt-Avalov (1877–1974), an aristocrat of Cossack lineage who declared that he would continue the anti-Bolshevik struggle. Taking command of the German forces in Courland, Bermondt's purported aim was to join up with the White army of General Nikolai Yudenich (see below), capture Petrograd, and reintegrate the Baltic territories into a monarchist Russia. However, Berlin's involvement in the scheme was so obvious that on November 25 the Ulmanis government declared that a state of war existed between Latvia and Germany. By this time, Bermondt's forces were spent, having failed to take Riga in October 1919 and then burning and looting the countryside during their retreat through Courland. By mid-December Bermondt's demoralized army was driven from the Baltic by the Latvian and Lithuanian armies with the aid of Estonian troops and Allied material aid. Soon afterward the Polish army drove the Bolsheviks from Latgale, leaving Latvia completely free of German and Russian armies.

If the Estonians had managed to liberate themselves from the Bolsheviks without help from the *Freikorps,* they did benefit from the assistance of Finnish, Latvian, and Baltic German forces, while also receiving aid from the Entente powers. Estonia also uncomfortably hosted a White Russian army headed by General Yudenich. The Whites, however, had no intention of recognizing the right to self-determination of any nationality of the old Russian Empire; they fought for a "Russia one and indivisible." While Yudenich's attempt to take Petrograd ultimately ended in defeat, by the spring of 1919 Estonia was cleared of Soviet troops and the Provisional Government was secure enough to elect a Constituent Assembly, which in turn voted unanimously to affirm Estonia's independence. Relations with Russia, however, remained questionable as the fractured giant's devastating civil war dragged on. Nevertheless, by early 1920 the Bolshevik government in Moscow (the new capital of Soviet Russia), concerned that the Estonians and others would join a united anti-Bolshevik front that would permit the victory of the White Russian forces, was ready to make peace with Estonia.

According to the terms of the Treaty of Tartu signed on February 2, 1920, Soviet Russia recognized Estonian independence *de jure* and forever renounced any rights to Estonian territory. Likewise, Latvia's Ulmanis government signed an armistice with the Bolshevik government after the liberation of Latgale in early 1920. A peace treaty followed on August 11, 1920, in which Moscow recognized Latvia's independence. Although many Latvian refugees returned from Russia between 1919 and 1927, at least 150,000 Latvians, many of whom were convinced socialists, decided to remain in the Soviet Union.[18]

Lithuania also endured a Soviet regime—the Lithuanian-Belorussian (Litbel) Republic, proclaimed in December 1918 following the withdrawal of German forces—but the Bolsheviks managed to occupy only about two-thirds of the country. Since Bolshevism had not produced a native organization in Lithuania as it had in Latvia and Estonia, the Lithuanians' war against the Red Army was truly a national rather than a civil war. Volunteer regiments were formed to fight for the country's independence, and by late August 1919 the Lithuanians were able to drive the tired and poorly supplied Red Army from their territory.

Like Riga, Vilnius changed hands numerous times during a profoundly turbulent era that witnessed the comings and goings of peoples (Russians being evacuated, Jewish refugees arriving), persistent food shortages, and waves of epidemics. The city was occupied by the Germans from 1915 until late 1918, then by the Bolshevik Lithuanian government (Litbel), and from April 1919 by Polish forces who claimed it and the surrounding region for Poland as they drove toward the Russian interior. A little more than a year later the situation was reversed: with Poland now losing its war against Soviet Russia, in July 1920, Bolshevik forces marched into Vilnius, following which they turned the city over to Lithuania in exchange for allowing the Red Army free passage through Lithuanian territory. Even after Polish forces returned to Vilnius in late October, the Lithuanian government refused to surrender its claim to the city.

Thus at various points in 1919–1920 the Lithuanians faced the Bolsheviks in the east, the Poles in the south, and White Russian (and

German) forces on the northern front. As a result, the resolution of the situation in Lithuania took longer than was the case in Latvia and Estonia. It was not until July 12, 1920, that the Lithuanian and Soviet governments at last concluded a peace treaty, with the latter recognizing Lithuania's claim to Vilnius (Poland's subsequent seizure of the city notwithstanding).[19]

No longer part of Russia, and freed from the dominance of the Baltic German elite, who now had nowhere to turn, the peoples of Estonia, Latvia, and Lithuania embarked upon the creation of independent states during a period of great uncertainty but with high hopes. But for the Baltic countries, it has never been possible to pursue the interests of nation and state completely independently of the will of their larger neighbors and other great powers. Indeed, while historian Georg von Rauch, writing 40 years ago, lauded the aspiring states for their "military prowess and political courage" at this critical moment in their collective history, it was, in the final analysis, the collapse of two great powers, Germany and Russia, which made possible the establishment of three sovereign states along the Baltic Sea.[20]

Although the Allied (Entente) powers were willing to provide some material help in their struggle against the Bolsheviks, the Baltic countries were able to secure Allied recognition only in 1921 and 1922—after the outcome of the Russian civil war had been decided. Having abandoned the cause of the various White armies who fought the united Bolshevik Red Army, the Allies now endorsed the idea of a *cordon sanitaire*—a belt of states that would confine Bolshevism to the east and keep Russia and Germany apart. In the postwar period, the requirements of the great powers would again play decisive roles in determining the fate of the Baltic peoples.

Few episodes in the history of the Baltic states are fraught with greater significance than the wars of independence that were fought between 1918 and 1920. From these wars emerged not only three new democratic states and three new national armies, but also a new pantheon of heroes and an institutionalized commemoration of the generation whose sacrifices brought liberty to the Estonian, Latvian, and Lithuanian peoples. Few could have been unaware that the political freedoms for which so many had sacrificed their lives could be quickly lost.

NOTES

1. The statistics used in this section were drawn from several sources. These include Andrejs Plakans, *The Latvians: A Short History* (Stanford,

CA: Hoover Institution Press, 1995), 88, 108; Andrejs Plakans, *A Concise History of the Baltic States* (New York: Cambridge University Press, 2011), 244–54; Toivo U. Raun, *Estonia and the Estonians*, 2nd ed. (Stanford, CA: Hoover Institution Press, 2001), 71–73; Andreas Kappeler, *The Russian Empire* (Harlow, UK: Pearson Education Limited, 2001), 397–407; Stephen D. Corrsin, "The Changing Composition of the City of Riga, 1867–1913," *Journal of Baltic Studies* 13, no. 2 (Summer 1982): 19–39.

2. Daina Bleiere, et al., *History of Latvia: The 20th Century*, 2nd ed. (Riga: Jumava, 2006), 39–51.

3. Overall, the demographic situation was bleak for the Baltic Germans. From 1881 to 1897 the total number of Baltic Germans in Estland, Livland, and Courland dropped from 180,423 to 152,936, partly due to Russification and also owing to some German emigration.

4. Alfonsas Eidintas, Vytautas Žalys, and Alfred Erich Senn, *Lithuania in European Politics: The Years of the First Republic, 1918–1940* (New York: St. Martin's Press, 1997), 17.

5. Edward C. Thaden, ed., *Russification in the Baltic Provinces and Finland, 1855–1914* (Princeton, NJ: Princeton University Press, 1981), 260.

6. See Toivu U. Raun, "The Revolution of 1905 in the Baltic Provinces and Finland," *Slavic Review* 53, no. 3 (Winter 1984): 453–67.

7. Latgale, an ethnically diverse and underdeveloped region of Latvia that was part of the province of Vitebsk, was less affected by the disturbances of 1905–1907.

8. Peter Gatrell, *A Whole Empire Walking: Refugees in Russia during World War I* (Bloomington: Indiana University Press, 1999).

9. At first *Oberost*, or *Ober Ost*, included only Courland, Lithuania, Bialystock-Grodno. With the Treaty of Brest-Litovsk in March 1918 it was expanded to include Estonia, Belarus, and the rest of Latvia.

10. See Vejas Gabriel Liulevicius, *War Land on the Eastern Front: Culture, National Identity, and German Occupation in World War I* (New York: Cambridge University Press, 2000).

11. Andrew Ezergailis, *The Latvian Impact on the Bolshevik Revolution* (Boulder, CO: East European Monographs, 1983).

12. After Russia lost Riga to the Germans in September 1917, the Riflemen were summoned by Lenin to Petrograd where they became his praetorian guard and arguably saved the revolution. But it wasn't long after returning to Latvia in the summer of 1918 that the Riflemen, whose ranks consisted mostly of landless peasants and small tenant farmers, became disillusioned with the Soviet experiment, having witnessed the betrayal of its promises of justice and fairness. The feats of the Latvian Riflemen would later be celebrated in Soviet Latvia, where monuments were erected in their honor. So great is their historical reputation that even many anticommunist Latvians accept the Rifleman as authentic Latvian heroes, even if they do not share many of the soldiers' commitment to Lenin's vision. See Geoffrey Swain, "The Disillusioning of the

Revolution's Praetorian Guard: The Latvian Riflemen, Summer-Autumn 1918," *Europe-Asia Studies*, vol. 51, no. 4 (June 1999): 667–86.

13. Bleiere, 120–21.

14. Georg von Rauch, *The Baltic States: The Years of Independence: Estonia, Latvia, Lithuania 1917–1940* (Berkeley: University of California Press, 1974), 58.

15. Mark R. Hatlie, "Riga's First Totalitarian Regime: January 3 – May 22, 1919." http://hatlie.de/pdf/korff.pdf (accessed July 9, 2014). Excerpts translated by Mark R. Hatlie.

16. Rüdiger von der Goltz, *Meine Sendung in Finland und im Baltikum* (Leipzig, Germany: K.F. Koehler, 1920), as appears in Puisāns, 193.

17. Amnestied in 1924, Niedra was expelled from the country only to return to Latvia during the later Nazi occupation.

18. Plakans (1995), 120. Among those who remained in Russia was the former Bolshevik Pēteris Stučka. From 1958 to 1990 the University of Latvia was officially named the Pēteris Stučka Latvian State University.

19. Although secretly authorized by Józef Piłsudski, the head of the new Polish state, the seizure of Vilnius by General Lucjan Żeligowski in October 1920 became known as Żeligowski's Mutiny. In 1922, the Lithuanian *Seimas* voted to incorporate Vilnius and the surrounding region into Poland, and afterward Piłsudski admitted that the "mutiny" had in fact been a planned operation carried out with his support.

20. Quote from Rauch, p. 75.

5

Independence, 1920–1939

Of the newly independent states that appeared in Europe after World War I, Estonia, Latvia, and Lithuania were among the most obscure to outsiders. Indeed, prior to World War I, it was common for Westerners, as it was for tsarist officials in St. Petersburg, to view the eastern Baltic region as an integral part of Russia itself; beyond the empire's western borders little was known of the languages and traditions of the Estonian, Latvian, and Lithuanian peoples. The empire's collapse in 1917–1918, however, offered the peoples of what are now called the Baltic states an entirely unexpected opportunity to pursue their own separate destinies apart from and independent of the empire. Yet even if the Allied and Associated Powers endorsed the principle of national self-determination during the war, they failed to commit fully to supporting the independence of the Baltic states, questioning the viability of such small states and hoping for Russia's stabilization under a friendly government. Nevertheless the Balts (a word that is henceforth used to include Estonians as well as the Latvians and Lithuanians) did receive some Western aid for their defense against Bolshevism. Indeed, it would be difficult to imagine a free and united Latvia without the support Latvian forces received from the Royal Navy.

Yet it was only in 1921–1922, after hopes for the emergence of a democratic Russia—within which, the Allies hoped, the Baltic peoples would enjoy national autonomy—had been dashed, that the new states were accepted as members of the League of Nations and given *de jure* recognition by the Allies. Concerned about the possible spread of Bolshevism beyond Russia, Allied leaders conceived of the Baltic republics, along with the other new states in central and eastern Europe, as part of a *cordon sanitaire,* a belt of buffer states intended to separate the German and Russian pariahs and to keep Bolshevism confined to the east. Otherwise the new countries were left to settle their own problems, including those with their neighbors.

These problems were indeed formidable. Estonia, Latvia, and Lithuania each faced the daunting task of building a viable and durable state while overcoming the extraordinary material and human losses each had endured during World War I and the wars of independence. They had to construct new political systems while the fighting was still taking place, rebuild their shattered economies, and settle their borders among themselves and with their larger Polish, German, and Russian neighbors. Moreover, with the new states having been created on the basis of national self-determination for the Estonian, Latvian, and Lithuanian majorities, those who had once controlled the political and economic life of the region—the Baltic Germans, Russians, and Poles—would have to accommodate themselves to the new circumstances. The parallels between the 1920s and 1990s, when the Baltic states attained their independence once again, are striking.

Although their experiments in parliamentary democracy ultimately failed as each of the republics succumbed to the lure of authoritarian government, the Baltic peoples managed to create viable and some might say thriving nation-states. Even a half-century of Soviet rule, beginning during World War II, would not be sufficient to erase the historical memory of two decades of independence.

RECONSTRUCTION AND REFORM

Of the Baltic countries the least damaged by the fighting of 1914 to 1920 was Estonia, whose prewar population of approximately 1,086,009 (1911) fell to 1,059,000 in 1920.[1] Thousands of Estonians, many of whom were communists, left for Russia, where they joined the tens of thousands of Estonians who had already been living there for several decades. Estonia's suffering was far exceeded by the staggering toll the wars took on Latvia and its people. From a prewar population of about 2.5 million, by 1920 the population of the Latvian areas, now reorganized as Kurzeme, Zemgale, Vidzeme, and Latgale, had plummeted to 1.6 million. Most of the decline is attributable to the large number of refugees—perhaps 760,000—who fled to Russia or elsewhere. Although most returned during the 1920s, many Latvians remained in Soviet Russia.[2] The physical destruction wrought by war and the prolonged sieges of Riga were accompanied by mass flight from the cities as the country's urban population fell from 40 percent to less than 24 percent between 1914 and 1920.[3] Once a bustling industrial and shipping center that served the needs of a sprawling empire, postwar Riga was transformed into the capital city and administrative center of a small, struggling Latvian state. From Liepāja in the west to Daugavpils in the east, the cities of Latvia were a shell of what they had been before 1914.

With its claims to Vilnius obstructed by Poland's seizure of the city in October 1920, Lithuania's provisional capital was Kaunas, a heavily fortified but otherwise neglected city under the tsars. Like parts of Latvia, Lithuania endured almost continual occupation by foreign armies between 1915 and 1920 and also like Latvia suffered from enormous material destruction and loss of life. In 1923, the population of the Lithuanian Republic was about 2,035,000—about 600,000 fewer than the number of people who lived in the Lithuanian *gubernii* (excluding the city and district of Vilnius) in 1897. Of those who remained about 84 percent were ethnic Lithuanians. The rest were mostly Jews, Poles, and Russians.[4] Likewise, Estonians (88 percent) and Latvians (about 75 percent) were clearly predominant in their respective states.

Serious economic disruptions due to the war were common to all three Baltic states and were compounded by the Allied blockade of Russia in 1919 as well as debts to Britain, France, the United States, and (in the Estonian case) Finland for their assistance during the wars of independence. In Latvia, where the fighting was heaviest, the economic situation was especially stark: most of the major industrial and transportation equipment had been moved to the Russian interior during the war and much of the agricultural land was devastated and lay fallow. Such conditions were aggravated by the fact that Baltic agriculture and industry had been heavily dependent on Russia, which was now suffering its own economic catastrophe and was effectively cut off from the Baltic states. Thus the Baltic economies had to be reoriented toward the countries of western Europe, whose entrepreneurs surely saw the Baltic region as a natural bridge to potential Russian markets.

With many rural areas in ruins and hundreds of manors abandoned during the fighting, one of the most pressing concerns for the Baltic leaders at the end of the wars of independence was the matter of land reform, by which they aimed to transfer control of the land from relatively rich landlords to the largely destitute peasantry. In 1918, most of the agricultural land in Estonia and Latvia was in the hands of large estate owners, and the vast majority of these large landed estates were held by Baltic Germans. In Lithuania, the land was traditionally held largely by Poles, as was the case in eastern Latvia. Thus a large proportion of Lithuanian, Latvian, and especially Estonian peasants remained landless at the end of the world war. Independence from Russia now offered the republics' new leaders the unprecedented opportunity to rectify this imbalance—and to break the political and economic hold that the nobility had enjoyed in the region for centuries. Moreover, in the wake of the Estonians' and Latvians' triumph over Bolshevism, land redistribution appeared to make good political sense, as it would blunt communism's appeal to the peasantry.

The subject of the debate was not whether land reform would take place, but rather how much land would be redistributed and what form compensation would take. The first and most sweeping experiment in Baltic land reform occurred in Estonia even before a constitution had been adopted. Under the terms of the agricultural law adopted in October 1919, 96.6 percent of the holdings classified as large estates—lands that together comprised more than half the farmland of the entire republic—were expropriated without compensation. The lands were then redistributed to small farmers, with priority going to veterans of the wars of independence. As a result of Estonia's land reform, the total number of Estonian farms more than doubled during the 1920s and Estonian land hunger was essentially satisfied even if the Baltic Germans, whose more modest proposal was overruled, were not.

In Latvia too the compromise solutions proposed by large estate owners were rejected. Convinced of the need for drastic reform—not only were the estates an anachronism, but maintaining them was politically impossible in light of the barons' support for the bitter campaign waged by the forces of Bermondt-Avalov in 1919—Latvian leaders, led by the then-dominant Social Democrats, introduced agrarian legislation in September 1920 under which all privately owned properties comprising more than 110 hectares would be nationalized and placed in a land fund for redistribution to landless peasants and veterans of the wars of independence. The parliament (*Saeima*) voted by a narrow margin that there would be no compensation to the estate owners, although estate owners whose properties were expropriated would be allowed to keep up to 50 hectares. While rural debt remained a problem in Latvia and the parcels were modest in size (no more than 22 hectares), the number of farmsteads doubled between 1922 and 1935 as Latvia, like Estonia, was transformed into a nation of small farmers. In both countries agricultural productivity, which had been higher on the small, independent farms than on the estates even before the war, steadily improved even as they lagged behind the more developed countries of western Europe.

In Lithuania, a country whose economy and society were more rural than either Latvia or Estonia, the main land reform law called for landlords to be left with no more than 80 hectares, later raised to 150. The rest was to be redistributed to veterans and peasants. Those estate owners, some of whom had supported the Poles in the war, who surrendered their property would be compensated over a period of 36 years. In reality little of this was ever actually paid and rural poverty remained a major social problem in Lithuania up to the outbreak of World War II.

These rural initiatives, which may well be the most sweeping land reforms ever undertaken by democratic governments, transformed the character of these three countries. Instead of consisting of masses of landless peasants dominated by a few wealthy landowners, Estonia, Latvia, and Lithuania now became nations of small farm owners, freed from the political and economic domination of the Baltic Germans and (in Lithuania) the Poles.

THE DEMOCRATIC YEARS

For the Baltic states the era between the two world wars may be divided into two distinct periods. The first was a democratic period, during which parliaments held the upper hand in state politics while national institutions were being built. The second period was authoritarian, beginning in Lithuania in 1926 and in Latvia and Estonia in 1934. Fearing the instability of parliamentary politics in the face of internal and external threats, authoritarian figures seized executive power in the name of the greater national good. These regimes, characterized by many historians as benign dictatorships, even as the Soviets labeled them "fascist," lasted until the region's occupation by Soviet forces in 1940.

Before turning to the rule of the dictators, however, let us consider the political arrangements that were created after World War I. In the 1920s citizens of the democratic Baltic countries enjoyed universal voting rights for men and women, equality before the law, and guarantees for the rights of minorities. True to the antiauthoritarian spirit of the early postwar era, the Baltic states adopted parliamentary forms of government in which executive power was weak. Constitutions were based in part on the model of Weimar Germany, which provided for proportional representation in the parliament on the basis of party lists. The result in each of the Baltic countries, as in numerous European democracies during the interwar era, was the proliferation of political parties and frequent government turnover.

The Republic of Estonia, where there was no independently elected president to balance the power of the legislature, was a textbook example of the sort of instability that plagued the newly created democratic governments of Europe during the 1920s. Adopted on June 15, 1920, the Estonian constitution provided for a State Elder (*Riigivanem*), who was effectively a prime minister, elected by the 100-member State Assembly (*Riigikogu*). Equipped with extensive powers, the *Riigikogu* could dismiss the government at any time without penalty. The *Riigivanem*, however, lacked even the basic power of veto over parliament, which could be dissolved only by popular referendum. Given the legislature's power over the government, the results were unsurprising: Estonian cabinets lasted less than nine months on average.

During the period of liberal democracy Estonia's politics were generally dominated by three parties. The main party on the left was the Socialist Workers' Party, a noncommunist labor party that formed in 1923 from a merger of the Social Democratic Party and the Independent Socialists. Further left was a tiny Estonian Communist Party, a Bolshevik-style organization that worked closely with Moscow.

The Estonian center was occupied by several parties, which consolidated themselves into the National Center in the early 1930s. Although a true conservative party did not exist during the 1920s in Estonia, the right was occupied by the Farmers' Assemblies (*Põllumeeste Kogud*), which consisted mainly of those farmers who had acquired land before the country had attained independence. After 1925–1926, the Farmers' Assemblies began to converge with the Settlers' Party (*Asunikkude partei*), and in 1932–1933, they were reorganized as the United Agrarian Party (*Asunikkude ning väikemaapidajate Koondis*), which briefly unified Estonia's right-wing parties.[5] Because of their small numbers, Estonia's national minorities received little representation in the *Riigikogu* and consequently carried little political weight in the country.

Despite the emergence by the early 1930s of what might be recognized as a three-party system, the presence of many other small parties in the *Riigikogu* made coalition-building a nearly impossible task throughout the democratic period. Governments frequently fell and *Riigivanem* rotated in office: Konstantin Päts (of the Farmers' and United

Agrarian Parties) was head of state five times, while Jaan Teemant (also of the Farmers' and United Agrarian parties) and Jaan Tõnisson (National Party and National Center) each served four times.[6]

During the democratic period the political center and right-center tended to dominate the politics of Estonia. Although the Socialist Workers' Party was the largest in the Estonian *Riigikogu* from 1926 to 1932, the radical left's popular appeal was somewhat tempered by extensive land reform in the early 1920s and its credibility was undermined by an attempted communist *coup* on December 1, 1924.[7] Following its failed attempt to seize power in Tallinn, the Estonian Communist Party was banned and even with new names its successor organizations exercised little influence on the country's political life

Latvia took longer to establish a permanent system of governance. Having declared the existence of an independent Latvian state in November 1918, a provisional government, the National Council (*Tautas Padome*), faced a series of challenges, not least of which were the military conflicts that threatened the very idea of an independent Latvia. In 1919, the National Council passed a citizenship law that made citizenship available to all persons born in the territories now comprising Latvia, citizens of the former Russian Empire who resided in Latvia, and citizens who were resident in Latvia on August 1, 1914; the hundreds of thousands of Latvian refugees scattered throughout Russia would thus be able to return home as citizens of the Latvian nation-state.[8] The National Council also inaugurated the sweeping land reforms that soon transformed Latvia into a nation of farmer-citizens and in April 1920 it organized elections to a Constituent Assembly. While 25 parties and political organizations participated in Latvia's first free elections, it was the left that prevailed—the Assembly's president was Jānis Čakste, a Social Democrat who had also presided over the National Council—and that determined the nature of Latvia's constitution. Adopted on February 22, 1922, the Latvian constitution provided for a unicameral *Saeima* of 100 members, each elected to three-year terms on the basis of an extremely democratic system of proportional representation that lacked any threshold for representation. While the rule of parliament was a fundamental feature of the constitution, Latvia had a president who was elected to a three-year term not by popular vote but by the *Saeima*—a feature that Latvia shared with Lithuania but not Estonia. First occupied by the experienced and flexible Čakste, who died in office in March 1927, the president had the responsibility of nominating a prime minister, subject to the approval of the *Saeima*; but in other respects the office was largely ceremonial.

If the purpose of these arrangements was to prevent an excessive concentration of authority, the result brought Latvia the same maladies of political division and government instability that plagued Estonia, demonstrated by the fact that 14 years of parliamentary democracy (1920–1934) in Latvia produced an equal number of governments. Just as unsettling was the corruption that often accompanied cabinet formation, a process that in all three Baltic states typically involved a rotation of familiar faces, for the people who created the new countries were the same as those who governed them in the 1920s and 1930s.

The extreme fragmentation that characterized Latvia's politics between 1922 and 1934 is well illustrated by the fact that no fewer than 27 parties were represented in the *Saeima* in 1925 and 1928. Nevertheless, several blocs were discernible. The left was led by the Latvian Social Democratic Workers' Party, a Marxist but noncommunist organization concerned primarily with the interests of trade unions and the urban proletariat. While its influence steadily declined through the 1920s—in part because it preferred to be in the opposition, for adherence to dogma was more attractive to the Social Democrats than the responsibility of governing—its fortunes revived somewhat during the economic crisis of the early 1930s. On the far left there was a small Communist Party, but it was illegal and many of its many of its activists had fled to Russia. Their leader Pēteris Stučka died of natural causes in Moscow in 1932, thereby avoiding the fate of the many comrades who were swept up in Joseph Stalin's Great Terror later in the decade.

The main grouping on the Latvian right was the agrarian bloc that was led by the Farmers' Union, which promoted agriculture as the backbone of Latvian economic life. Led by Kārlis Ulmanis, who chaired it, and Zigfrīds Anna Meierovics (1887–1925), who was Latvia's foreign minister from 1918 to 1925 and twice was the country's prime minister, the Farmers' Union was well represented in all Latvian governments: three of the country's four interwar presidents and 10 of its 13 prime ministers were from the Farmers' Union.

Occupying the center of Latvia's political spectrum was the Democratic Center, a coalition of three bourgeois parties that managed to elect only a few of its representatives to the parliament. Also represented in the *Saeima*, where they often allied with the Social Democrats against the Farmers' Union, were a series of regional peasant-based parties in Latgale as well as the parties of Latvia's national minorities: these included a relatively strong German party as well as Russian and Jewish parties. In general, Latvian governments during the democratic years tended to be Farmers' Union–led alliances of disparate parties united in their distrust of the Social Democrats. The hostility to the left was particularly pronounced among the Home Guards (*Aizsargi*), a volunteer paramilitary organization that was formed during the civil war and continued to be funded by the state for no apparent purpose.

The Lithuanian system that finally emerged in 1922 was similarly characterized by a strong legislature, a weak executive, and a proportional representation system in the *Seimas*. A feature that distinguishes the Lithuanian system from those of its neighbors, however, was the Catholic Church's crucial role in politics. Throughout Lithuania's brief period of liberal democracy, until the end of 1926, Christian Democratic coalitions dominated, presided over by Aleksandras Stulginskis (1885–1969), who was one of the party's founders and Lithuania's second president (1920–1926) after Antanas Smetona (1919–1920, 1926–1940).

Because of its emphasis on the public role of the Catholic Church, the Christian Democratic Party encountered opposition from sectors of society that might otherwise have supported it for its nationalist, anti-Polish, and anticommunist positions. Peasants tended to share these views, but most joined the Lithuanian Peasant Populist Union (*Lietuvos valstiečių liaudininkų sąjunga*), a secular party of the left that in December 1922 united two existing peasant-based parties. Opposed to what they saw as the Catholic Church's excessive influence in education and state administration, Populists, led by Mykolas Sleževičius (1882–1939) and Kazys Grinius (1866–1950), nevertheless often worked together with Christian Democrats in government coalitions. A falling out between the two blocs in 1926 over this issue, however, helped pave the road for the establishment of a nationalist dictatorship in Lithuania.

While the center and right dominated Lithuania's political life in the 1920s, on the far left a small, illegal Communist Party worked closely with Moscow. Although some Lithuanian leaders were preoccupied by the specter of a Bolshevik-style coup, the appeal of a socialist workers' state in this overwhelmingly rural country was in fact very limited. Indeed, in the absence of a large proletariat, even the more moderate Social Democratic Party lacked a large social base and never won more than 17 percent of the vote (1926).

The National Progress Party (NP) of Antanas Smetona and Augustinas Voldemaras (1883–1942) was on the far right of Lithuania's interwar political spectrum. In its early days the NP bucked the tide of popular opinion by opposing land reform and remained on the political periphery during the early period of independence. In August 1924, the NP merged with the Lithuanian Farmers' Union (*Lietuvos ūkininkų sąjunga*) to form the Lithuanian Nationalist Union (*Lietuvių tautininkų sąjunga*), a movement that was open only to ethnic Lithuanians. While the *tautininkai*'s ideas about "national unity" resonated with many ethnic Lithuanians, during the parliamentary period it remained an outside critic of government rather than a participant. Its opportunity arrived with the putsch of December 1926.

AUTHORITARIAN GOVERNMENT

Following the example of General Józef Piłsudski's successful coup in Poland in May 1926, Lithuania was the first of the Baltic states to turn to an authoritarian solution. On December 17, 1926, Dr. Kazys Grinius, elected president earlier in the year and now preparing for a reception to celebrate his 60th birthday, was placed under house arrest in what observers remembered as a quick and orderly military coup. He and Prime Minister Mykolas Sleževičius resigned that evening in favor of Smetona and Voldemaras, whose own roles in the coup remain unclear. While the putsch launched Lithuania on the road to authoritarian government, it was not until 1928 that the cautious Smetona, regarded by some as little more than a figurehead at first, annulled the 1922 constitution and consolidated the first of the Baltic dictatorships.

For many Lithuanians, exasperated by the continuing animosity between the major political parties and the institutional weakness of executive authority, abandoning liberalism appeared to be the only way to save the country from falling into the hands of extremists. While the Lithuanian putschists claimed to have saved the country from a communist coup (to underline the point the new government executed several communists), the army's support may been bought with the promise that it would not suffer from the government's efforts to balance the budget. Both the Christian Democrats and the Nationalists supported the move, but even if the Christian Democrats initially participated in the post-coup government it was the *tautininkai* whose political interests benefited the most from the seizure of power.

Estonia and Latvia did not succumb to dictatorship until 1934, but the economic decline of the early 1930s provided fertile soil for the growth of extreme nationalist groups, both in the Baltic states and elsewhere in Europe. In Estonia, the most popular of these was the League of Independence War Veterans (*Eesti Vabadussõjalaste Liit*), whose development paralleled that of the far-right Lapua movement in neighboring Finland. Founded in 1928 and nominally led by Andres Larka (1879–1943), the League, commonly known as VAPS, was primarily concerned with the material welfare of the war veterans during its early years. But as it evolved into an ambitious and influential political organization in the early 1930s—one that loathed corruption, communism, and parliamentary politics, but was fond of uniforms, Nazi-style salutes, and street parades—VAPS gained popular support at the expense of the Farmers' and Socialist Workers' parties.[9]

Sensing the antiliberal mood of the Estonian populace, in autumn 1932 VAPS, whose driving force by now was the demagogue Artur Sirk (1900–1937), proposed a revamping of the constitution to give the country a strong chief executive, independent of parliament with the power to rule by decree. Similar constitutional changes were being debated in other European countries at this time—notably Weimar Germany, which succumbed to the Nazi dictatorship in 1933. While its opponents alleged that VAPS intended to create such an arrangement in order to attain power for itself, VAPS's defenders countered that it was a necessary measure to counteract government instability. As the increasingly unpopular Tõnisson-led government cracked down on the movement, constitutional referenda were held in June and October 1933, the results of which overwhelmingly favored VAPS's proposals. Following this victory, in January 1934 a new constitution went into effect that reflected VAPS's preferences for a popularly elected president with the power to rule by decree if necessary. Konstantin Päts, head of the government coalition since the previous October, was made acting president.

The next step in the extinguishing of parliamentary democracy in Estonia came in the wake of a VAPS victory in the local elections that had just been held in the country's three largest cities. With Andres Larka now threatening to win the forthcoming presidential election, on March 12, 1934, Päts declared martial law and prohibited all political activity in the country. Suspected of planning an armed coup, VAPS was shut down and hundreds of its leading members were arrested.[10] Thus began what Estonians refer to as the "Era of Silence," which lasted until the arrival of Soviet troops in 1940.

In Latvia it was a growing fear of the left that was used to justify an authoritarian coup, but similar conditions—the sharp economic downturn of the early 1930s, growing unemployment, political instability, a loss of confidence in the *Saeima*, the rise of extremist parties with their own paramilitary organizations—militated in favor of an authoritarian solution. Although rumors of an impending putsch had been floating around since 1932, Kārlis Ulmanis, leader of the Farmers' Union and Latvia's prime minister, did not act until May 15, 1934, two months after Päts seized power in Estonia. As in Lithuania and

Estonia, the Latvian coup occurred in the midst of a constitutional crisis, encountered little opposition, and was essentially bloodless. The coup found particular support among the *Aizsargi*, whose membership grew as Ulmanis consolidated his dictatorship. Although Alberts Kviesis (1881–1944), who was president at the time of the coup, was allowed to serve out his term to 1936, Ulmanis ultimately merged the offices of president and prime minister in his own person.

In all three countries the essential features of authoritarian government were quickly introduced, including martial law, press censorship, and strict limitations on political activity. Parliaments were subordinated to a vastly strengthened executive, against which overt opposition could not be expressed publicly. Following the examples of other east central European countries like Poland, Hungary, and Bulgaria, parliament was ignored (Lithuania and Estonia) or shut down all together (Latvia). What is striking, however, was how willingly the citizens of the Baltic states surrendered to authoritarianism. As the Latvian scholar and diplomat Alfred Bilmanis aptly remarked, "The people came to look upon themselves as grossly betrayed by their politicians, whom they had elected but over whom they had no control in ultra-liberal parliaments. . . . An unfettered executive authority with emergency powers made a strong appeal to peoples confounded by free-for-all politics."[11] The sad fact was that 15 years was not long enough for a democratic tradition to develop that could withstand the appeal in a time of crisis of authoritarian government based on an ideology of national unity.

Likewise, Lithuania's authoritarian turn was commonly understood to be a necessary solution to government instability, the dangers of communism, and the threat posed by irredentist neighbors. Indeed, many Lithuanian and Western historians view take a sympathetic view of Nationalist rule, portraying Antanas Smetona as an intellectual—an image he liked to cultivate, having lectured at the University of Lithuania (in Kaunas) before returning to the presidency—who behaved with restraint and remained above the political fray. For two years Smetona worked closely with Prime Minister Augustinas Voldemaras, who headed the fascistic Iron Wolf Association (*Geležinis Vilkas*), but then after a power struggle the latter was dismissed in September 1928, leaving Smetona to be the sole dictator.[12] With the adoption of a new constitution in May 1928, the president was no longer chosen by the *Seimas* but by "extraordinary representatives" of the nation, who reelected him in 1931 and again in 1938.

While lacking Mussolini's charisma and flair for the dramatic, the pensive Smetona enjoyed broad popular support, for with the

Lithuania became the first of the Baltic states to establish an authoritarian regime when Antanas Smetona (1874–1944) was installed as the country's president in December 1926. Smetona's relatively soft dictatorship came to an end when Lithuania fell under Soviet occupation in 1940. (Library of Congress)

exception of some Catholic organizations there was little overt opposition to the Smetona regime. However, only the *tautininkai* and related youth organizations were permitted a great deal of latitude in their operations; unassociated political parties and organizations were either shut down or found their activities sharply circumscribed. While the *Seimas* was allowed to function, it was reduced to little more than a consultative body.

Likewise, shortly after the preemptive coup of Konstantin Päts, political parties were banned in Estonia and newspapers that criticized government policy were shut down, including Jaan Tõnisson's *Postimees*. Ignoring the parliament, in March 1935 Päts attempted to concentrate state power by creating the Fatherland League (*Isamaaliit*), a pro-government party that was intended to promote stability and national unity. Being little more than a propaganda vehicle for the regime, the Fatherland League failed to capture the popular imagination.

In January 1937, Päts attempted to legitimize his authoritarian approach to government—some say he was in fact dismantling his dictatorship—with the adoption of a new constitution that created a powerful chief executive and divided the *Riigikogu* into a bicameral legislature. The upper house, a 40-member chamber called the State Council (*Riiginõukogu*), was designed as an appointive body to represent the various institutions of Estonian society, such as the army, churches, industry, and local governments. The lower house, called the Chamber of Representatives (*Riigivolikogu*), consisted of 80 delegates elected by popular vote. Despite this government overhaul, no parties save the Fatherland League were permitted to engage in political activity. By 1938 it appeared to many Estonians that the state of emergency was soon to end and democratic rights would be restored, but this failed to take place before the Soviet occupation in 1940.

Like his counterparts in Lithuania and Estonia, Latvia's Ulmanis portrayed himself as a truly national figure, above the rough and tumble of ordinary politics. Yet among the Baltic dictators, all of whom emerged from the peasantry, it was Ulmanis, embracing the title *Vadonis* (leader), who came the closest to creating what might be called a personality cult. Convinced of their leader's commitment both to democratic ideals and to protecting the interests of the ethnic Latvian *tauta*, many Latvians at that time believed that Ulmanis was motivated less by greed for personal power than by an unswerving commitment to the welfare of his nation in its time of need. Others take a dimmer view, seeing Ulmanis as a power-hungry opportunist and conspirator who spent nearly a year carefully preparing his coup.[13] Whatever his motives, Ulmanis swiftly neutered the left as hundreds of Social Democrats were arrested and thousands of civil servants (mostly Social Democrats) dismissed. However, the regime did not persecute its Jewish or Baltic German minorities, even if some of Ulmanis's measures had the effect of reducing their economic power. While the monuments to Europe's other interwar dictators disappeared long ago, a controversial statue of Ulmanis was erected in central Riga in 2003 and six years later a musical about the Latvian dictator, *Vadonis*, debuted in the Latvian National Theater.

Yet the Ulmanis regime was one of the most antidemocratic of Europe's authoritarian governments: even Benito Mussolini and Adolf Hitler maintained the pretense of popular representation by maintaining the Chamber of Deputies and the Reichstag. But whereas *il Duce* and *der Führer* headed parties that embodied and executed their will, Ulmanis proscribed political life altogether: the cabinet was to rule alone. Meanwhile, all the country's political parties were disbanded, including Ulmanis's own Farmers' Union and the fascistic *Pērkonkrusts* (Thunder Cross) organization. Although authoritarian Latvia also had a political police and press censorship, the regime's enemies were not killed and most of its political prisoners were soon released.

Like his Estonian counterpart, Latvia's dictator attempted to create a corporative form of government according to which a series of newly created councils were to collaborate with their respective government departments.[14] With the government taking a leading role in the economy as the worldwide depression eased, Latvia was put back on the track to prosperity—an achievement that earned Ulmanis much popular acclaim. Unlike Päts, however, Ulmanis ended the state of emergency in Latvia in February 1938, well before the country fell under Soviet occupation.

If one of the main objectives of the Baltic dictatorships was a more Latvian Latvia, a more Lithuanian Lithuania, and a more Estonian Estonia, the process was underway well before the dictators took control of the machinery of the state. From the moment of their foundation, the new republics were conceived as national states in which the needs of the titular nationality were considered first and foremost, even if national minorities were guaranteed certain constitutional protections. Thus the capitals of the Baltic states, long associated with the domination of foreigners, were modestly renovated in an effort to transform them into national administrative centers and to emphasize the status of the dominant nationality. In Kaunas, a largely Jewish and Polish city prior to the war but now Lithuania's provisional capital, the erection of a series of showpiece public buildings in the modern functionalist style was intended to represent a distinct architectural style in celebration of the country's independence. A city "with fine broad streets and splendid surroundings," a U.S. diplomat recorded in his diary in 1926, all Kaunas needed was "an assured political future and favorable economic conditions" to assure its development into an "imposing and attractive city."[15] Thus a neglected town that was practically devoid of modern architecture (or a sewage system) prior to the World War I became a showcase city for a modernizing country, featuring dozens of modern residential and industrial buildings designed by architects such as Mykolas Songaila (1874–1941) and Vytautas Landsbergis-Žemkalnis (1893–1993). While some were damaged during World War II, many of Kaunas's architectural gems have survived to the present day.

The nationalizing imperative was particularly evident in Riga. A handsome city with a distinctly Germanic architectural heritage that dates to the Middle Ages (it still has one of Europe's most spectacular collection of *Jugendstil* buildings, constructed around the turn of the 20th century), Riga was the focus of the government's efforts to create a more Latvian Latvia. The centerpiece of this project was the erection of the Freedom Monument, which at 350 meters in height came to dominate the city center. Located on the site where a statue of Peter the Great, an unabashed symbol of tsarist power, had stood from 1910 to 1915, the monument consists of a tall granite column on top of which stands a westward-facing woman who holds three golden stars over her head representing Latvia's three cultural regions (Courland, Vidzeme, Latgale). At the monument's base are several sets of figures, each of which tells a story about the Latvian nation. While the idea for project was conceived shortly after the achievement of Latvian independence, it was not completed until 1935, by which time "Latvia for Latvians!" had become a rallying cry for the country's nationalists under the Ulmanis dictatorship. It was during this era that the first serious archaeological excavations were undertaken in Riga, whose purpose was to demonstrate the non-German origins of what was now Latvia's capital city.

Despite the nationalizing thrust of the Baltic governments and the fundamental lack of political freedoms under Smetona, Päts, and Ulmanis, the Baltic dictatorships were mild in comparison to many other authoritarian regimes in Europe during the 1930s: if the temporary imprisonment of political enemies was common to all three states, harsher measures were rare. The common claims that the Päts regime saved Estonia from the potential tyranny of the League of Independence War Veterans, and that Ulmanis saved Latvia from communism are indeed subject to debate, but there is little doubt that given the ineffectiveness of parliamentary government in the early 1930s, the mild authoritarian governments in Kaunas, Tallinn, and Riga were far preferable to the monstrous totalitarian regimes in Berlin and Moscow that would decide the fate of the Baltic states in August 1939.

View of Riga, Latvia. In the background is the Nativity Cathedral, built in the 1880s to serve the city's growing Orthodox population. To the right is the Freedom Monument, erected in 1935 on the basis of a design submitted by the Latvian sculptor Kārlis Zāle. Before World War I a statue of Tsar Peter the Great stood at the same location. (Shutterstock.com)

ECONOMIC DEVELOPMENT

The transformation of the local economies began during the war, when much of the region's industry was destroyed or dismantled and the manufacturing capability of the Baltic states was left in a sorry state. While independence from Russia was an enormous political achievement, economic independence was crippling, for prior to 1917 Russia had been the Baltic region's main market. The Latvian ports of Riga, Liepāja, and Ventspils alone accounted for one-third of Russia's imports and exports. But Russia's total economic collapse, compounded by the Allied blockade of 1919, meant that there were few goods to be exported from the Union of Soviet Socialist Republics (USSR), as the communist state was renamed in late 1922. A telling example is the fate of the Krenholm mill in Narva, located in northeastern Estonia. Before World War I, Krenholm was the largest cotton mill in the Russian Empire, employing more than 10,000 people and manufacturing 70 million yards of semi-finished cotton cloth each year for use in Russia. But postwar conditions in Russia deprived Krenholm of its market and the mill nearly closed.[16]

To compensate for the loss of this huge market, the Baltic countries had to expand their domestic markets and find new foreign markets, which in practice meant that the region's trade had to be reoriented toward western Europe—in particular Britain and Germany, which soon became the main consumers of Baltic goods. Within a decade, the tiny Baltic republics managed to develop their agricultural and manufacturing bases while securing a place in the European system as exporters of raw materials and agricultural products.

Estonia's steady economic recovery during the 1920s was aided in part by the 15 million gold rubles paid by the Soviet regime as war reparations, in addition to significant foreign investment, mostly from Britain. Taking 1929 as a base, the top branches of Estonian industry were textiles (the Krenholm mill once again became the country's leading textile manufacturer), foodstuffs, paper, metallurgy, and woodworking. Meanwhile, with the exploitation of the country's massive oil shale deposits located in the region between the Gulf of Finland and Lake Peipsi, Estonia became an energy exporter in the 1930s, its chief customers being Germany and its neighbors in the Baltic Sea region.

Otherwise blessed with few industrial raw materials, Estonia had to trade for most of the metals, chemicals, dyes, and paints necessary for the country's economic development. Yet Estonia, like the other Baltic states, remained a predominantly agricultural country, with about two-thirds of the working population employed in the agricultural sector during the 1920s. This proportion began to decline significantly only during the industrial expansion of the late 1930s. During the interwar period Estonia's major exports were foodstuffs (butter, meat, and livestock), timber, flax, paper products, and textiles, and its principal trading partners were Germany and Great Britain, followed by the Scandinavian and other west European countries, and the United States. By 1935 trade with the Soviet Union, which had accounted for 25 percent of Estonian trade in 1922 before Stalin made a priority of economic self-sufficiency, was hardly a factor. Because the Baltic economies competed against rather than complemented each other, the volume of Estonia's trade with its southern neighbors, Latvia and Lithuania, remained modest throughout the interwar period.

Latvia experienced a pattern of economic development similar to that of Estonia: slow but steady growth in the 1920s, depression in 1929–1933, and recovery and industrial expansion during 1933–1939. It is important, however, to consider the conditions under which Latvia, whose population remained primarily rural (62 percent in 1935) throughout the interwar period, began to develop its shattered industrial sector after World War I. As noted earlier, of the three Baltic states to emerge from World War I and the wars of independence it was Latvia that suffered the most extensive damage. The following chart indicates how key sectors of the manufacturing economy developed in Latvia's most populous and most industrialized city during this period.[17]

On the eve of the Great Depression the main industries in Riga, and in Latvia as whole, were metal production, woodworking, food processing, and textiles manufacturing. While a recovery was undoubtedly taking place during the first decade of Latvian statehood, thanks in part to the introduction of the *lats* as the official currency in August 1922, at the end of the decade the total number of workers employed in the industries of its largest city was still little more than half the prewar total. Other Latvian cities experienced similar trends if on a much smaller scale. By 1930, the last year before the world economic crisis strongly affected Latvia, industry had begun to recover even if it was still less productive than it had been in 1913. The Great Depression, however, could only devastate a nation so dependent on exporting its goods as many countries, including those that traded with Latvia (especially Britain), reacted to the crisis by raising tariffs and introducing quotas on imports.

In each of the Baltic republics the state played a leading role in directing the country's economic development through tax, price, and credit policies. Such intervention intensified in the wake of the economic crisis. Nowhere did the state intervene in the economy more actively than in Latvia, where the State Electrotechnical Factory (VEF) was established in Riga in 1919. Soon VEF began producing telephones and radio receivers for the domestic market, but in the 1930s it benefited from enormous state investment and became the prize of Latvian industry, famous for producing the Minox, a subminiature camera (then the world's smallest) invented by the Baltic German Walter Zapp and introduced to the market in 1938. Even in the decades following the

Table 5.1

Riga and suburbs	1913	1920	1929
Total population	517,522	181,443	377,917(a)
Workers (total)	87,607	8,921	47,276
Metal industry workers	28,343	2,005	7,293
Chemical industry workers	19,835	114	4,616
Exports (millions kg.)	1,996	143(b)	852

(a) Population of Riga in 1930.
(b) Riga's total exports in 1921.

country's absorption by the USSR, VEF remained Latvia's largest electronics manufacturer as it supplied the Soviet military with electronics and telecommunications equipment.

State intervention in the economy was most notable in the struggling banking sector and was especially pronounced during the Ulmanis years, when the government nationalized most of Latvia's private banks and focused on intensive industrialization with the goal of achieving greater economic self-sufficiency. State policy simultaneously focused on intensifying the country's agricultural development by providing agricultural credits to Latvian farmers and cooperatives. The state also regulated the production and marketing of agricultural produce, with an eye to foreign (especially British and German) markets. Latvia's leading exports were primarily agricultural and were nearly identical to those exported by its neighbors, including butter, bacon, and eggs. Fur, flax, timber, and wood products were also significant Latvian exports, and later wheat and rye, a commodity that used to be imported.

Starting from a weaker base, industrialization and urbanization proceeded more slowly in Lithuania than in Latvia and Estonia. Since the Smetona government was cautious about industrial expansion (perhaps, it has been suggested, partly because many of the larger industrial concerns were in the hands of Germans and Jews rather than Lithuanians), state policy did little to promote manufacturing; as late as 1936 only 6.4 percent of Lithuania's laborers were employed in industry. As in Latvia and Estonia, the Lithuanian ideal was the small family farm. The state did much to promote this vision of rural prosperity by supporting agriculture, a policy that favored ethnic Lithuanians, with particular emphasis on dairy farming.

Even if the Smetona government never committed itself to the kind intensive industrial development encouraged by the other Baltic dictators, Lithuania nevertheless witnessed a doubling of its own industrial capacity during his rule. A contributing factor was the country's seizure in early 1923 of Klaipėda (Ger. *Memel*), an act (see page 138) that gave Lithuania its first major port and industrial center. However, the products created in the paper, food-processing, and textile-producing factories that were built in the 1930s were oriented principally toward the internal market, not for export. Lithuanian exports were mainly agricultural products, including dairy products, bacon, eggs, processed foods, flax, and timber—products that mirrored and competed with those of Estonia and Latvia. Lithuania also had the same buyers for her products: in the 1920s it was mainly Germany, and after 1932 Britain—a consequence of the economic slump and Lithuania's political difficulties with Germany over Klaipėda. (In 1934, Britain concluded treaties with all three Baltic republics intended to make them buyers of British goods as well.) Yet unlike her northern neighbors, Lithuania maintained close economic links with the USSR, from which it obtained a large share of its imports.

Whatever their differences, the economic policies of the authoritarian regimes of the 1930s were generally similar: all were based on strong state intervention and economic nationalism, yet all three retained a market economy whose leading sector was agriculture. And in all three Baltic states a common narrative later emerged that idealized the late 1930s as a period of common prosperity in which food was plentiful, incomes were high, and life was good. Few could have foreseen the difficulties that foreign powers would bring after 1939.

NATIONAL MINORITIES

Since the Baltic republics were founded on the basis of the national principle, one of the main social issues confronting each of them was the matter of reconciling their national minorities with the Estonian, Latvian, and Lithuanian majorities. During the interwar period, national minorities shared the goal of securing and maintaining social autonomy in a complex and sometimes hostile national and international environment. In this respect the German, Russian, Jewish, and Polish minorities achieved some successes, gaining representation in Baltic legislatures and exercising at least a modicum of influence on state policies during the early period of liberal democracy. However, enduring prejudices rooted in the region's troubled national–ethnic history did much to undermine relations between the republics' predominant nationalities and the minorities whom they sometimes distrusted. Yet on the whole conditions for the Baltic minorities were no worse, and in fact were often better, than those for the national minorities of the other nation-states of central and eastern Europe.

In the Latvian and Estonian republics the main nationality issue concerned the Baltic Germans, who were the principal objects of the natives' resentment. In Latvia Germans officially constituted 3.7 percent of the population (58,000, including more than 5,000 foreign-born Germans) and in Estonia only 1.5 percent (16,000). While far more Baltic Germans lived in Riga than in all of Estonia (or for that matter Lithuania, which 29,000 Germans called home in 1923), it is likely that their numbers were underreported everywhere. With the ancient

Ritterschaften disbanded and nobody to support their claims to the land, most of which was expropriated during the land reforms discussed at the beginning of the chapter, the Germans who had dominated Baltic society for centuries had little choice but to accept this reversal of fortunes.

Defeated in war and suffering from the stigma of "war guilt," the German state was in no position to help and in any event it was inclined to do little more than support Baltic German cultural organizations while trying to maintain economic ties with the Baltic German commercial class. Around 20,000 Baltic Germans had emigrated to Germany during the wars of independence, but with the country already suffering from a dearth of employment opportunities it was the Weimar government's policy to discourage more refugees from settling in Germany. Aiming for a recovery of the country's foreign trade, including trade with the Baltic region, the Weimar government hoped to return as many émigrés as possible and encouraged the Baltic Germans to be loyal to their new states. During 1920–1921, perhaps half returned to Latvia and Estonia, where they had to settle for positions of formal equality with those they had once ruled.

Under the constitutions of the new governments, Baltic Germans and other minorities were assured cultural autonomy, including the right to set up schools in which education was conducted in the mother tongue. Land confiscation may have destroyed much of the Germans' wealth, but the German bourgeoisie remained strong in Baltic cities. Some Germans, however, found their professional careers blocked, especially in the civil service and army, and in the 1930s such people often chose to emigrate to Germany. While on the whole the Baltic German community was never reconciled to its loss of dominance and its status as a minority, there were individuals like Paul Schiemann (1876–1944), a liberal patriot who admired Latvia's diversity and devoted his life to defending minority rights there, who remained strongly attached to their host countries.[18] Although the situation took some getting used to, before 1933 many Baltic Germans accepted parliamentary democracy and as a group they were well represented in the *Riigikogu* and *Saeima*.

Deprived of the backing of a strong state and lacking any tradition of self-governance, Russian minorities were less able to assert themselves in Baltic politics. Russians were the largest ethnic minority in both Estonia and Latvia: in Estonia they constituted just over 8 percent of the population throughout the interwar period, while in Latvia the number of Russians grew from 7.8 percent of the Latvian population in 1920 to 12 percent in 1934. Russian communities, as well as

Belarusian, Polish, and Jewish ones, were concentrated in Latgale, the easternmost and least economically developed part of Latvia, where most were engaged in agricultural pursuits. Although today most of Estonia's Russians live in Tallinn and the northeastern cities, during the interwar period the Russian population in Estonia was far smaller and was more evenly dispersed throughout the country. Organized into a large number of competing splinter parties, Baltic Russians were never able to achieve political representation commensurate with their growing numerical strength and few worked in state institutions. Unlike Baltic Germans or Jews, Russians were also underrepresented in local institutions of higher education, largely because Russians lacked their own universities and only a small minority could speak Latvian, Estonian, or Lithuanian.

Jews constituted a third important national minority in the region. Although few Jews lived in Estonia and nearly all lived in its capital city, they were vital to the economies of all three Baltic states, particularly Lithuania, which had by far the greatest number of Jews. The census taken in Lithuania in 1923 showed a total of 153,332 Jews in the country, equivalent to 7.6 percent of the total population; however, it is likely that the real number was higher, and it certainly would have been still greater had the Vilnius region, administered by Poland until 1939, been considered. In the larger Lithuanian towns, Jews formed a quarter to one-third of the population.

Latvia also had a significant Jewish population. However, because many Latvian Jews became refugees during World War I the Jewish population of Latvia in the 1920s was less than half of what it had been prior to 1914, when 170,000 Jews lived in the territory of Latvia. While the German-speaking Jews of Courland were relatively affluent, the Russian- and Yiddish-speaking Jews of Latgale were generally poor. In the middle were the 46,000 Jews of Riga (1940), who comprised half of Latvia's Jewish population.

Throughout the Baltic region Jews continued to play an important role in industry, commerce, and banking, as they had before World War I. Moreover, like the region's other national minorities, Jews in the Baltic states initially enjoyed cultural autonomy. In Lithuania, for example, Jewish autonomy was ensured with the creation of a Jewish National Council, which in conjunction with the Ministry of Jewish Affairs administered Jewish autonomous institutions such as the expanding network of Hebrew- and Yiddish-language elementary and secondary schools. Despite such promising beginnings, conditions for Jews were gradually eroded by the collapse of democracy, the adoption of state policies designed to improve the economic position of the national majorities, and the growing expressions of resentment directed against national minorities and the communal rights they were guaranteed in the constitutions of the new states. Formal autonomy for Lithuania's Jews ended with the closing of the Ministry for Jewish Affairs in 1924, following which the National Council was dispersed by the police.

While no Baltic government officially sanctioned antisemitism, the region's Jews nevertheless endured growing resentment, often fomented by extremist groups operating in an increasingly xenophobic European political landscape. If the conspicuous presence of Yiddish-speaking Jews in the cities of Lithuania was a source of irritation for ordinary Lithuanians who conceived of their country as a nation-state for the Lithuanian people, the coming to power of the *tautininkai* after the coup of December 1926 seems to have exacerbated the frictions between these communities. Although Jews managed to retain a modicum of autonomy, including control over the Jewish educational system and a Jewish network of banks, economic discrimination against Jews worsened in the 1930s as the Smetona regime attempted to increase ethnic Lithuanian participation in the economy. The growth of cooperatives, which took over Lithuania's export trade in agricultural products, deprived thousands of Jews of their livelihoods and contributed to a steady decline in the number of Jews engaged in trade, industry, and crafts. If in 1923 Jews owned seven shops for every shop owned by a Lithuanian, by the mid-1930s the proportion had become more or less equal.[19] Despite such conditions, which it should be noted were probably no worse than in most of the rest of eastern and central Europe, Jews enjoyed Smetona's protection: even if he was no democrat, the Lithuanian president detested antisemites and discouraged attacks on Jews.

Poles were the second largest minority in Lithuania, officially comprising about 3.2 percent of the population in 1923, although Polish authorities falsely claimed that the accurate figure was closer to 10 percent. Polish national life in Lithuania was complicated by the country's troubled relationship with Poland, as a result of which organized political activity for its Polish citizenry was circumscribed in Lithuania, even if Poles were able to elect their own representatives to the *Seimas*. Discouraged by the government in Kaunas, Polish-language education gradually declined in the 1920s and laws enacted in the 1930s restricted such education only to children who had two Polish-speaking parents.

In general, tolerance for national diversity declined under the authoritarian regimes. The demise of the proportional representation systems meant less minority representation in government at a time when national cultural autonomy was being curtailed. While Lithuanian nationalism was directed against the Poles and Jews, in the other Baltic states the object of nationalist hostility was the Baltic German community, manifested in Latvia's language laws of 1934–1935 that prohibited the use of German names on street signs, the state's expropriation of some Baltic German churches, and the closure of Baltic German agricultural associations. The subsidies for Baltic German activities provided by Hitler's Third Reich after 1933 only exacerbated the mistrust. With help from Nazi Germany the area's National Socialist sympathizers came to exert increasing influence over existing Baltic German institutions and especially over the Baltic German parties of Estonia and Latvia, which quickly became Nazified as their members succumbed to Nazi ideas about a German national revival. Yet it was also Hitler who, having just agreed to a nonaggression pact with the USSR in August 1939 acted to evacuate Baltic Germans from Latvia and Estonia the following autumn—a decision that, contrary to Hitler's long-term plans, served to remove German influence in the region permanently.

CULTURE, EDUCATION, AND RELIGION

No longer inhibited by tsarist rule and yet to be absorbed by the USSR, for two decades national cultures flourished in the Baltic countries. In each case the state played an important role in the organization and finance of theaters, the performing arts, symphony orchestras, radio stations, libraries, and museums. While the Baltic artistic world prospered like never before, intellectual and cultural life was enriched by an expanding body of literature and the proliferation of newspapers, magazines, and professional, scientific, and scholarly journals.

Literature was at the heart of the national project in each of the Baltic states. Not only were writers considered the conscience of the nation, but their works were understood as the embodiment of the national experience. Unlike England, France, or the United States, these countries had few political or military heroes to celebrate; it fell to writers, playwrights, and artists to give expression to the nation's tragedies and aspirations. Accordingly, literary pantheons were quickly established in each of the new states. Before the war the Latvian literary elite included the dramatist and short-story writer Rūdolfs Blaumanis (1863–1908), Augusts Deglavs (1862–1922), the author of the *Riga* trilogy (1909–1922), and the revolutionary poet and dramatist Aspāzija (1865–1943). Towering over all of them was Aspāzija's husband Jānis

Rainis (*née* Pliekšans, 1865–1929), a political radical whose enduring play *Fire and Night* (1905) was based on the Latvian epic *Lāčplēsis*. After the Revolution of 1905 Rainis emigrated to Switzerland, returning after the war to Latvia, where he busied himself with political affairs (while directing the Latvian National Theater) in the unrealized hopes of becoming the country's president. To this existing pantheon Latvia's nation-builders added the short-story writer Jānis Jaunsudrabiņš (1877–1962) and Kārlis Skalbe (1879–1945), a writer and journalist who had been imprisoned by tsarist authorities for his revolutionary activities before fighting as a Latvian Rifleman during the war. One of the founders of the Latvian state, Skalbe continued to publish fairy tales for adult audiences during the interwar era.

The Estonian literary canon is also filled with writers who made their mark during, and often before, the era of independence. If Hansen Tammsaare (1878–1940), the acclaimed author of a series of naturalistic stories that depict the country's rural life, is the Estonian Shakespeare, then Oskar Luts (1887–1953) is its Mark Twain, for Luts's entertaining books about the farm boy Toots have been read by generations of Estonians. Among the outstanding Lithuanian writers of this era was the playwright and poet Vincas Krėvė-Mickevičius (1882–1954), many of whose stories were based on Lithuanian mythology and legends. Like a number of left-leaning intellectuals in the Baltic states, Krėvė was briefly enlisted by the Soviet regime to work in the People's Government established during the summer of 1940 (discussed in chapter 6).

The basis of this cultural upsurge was an expanded educational system, which, once schools were rebuilt (in Latvia and Estonia many manor houses were converted into schools) and enough qualified teachers could be found or trained, also became one of the main agencies in the dissemination of patriotic and nationalist sentiment in the Baltic countries. The emphases on de-Russification and on instilling patriotic attitudes was evident, for example, in the Latvian conception of a program called "Native Land Studies," which included lessons on the country's industries, government, and other topics related to the "native land."[20] In all three Baltic countries the native language was elevated to the primary language of instruction, although allowances were made for minority nationalities to use their own languages in separate school networks.

Estonia's educational network, like those of its southern neighbors, was vastly expanded after the war. Already high at the time of independence, the Estonian literacy rate approached universal by the mid-1930s. Successes in primary and secondary education were matched at the university level: on December 1, 1919, the University of Tartu, founded as a German institution (*Universität Dorpat*) and then Russified in the late 19th century, was reopened as the country's main research center. Although initially the faculty was composed mostly of Baltic Germans and Russians, by the mid-1930s the curriculum was overwhelmingly Estonian, as was its student body. By 1926, a higher proportion of Estonians, 1 in 280, attended university than did Germans, Swedes, or Finns in their respective countries.[21]

Latvia experienced similar educational successes: between 1920 and 1933 the number of primary schools in Latvia more than doubled and the number of secondary schools rose from 36 to 96. By 1926 the illiteracy rate was down to 14.3 percent and dropped still further in the 1930s. Meanwhile, the eastern province of Latgale, which was less developed than many other Baltic regions and whose inhabitants spoke, and still speak, a distinct dialect of Latvian, was the recipient of immense investment, especially in education, in an effort to bring about the region's full integration into Latvia.

Latvian higher education also made impressive advances. Before 1919 there had been no specifically Latvian institution of higher education, since under Russian rule the University of Tartu, where Russian had been the main language of instruction since the 1890s, was to serve all the Baltic provinces. While Riga had for half a century been the home of the Riga Technical University, (a German-language institution that was established in 1862, it was renamed the Riga Polytechnical Institute in 1896 as Russian became the language of instruction), it was evacuated to Moscow in 1914, leaving Latvia without any universities at all. Upon obtaining national independence this shortcoming was immediately redressed with the opening of the University of Latvia, in which more than 7,000 students were enrolled by 1939. Meanwhile, Latvia's Germans founded their own private university, the Herder Institute, and had their own daily newspaper, *Rigasche Rundschau*, whose chief editor was the liberal journalist Paul Schiemann. While Latvia's Russians lacked both a university and influential politicians, their newspaper *Segodnia* (Today) was one of the best-circulated Russian-language newspapers outside Russia in the 1920s.

As in most areas of national development, in educational matters Lithuania started at a lower base than either Latvia or Estonia. As late as 1923 nearly one-third of the Lithuanian population was unable to either read or write. A doubling of the number of primary schools between 1919 and 1931 helped the country to combat illiteracy; compulsory education, however, was not introduced until 1931. Higher education was limited to the University of Lithuania, which was set up in Kaunas in 1922. Eight years later it was renamed Vytautas the Great, a reflection of the interwar state's veneration of Grand Duke Vytautas, to whom monuments were built everywhere in an effort to demonstrate the medieval origins of Lithuanian statehood.

Throughout the independence era the Catholic Church continued to play an important role in primary education in Lithuania. But the Church's function was not limited to providing spiritual and educational nourishment, for in Lithuania, as in much of western Europe, Catholicism occupied a prominent position in the country's social and political life and was often at the center of the country's most pressing political questions. The country's second most important religion was Judaism, but neither the faith nor Lithuania's Jewish leaders played a role in Lithuanian politics. Lithuania also had a substantial Russian and Orthodox minority; many of these were Old Believers whose ancestors, forbidden to practice their religion in the Russian Empire, had arrived in the region in the 17th century.

In Latvia, Evangelical Lutheranism was the religion of more than half of the population. However, during the independence era Latvians' attachment to organized religion appeared to weaken. Although this in part reflected a general European trend toward secularization, it is probably also related to the fact that in Latvia the churches had been historically dominated by German clergymen. Thus, during the independence era attempts were made to Latvianize the Lutheran church: while ethnic Latvian clergy became predominant, original Latvian hymns were composed to replace the old German hymns and the New Testament was translated into modern Latvian. The Latvianization of the country's churches was also accomplished by expropriation: the Latvian state, like the Estonian state, simply seized some of the country's Lutheran and Russian Orthodox churches, notably the Church of St. James (1923) in Riga and the Riga Cathedral (1931).[22]

Of Latvia's remaining population, nearly one-fourth were Roman Catholics, most of whom resided in Latgale, where much of Latvia's Orthodox and dissenting Old Believer communities lived as well. Russians and other Slavs constituted the bulk of the country's Orthodox believers, who made up about 9 percent of the total population. Jews, constituting about 4 percent of the country's population, were concentrated in Latvia's largest cities, with about half living in Riga.

In Estonia, Lutheranism continued to predominate. According to the 1934 census, 78 percent of Estonian citizens claimed to be Lutherans. A further 19 percent, mostly Russians but also a significant number of Estonians, were Orthodox. Old Believers living near Lake Peipsi were almost exclusively Russian. Estonia also had smaller numbers of Baptists, Evangelical Christians, Roman Catholics, Adventists, Methodists, and about 4,300 Jews, most of whom would flee to the USSR to escape the Nazis in the cataclysm that brought an end to Jewish life in the Baltic states.

INTERNATIONAL RELATIONS

The Baltic states began their existence under precarious circumstances—as buffer states between two defeated and resentful pariahs, Germany and Russia. As part of a *cordon sanitaire* designed to contain Bolshevism to the east and keep their two larger neighbors apart, the Baltic republics' prospects for long-term survival appeared grim at the outset. Their security was further undermined by their subordinate position to Poland in the *cordon sanitaire* and the weakness of the League of Nations, which could offer them little protection against carnivorous neighbors. Moreover, Baltic leaders failed to cooperate with each other on economic, political, and defense issues in a consistent and systematic way.

In the early days of the independence era all three republics declared the creation of a Baltic union—one that included Finland, Sweden, and Poland as possible partners—to be a high priority; however, this aim was never realized. Instead of a larger Baltic alliance, the links that were developed in the region tended to be bilateral arrangements. While generally taking neutral positions in their foreign policies, Latvia and Estonia tended to gravitate toward the leadership of Poland, which sought to play the role of a "great power" in the region. As defenders of the status quo, the northern Baltic republics were concerned mostly with their own survival in an uncertain international climate; the main objective was to avoid being drawn into the struggles of their larger neighbors.

For Lithuania, the main foreign policy questions concerned Klaipėda, an industrial and port city located at the mouth of the Nemunas River, and Vilnius, for centuries the capital city of the Grand Duchy. At the Paris Peace Conference in 1919 Lithuanian delegates made a case for the inclusion of the Klaipėda territory, covering 1,100 square miles, in their new state. Although the proportion of Lithuanian residents who lived in the region was fairly low, the Lithuanian government believed that it nevertheless had a strong claim: Germany was going to lose territory anyway, and, as peace conference chairman and French premier Georges Clemenceau argued, Klaipėda would be Lithuania's main outlet to the sea. Nevertheless, having detached Klaipėda and its

140,000 inhabitants from Germany, the peacemakers decided to place the district under French administration for the time being.

Responding to a propaganda campaign that warned of an imminent Polish takeover, in January 1923 the Lithuanian military organized an insurrection and seized the city. With little resistance from the French and the German population of Klaipėda remaining mostly passive, the coup was swift and bloodless. Then preoccupied with problems in the Ruhr district, which the French army occupied in an effort to force Germany to pay war reparations, the Weimar government did not register an objection to the Lithuanian seizure, perhaps reasoning that it would be better for Klaipėda to go to Lithuania than to Poland, whose leaders had also staked a claim to the region. Soon after the Lithuanian takeover, the Western powers blessed it by transferring to Lithuania legal rights to the Klaipėda territory. Now Lithuania at least had a port and industrial center, but the Vilnius issue remained.

As discussed in chapter 4, Vilnius changed hands several times during the wars of 1914–1920 but was ultimately seized by Polish forces in October 1920. Despite Lithuania's historical claims to the city, neither the demographic nor the international situation worked to its advantage as Vilnius's tiny population of ethnic Lithuanians was dwarfed by the vastly larger numbers of Poles, Jews, and Belarusians residing there. Moreover, the Polish state enjoyed the backing of France, which was the guarantor of Europe's postwar security system. Refusing to relinquish the contested city, the Polish administration in Vilnius held elections in January 1922 that produced a provincial legislature that in turn overwhelmingly voted for union with Poland. But Lithuania refused to recognize the legitimacy of this act and brought its case before the International Court of Justice in The Hague, which produced no firm opinion. In an attempt to lay the matter to rest once and for all, the Allies recognized Polish sovereignty over Vilnius in March 1923. Only the Soviet Union, Poland's implacable enemy, recognized Lithuania's claim to Vilnius.

Polish-Lithuanian relations went from bad to worse during the 1920s and in November 1927 war appeared imminent. Polish authorities in Vilnius restricted activities in Lithuanian schools and institutions while Lithuanian authorities returned the favor to the country's Polish minority. A heightened sense of nationalism gripped Lithuania and its Polish minority came to be regarded as an internal enemy. Although direct negotiations between Poland's president Józef Piłsudski and Lithuania's prime minister Augustinas Voldemaras took place in December 1927, nothing came of them. The estranged governments were on the verge of trying again in 1935, but the death of Piłsudski aborted this initiative. Meanwhile, Poland reinforced its claim to Vilnius by settling thousands of Poles in the region during the interwar years.

Due to its simmering conflicts with Poland, Lithuania could not be a full partner in any Baltic alliance that included its nemesis. Instead it sought the support of the great powers in the region, namely Soviet Russia and Germany, each of whom also bore grudges against Poland. Yet it was Germany and the Soviet Union, far more than Poland, that were the most significant threats to the independence of all three Baltic states. However, thanks to their unusual weakness in the wake of World War I, the danger from Soviet Russia and Germany did not materialize for nearly two decades, and then under very different circumstances. Indeed, if it was in the interests of the Baltic states to pursue cooperative relationships with their more powerful neighbors, the reverse was also true: the USSR and Germany, at least during the life of the Weimar Republic (1919–1933), respected the independence of the Baltic republics and attempted to build constructive diplomatic and economic relations with them.

By the mid-1920s Soviet Russia had turned its energies inward, focusing on building "Socialism in One Country" rather than actively inciting revolution in foreign lands. During the 1926–1933 period, the USSR signed bilateral trade agreements and nonaggression treaties with most of its western neighbors. Nonaggression treaties were signed with Lithuania in September 1926, a maneuver that incited the student protests that may have been a factor in the Smetona coup at the end of the year, and later with Latvia (February 1932) and Estonia (May 1932). Originally intended to last for five, four, and four years, respectively, in 1934 the Soviets extended the agreements to the end of 1945 in the hopes of keeping the eastern European states divided. For the Baltic states, the objective was to ensure peace and stable relations with the much more powerful Soviet Union. Only after the fall of the Weimar Republic in January 1933 was Baltic security seriously threatened by the two major irredentist powers.

Throughout this period many Baltic leaders were convinced that should the need arise, Britain could be counted on for their defense, the British Foreign Office's formal statements to the contrary notwithstanding. As historians John Hiden and Patrick Salmon wrote, the Baltic governments "suffered from the understandable optical illusion that a relationship which was of paramount importance to them was equally important to Great Britain." Despite the significance of the Baltic trade, Britain refused to commit itself to the defense of these states.

Indeed, until the early 1930s its Foreign Office was convinced that they would ultimately be reincorporated into Russia one way or another.[23]

THE MOLOTOV–RIBBENTROP PACT

Hitler's foreign policy initiatives in the mid-1930s upset an equilibrium that had earlier allowed the Baltic states to enjoy generally peaceful relations with both the Germans and Soviets. As part of the Reich's efforts to reassert its economic influence in the region in the late 1930s, Germany signed trade treaties with the Baltic states that secured access to raw materials such as Estonian oil shale, essential for the German war machine. More ominous still was Nazi support for the claims of dissatisfied Baltic Germans, who suffered from the centralization policies then being pursued by the governments of Estonia and especially Latvia. Some felt that their futures would be better secured if the republics were attached to Germany, which long before Hitler's appointment had contributed to the financing of many of their educational and cultural institutions.

As Berlin worked to consolidate a sphere of political and economic influence in central and southeastern Europe and the Soviets worked to end their diplomatic isolation, in September 1934 the three Baltic states jointly signed a Treaty of Friendship and Cooperation. While the resulting Baltic Entente provided for collaboration in foreign affairs, it fell far short of a full military alliance, since Estonia and Latvia did not wish to be drawn into Lithuania's unresolved disputes with Poland and Germany over the Vilnius and Klaipėda territories. Even with a potential combined defense force of 500,000 men (the number of men on active duty was always far smaller), the three republics lacked a unified command structure and could not have stopped an attack by any of the great powers. Thus the Baltic states continued to emphasize their neutrality and their desire not to get in the way of Europe's great power struggles.

Whether the USSR's entry into the League of Nations in September 1934 signaled Moscow's acceptance of European diplomatic norms or simply a new approach to the same ends—maintaining state security while encouraging communist sedition abroad—its subsequent treaties with France and Czechoslovakia, both in May 1935, did little to deter Germany's ambitions, which were hardly satisfied with Berlin's remilitarization of the Rhineland in March 1936 and the annexation of Austria two years after that. A far more significant setback to European stability, and hence the security of the Baltic region, was the Munich Pact of September 1938. In a failed effort to satisfy Hitler's territorial

demands in Europe peacefully, the leaders of Italy, Britain, and France
acceded to the dismemberment of Czechoslovakia by granting Germany the Sudetenland, an area that contained most of the country's
three million Germans, whose rights Hitler claimed to be defending.
It quickly became clear that the *Führer* would also demand new arrangements for other areas lost to Germany after World War I, such as
Gdańsk (Ger. *Danzig*) and the neighboring "Polish corridor" as well
as Lithuanian-occupied Klaipėda. Immediately after German troops
marched into Prague in March 1939, Berlin demanded that Lithuania
surrender Klaipėda to the Reich. Fearing German occupation of the
whole country, Kaunas immediately complied. The Western powers
upon whom the Baltic countries relied for their security did little more
than murmur a word of protest; indeed, it was not long before Britain,
consistent with its policy of appeasing Hitler, granted *de jure* recognition of Germany's seizure of Klaipėda.

To London and Paris it was Poland's security, rather than that of the
Baltic countries, that was the key to maintaining peace in Europe. In
the hopes of averting further German aggression, at the end of March
1939 Britain and France gave Poland a joint guarantee; its effectiveness,
however, would have required both an actual commitment to military
action and Soviet support. Likewise, from the German perspective, a
war against Poland could be carried out successfully only with an as-
surance that the Soviets would not intervene. Thus both the Western
powers and Germany courted Stalin, but for different reasons.

But Stalin was extremely mistrustful of the British, who seemed
capable of little more than appeasing Germany's dictator. While also
distrusting Hitler, the Soviet leader understood that his own interests,
at least with regard to the lands between them, were more in line with
Hitler's than with those of the Western powers, who in the end seemed
to have little to offer. For the Western powers, any agreement with
the Soviets had to include a guarantee of the sovereignty of the Baltic
states that included Finland but not Lithuania, which did not share a
common border with the USSR. For the Soviets, however, the ports
and naval facilities of the Baltic states were essential for the defense
of Leningrad (formerly Petrograd, and before that St. Petersburg, as
it is again today), the country's second largest city and an important
center of military industry. Distrust between the West and the USSR,
arising in part from Stalin's resentment of the Munich agreement and
in part from the long-standing anticommunism of the West, prevented
the conclusion of an anti-German alliance. The Baltic states thus remained caught between two great powers who appeared to be moving
steadily toward war.

Posing as a concerned supporter of the Baltic states' continued independence, Germany pressured Estonia and Latvia into signing nonaggression pacts on June 7, 1939. With Britain and France seemingly powerless to influence events in central Europe, the only choices available to the leaders of the Baltic republics were to lean toward the Soviets or toward the Germans, for these states had once again become the region's dominant powers. However, the signing of these pacts appeared to imply that Latvia and Estonia had now become part of Germany's security system, which was surely suspicious to the Kremlin. Whereas Latvia and Estonia were coerced into making pacts with Germany, Lithuania tried to maintain its neutrality, all the while hoping to retain Vilnius in the event that a Polish-German conflict should break out.

Half-hearted negotiations between the USSR, Britain, and France in the summer of 1939 to deal with the Nazi threat produced nothing. However, behind-the-scenes negotiations between the Soviet Union and Germany resulted in the signing on August 23 of a nonaggression treaty, often referred to as the Molotov–Ribbentrop Pact in honor of its signatories, People's Commissar of Foreign Affairs Vyacheslav Molotov (1896–1986) and German defense minister Joaquin Ribbentrop (1893–1946). For Hitler, the pact meant insurance against Soviet interference during the coming German-Polish war. For Stalin, the pact bought time to build up Soviet defenses while offering the USSR something the Western powers could not—a sphere of influence in eastern Europe. The fate of the Baltic states was decided with the conclusion of a supplementary protocol to the Nazi-Soviet pact, according to which Poland would be divided between Germany and the USSR; Finland, Estonia, and Latvia would fall under the Soviet sphere; and Lithuania would fall under the German sphere of influence. With the signing of these "secret protocols"—they were unknown although widely suspected at the time and their existence continued to be denied by Soviet authorities until 1989—and London's refusal to offer the Baltic states security guarantees, the option of choosing between German guarantees against Russia or vice versa was removed.

Having succeeded in assuring Moscow's benevolence, Germany launched a massive and successful attack on Poland on September 1, 1939. This opening act of World War II was followed two days later by declarations of war on Germany by Britain and France in fulfillment of their obligations to Poland. However, at this point all they could do was blockade the Reich so as to prevent her from importing food and raw materials. Meanwhile, as Polish refugees flowed into Lithuania, Berlin pressured the Smetona government to aid in the attack on Poland

and to occupy Vilnius, but the Lithuanian president refrained and cautiously declared his country's neutrality. While the German *Wehrmacht* and *Luftwaffe* demolished western Poland, Soviet forces drove in from the east on September 16 and three days later entered Vilnius, which like Kaunas now became a haven for fleeing Jews. With little delay Moscow arranged for the incorporation into the USSR of the territories inhabited primarily by Poland's Ukrainian and Belarusian populations, whose alleged need for protection justified the Soviet invasion. Having helped Hitler destroy the Polish state, Stalin soon suggested a change in their respective spheres of interest that was quickly accepted by the Germans. According to the resulting supplemental (and secret) treaty on borders and friendship, signed on September 28, Germany would get a larger piece of Poland, including the Lublin district, and Lithuania would be transferred to the Soviet sphere.

The economic helplessness of the Baltic states was now as great as their military vulnerability, for the Baltic Sea was closed to commerce and their trade connections to Great Britain were severed as Moscow began to pressure them (and Finland) to conclude "mutual assistance treaties" that would enable the Red Army to occupy strategic bases in the region. Assured that their sovereignty would remain intact, the Baltic republics had little choice but to accede to Soviet demands. That Moscow was willing to back these demands with force was made clear to the Estonian government as the Soviets moved 160,000 troops from Polish territory to the border of Estonia, the smallest of the Baltic states and the furthest away from Germany.[24] A Soviet-Estonian treaty was signed on September 28 that allowed the Soviets to establish military bases on Estonian soil and to station 25,000 Soviet troops; similar treaties were signed by Latvia on October 5 and Lithuania on October 10. Significantly, the last of these treaties allowed for the transfer of the Vilnius region with its 457,500 mostly Polish, Belarusian, and Jewish inhabitants to Lithuanian control. The price that Lithuania would have to pay for the return of Vilnius, a city where few people actually spoke Lithuanian, would only become fully apparent the following spring and summer as Moscow engineered the incorporation of the three Baltic republics into the USSR.

Meanwhile, if Hitler still entertained any hopes of taking the eastern Baltic littoral for Germany, his improvised invitation to Baltic German *Volksdeutsche* in early October to leave the Estonian and Latvian republics for their German "homeland" suggests that he had abandoned such ambitions, at least for the time being. Hitler's main concerns were diplomatic—he hoped to avoid any chance that the Baltic Germans would be a point of contention between himself and Stalin—and racial: the German populations in the Baltic would begin the process

of Germanizing the *Lebensraum* ("living space") he had seized in Poland.[25] In the autumn and winter of 1939–1940 some 13,700 Germans
from Estonia and 50,000 from Latvia, including many people who
tried to pass themselves off as Germans, hastily boarded ships bound
for the Reich, taking with them only their personal possessions. Despite the profusion of propaganda encouraging the Germans to leave,
several thousand refused to go. A second exodus took place in early
1941 during which another 11,000 or more Germans left Latvia and
more than 50,000 people departed from Lithuania—a country that had
barely 35,000 Germans at the time.

While it is true that many Baltic Germans sympathized with the Nazi
regime, it would be a stretch to say that the departure of tens of thousands of people was motivated by a commitment to the Nazi cause,
for most of the German inhabitants of the Baltic states were above
all afraid of what would happen if the Soviets took over. Discussing
the declining fortunes of her family, who made their living from their
ownership of a taxi company, Eva Brennere (*née* Weiss, b. 1930) recalled
that after the arrival of Russian soldiers in the summer of 1940:

> We succeeded in selling off the one remaining taxi, and used the
> money to bribe the officials and receive an emigration permit.
> In March 1941, we left Latvia by ship from Liepāja, together with
> a large number of other people seeking to escape in order to save
> their lives. Germany at war seemed much more acceptable than the
> torture chambers of the Soviet secret police, forced exile, or even a
> death sentence.[26]

While Eva Brennere's family was temporarily moved to Saxony before making its way to the British zone of occupied Germany at the
end of the war (the family ultimately ended up in Australia), the fate
of the majority of the exiting Germans, at least temporarily, was settlement in that area of Poland recently annexed by Germany known
as the Warthegau. Meanwhile, ethnic Poles who lived in the annexed
territory were being expelled to an area known as the General Government, a sort of dumping ground for racial undesirables, to make way
for the arriving Germans. Due to chaotic conditions, endemic shortages, and the generally lower standard of living they experienced in
the Germanized part of Poland, many of the settlers were dissatisfied
with the arrangement and longed to return to their birthplaces following the anticipated German victory. These "repatriations" of the
Baltic Germans were the first in a series of transfers of several hundred
thousand *Volksdeutsche* from the states of eastern Europe to areas that

were militarily controlled by Germany. Few would ever return to their ancestral homelands.

But what were Stalin's intentions in the Baltic region? Was his goal all along to absorb the Baltic republics (along with eastern Poland and Bessarabia) in an effort to reestablish, more or less, the western boundaries of the old Russian Empire? Was his intention to create a series of new Soviet republics along the lines of the eastern European people's democracies that emerged after the war?[27] Or was he merely trying to draw a defensive line in eastern Europe to protect the USSR against a future German invasion? Whatever Stalin's intentions, he was, as neighboring Finland soon found out, unwilling to brook resistance of any kind—least of all the kind that involved rejecting his demands for bases and territory. The Winter War of 1939–1940 was a direct consequence of Finland's refusal to bow to the Kremlin's demands, and as poorly as the Red Army performed during the fight with Finland, where 127,000 Soviet soldiers died compared to 26,000 Finns, Moscow succeeded in revising the Finnish border to its own strategic advantage, using its newly acquired air and naval bases in Estonia to bomb Helsinki and other Finnish cities.

While the Finns bravely defended their homeland from the Red Army, for nearly two years the Baltic states existed in a twilight zone between independence and foreign occupation. Officials in all three Baltic countries attempted to pacify their populations, calling upon the people to support their respective governments and national unity. Hoping to avoid being embroiled in a conflict with either the Germans or the Soviets, Baltic leaders maintained correct working relations with both and instructed their newspapers to maintain a neutral and objective line. If the locals were surprised by the poor discipline of the arriving Soviet military personnel and the meager quality of their equipment and vehicles, at least it can be said that for the first few months of this forced arrangement the Soviet units stuck to their own leased areas and avoided contact with local populations.[28] Talk of the "Sovietization" of the Baltic countries, declared Molotov on October 31, 1939, would be "useful only to our common enemies and to all sorts of anti-Soviet provocateurs."[29]

NOTES

1. Toivo U. Raun, *Estonia and the Estonians*, 2nd ed. (Stanford, CA: Hoover Institution Press, 2001), 90, 129.

2. The 1926 Soviet census showed that 154,410 Latvians resided in the USSR, with significant concentrations in the Leningrad, Moscow, and

Siberian regions as well as Belarus. All together there were 372 Latvian colonies in Soviet Russia with some 12,000 farms. Many of these Latvians had settled in Russia in the 19th and early 20th centuries.

3. Artis Pabriks and Aldis Purs, *Latvia: The Challenges of Change* (London and New York: Routledge, 2001), 16; Andrejs Plakans, *The Latvians: A Short History* (Stanford, CA: Hoover Institution Press, 1995), 112, 124, 131–32.

4. Alfonsas Eidintas, Vytautas Žalys, and Alfred Erich Senn, *Lithuania in European Politics: The Years of the First Republic, 1918–1940* (New York: St. Martin's Press, 1997), 16; Georg von Rauch, *The Baltic States: The Years of Independence: Estonia, Latvia, Lithuania 1917–1940* (Berkeley: University of California Press, 1974), 85.

5. Other authors sometimes use alternative English translations for the names of some of the political organizations mentioned in this book. For example, the United Agrarian Party is sometimes, and more precisely, rendered in English as the Union of Settlers and Smallholders.

6. Raun, 114.

7. The leader of the attempted communist revolt, Jaan Anvelt, escaped to the USSR and was executed during the Stalinist repression of 1937.

8. Daina Bleiere, et al., *History of Latvia: The 20th Century*, 2nd ed. (Riga: Jumava, 2006), 146–47.

9. See Andres Kasekamp, *The Radical Right in Interwar Estonia* (New York: St. Martin's Press, 2000).

10. The arrested individuals, including Larka, were later freed. Sirk, however, managed to escape prison and fled to Finland.

11. Alfred Bilmanis, *A History of Latvia* (Westport, CT: Greenwood Press, 1951), 357.

12. In 1934 Voldemaras attempted to regain power during a coup attempt, but this failed and after being released from prison in 1938 he settled in France.

13. Bleiere, 165–69.

14. In 1936 a State Cultural Council (consisting of the boards of the Chambers of Professions and of the Chamber of Literature and Art) and a National Economic Council (consisting of the boards of the new chambers of commerce, industry, agriculture, artisans, and labor) were formed for the purpose of better coordinating the various sectors of the Latvian state and society.

15. Robert W. Heingartner, *Lithuania in the 1920s: A Diplomat's Diary* (Amsterdam and New York: Rodopi, 2009), 24. Heingartner's diary contains detailed descriptions of life in Kaunas in the 1920s.

16. United States Bureau of Markets, "Estonian Cotton Mills May Close," *The Market Reporter*, vol. 4 (July–December 1921), 127, http://books.google.com/books?id=EWkuAAAAYAAJ&pg=PA127#v=onepage&q&f=false (accessed June 10, 2013).

17. The main source for these statistics on Riga is E. Bulmerinks, "Rīgas rūpniecība," in *Rīga kāLatvijas galvas pilsēta: Rakstu krājums Latvijas*

Republikas 10 gadu pastāvešanas atcerei, ed. Teodors Līventāls (Rīga: Rīgas pilsētas valdes izdevums, 1932), 123–36. A useful overview of the Baltic economies as a whole during the interwar period can be found in John Hiden and Patrick Salmon's *The Baltic Nations and Europe: Estonia, Latvia and Lithuania in the Twentieth Century* (London and New York: Longman, 1991), 76–87.

18. See John Hiden, *Defender of Minorities: Paul Schiemann, 1876–1944* (London: Hurst, 2004).

19. Violeta Davoliūtė, *The Making and Breaking of Soviet Lithuania* (London and New York: Routledge, 2013), 23.

20. See Gaston Lacombe, "Nationalism and Education in Latvia, 1918–1940," *Journal of Baltic Studies* 28, no. 4 (Winter 1997): 309–38.

21. Raun, 134; Rauch, 128–29; F.W. Pick, "Tartu. The History of an Estonian University," *American Slavic and East European Review* 6, no. 3/4 (Nov. 1945): 150–61.

22. Rauch, 169.

23. Hiden and Salmon, 73–74.

24. Rein Taagepera, *Estonia: Return to Independence* (Boulder, CO: Westview Press, 1993), 60.

25. Valdis O. Lumans, *Latvia in World War II* (New York: Fordham University Press, 2006), 71–75. Synthesizing a wide range of scholarship in multiple languages, this book offers the most extensive treatment available of Latvia's experience in the war.

26. E. Smalkais and J. Vējiņš, eds., *Latvia through the Centuries* (Riga: A/S Preses Nams), 2007.

27. See Elena Zubkova, *Pribaltika i Kreml'. 1940–1953* (Moscow: Rosspen, 2008).

28. See the essays by Magnus Ilmjärv, Valters Ščerbinsky, and Toomas Hiio in *Northern European Overture to War, 1939–1941: From Memel to Barbarossa*, ed. Michael H. Clemmesen and Marcus S. Faulkner (Leiden and Boston: Brill, 2013).

29. Alfred Erich Senn, *Lithuania 1940: Revolution from Above* (Amsterdam, NY: Rodopi, 2006), 65.

6

World War II and the Totalitarian Experience, 1939–1953

Simultaneously admitted into the League of Nations on January 21, 1922, Estonia, Latvia, and Lithuania enjoyed a sense of security that, while always precarious, was never directly challenged until September 1939, when the Polish state was obliterated by its more powerful neighbors. As the summer turned to autumn the clouds darkened over the three small states located along eastern shores of the Baltic Sea, for their inhabitants too would soon become the victims of unprovoked aggression. First it was the Union of Soviet Socialist Republics (USSR), whose unquenchable thirst for security left no room for the independence of the Baltic states. Then came the Germans, whose rulers planned to seize "living space" in the east for future "Aryan" habitation. Three years passed before the Red Army was able to drive back the Wehrmacht and retake the bases it originally acquired in 1939–1941. The Soviet and Nazi occupations fundamentally altered the Baltic societies' political systems, economies, social order, and demographic profiles. Few survived unscathed by, and many were complicit in, the totalitarian experience that lasted without interruption until Stalin's death in 1953.

This is a discrete period in the region's history that warrants a detailed examination, for the hardships and unrelenting terror of Soviet and Nazi occupation gave the Estonians, Latvians, and Lithuanians a shared historical experience that in turn gave rise to a collective identity, even if such an identity was largely imposed upon them from the outside and was never really embraced by the "Balts" themselves. For nearly half a century the territories they inhabited were collectively known to the outside world as the "Baltic republics" and to Moscow as *Sovetskaya Pribaltika*. All three republics experienced the Sovietization of their political, economic, religious and cultural lives, and all three lost significant parts of their population to war, flight, and deportation. Familiarity with the events and controversies of this era is essential for anyone who wishes to understand the contemporary Baltic states and the peoples who live in them.

THE YEAR OF TERROR

Although the independence of the Baltic states formally came to an end in the summer of 1940, their fate was in fact decided in August and September 1939 by the Molotov–Ribbentrop Pact, a nonaggression treaty whose secret protocols divided eastern Europe into German and Soviet spheres of influence (see chapter 5). Not only was the arrangement a perfect reflection of Stalin's belief that the fate of small states was to be decided by their larger and more powerful neighbors, the deal with Hitler was better than anything being offered by the hesitant West, as it gave Stalin the opportunity to expand the USSR's strategic presence into those areas of eastern Europe lost to Russia after World War I, including the eastern half of Poland, Finland, Bessarabia, Estonia, Latvia, and Lithuania. For Hitler the overriding concern was securing a free hand in western Poland, which the Germans invaded on September 1, just a week after concluding the agreement with Moscow.

Holding up their end of the bargain, the Soviets occupied eastern Poland during the second half of September, following which they forced "mutual assistance" treaties on the Baltic states. Similar demands were made of Finland, whose resistance prompted a Soviet attack on November 30. Two weeks later the USSR was expelled from the League of Nations. Defeated after three and a half months of fighting, Finland was forced to cede strategically valuable territory that would allow the Soviets to better protect both Leningrad, a hub of the Soviet armaments industry, and the railroad that led to Murmansk on the White Sea. Although Finland, which like the Baltic states had been part of the Russian Empire before World War I, managed to maintain its independence, then and after World War II, it is likely that the Red Army's poor performance there influenced Hitler's decision to attack the USSR in 1941.

Despite the installation of Soviet military bases within their borders in late 1939, the Baltic protectorates were allowed to conduct their domestic affairs without Soviet interference while Moscow scrupulously observed the terms of the mutual assistance treaties.[1] Then in the spring of 1940, while the world's attention was riveted on the victorious Nazi campaigns in Holland, Belgium, and France, Moscow began to ratchet up the pressure on the three Baltic republics. In late May and early June the Soviet minister of foreign affairs Vyacheslav Molotov repeatedly accused the Baltic governments of unfriendliness and of conspiring together against the USSR. Alleging their inability to carry out the terms of the mutual assistance pacts, Moscow issued ultimatums to each of the Baltic countries, demanding that they form friendly governments capable of fulfilling their treaty obligations. The accusations were merely a pretext to mask the Moscow's real intentions of taking over the Baltic states in order to secure the USSR's direct and permanent access to the Baltic Sea.

Accused of abducting several Red Army soldiers who had strayed from one of the Soviet-occupied military bases, Lithuania was the first to be presented with an ultimatum, just before midnight on June 14. In what was surely a coordinated effort, a few hours later Soviet security forces (NKVD) staged a series of provocations at Latvia's Masḷenki border station. That these incidents occurred just as German troops marched into Paris was hardly accidental; it is possible that the ease of the Nazis' victories in the West caused Stalin to move more decisively to consolidate the USSR's position in the Baltic. However, it is unclear exactly when the Soviet leadership decided on the actual incorporation of the Baltic states into the USSR.

With invasion imminent, President Antanas Smetona tried to convince his cabinet and army that Lithuania, with its 26,000 active and 120,000 reserve soldiers, should at least organize a symbolic resistance to the Soviets, but he was overruled. On June 15, the Red Army overran the country as the president escaped to Germany, where the authorities offered him little more than temporary refuge. Continuing to insist that he symbolized independent Lithuania, Smetona died in a house fire in Cleveland in 1944.

On June 16, as 80,000 Latvians gathered in Daugavpils for a national song festival at which the beleaguered President Ulmanis made a brief appearance, Molotov issued similar demands to the Latvian and Estonian ambassadors in Moscow. Fully understanding the futility of military resistance, Baltic leaders had little choice but to accept the USSR's ultimatums. As in Lithuania, the occupation of Latvia and Estonia by the Soviet armed forces immediately followed. Within days more than 300,000 Soviet soldiers fanned throughout the Baltic states. "This is a temporary phenomenon that we will get over after a few days," Latvia's president told his people on June 17. "I will stay in my place, you stay in yours."[2] On June 21 Ulmanis was forced to resign. On the following day Konstantin Päts, the man who did more than anyone to create the Estonian state, signed the documents that for all practical purposes ended the country's independence and resigned his office. A month later Ulmanis was deported to Voroshilovsk (currently Stavropol) before reportedly dying in Turkmenistan in 1942. Päts, who did a brief stint in a tsarist prison in the earlier part of the century, was also exiled to the Soviet interior before dying in an NKVD psychiatric hospital in Kalinin (now Tver') in 1956.

The Soviet justification of the occupation, written in history books published in the postwar period, ignored Soviet belligerency in these events, instead emphasizing the "class struggle" then allegedly taking place in each of the Baltic countries. As one Soviet historian later wrote of the situation in Latvia:

> In June 1940, a revolutionary situation penetrated Latvia. Outwardly there was a crisis in the internal and external affairs of the dominant class; further, the oppressed classes were absorbed in poverty and disaster. Attempting to maintain power, the fascist government on June 17 enforced a state of siege in the country and intensified a bloody terror against the workers. On this day, the police resumed their fierce punishment of workers in Riga, who went out into the streets to greet part of the Red Army.[3]

"Spontaneous demonstrations" broke out in each of the Baltic capitals as the old order gave way to a new one. One such demonstration took place on June 21 in Tallinn, where observers were under the impression that the vast majority of the demonstrators were Russians and that at least some of these were Soviet troops clad in civilian clothing.[4] Similar conditions were reported in Riga. Such public demonstrations of support for Soviet power were important for Moscow to defend what would later become its official claim that the "fascist" regimes in the Baltic were swept away by indigenous socialist revolutions. That the legal transfer of power took almost identical form in all three Baltic states is indicative of the thinness of Soviet assertions.

Within weeks of the invasion, parliamentary elections were organized whose purpose was to confirm the voluntary nature of the Baltic republics' acceptance of socialism and their entry into the Soviet Union. To prevent the formation of an organized opposition, the countries were quickly Sovietized. In Riga the process was overseen by Andrei Vyshinsky, who in the 1930s had organized the Stalinist trials of the "enemies of the people." In Tallinn politburo member and Stalin favorite Andrei Zhdanov took charge, while Deputy Foreign Commissar Vladimir Dekanozov, an NKVD operative who was responsible for overseeing the purges in the Red Army in 1937–1938, was dispatched to Kaunas. It was their responsibility to pressure the legal cabinets to resign, to replace them with Soviet-approved appointees, and to create a new order—one that for the moment showed no sign of being controlled by the local (and miniscule) communist parties.

In Lithuania, the left-wing but noncommunist journalist Juozas Paleckis was selected as the country's new prime minister while the popular writer Vilis Lācis (1904–1966) was appointed Latvia's minister of the interior. Such people were needed by the Soviet regime to bolster the legitimacy of the People's Governments and to lend their signatures to the documents that would determine the sad fate of the Baltic countries.[5] Indeed, the primary task of the new governments was not to govern but to prepare the way for a complete communist takeover. The police and army were immediately neutralized in all three republics as the republics' political prisoners, mostly members of the underground communist parties, were released. Itching for revenge, they had to wait, biding their time by organizing workers' demonstrations while the Soviet authorities made their plans.

With new "elections" scheduled for July 14–15, the occupying authorities immediately carried out purges of noncommunist political organizations and other institutions. Just days before the elections were to take place, the People's Government of Lithuania waged a "class struggle" that resulted in the arrests of as many as 2,000 activists with suspect loyalties. Many of the arrested had entertained hopes of reestablishing the constitutional order that had existed in their country prior to the establishment of the Smetona dictatorship, but were dismayed at having been duped by a Soviet regime that was now bent on annexation masked by only the thinnest veneer of Soviet legality.

As popular manifestations of antisemitism grew during the two months of the People's Government, many Lithuanians linked the punishments meted out by the new authorities to Lithuania's Jewish population, which had grown substantially since the 1939 acquisition of Vilnius. Not a few Lithuanians were convinced that Jews had welcomed the Red Army and had both abetted and benefited from what was amounting to a Soviet takeover. The reality is that Jews, too, were frequently victims of the new order that was descending on Lithuania, for the Soviets considered *all* members of the bourgeoisie to be class enemies. This included Jews, even if on the whole the country's Jews, who were particular targets of the Nazis' racist ideology, supported the People's Government (and then the Soviet regime) more than the ethnic Lithuanians did. Such perceptions of Jewish collaboration likely fueled the horrific pogroms unleashed by Lithuanian "patriots" in Kaunas a year later. Jews in Riga were similarly suspected of greeting the arrival of the Red Army with great enthusiasm, but as in Lithuania it seems likely that such pro-Soviet sympathies were based less on a preference for communism than on a growing recognition of the Jewish experience with the Nazis in Europe, against which Moscow offered the best hope for protection.

Meanwhile, with Soviet soldiers and tanks in full sight seemingly everywhere, Moscow dispatched agents into the Baltic states to foment antigovernment agitation as left-leaning popular fronts—for example, the Latvian Working People's Bloc—were organized to provide cover for the communist parties in the upcoming elections. But the main goal of Soviet elections in the Baltic republics was not to offer a choice or to elect a new government but to disguise the fact that their fate had already been determined. All that was left to the local populations was to make public demonstrations of their support for a Soviet government and "vote" for it. While nobody today takes seriously the official claims that 99.2 percent of voters in Lithuania voted for the approved lists, or that 97.2 percent of Latvian voters and 92.8 percent of Estonian voters did the same, it is hard to imagine any sober-minded person taking such figures at face value in the summer of 1940 either.

The desired outcome having been achieved, the popular fronts disappeared, leaving the communists in sole control. Symbols of the independent Baltic states—their flags, national hymns, and so on—were banned as the authorities organized rallies to demonstrate popular support for their countries' admittance to the Soviet Union. On July 21–22, each of the new parliaments issued resolutions in which they declared themselves Soviet republics. Lithuania was admitted to the USSR on August 3, Latvia on August 5, and Estonia on the following day as Zhdanov, Vyshinsky, and Dekanozov returned to Moscow.

Whether the annexation of the Baltic states offered the USSR any greater advantages than maintaining them as satellites on the order of Mongolia remains an open and perhaps unanswerable question. But Soviet republics they now were, and as long as Germany was ravaging the continent the independence of the Baltic republics was hardly a main concern of either Britain or the United States. Nevertheless, on July 23, 1940, the U.S. State Department issued a declaration in which it refused to recognize the USSR's incorporation of the Baltic countries. Under the circumstances, this had no effect on Soviet policy in the region, as the USSR was not yet an ally of Britain and the United States. On the contrary, from August 1939 until June 1941 Stalin and Hitler were effectively partners in the division and subjugation of Europe. Even after the Nazi invasion of the USSR, Britain and the United States continued to take a pragmatic approach to the region, accepting the *de facto,* if not *de jure,* loss of the Baltic states' independence.

Their most prominent interwar leaders having been deported to the USSR, the Baltic countries were given new rulers, chosen from among sympathetic (or opportunistic) natives and cadres imported from the other Union republics, primarily the Russian republic, or RSFSR (Russian Soviet Federative Socialist Republic). The importation of administrators was necessary partly because few native communists were residing in the Baltic countries on the eve of the Soviet occupation: the Communist Party of Lithuania emerged from underground with 1,741 members; the Latvian Communist Party could claim 967 members, even if far fewer were actually in Latvia; tiniest of all was Estonia's Communist Party, with only 133 members in the spring of 1940.[6] Moreover, Baltic communists could count on only limited help from the thousands of Estonian, Latvian, and Lithuanian communists who had spent the interwar years in the USSR, as many of them had been eliminated during the purges of the 1930s. Nevertheless, until the ranks of the local communist parties (now folded into the Communist Party of the Soviet Union, or CPSU) were replenished, the communists Moscow sent to the Baltic capitals in the summer of 1940 were indispensable for the Sovietization of the Baltic states. To these were added the opportunists who joined the party in droves. By June 1941 the Communist Party of Estonia (ECP), for example, had grown to 3,732 members—a nearly 30-fold increase over the course of a single year.[7]

The new governments immediately began to align their policies with current Soviet practices, the basis of which was Marxist-Leninist ideology. The old "bourgeois" societies had to be destroyed so that new "socialist" societies, run by loyal Soviet citizens, could be constructed in their place. The reconstituted parliaments quickly proclaimed the nationalization of large enterprises, transportation, banks, private housing, and commerce in general. Although land was now considered the property of the people, for the time being the Soviet regime limited itself to expropriating only those holdings comprising 30 or more hectares (about 75 acres). The rest was placed in republic land banks, which then distributed some of the property to landless peasants and farmers with the smallest holdings.

If the main goal of the Baltic land reforms of 1919–1920 had been to create a class of independent farmers (while undercutting the power of the Baltic Germans), the policies pursued by the Soviet regime in 1940 aimed to dispossess the very same class in an effort to temporarily strengthen the smallholders and landless rural laborers. However, by creating large numbers of small, unviable farms, the Soviet regime intended over time to weaken the institution of private landholding and build support for Soviet power among the poorest farmers so that later collectivization, a program of agricultural consolidation that was undertaken in the USSR a decade earlier with horrifying results, could be presented as an efficient and popular alternative. Although large-scale collectivization was not yet attempted, a few experiments were undertaken during the final months of the "Year of Terror."[8]

Meanwhile, with the arrival of the Red Army, which quickly absorbed and attempted to indoctrinate the military forces of the Baltic states, accompanied by an influx Soviet security forces (NKVD), came strict censorship and press control along with the confiscation of items such as radios and bicycles. If the working class, the regime's primary constituency, was rewarded with increased wages, then the price increases, shortages, and the introduction in November of the ruble as legal tender in the Baltic republics soon canceled out such gains. In Riga and the other capitals housing became scarce as large apartment buildings were appropriated and reallocated to officials from the USSR. Everywhere the streets were renamed after Soviet heroes—a practice repeated by the Germans in 1941 and once again by the Soviets after the war. Organized religion, anathema to the atheistic Soviet state, also came under attack, for in each of the new Soviet republics churches and ecclesiastical property were nationalized, religious education and religious publications were forbidden, seminaries and monasteries were seized (often to quarter the Red Army), and many clergymen were arrested.

The greatest blow to the Baltic clergy, whether Lutheran, Catholic, or Orthodox, was dealt in mid-June 1941, when large numbers of priests and pastors were deported to the Soviet hinterland. This was part of a sweeping deportation that simultaneously affected all three Baltic republics and which targeted entire categories of people on the basis of lists prepared by the NKVD. These included former employees of the pre-Soviet Baltic governments, individuals who had been expelled from the communist parties, members of noncommunist parties active during the independence era, former police and prison officials, former large landowners and business owners, heads and active members of labor unions, and former officers in the armed forces.[9] Beginning on the night of June 13–14 and lasting for only a few days, the operation involved the shooting of hundreds of army officers and the deportation of about 15,000 people from Latvia, 10,000 from Estonia, and 18,000 from Lithuania, among them many Russians, Jews, and others.[10] Packed into boxcars for a journey of several weeks to northern Russia, Central Asia, or Siberia, many of these alleged class enemies, which included women and children, died along the way.

While these events have sometimes been described as the beginning of an attempted genocide—and some have noted the prominent role of Jewish NKVD officials—the fact that thousands of Jews, Russians, and others were on the NKVD deportation lists calls such assertions into question. Whatever the nationality of the repressed, any properties they held—farms, vehicles, precious metals, libraries, musical instruments—were "requisitioned for the working masses for the good of the state." Many who faced imminent arrest fled to the woods. Similar operations were planned for later that month, but the approach of the German army prevented them from being carried out.

If the republics' Soviet-censored newspapers ignored these events at the time, they were known to the local populations and even today remain deeply embedded in the historical consciousness of the Estonian, Latvian, and Lithuanian people, whose leaders continue to view Moscow as guilty of criminal acts for which it has yet to take full responsibility. The "Year of Terror," echoing and amplifying the Red Terror that took place in the Soviet republics of Latvia and Estonia in 1918–1919, defined the Baltic peoples' understanding of what it meant to be a citizen under a communist government and helps to explain why so many greeted the arriving German army as liberators in 1941—and why some locals resisted Sovietization when the Red Army returned in 1944. Indeed, the events of 1940–1941, as well as the deportations of 1948–1949 (see pp. 178–179) created a legacy of mistrust between the Baltic states and Russia that is still felt in present times.

OSTLAND

On June 22, 1941, only a week after the massive deportation operations, Nazi Germany broke the nonaggression pact with the USSR and launched Operation Barbarossa. This being Hitler's plan all along, the only person who seemed to be genuinely surprised was Stalin, a paranoiac who could hardly be accused of lacking vigilance. Nevertheless, despite having hundreds of thousands of their soldiers stationed in the recently annexed border areas, including 375,000 in the Baltic republics, the Soviet army, still reeling from the destruction of much of its top brass during the purges of 1937–1938, was unprepared for a defensive war. Lulled into a false sense of security by the Molotov–Ribbentrop Pact and faithfully delivering goods to Germany on the basis of trade agreements concluded in 1940, the Soviets based their strategy on the assumption that there would be no war in 1941 and that they had time to prepare for what even Stalin realized was a likely confrontation with his partner—one in which he apparently expected to take the offensive. Indeed, a few historians believe (even if they have not yet convinced the rest) that it was Stalin's plan to attack first—to take the war to the enemy rather than allow the Soviet homeland to be invaded—that prompted Hitler to break the pact.[11]

Launching the largest land invasion in history with the assistance of a half million troops from allied Hungary, Romania, and Finland (as well as volunteers from Italy, France, and other countries), approximately three million soldiers of the Wehrmacht, backed by 3,000 tanks and 2,500 airplanes, pummeled the USSR's western borderlands, capturing thousands of tanks and hundreds of thousands of stunned and misled Red Army soldiers. Much of the lauded Soviet air force was destroyed on the ground in the first hours of the war.

Many citizens of the Baltic republics, much like many western Ukrainians and other inhabitants of the USSR's recently acquired border territories, were at first overjoyed by the invasion, believing that the Germans had arrived as "liberators" from Soviet oppression. As one witness in Latvia recalled of the first days of Operation Barbarossa, "Few cities had ever welcomed their own bombing as Riga."[12] While German propaganda later portrayed the destruction of part of Riga's medieval Old Town as the work of the retreating Red Army, this wasn't a Soviet act; it was the German air raids that began on June 23 that destroyed the wooden spire of St. Peter's Church and other important architectural monuments. Meanwhile, as the Red Army retreated, tens of thousands of civilians, many frightened Jews among them, headed east for the Russian border.

On July 1 the Wehrmacht reached Riga, entering Estonia on July 5. Having just deported tens of thousands of Estonians, Latvians, and Lithuanians in mid-June, panicked Soviets forces committed a final act of barbarity before abandoning their posts. As the Red Army prepared its hasty retreat, NKVD operatives evacuated the prisons that they expected would soon fall into German hands. The Chekists shot hundreds of political prisoners in the Tartu prison, dumping the bodies in makeshift graves. Locals soon found the courtyard of the Central

Riga Prison littered with exhumed corpses. Lithuanians encountered similar grisly scenes at the Lukiškės Prison in Vilnius and Pravieniškės Prison near Kaunas. It should come as little surprise, then, that the German attack stirred the Baltic peoples' hopes for permanent liberation from Soviet terror.

By the time the Army Group North blazed into the Baltic republics, native groups had already organized, hoping to restore the independence of their countries. In Lithuania, the revolt against Soviet authorities began on June 23, as insurrectionist forces headed by the Lithuanian Activist Front (LAF) took over police stations and several arsenals in Kaunas while some took their revenge on local Jews. Meanwhile, revolts involving thousands of partisans broke out in Latvia and Estonia, which the Germans began to occupy in early July, capturing Tallinn, home to much of the Soviet Baltic fleet, in August, with the intention of moving on Leningrad. It wasn't until October that the Wehrmacht secured the larger Estonian islands.

With the partisans taking action into their own hands, and in doing so contributing to the stunning speed of the Germans' advance, local activists hoped that Germany would be forced to recognize the independence of their countries. Most notably, the underground LAF, having established contacts with the Germans well before the invasion, expected that in return for its help against the retreating Red Army Lithuania would regain its freedom. A Lithuanian Provisional Government was declared at the moment of the June Uprising, but the Nazis ignored it. They had their own plans for the region.

A popular view of the Nazi regime as being exceptionally well organized under a decisive and all-powerful leader belongs more to myth than fact. Indeed, the occupation of the Baltic region is a textbook case of the Nazi occupation regime's structural incoherence. On the whole the Germans' occupation policy was muddled, fraught with jurisdictional rivalries and a neglect of political planning. In its bare essentials, the goal was to eradicate the Soviet regime and create *Lebensraum* ("living space") for Germans in the European parts of the USSR. Joined together with the Belarusian region, the former Baltic states formed a civil administrative unit called *Reichskommissariat Ostland* under the rule of Hinrich Lohse (1896–1964) in Riga. Lohse was the choice of Alfred Rosenberg (1893–1946), Germany's Minister for the Occupied Eastern Territories, to whom he reported. A Baltic German from Tallinn and a longtime Nazi ideologist, Rosenberg was the leading civilian authority in *Ostland,* but in jurisdictional disputes he had to contend with the army, the elite SS (*Schutzstaffel*) organization headed by Heinrich Himmler (1900–1945), who was also Reich

Commissioner for the Strengthening of German Nationhood, and Hermann Göring (1893–1946), who as plenipotentiary of the Four-Year Plan was in charge of the Reich's economic concerns.[13] Each had their own prerogatives and priorities.

According to the *GeneralPlan Ost* (1942), which was essentially a master plan for ethnic cleansing that gave priority to the racial objectives of the SS, the region was to be exploited and completely Germanized within the next 25 years in preparation for its ultimate absorption by the Reich. Rosenberg's loopy racial theories placed Estonians, whom he regarded as largely Germanized, at the apex of the Baltic racial hierarchy. Some Latvians and fewer Lithuanians could be assimilated, but like the Slavs most would have to enslaved, transferred to the Russian hinterland, or simply eliminated. The resulting vacuum would be filled by colonizing Germans, thousands of whom were in fact brought from the Reich to settle on some of the expropriated farms. (Rosenberg and Hitler did not allow Baltic Germans to participate in the political administration of *Ostland*.) Rosenberg's plans, often ignored by Hitler for being too sympathetic to certain non-German populations, called for these colonists to be joined by the Baltic Germans who had departed from Estonia and Latvia at the end of 1939. For the time being, however, they were more useful in the territories annexed from Poland (the Warthegau), to which the Baltic Germans were expected to bring "civilization."

Yet with Hitler focusing on military matters and leaving the implementation of his vision to competing subordinates—a hallmark of his leadership style—occupation policies tended to be improvised and then altered as the *Führer*'s henchmen attempted to divine his will. For example, in February 1942 Rosenberg, working from his desk in Berlin, agreed to the establishment of a Latvian Self-Administration (*Landselbstverwaltung*) under General Oskars Dankers (1883–1965), a pro-German veteran of Latvia's War of Independence who left Latvia when the Soviets took over and then returned to the country after its "liberation" by the Wehrmacht.[14] Such administrative autonomy, symbolic as it was, was also granted to the Estonians and Lithuanians but was denied the other peoples of the Soviet Union. Its primary purpose was not actual governance but to provide the Nazis with willing and subordinate collaborators whose desire to restore local independence could be easily manipulated and otherwise ignored.

The potential for such a partnership between occupiers and the occupied was scarcely entertained by the Nazis in the summer and fall of 1941 as the Red Terror gave way to the New Order and Sovietization was replaced by Germanization. Rigans who had greeted the Germans as liberators in July were appalled at the renaming of the city's streets, parks, and squares (Liberty Avenue became Adolf Hitler Street, and so on), intended to underline the Nazis' goal of restoring "the ancient German character of the Baltic lands."[15] The hope that had accompanied liberation gradually turned to hostility as it became clear that a new evil had replaced the previous one. Even if the Germans made occasional concessions to the Latvian Self-Administration and repeatedly dangled the prospect of expanding self-rule in the Baltic lands, most likely for the purpose of increasing requisitions, Hitler could never conceive of true political autonomy for Latvia or the other occupied territories. Nevertheless, as the war went on circumstances compelled the Nazi leadership to reconsider what had previously been a purely ideological approach to the Nazi occupation of *Ostland*.

THE HOLOCAUST

One thing remained absolutely consistent after the summer of 1941, and that was the Nazis' commitment to eliminating the Jewish populations of the conquered territories. While the number of Jews living in the Baltic states paled in comparison to Poland, home to 3,474,000 Jews in 1939, there were significant Jewish populations in both Latvia and Lithuania, although not in Estonia, whose 4,300 Jews comprised less than one-half of 1 percent of the population.

Jews have lived in the Latvian lands since the 16th century and in Lithuania still longer (see chapter 2). The 1935 census in Latvia reported 93,479 Jews in Latvia (about 4 percent of the total population), down from 185,000 on the eve of World War I. Nearly half (43,672) lived in Riga, with most of the rest residing in the Latgale region (27,974). Of the approximately 210,000 Jews living in Lithuania in 1939, the recently acquired Vilnius area alone contained up to 80,000 Jews (and almost no Lithuanians). Most lived in cities and were engaged in trade, commerce, and industry; only a very few Jewish farmers exemplified the agrarian ideals extolled by the interwar Baltic governments. Jewish minorities, like all Baltic national groups, enjoyed had constitutional protections in the 1920s (see chapter 4), but Jewish cultural autonomy and economic influence were curtailed under the nationalizing dictatorships of the 1930s. In both interwar Latvia and Lithuania Jews had been excluded from the civil service and had limited options in the military.

Even if the populations of the Baltic states were not immune from the wave of antisemitism that engulfed Europe after the rise of the Nazis in Germany, prior to the war Jews were not singled out for repression, and when attacks on Jews occurred they were almost always verbal. However, the experience of Soviet terror in 1940–1941 created bitter resentments in the Baltic states, where the myth of the Jewish commissar took hold of the popular imagination as antisemitism began to spread to the wider population even before the arrival of the German army. It should be noted that this myth was born not in 1940–1941 but in 1918–1919 when Bolshevik governments in the Baltics carried out a brief but bloody Red Terror. Moreover, the myth was partially substantiated by the fact that the Soviet regime did indeed open up opportunities previously unavailable to Jews in 1940–1941 and the security services did attract a disproportionate number of Jews.

It is also worth noting that before World War II many Jews in Latvia and Lithuania tended to be friendly toward German culture, most speaking the German-based Yiddish language and often looking down on the uncultured peasants whose villages surrounded the more cosmopolitan cities where many Jews lived and worked. While many of the region's Jews could communicate in German (and some in Russian as well), few spoke Latvian or Lithuanian. Christian and Jewish communities lived alongside each other and were economically interdependent but generally maintained a social distance.

Far from reciprocating the guarded admiration many Jews, especially those in Lithuania and Courland, had for Germany and Germans, the Nazis viewed the Jews as degenerate *Untermenschen* (sub-humans). In Hitler's view the Jews were aliens, economic parasites, and cultural imperialists who existed outside the *Volk* (nation) and posed the most serious threat to the biological purity of the master Aryan race. If Nazi policy in occupied Poland between 1939 and 1941 focused mostly on ethnic cleansing—the removal and ghettoization of undesirable populations to isolate them and make room for incoming Germans—by the summer of 1941 the goal had become extermination.[16]

The task of annihilating Soviet and Baltic Jewry fell to the SS *Einsatzgruppen*—the mobile killing forces founded in May 1941 by Himmler and Reinhard Heydrich (1900–1942), who along with Hitler were the main architects of the Holocaust. Organized into four units that followed the advancing German army into Soviet territory, the *Einsatzgruppen* were charged with restoring order, maintaining security, killing communist functionaries, and fighting partisans. Owing to the myth of Jewish collaboration with the Soviet regime, such targets became synonymous with the Nazis' foremost enemy, the Jews, whom the SS had full license to annihilate.

Upon the arrival of the Wehrmacht, tens of thousands of Lithuanian and Latvian Jews fled toward Russia. The arrival of SS Brigadier

General Dr. Walther Stahlecker (1900–1942) in Kaunas on the morning of June 25 coincided with local pogroms in which 5,000 Jews were killed. There is some controversy as to whether these pogroms were spontaneously initiated by the local population or were instead incited by the Nazis and made to look like a local action. While the fact that Lithuanians participated in the massacre (as did hundreds of Latvians in German-organized mass killings throughout Latvia) is now beyond dispute, the explanations for the murderers' behavior range, according to one historian, "from sheer opportunism to sincere and deep-rooted lust to avenge the Crucifixion and retaliate for persecutions suffered under the Soviets."[17]

If the Nazis disdained to consider any kind of political collaboration with the peoples of the occupied territories beyond the creation of powerless "Self-Administrations," they did not hesitate to recruit local collaborators to help them complete the gruesome task of annihilation, which local participants likely viewed as revenge rather than genocide. Following the trail blazed by Army Group North into the Baltic lands, Stahlecker's *Einsatzgruppe A* next moved into Latvia, reaching Riga on July 1. Accompanying these forces were hundreds of uniformed Latvians returning from Germany who became the core of the Latvian SD (Security Service). Immediately Stahlecker began to recruit locals into auxiliary police units made up of former soldiers and policemen as well as former members of the *Aizsargi* (Home Guards) and *Pērkonkrusts* (Thunder Cross), which was Latvia's largest fascist-type organization until its suppression by the Ulmanis regime in 1934. The most notorious of the Latvian auxiliary police units was the Arājs Kommando, which historian Andrew Ezergailis described as "a unique unit with no exact counterpart in occupied Europe." Led by a vicious opportunist named Viktors Arājs (1910–1988), its 300 or more volunteers went as far as Minsk in search of victims and were responsible for the murder of at least 26,000 Jews in Latvia and still more in Lithuania and Belarus.[18]

The first wave of Jewish persecution in Riga began with the arrival of *Einsatzgruppe A* as uniformed Latvians "forced their way into the homes of prominent Jewish citizens, abducted lawyers, rabbis, doctors, and other Jewish citizens and took them away"—a procedure that closely matched the *Einsatzgruppen's* original orders to take action first against members of the elite.[19] The city's Central Prison was quickly filled with ex-Soviet authorities and Jews suspected of cooperating with them. Over the next two weeks trucks belonging to the Arājs Commando routinely picked up Jewish men from the prison and brought them to the Biķernieki forest to be shot in secret.

Accounts of mass killings like this one frequently mention the role of alcohol in fortifying the executioners' nerves. Having cut off the escape route to the east with the capture of Daugavpils at the end of June, German forces trapped all of Latvia's Jews, as well as Jewish refugees from Lithuania, but an estimated 10,000 to 15,000 who managed to flee to Russia.

Although Heydrich's orders to the *Einsatzgruppen* gave them license to carry out reprisals against Jewish-Bolshevik elites and to quash any resistance behind the front lines, with the region's transfer to civilian control on July 17 (later in Estonia), the Nazis lacked a unified policy as to what should be done with the Jewish populations as a whole. If the preference of *Ostland*'s governor Hinrich Lohse was to ghettoize the Jews and use them as a skilled labor force, SS leaders preferred immediate liquidation—a "comprehensive pogrom." The Nazis did both. Throughout the occupied territories urban Jews were crowded into ghettos, which were eventually sealed by barbed wire; these were organized by Lohse and his civilian government. Meanwhile the *Einsatzgruppen* with their Latvian collaborators conducted "cleansing operations" in the smaller towns and villages. A typical ploy the Germans used to induce the locals to take action was to force Jews to dig up the graves of Soviet victims, counting on Latvians to be so incensed that revenge was inevitable.[20]

By July 17 Stahlecker was able to report that all the synagogues of Riga had been destroyed. Within another three months nearly half of Latvia's Jews had been murdered.[21] Now only 29,000 frightened and destitute Jews—the Germans and their Latvian collaborators robbed them of anything of value—remained alive in the isolated Riga ghetto, which became a crowded, unhygienic dumping ground in one of the poorest sections of the city. Easily identified by the yellow Star of David they were forced to wear on their chests and backs, ghetto Jews were compelled to work. A total of 7,000 Jews remained in the Daugavpils ghetto, and fewer than 4,000 in Liepāja, Latvia's second largest city. The latter became the site of a filmed massacre of Jewish women in which a Latvian police battalion participated. Its viewers will confront a deeply unsettling window into the horror show that was the Nazis' "New Order."[22] Having overseen the murder of many thousands of Jews in Latvia and Lithuania (although not quickly enough for Himmler), Dr. Stahlecker was reassigned to the Russian front where he was killed in an action against Soviet partisans.

Meanwhile, with 24,000 of the Latvian Jews in Riga shot in massacres in the Rumbula forest just outside the city on November 30 and December 8, only a few male skilled laborers remained in the ghetto. The first of these massacres occurred just hours after the arrival of a thousand Jews from Germany ("Reich Jews"), who were immediately liquidated. Further transports arrived in the winter of 1941–1942 carrying 18,000 or more Reich Jews who were shot in Latvia largely because of its remote location. Thousands of Latvian Jews were also sent to labor in other parts of eastern Europe.

Much of the killing that took place during the fall and winter of 1941–1942 was supervised by SS Lieutenant General Friedrich Jeckeln (1895–1946) who, having developed an efficient system of killing in Ukraine, was brought to Riga in November 1941 to speed up the process. By the time Heydrich's infamous Wannsee Conference was held on January 20, 1942, to ensure the cooperation of Germany's various government departments in the final solution of the Jewish question—that is, to clarify the process whereby Jews would be transferred to the facilities in the east for extermination—nearly all of Latvia's Jews had been eliminated or transferred outside the country to perform labor.

For many months after the Jewish presence in Riga was almost completely eradicated (the ghetto was not liquidated until November 2, 1943), a few thousand Latvian and Reich Jews continued to labor for the Reich in the camps established at Mežaparks (Ger. *Kaiserwald*), Salaspils, and elsewhere. Most of them also died, mostly from starvation, overwork, and lack of any kind of medical care. It is also worth noting that Jews, of whom only a thousand survived the war, were not the only ones to perish in German camps in Latvia. The estimated 100,000 Latvian and foreign Jews (from Germany, Austria, Hungary, Lithuania, and elsewhere) killed in Latvia were joined in death by 330,000 Soviet prisoners of war, whose camps were likewise scattered throughout the country.[23] No country in Europe had a higher rate of eradication than Latvia.

The execution of the final solution was no less horrific in Lithuania, but the scale was greater owing to the larger size of the Jewish communities in Lithuanian cities. As mentioned above, on June 25–26 Kaunas was the scene of the first large-scale massacres; these coincided with the arrival of the Germans, who further goaded the Lithuanians violence against the Jews. While the attacks that took place on these two days are well documented in photographs and memoirs, there is also evidence that from the moment of the insurgency on June 23, before the Germans arrived in Kaunas and other Lithuanian towns, local nationalists were already killing their neighbors. As Solly Ganor, a Jewish resident of Kaunas at the time, recalled:

Even with huge numbers of Soviet troops still in Kaunas, gangs of Lithuanians armed with rifles and revolvers were roaming the streets. They called themselves "Siauliai," or "Patriots," and although they occasionally fought the Russians, for the most part they were robbing and beating up Jews. Our neighbors had turned against us, and the Germans hadn't even arrived.... The retreating Soviet army was only a few hundred yards away, and the Lithuanians were murdering the Jews under their very noses.[24]

Vilnius was one of the few larger cities where such pogroms did not occur, owing to the large number of Jews and small number of Lithuanians living in the city. By the end of June the Germans had disarmed most of the anti-Soviet bands and incorporated them into their own auxiliary units for the purpose of continuing the struggle against the Jews in a more orderly, controlled, and thorough manner.

On the whole, the Holocaust unfolded in Lithuania much the same way it did in Latvia, yet Lithuania was the first place in Nazi-occupied Europe where Jews were executed by the thousands. Indeed, the way the Nazis carried out the business of genocide in Soviet territory, largely through shootings, differed markedly from their methods in western Europe and occupied Poland. If the latter became the site of the infamous death camps established beginning at the end of 1941 at Chelmno, Bełżec, Majdanek, Sobibór, and Treblinka, where Polish Jews were gassed using modern industrial methods to kill as many Jews as quickly and as efficiently as possible (Jews living in western countries were usually sent to Auschwitz-Birkenau, which became the largest of the death factories), Soviet Jews, including the Jews of Lithuania and Latvia, were destroyed in mass shootings in a "Holocaust by bullets" that claimed the lives of 1.5 million Jews overall.[25] There was not one Holocaust, but two, and perhaps many.

The evidence that a small number of Lithuanian "freedom fighters" staged pogroms and killed Jews at random in the interval between the Red Army's evacuation and the Germans' establishment of mastery over the country is nearly incontrovertible. The gruesome displays of frenzied hatred in Kaunas on June 25–26 even disturbed some of the arriving Nazis, who encouraged the attacks even if their haphazard nature violated the Germans' sense of order. Establishing his Kaunas office on July 25, Reichskommissar Lohse dashed any hopes the Lithuanians had of regaining their independence and instead treated Lithuanian nationals as inferiors; yet, as in Latvia, the Nazi administration in Lithuania needed local volunteers to help the accomplish the task of making the country *Judenfrei* (cleansed of Jews). This largely accomplished by the spring of 1942, the first group of 20,000 farmers from Germany arrived in May. It was they, the Germans and not the

Lithuanians, who were to benefit from the seizure of Jewish properties and the looting of their possessions.

A massive relocation to the ghettos, intended in part to shut Jews off from mixing with local populations, occurred in August 1941, as other Lithuanian Jews were sent to labor camps outside the cities. The Kaunas ghetto became the prison of 35,000 to 40,000 Litvaks, to which the Germans communicated their orders through a Jewish Council (*Judenrat*), whose elderly members acted as intermediaries between the authorities and ghetto inmates in the hopes of providing the latter with some modicum of safety and security. Council members frequently convinced themselves that the Germans would spare the Jews if they provided them with reliable labor. "Helpless in the face of their all-powerful enemies, the Jews in the ghettos, tortured by hunger, insecurity and fear, teetered between despair and hope. Death from starvation, cold, and disease, was an everyday occurrence, and the death toll rose with each passing day."[26]

Such was also the fate of the 38,000 Jews herded into the two Vilnius ghettos, established on September 21, 1941, just weeks after some 25,000 Jews were murdered in the nearby forests of Ponary (Lith. *Paneriai*).[27] While the Germans coordinated the massacres at Ponary, Lithuanian volunteers did much of the killing. Afterward the pace of the killings slowed due to the need for slave labor in Latvia and Estonia, until in March 1943 the Nazis decided to liquidate the Jewish communities in the small towns and transfer their remnants to the crowded Vilnius ghettos and labor camps further north. Three months later Himmler ordered the liquidation of all the ghettos in *Ostland*.

These actions were being undertaken at roughly the same time as the Nazis attempted to suppress an uprising in the Warsaw ghetto. News of this event, the greatest act of Jewish resistance during the Holocaust, soon reached the Jews of Vilnius. "A few rumors still come from Warsaw: Warsaw is still fighting, the Warsaw Ghetto has already given up the struggle, and the final cord—the Warsaw Ghetto has finally been silenced," reads the May 25th entry of a diary by Herman Kruk, written in Yiddish. "Now the radio says they are searching for Jews in Warsaw, outside the ghetto. For pointing out a Jew you receive . . . 10 kilos of sugar. A Jewish head is worth 10 kilos of sugar."[28] Clashes between German units and members of an underground group occurred in Vilnius on September 1, but this only bought the Jews of Vilnius a few weeks' time as the ghetto was liquidated on the 21st, its remnants sent either to the death camp at Majdanek or to the labor camps in Estonia.

Despite the aid offered by a few sympathetic Lithuanians who helped Jews survive by concealing them in their homes and caring for them at tremendous personal risk, some 90 percent of Vilnius's 76,000 to 80,000 Jews perished during World War II. The proportion is even greater for Lithuania as a whole, as scholars estimate that 195,000 of the 210,000 Jews living in Lithuania in 1939 were killed during the Holocaust between 1941 and 1944. (The Nazis also killed 45,000 ethnic Lithuanians.) Jewish Vilna, the "Jerusalem of Lithuania," one of the great cultural symbols of the Jewish diaspora in Europe and for hundreds of years a leading center of Jewish learning, was lost forever. Disdaining to show even the slightest interest in the city's Jewish history, the Soviet regime, having resettled most of the city's Polish population after the war, later bulldozed what was left of Jewish Vilna, for the city was now Vilnius, the capital of the Lithuanian Soviet Socialist Republic (SSR); there was no need to commemorate its Jewish (or Polish) heritage.

The first region the Nazis declared *Judenfrei* in the summer of 1941, Estonia, was an anomaly in the history of the Holocaust, for owing to the tiny number of Jews in the country there was less antisemitic hatred among the locals for the Nazis to exploit. While Estonia began to feel the influence of Nazi Germany toward the end of the 1930s, and while many Estonians had lived through the events of 1918–1919 and 1940–1941 and some also equated the Jews with Bolshevik terror, the reality is that with its miniscule Jewish population the conditions did not exist for the "perfect storm" that swept through Lithuania and Latvia in the summer of 1941.

About 1,000 Estonian Jews were killed at the hands of *Einsatsgruppe A* and the Nazis' local collaborators, the remainder either having been deported by the Soviets in June 1941 (415 Estonian Jews) or fleeing to Soviet Russia at the start of the German invasion. While this is a tiny number when compared to the six million European Jews who perished during the Holocaust, these were not the only Jews to die on Estonian soil during World War II. Latvian and Lithuanian Jews who fled to Estonia or were deported to its labor camps, as well as Jews from the Reich and elsewhere in Europe, also met their end in this remote corner of northeastern Europe. The camp established at Klooga, established late in the war, was where the diarist Herman Kruk was killed in September 1944 as the Red Army advanced once again into Estonia. This was one of the 22 concentration and labor camps established in Estonia where foreign Jews and Soviet prisoners of war (POWs) were used as slave labor. The largest of these, the Vaivara camp complex, processed 20,000 Jews from Latvia and the Lithuanian ghettos in its capacity as a transit camp. Its prisoners then worked in the nearby forest, in the quarries, or in the oil shale mines of northeastern Estonia.

If, from the Nazi point of view, Estonians occupied a higher position in the racial hierarchy than did the Latvians or Lithuanians, the Estonians, for their part, trusted the Germans better (or at least distrusted them less) than they did the Russians. Historian Anton Weiss-Wendt asserts that "A majority of the Estonian population backed the Germans until the very last day of the occupation" and convincingly argues that Estonians embraced the Nazi cause not out of antisemitism but a heightened sense of nationalism.[29] Nevertheless, as in the other Baltic countries, the Nazis could not have completed their work in Estonia without the services provided by local auxiliaries who guarded the camps filled with Jews and Soviet POWs. It must be added, however, that the mass-shooting of the 2,000 prisoners at Klooga was carried out by German units.

Also like its southern neighbors, Estonians suffered from a similar collective amnesia about the events of that time. Concerned above all with restoring an independent Estonian state, they accepted Hitler as the lesser of two evils and sought to prove the superiority of their culture over that of the Soviets. It was not until 2002, more than a decade after Estonia was freed from Soviet rule, that the Estonian government officially commemorated the Holocaust.

Used to playing the part of victim, the courageous David to the Russian and German Goliaths, segments of the populations in all three Baltic countries, not least their governments, have found it difficult to engage in an honest assessment of those times when their co-nationals, too, had been victimizers. But this is changing as the commemoration of the tragedy becomes increasingly institutionalized. Since the restoration of independence Latvia has observed July 4 as the official commemoration day for Jewish Victims of Genocide in Latvia. The seriousness with which this is taken by the Latvian government is indicated by the annual appearance of Latvian presidents and other dignitaries at the ceremony, which takes place at the site where a synagogue was burnt down in Riga on July 4, 1941. Likewise, Lithuania has been commemorating the National Memorial Day for the Genocide of Lithuanian Jews since September 23, 1994, four years after its government first officially admitted Lithuanian involvement in the Holocaust.

EXPLOITATION AND COLLABORATION

If many locals saw Nazi tyranny as an improvement over Soviet tyranny, this was due in some measure to the limited concessions the Germans granted with regard to cultural autonomy and basic freedoms for Christian religious believers, whose congregations were allowed to resume their services, even if unreliable clergymen were regularly repressed. But the Nazis' main concern, second only to the racial reorganization of Europe, was economic exploitation. Thus while Jews were targeted for extermination, the economic centralization and strict labor policies earlier instituted by the Soviets remained in place: confiscated commercial and industrial enterprises remained nationalized, workers remained tied to their workplace and were denied the right to strike, and efforts by former landowners to reacquire their confiscated lands met with little success.

While Baltic industries were expected to contribute to the Reich's war needs, it was agriculture that predominated in German planning. The dairy products, pork, and poultry produced in *Ostland* were intended first and foremost to feed the German armed forces and secondly to feed the Reich itself. Indeed, the assumption at the heart of *GeneralPlan Ost* was that many of the inhabitants of the occupied territories would starve. It was through deliveries of agricultural goods to the occupying authorities that Baltic farmers were expected to show their gratitude for having been liberated from Soviet rule. With the Germans setting the prices and instituting nonnegotiable quotas, all while introducing food rations that favored German administrators over local inhabitants, the system did not substantially differ from the one imposed by Moscow. Yet not even the Soviets went so far as to plunder the local livestock and horses. Shortages, especially of food, grew more critical with each passing month as barter largely replaced the monetary economy. For example, on the farmsteads of occupied Estonia thousands of illegal distilleries produced moonshine for personal consumption, to bribe officials, and as currency for the exchange of goods—a practice that endured until the collapse of the USSR.[30]

Problems with the food supply were connected to *Ostland*'s endemic labor shortage, which in turn was caused mostly by flight and by the absence of the seasonal agricultural laborers upon which Latvia in particular relied. While the deficit was partly made up for by the use of Soviet prisoners of war to work on the farms (as well as the exploitation of Jewish labor in the ghettos), the Nazis exacerbated local labor shortages by deporting tens of thousands of workers to the Reich to labor in German industries as so-called *Ostarbeiter,* a practice felt more acutely in occupied Ukraine. At first recruitment was semi-voluntary—the material incentives the Nazis offered the locals to sign up to work in Germany were always backed by the credible use of force—but by 1943 labor was regularly being conscripted in the Baltic territories. Thousands avoided mandatory service by taking refuge in the woods.

Yet the biggest drain on labor resources in *Ostland* after 1942 was the military struggle then being waged against Soviet Russia, for the war dragged on far longer than the Germans expected and created a need for more men in uniform. By 1942, having already resorted to summoning into active service German reserve policemen well into their 30s and 40s, the Nazis, or rather the leaders of the Wehrmacht and the SS, had little choice but to reevaluate the official stance on military collaboration with the locals, even if Hitler had made clear his opposition to the arming of non-Germans.

The first such experiment occurred in Estonia, where at first the locals were recruited on a voluntary basis. An Estonian Waffen-SS unit, called the Estonian Legion, was created in August 1942, but by mid-October it could claim only 500 recruits.[31] Turning to forced mobilization when the war began to go badly, the Germans conscripted several thousand Estonian men and sent them to the eastern front in 1943, but thousands more were able to avoid being drafted by fleeing to Finland. Nevertheless, when the Red Army threatened once again to cross the Estonian border in February 1944, Hjalmar Mäe (1901–1978), the head of the Estonian civilian administration (and a former propagandist for the fascistic League of Independence War Veterans), was able to enlist or conscript up to 38,000 men to fight a "new war of independence." When one considers the tiny size of the Estonian population and the existing demands on the young men of Estonia, this is an impressive number indeed.[32] German mobilization efforts met with similar success Lithuania: tens of thousands of Lithuanians volunteered to fight the Soviets, but unlike Latvians and Estonians, Lithuanians did not join the Nazi SS-Legions.

The Nazis' greatest recruitment success was in Latvia, for perhaps 100,000 men or more were mobilized into the Latvian Legion and other auxiliary forces; as in Estonia, those who did not wish to fight could choose labor service instead.[33] The legacy of the Latvian Legion remains one of contemporary Latvia's most divisive historical subjects, for the Legion was the enemy of the victorious Soviet Red Army to which memorials all over Latvia were dedicated during the Soviet era. If Russian Latvians tend to remember the Legion's soldiers as fascist lackeys of the *Führer* (their commanders were almost always German members of the Waffen-SS, but subordinate officers were Latvian), many ethnic Latvians defend them as patriots who died heroically fighting for the Fatherland, no matter what uniform they were forced to wear. But "[p]articipation in the German armed struggle was more a matter of choice than many postwar Latvian apologists care to admit," writes historian Valdis Lumans, noting Lithuanians' resistance to the formation of SS units. "The Latvians too could have said no if they had chosen that course."[34] But even if those who said "yes" had a variety of motivations, and some surely committed war crimes, who else but the Germans could have prevented the return of the Soviets? Being on the same side, the Legion's defenders have argued, is not the same as being allies. Moreover, had Britain and the United States not partnered with the Soviet Union, which had illegally absorbed the Baltic states and had committed countless outrages, to fight what the West at the moment regarded as the greater evil?

By the time the Hitler reluctantly agreed to the Legion's formation in February 1943, it was too late, for the Wehrmacht was reeling from its defeat at Stalingrad and would never regain the initiative. Yet even as Hitler's exhausted and hungry forces retreated in 1943 and 1944, the Nazis spared no efforts to mobilize the local populations for total war while simultaneously murdering the remnants of the Jewish population that had reliably supplied them with labor.

DEVASTATION

When the Soviets returned to the Baltic states in 1944 the people they encountered were divided. If hundreds of thousands of Estonians, Latvians, and Lithuanians had volunteered (or been conscripted) to fight with the Germans against the advancing Soviets—which likely helped delay the latter's occupation of their countries—a comparable number of local inhabitants fought wearing the uniform of the Red Army. It has been estimated that 30,000 Estonians, 75,000 Latvians, and 82,000 Lithuanians belonged to the Red Army during the latter stages of the war; these included men who had formerly served in the forces created by the Germans.[35] To the German- and Soviet-led forces one must add another category of combatants: the anti-Soviet partisan units, some of which had been organized and trained by the Germans. Hiding in the forests of the lands being retaken by the Red Army, the partisans were a drain on Soviet resources but were too insignificant and disunited to secure control over their respective countries or even to significantly impact the course of the war.

Nazi Germany's domination of the Baltic Sea met its first serious challenge in January 1944 when Soviet forces lifted the 872-day siege of Leningrad, thereby opening up Russia's window to the West at the cost of a million Soviet soldiers' lives. By the end of September 1944 Finland had switched sides, turning against its German ally, while nearly the entirety of the contemporary Baltic states (Hitler obstinately held onto Courland in western Latvia until the war was lost) was overrun by the Red Army, whose soldiers encountered scenes of utter devastation as they reoccupied the western borderlands now being reclaimed for the Soviet Union. The Germans' scorched earth policy left much of the shattered empire in ruins: 1,700 Soviet towns and 70,000 villages were destroyed, 26 million Soviet citizens were dead, and nearly an equal number were left homeless.[36] Soviet forces arrived in Europe bent on revenge, frequently taking it at the expense of unprotected civilian populations, especially those who were German and female. Estonia, the first of the Baltic states to be "liberated," was not spared Soviet atrocities; nor were Latvia and Lithuania.

Nor was the Baltic region spared the physical destruction and population losses experienced by the other parts of the USSR, for what the Nazis didn't loot they simply destroyed. As the Nazi SS hurried to finish off its emaciated prisoners and destroy the forced labor camps before they could be liberated by the Soviets, the Wehrmacht did the job of reducing countless towns and villages in Latvia and Lithuania, like those in Ukraine and Belarus, to smoldering ruins. Meanwhile, Soviet bombing during the final stages of the war nearly obliterated the Estonian border city of Narva and the Lithuanian town of Šiauliai while also causing heavy damage to Tallinn and Tartu.

But the physical destruction and the movement of peoples did not end on May 8, 1945, the date that officially commemorates the end of World War II in Europe (in Russia the announcement of "Victory Day" was delayed for one day and to this day it is celebrated on May 9). When the Red Army liberated Klaipėda on January 28, it is said to have found a nearly deserted city, for the Germans who inhabited the city had fled. Within a few years these were replaced by Lithuanians and Russians as the Soviets obliterated the city's architecturally German character and destroyed the city's churches. Indeed, the fate of Klaipėda mirrored that of the entire region, where physical destruction and demographic transformation went hand in hand. Entire ethnic communities were uprooted or destroyed, including the Baltic German and Jewish communities, depriving the region of much of its ethnic and cultural diversity as well as many of its most educated and socially active individuals.

Some in the Baltic lands had the opportunity to escape before Soviet forces could fully take control of the region. During the war's final ten months as many as 64,000 Lithuanians, 80,000 Estonians, and 160,000 Latvians, fled westward to Germany or boarded fishing boats and other small vessels to reach Sweden—the only country aside from Nazi Germany that legally recognized the Soviet incorporation of the

Baltic states—rather than live under a restored Soviet regime. In this way many of the region's surviving intellectuals, property owners, and cultural and religious leaders were able to escape the mass executions and deportations—ostensibly for having collaborated with the Germans—that followed the Soviet reoccupation of the Baltic region. In Courland, where a battle raged for eight months costing the lives of 320,000 Soviet and 150,000 German soldiers, the Soviets rounded up all enemy soldiers and every surviving male over the age of 16 and sent them to "filtration camps" for political screenings. Thousands did not return home for years; an unknown number never returned at all.

Total human losses are difficult to estimate, but it seems that on the whole the Baltic countries lost about 20 percent of their population during World War II, due to a combination of flight to the West, losses of territory, deportations, and deaths caused by war and occupation. Few regions suffered greater losses in terms of population—not even Poland, where over 16 percent of the population perished, or Yugoslavia, whose human losses approached 11 percent. If just over 1.5 million Latvians lived in Latvia in 1939, the corresponding figure for 1950 was closer to 1.3 million. About one million Estonians lived in Estonia in 1939, but by 1950 the number had dropped to 845,000. While an accurate count of Lithuanians is muddled by the return of Vilnius in 1939, it seems that the number of Lithuanians living in Lithuania (including Vilnius) dropped from about 2.36 million to approximately 1.93 million in 1950.[37] The Jewish population was eliminated in its entirety.

Survivors had to adjust to a new reality, whether in the displaced persons camps in western Germany—for 200,000 Baltic refugees these were arguably the safest places to be in Europe in the spring of 1945—or in the reconstituted Estonian, Latvian, and Lithuanian SSRs. Neither Britain nor the United States were willing to risk alienating their Soviet partner when it came to the fate of the Baltic states. This much was clear at the Yalta Conference of February 1945, when Stalin's partners Franklin Roosevelt and Winston Churchill chose stability over principle and allowed the Soviet dictator to strengthen his conquests in eastern Europe. The Western countries even complied with Soviet demands for the return of refugees, many of whom were deported to various parts of the USSR. As the historian Modris Eksteins wrote with remarkable elegance 1945 was *Stunde Null*, the zero hour, a low point in the history of Western civilization. "Collaborators, resistance fighters, SS soldiers, Jews, peasants, professors, children, paupers, bankers, criminals, clergymen. Every nationality, age, social class, type. They were all present amidst the devastation."[38]

SOVIETIZATION AND RESISTANCE

The returning Soviets did not treat the Baltic states as liberated republics of the USSR but as occupied territories populated by enemies of Soviet power. Not only were they denied independence of any kind, the reincorporated SSRs were forced to accede to minor but unfavorable border changes. Yet the transfers of territory that took place between the USSR and the Baltic republics must be seen in the context of the new borders being drawn throughout eastern Europe that were favorable to the Soviet Union, whose leaders sought to maximize their security and influence in postwar Europe. Germany was forced to cede a large portion of East Prussia, renamed the Kaliningrad *oblast'* in 1946, to Soviet Russia. Poland was shifted westward: while absorbing a large amount of eastern German territory, Poland lost its own eastern regions to the Ukrainian, Belarusian, and Lithuanian SSRs. In nearly all the countries bordering the USSR there were population exchanges involving millions of people to ensure that the countries of eastern Europe were more ethnically homogenous. No ethnic group was affected by this more than the Germans, who were the objects of revenge all over the continent.

In comparison to the overhaul which Germany and Poland received, the outlines of the Estonian and Latvian republics were not drastically altered by Stalin's blue pencil. Estonia ceded to the Russian republic (RSFSR) eastern territories located both north and south of Lake Peipsi, including most of the Petserimaa district and all the territory east of the Narva River. These areas constituted about 5 percent of the prewar territory of the Republic of Estonia and were home to about 70,000 residents, mostly ethnic Russians. Latvia was forced to cede to the RSFSR the Abrene region, a thin sliver of territory in the northeast that contained relatively few Latvians.

Among the Baltic republics, Lithuania experienced the most significant territorial adjustments, for the earlier acquisition of the Klaipėda (1923) and Vilnius (1939) territories were made permanent. Related to these changes was the ethnic homogenization of the country that occurred between 1940 and 1945. Owing to the nearly complete destruction of Lithuania's once large Jewish community and the removal of more than 200,000 Poles (mostly from Vilnius and its suburbs) to the new Poland following Soviet reoccupation, the postwar Lithuanian SSR was both territorially larger and, owing to the catastrophic population losses, far more ethnically homogenous than the prewar state. Likewise, the construction of a Soviet Lithuanian Vilnius, a city that was earlier claimed by Poles and Jews, as well as by Russians and Belarusians, but was heavily populated by Jews, was made possible owing to these very same tragedies.

Since all three Baltic states suffered devastating human losses, the Soviet authorities once again faced the challenge of recruiting personnel for the management of the Baltic governments and economies. Most pressing was the matter of the communist parties, which were to resume their leading role in the re-Sovietized republics despite the thinness of their ranks. As in 1940, the importation of cadres from the interior provided a convenient solution. While this temporarily swelled the ranks of the Baltic communist parties with nonnatives, mostly Russians, the communist parties were gradually able to attract cadres from among the titular populations. The Communist Party of Lithuania best reflected this trend: only 16 percent of its members in 1947 were Lithuanian, rising to 38 percent by 1956 and nearly 56 percent in 1959.[39] While first secretaries were usually Russian-trained natives, throughout the Soviet era the second secretaries in the republics were always Russians and usually exercised at least as much power as their nominal superiors.

Since Stalin was unconvinced of the reliability of cadres in the Baltic SSRs, the threat of a purge, like those that were carried out in the satellite states of eastern Europe in the 1940s and early 1950s, was ever present. The most drastic case among the Baltic parties was the ECP, from which "bourgeois nationalists"—communists who were believed to favor Estonian interests over those of Moscow—were purged in 1950–1951. They were replaced by Estonians whose families had emigrated from Estonia to Russia in the decades before 1920. Most notably, during the purge Nikolai Karotamm (1901–1969), who had survived the Great Terror in Moscow and was appointed ECP first secretary in 1944, was removed for his supposed lack of vigilance in the face of class hostility; his real crime, however, was pleading for a slower pace of collectivization. Karotamm's replacement was Jonannes Käbin (1905–1999), an Estonian who had been born in his homeland but had risen through the party bureaucracy in Soviet Russia, only to return during the first Soviet occupation. As long as Stalin lived, political life in the Estonian republic was dominated by a "Russian Estonian mafia"—Russified Estonians who had risen to the top of the ECP—that served Moscow's interests alone.[40]

In Latvia and Lithuania the makeup of the Communist Party leadership showed signs of greater stability. From 1940 to 1959 the first secretary of the Communist Party of Latvia was Jānis Kalnbērziņš (1893–1986), who like Käbin had resided in the USSR before 1940. Still steadier was the Lithuanian leadership, whose first secretary Antanas Sniečkus (1903–1974) retained his post until his death in January 1974. Such leaders, most notably Sniečkus, have sometimes been credited with defending the interests of their republics by mitigating the harshest aspects of Soviet rule. However, it should be remembered that these very same leaders were also partly responsible for the repressions and deportations of the 1940s while at the same time executing Moscow's policies of collectivization, industrialization, and Russian colonization.

Meanwhile, as the Baltic republics were being assimilated into the USSR, the war against Soviet reoccupation continued to smolder in the forests. It will be recalled how the Baltic states were too weak and disunited to resist the first Soviet occupation in 1940–1941. However, three more years of Nazi occupation provided the Baltic peoples with the time and resources to develop an impressive if ultimately unsuccessful resistance to another round of Sovietization. At their peak in 1944–1946, anti-Soviet partisans called "forest brothers" dominated the Baltic countryside. Although it is difficult to say with any certainty how many guerillas were active at any one time—and there is a tendency to exaggerate the numbers—it is estimated that as many as 30,000 Lithuanians, and smaller numbers of Estonians and Latvians (including former members of the Latvian Legion), took up arms against the Soviet authorities.[41] Emerging from their forest hideouts, partisans shot at Soviet uniformed personnel and party cadres while inflicting substantial damage on buildings, especially in rural areas. Encouraging the local populations to resist Soviet rule, the forest brothers also published and disseminated underground literature— and executed hundreds of suspected collaborators.

Despite being vastly outnumbered, undersupplied, and isolated, some partisan bands rejected repeated Soviet offers of amnesty and a few held out in the forests until as late as 1955, by which time they certainly could not have expected to drive the Soviets out. Holdouts were motivated by the hope, encouraged by foreign radio broadcasts (Radio Free Europe and Voice of America were established in 1949 and 1951) suggesting that Soviet communism would soon collapse and that the Western Allies would help them restore Estonian, Latvian, and Lithuanian statehood.[42] Nevertheless, the main partisan formations, strongest in Lithuania, were broken by 1948, after which the guerillas were deprived of recruits and food supplies due to the mass deportations that accompanied the collectivization of the Baltic countryside.

AGRICULTURAL COLLECTIVIZATION

One of the Soviet Union's crowning achievements and most heinous crimes was agricultural collectivization. A system that was predicated on Marxist-Leninist theories concerning rural modernization and class struggle in the countryside, collectivization had earlier brought tragedy to Ukraine and other parts of the USSR and was eventually extended to the satellite states of eastern Europe after World War II. Although the farmers of Estonia, Latvia, and Lithuania were spared large-scale collectivization during the first Soviet occupation in 1940–1941, the second occupation saw a vigorous application of the devastating agricultural policies that had first been imposed on Soviet farmers around 1930. Since the emphasis in the Baltic republics, Estonia and Latvia in particular, was on rapid industrialization, planners in Moscow at first accorded a low priority to Baltic agriculture. However, once the situation in the Baltic region stabilized, collectivization was to serve several purposes: in principle, the collective farms (*kolkhozy*), supplied with tractors and other equipment normally beyond the reach of ordinary family farmers, would provide Baltic agriculture with economies of scale that would permit the transfer of excess rural labor to the new industrial concerns. However, the political benefits of this policy may have been even more important, as collectivization was also a means of ending partisan resistance in the Baltic countryside.

After a delay of several years, Soviet land reform in the Baltic territories picked up where it had left off in 1940–1941. During the 1944–1947 period, the Soviets continued to eliminate farms larger than 30 hectares (including farms formerly belonging to German colonists and native landowners who had fled to the West), while expropriating the land, livestock, and property of the *kulaky*—the so-called "rich" farmers. Such *kulaky*, who were usually labeled as such not because they were actually wealthy but because of wartime activities the Soviet authorities deemed suspicious, were ostracized and forbidden from joining the *kolkhozy*. Only in 1947 were the first postwar collective farms set up in the Baltic republics. By the end of 1948 there were more than 500 *kolkhozy* in both Latvia and Lithuania, but less than half that in Estonia, where collectivization was slowest.

To induce the modestly successful farmers to join the collectives Soviet authorities raised tax rates on farms to a level where it became impossible for them to continue functioning, leaving many little choice but to join the *kolkhozy* along with the poorer strata. Meanwhile, the *kulaky* were liquidated as a class. Many were sent into internal exile, which often meant certain death. In late March 1949, at the height of the collectivization drive, more than 94,000 rural Estonians, Lithuanians, and Latvians—more than half of them women and children—were deported and dispersed to various locations throughout the USSR.[43] That 42,133 Latvians were rounded up in the course of just a few days gives one pause to consider the arbitrary nature of Soviet power, its wanton cruelty, and its appetite for vengeance. Whether motivated by ideology, the desire to settle scores, or simple greed, Latvians too were involved in the process of compiling deportation lists.[44] Victims who received permission to return to their homelands after 1954 still had to live with "spoiled biographies" for decades, as returnees experienced great difficulty finding work, opportunities to study, or even places to live.

While there is little doubt that the impetus for rural reform came from Moscow, recent scholarship has shown that de-kulakization proceedings were often carried out locally. In her study of collectivization and de-kulakization in Soviet Estonia, historian Anu Mai Kõll shows that the struggle against the kulaks was a public process that invited popular participation. The late 1940s was a time of conflicting loyalties and uncertain outcomes; as yet the local community "was not united against Soviet officials; it was still negotiating the boundaries of the permissible."[45] Whatever the role of local participants in the de-kulakization process, the reality for most of the region's farmers was a second enserfment, for *kolkhoz* members were now tied to the collective, forbidden from changing residence without a special permit.

However, Soviet officialdom often looked the other way when young men fled the *kolkhoz* to seek employment in industry or construction where labor shortages were chronic. Other common responses to collectivization were shirking one's duties, pilfering materials from the *kolkhoz*, and producing moonshine to generate some income. While collective farms workers tended to shun mandatory labor on the *kolkhoz*, they put considerably more effort into their private garden plots, which generated the largest part of their incomes.[46]

Once begun in earnest, collectivization was rapidly completed, and by the end of 1950 the vast majority of Estonian, Latvian, and Lithuanian peasants had joined the collective farms mandated by Moscow. Along with this achievement the Soviet regime could rejoice in having nearly completely eliminated the guerilla resistance movements in the Baltic countryside. The negative consequences of collectivization, however, should have been foreseeable. Although farmers did not resort to the large-scale slaughter of livestock as Ukrainian farmers did in the early 1930s, and the peoples of *Pribaltika* did not starve, there was by every conceivable measure a catastrophic drop in agricultural production in each of the Baltic republics between 1948 and 1955. If Baltic agriculture began to recover during the second half of the 1950s, the same could not be said of the thousands who suffered the tragedies of collectivization and de-kulakization, deportation and exile, and the loss of homeland as Moscow imposed its system, its administrators, its values, and its version of recent historical developments on its three newest republics.

INDUSTRIALIZATION AND URBANIZATION

Sovietization began to transform the cities of the Baltic republics well before its power was fully felt in the surrounding countryside. Because of the region's skilled labor reserve and the existing industrial infrastructure, the focus of Soviet economic policy in the cities was rapid industrial development. Moscow's objective was to integrate the Baltic republics into the centralized Soviet economic system; they would then serve as a source of energy while producing a range of industrial and agricultural products for export to the rest of the USSR. But first existing industry had to recover from the destruction it had suffered during the war. This was mostly completed by 1950, partly aided, especially in Estonia, by the use of German prisoners of war as laborers and by the importation of industrial plants dismantled by the Soviets in their occupation zone in eastern Germany.

Concentrated in Riga, Latvian industry focused on the production of steel and agricultural machinery, electric motors, and diesel engines. While the State Electrotechnical Factory (VEF) in Riga was heavily damaged and looted during the war, the Soviets saw it as essential for its reindustrialization efforts and reopened it to produce telephones and radios for sale in Latvia and the other republics. VEF's radios were an important means of getting of information about the outside world, for some models were capable of receiving Voice of America, Radio Free Europe, and other Western propaganda stations. In Estonia, Soviet planners emphasized the expansion of one of interwar Estonia's most successful interwar enterprises—the oil shale industry. Immediately placed under the direct control of the All-Union Ministry of the Coal Industry, Estonian oil shale was to serve as a fuel source for the northwestern region of the USSR. With the construction in 1948 of a pipeline linking the oil shale region of Estonia to Leningrad, Estonia's most important natural resource began flowing to the RSFSR.

As its industrial base was still weaker than that of her northern neighbors, Lithuania received less capital investment than did Latvian and Estonian industry. There Soviet economic policy during the first postwar decade focused on light industry and food processing.

Intensive industrialization focusing on heavy industry was delayed until after Stalin's death in 1953, thanks in part to the efforts of First Secretary Antanas Sniečkus. A career communist bureaucrat who was intensely loyal to party authorities in Moscow, he is nevertheless often credited with sparing the Lithuanian republic from some of the negative effects of intensive industrial development and from the kind of massive Russian immigration endured by Estonia and Latvia.

The migration of Soviet citizens to the Baltic republics was due in large measure to the labor requirements of the industrialization drive. However, while claims that Moscow was bent on ethnocide through immigration are sometimes overstated, there was undoubtedly a political motive as well, for the presence of a large Russian-speaking community would reinforce Soviet political control over the Baltic republics. In fact, precisely as large numbers of Estonian, Latvian, and Lithuanian peasants were being deported eastward into the Soviet hinterland during the collectivization drive, thousands of Soviet citizens were moving westward into the cities of the Baltic republics to work in the revitalized and expanded local industries. These immigrants included significant numbers of Estonian Russians and Latvian Russians who had spent the interwar period in Soviet Russia. The lion's share of immigrants, however, were Slavs from the Ukrainian and Belarusian SSRs, and most of all from the Russian republic.

The peak influx came during the immediate postwar years and contributed to the housing shortage that became a permanent feature of life in Baltic cities during the Soviet era. The most extreme example was the Latvian SSR, which received hundreds of thousands of mostly non-Latvian immigrants in the 1940s and 1950s. As a result the Latvians' share of the republic's population declined from about 84 percent in 1945 to 60 percent in 1953; by the end of the Soviet era Latvians comprised a bare majority of the inhabitants of the republic that bore their name. Perhaps four million people altogether passed through Latvia during the Soviet period. While migration tended to be rotational, with constant migratory movements between the Latvian SSR and the other Slavic republics, at least 700,000 people of other nationalities settled in Latvia permanently during the Soviet era.

Soviet Estonia's demographic profile was similar. As in Latvia, the peak period of immigration was 1945–1947, when approximately 180,000 non-Estonians, including a significant number of ex-convicts from Russia, flooded into the tiny Estonian SSR. Most settled in northeastern Estonia and urban centers such as Narva, whose medieval ruins stood for years before the Soviets, opting not to restore them, sent in the bulldozers. As a result of this massive immigration Estonians were pushed out of the country's resource-rich border regions and the titular nationality's share of Estonia's population dropped dramatically, from about 94 percent in early 1945 (after Estonia ceded regions largely inhabited by Russians to the RSFSR) to 72 percent in 1953, and finally to 61.5 percent in 1989.[47] That imperialist considerations outweighed economic ones is beyond debate; less clear is whether Moscow intended to flood the region with so many immigrants that in the long run the Estonians, Latvians, and Lithuanians would naturally assimilate into a Russian-speaking Soviet people.

The experience of Lithuania, where immigration, like industrialization, occurred on a somewhat smaller scale, suggests otherwise. In 1939, Russians accounted for 2.3 percent of the Lithuanian population, rising to 9.4 percent over the next 50 years, while the ethnic Lithuanian population stabilized at around 80 percent. However, while immigration did not seriously alter Lithuania's ethnic balance, in other respects the experience was the same, for many of these immigrants were government and party officials, industrial managers, engineers, and professionals. As such they were accorded priority in the awarding of scarce urban housing, thus contributing to the natives' resentment of the Russian-speaking arrivals and the belief that the Russians were colonizing their homelands.

The waves of migration were a principal feature of a more general influx into the cities that transformed Latvia and Estonia into two of the USSR's most urbanized republics: by the early 1950s more than half the residents of Latvia and Estonia could be classified as urban residents. Riga's population doubled from 228,000 at the end of World War II to 482,000 in 1950; likewise, the population of Estonia's largest city, Tallinn, more than doubled to 283,000 between 1944 and 1959, as did Vilnius, whose population during the same period rose from 110,000 to 236,000. Russians as well as Latvians flooded into Riga, with many of the Soviet migrants moving into buildings in the Moscow district once inhabited by Jews. Still others settled in Daugavpils and Liepāja. While Russians had always been a large component of Narva's ethnic makeup, Slavic migrants from the Soviet interior soon became the second most populous community in Tallinn.

But it was Lithuania's cities, having lost their Polish, German, and Jewish populations, that were the most radically altered by the war and its aftermath: Vilnius's Poles were resettled by the Soviets in 1944–1946, the Germans of Klaipėda and elsewhere fled to escape the Soviets, and Jews everywhere were shot by the Nazis and their accomplices. While the Russian presence in Lithuania's cities increased after the war, the vast majority of the new urban residents were Lithuanians who were rapidly being uprooted from their rural communities. That the first 14 years after the war saw the urban population of Lithuania increase by 173 percent reveals the astonishing pace of Soviet modernization in this traditionally rural country. The scale of this exodus to Lithuania's cities and towns dwarfed even the deportations to the Soviet interior or the earlier flights to the West, and in some ways was no less traumatic to those who experienced it.[48] Yet it was not until 1970 that Lithuania's urban population outnumbered its rural population (and gradually Lithuanians arriving from the village became the majority population of Vilnius), by which time Estonia had become the most urbanized of the Soviet republics, with 65 percent of its population living in cities.

By 1953 the Baltic republics had each become nearly fully integrated into the political and economic structures of the Soviet Union. Even if the era of totalitarian terror had come to an end with Stalin's death that March, Soviet rule appeared to be a permanent condition of life in the Baltic republics. With no hope for the restoration of independence, for the next several decades their inhabitants had little choice but to accommodate themselves to the realities of Soviet colonization while attempting to maintain their ethnic identities and cultural traditions.

NOTES

1. By March 1940 there had been a number of incidents between Soviet troops and locals in Estonia. See Andrejs Plakans, ed., *Experiencing Totalitarianism: The Invasion and Occupation of Latvia by the USSR and Nazi Germany 1939–1991: A Documentary History* (Bloomington, IN: AuthorHouse, 2007), 16–19.

2. Plakans (2007), 35.

3. D. Y. Stradins, ed., *Istoriia Lativskoi SSR* [History of the Latvian SSR] (Riga: Academy of Science of the Latvian SSR, 1955), 481, as appears in I. Joseph Vizulis, *Nations under Duress: The Baltic States* (Port Washington, NY: Associated Faculty Press, 1985), 46.

4. Toivo U. Raun, *Estonia and the Estonians*, 2nd ed. (Stanford, CA: Hoover Institution Press, 2001), 144.

5. In the wake of Latvia's annexation by the USSR in 1940 Lācis became chairman of the Council of Ministers of his republic—equivalent to a prime minister, except the office lacked real power. Resuming this post after World War II, he retained it until 1959.

6. Romuald Misiunas and Rein Taagepera, *The Baltic States: Years of Dependence 1940–1990*, expanded and updated edition (Berkeley and Los Angeles: University of California Press, 1993), 359.

7. Raun, 150.

8. See Geoffrey Swain, *Between Stalin and Hitler: Class War and Race War on the Dvina, 1940–46* (London and New York: Routledge, 2004), 32–39.

9. The original plans for the deportation of "anti-Soviet" elements were written in October 1939. The document is reproduced in Vizulis, 99–101.

10. The exact figures for these deportations will never be known. All together around 34,250 people from Latvia, 39,000 from Lithuania, and 61,000 from Estonia are thought to have faced arrest and deportation during the "Year of Terror." Valdis O. Lumans, *Latvia in World War II* (New York: Fordham University Press, 2006), 138.

11. The publication in 1990 of *Icebreaker* by former Soviet intelligence agent Viktor Suvorov stimulated a debate about Soviet intentions vis-à-vis Germany in 1939–1941. While Suvorov believes that Stalin was planning to strike first, most historians have resisted this view.

12. Quoted in Lumans, 158.

13. Rosenberg studied architecture at the Riga Polytechnical Institute, emigrating to Germany in 1918 in the wake of the Bolshevik seizure of power. Arriving in Munich he became one of the earliest members of the Nazi Party and influenced the young Hitler. While his appointment as minister for the Occupied Eastern Territories revived a flagging career, Hitler frequently disregarded his views. See Michael Kellogg, *The Russian Roots of Nazism: White Émigrés and the Making of National Socialism, 1917–1945* (New York: Cambridge University Press, 2008).

14. Riga was treated separately from the Self-Administration. Denied self-government, it was the hub both of German administration and of the Nazis' Germanization efforts in Latvia.

15. Andrejs Plakans, *A Concise History of the Baltic States* (New York: Cambridge University Press, 2011), 100.

16. Christopher Browning, *The Origins of the Final Solution: The Evolution of Nazi Jewish Policy, September 1939—March 1942* (Lincoln: University of Nebraska Press, 2004).

17. Karen Sutton, *The Massacre of the Jews of Lithuania: Lithuanian Collaboration in the Final Solution 1941–1944* (Jerusalem: Gefen, 2008), 121.

18. Andrew Ezergailis, *The Holocaust in Latvia 1941–44: The Missing Center* (Washington DC: United States Holocaust Memorial Museum, 1996), 22, 173–202.

19. Andrej Angrick, Peter Klein, and Ray Brandon, *The "Final Solution" in Riga: Exploitation and Annihilation, 1941–1944* (New York: Berghahn Books, 2009), 68.

20. Lumans, 243.

21. Bernhard Press, *The Murder of the Jews of Latvia 1941–1945* (Evanston, IL: Northwestern University Press, 2000), 46, 53. An eyewitness to the Holocaust in Riga, Press emphasizes the Latvians' betrayal and bloodlust, going so far as to assert that "the majority of the Latvian people" supported the mob actions and "also actively participated themselves"

(p. 52). Press argues that Latvians began killing Jews even before the arrival of the Germans. This contention is refuted by Andrew Ezergailis, cited earlier, who agrees that Latvians were active participants but maintains that it was the Germans who gave the orders.

22. Holocaust Encyclopedia, "Introduction to the Holocaust—Historical Film Footage." United States Holocaust Memorial Museum, http://www.ushmm.org/wlc/en/media_fi.php?ModuleId=10005143&MediaId=183 (accessed June 25, 2014).

23. Lumans, 259.

24. Solly Ganor, *Light One Candle: A Survivor's Tale from Lithuania to Jerusalem* (New York: Kodansha International, 1995), 53, 57.

25. Patrick Desbois, *The Holocaust by Bullets: A Priest's Journey to Uncover the Truth Behind the Murder of 1.5 Million Jews* (New York: Palgrave Macmillan, 2009).

26. Masha Greenbaum, *The Jews of Lithuania: A History of a Remarkable Community 1316–1945* (Jerusalem: Gefen Books, 1995), 321–22.

27. Of the two Vilnius ghettos, one was established for elderly and sick people incapable of performing labor, but it existed for only 45 days before its inhabitants were taken to Ponary to be shot. The other was for those able to work.

28. Herman Kruk, *The Last Days of the Jerusalem of Lithuania: Chronicles from the Vilna Ghetto and the Camps,* ed. Bejamin Harshav (New Haven: Yale University Press, 2002), 551.

29. Anton Weiss-Wendt, *Murder without Hatred: Estonians and the Holocaust* (Syracuse, NY: Syracuse University Press, 2009), 77.

30. Olaf Mertelsmann, *Everyday Life in Stalinist Estonia* (Frankfurt am Main, Germany: Peter Lang, 2012), 46–47.

31. The Waffen-SS were combat units composed of Reich Germans, *Volksdeutsche,* and other nationalities. These units were subordinate to the leadership of the SS but fought under the army military command.

32. Raun, 159.

33. Misiunas and Taagepera, 59; Plakans (2007), 139; Plakans (2011), 357; Lumans, 295–96.

34. Lumans, 298.

35. Plakans (2007), 92; Plakans (2011), 357.

36. Ronald Gregor Suny, *The Soviet Experiment* (New York: Oxford University Press, 1998), 333.

37. These figures are based on estimates provided by Misiunas and Taagepera, 353.

38. Modris Eksteins, *Walking since Daybreak: A Story of Eastern Europe, World War II, and the Heart of Our Century* (New York: Mariner Books, 1999), 220.

39. Misiunas and Taagepera, 359–60.

40. Rein Taagepera, *Estonia: Return to Independence* (Boulder, CO: Westview Press, 1993), 86.

41. Arvydas Anušaukas, ed., *The Anti-Soviet Resistance in the Baltic States*, 3rd ed. (Vilnius: Akreta, 2001).

42. In an early Cold War operation between 1949 and 1955 the CIA worked with the British MI-6 to insert Polish, Lithuanian, Latvian, and Estonian agents into Poland and the Baltic states to link up with the anti-Soviet partisans, but the KGB was able to capture or kill nearly all the 42 agents who had landed in the Baltic.

43. Approximations of the number of people deported from the Baltic states during this period vary. Lithuania, which alone experienced 35 waves of deportations between 1941 and 1953, lost approximately 41,000 people to exile in the deportations of May 22–27, 1948. All together at least 200,000 people were deported from the Baltic states in 1940–1953.

44. Dovile Budryte, *Taming Nationalism? Political Community Building in the Post-Soviet Baltic States* (Burlington, VT: Ashgate, 2005), 189.

45. Anu Mai Kõll, *The Village and the Class War: Anti-Kulak Campaign in Estonia* (New York: Central European Press, 2014), 86, 184.

46. Mertelsmann, 89–97.

47. Misiunas and Taagepera, 112.

48. Violeta Davoliūtė, *The Making and Breaking of Soviet Lithuania* (London and New York: Routledge, 2013), 50–51.

7

Soviet Republics, 1953–1991

Chapter 6 examined the "totalitarian experience" of the Baltic states that began during World War II and concluded with Stalin's death in 1953. Although the arbitrary arrests, deportations, and mass mobilizations that defined the totalitarian era subsided, Soviet tyranny did not end with the tyrant's inevitable demise, for the center's priorities continued to take precedence over local ones, and the instruments of repression—the Communist Party, Soviet security forces, central planning institutions in Moscow—remained firmly in place for another 35 years.

Yet the decades between the Stalinist dictatorship and Gorbachev's liberalization may also be seen as a period of incubation—an era when Estonians, Latvians, and Lithuanians became increasingly educated and to a limited extent "Sovietized" while at the same time remaining aware of their national distinctiveness. If the local cultures suffered the indignities of Moscow's misguided attempts to create *homo sovieticus*—the Soviet Man, shorn of religious and national affiliations and committed to the realization of Lenin's dream of a socialist paradise—exile communities in the United States, Canada, and Australia helped keep alive the traditions of the Estonian, Latvian, and

Lithuanian peoples during a period of cultural grayness at home. For more than four decades the two worlds, the Baltic republics of the Union of Soviet Socialist Republics (USSR) and the exile communities abroad, remained separated by vast oceans and Soviet censors.

Despite the efforts of the republics' small dissident communities, the authoritarian single-party Soviet state ensured that this was largely an era of silence for the Baltic republics. But the world would come to hear their voices during the "Singing Revolution" that gently heralded the end both of foreign domination and of the once-mighty Soviet empire itself.

THE BALTIC COMMUNIST PARTIES

As instruments of control and repression, and as avenues for upward social mobility, the communist parties were the focal point of political and economic life in the Baltic republics throughout the Soviet era. The Communist Party of the Soviet Union (CPSU) imposed service obligations and ideological conformity on its members, but it also rewarded them with status and career opportunities. While an individual could usually choose whether or not to join the party, he or she could not hope to avoid its influence over the most personal aspects of daily life, ranging from access to higher education, housing, and consumer goods, to matters of ideology, religious belief, and individual conscience. Led by Marxist-Leninists eager to please Moscow, the local communist parties were the Balts' jailers and acted as mediators between themselves and the larger CPSU.

Despite the iron grip of the Communist Party, after 1953 life in the Baltic republics, as in the Soviet Union as a whole, became somewhat more relaxed. Following a bitter power struggle with his Politburo rivals, the proletarianized peasant Nikita Khrushchev (1894–1971) emerged as the new master of the Kremlin. The first part of the Khrushchev era was known as the "thaw" (Rus. *ottepel'*), a period of de-Stalinization of intellectual life and limited decentralization of the Soviet economy. While the regime's use of terror as an instrument of social control diminished substantially, Khrushchev's distrust of local nationalism meant that political power remained concentrated in Moscow. Despite the preponderance of power enjoyed by the CPSU, the thaw afforded the leaders of the Baltic communist parties an opportunity to try to block those policies, namely, breakneck industrialization and Russification, which they believed to be harmful to their republics.

Among the leading ideologues of Latvian "national communism" was Pauls Dzērve (1918–1961), a director of the Economics Institute in the Latvian Academy of Sciences in the late 1950s whose goal was to orient the republic's economy toward local needs by curtailing the existing stress on heavy industry (which required an imported labor force) and instead emphasizing consumer goods and the development of production in areas that corresponded with the local human and natural resource profiles.[1] A conflict began to take shape at the highest levels of the Communist Party of Latvia (LCP): while Dzērve's views were supported by Eduards Berklavs (1914–2004), a secretary of the Riga party organization and deputy chairman of the Latvian Council of Ministers from 1956 to 1958, the main spokesman for the Kremlin's viewpoint was Arvīds Pelše (1899–1983), a pro-Moscow Latvian who criticized such manifestations of local nationalism. The struggle was highlighted by the issues concerning the Pļaviņas Hydroelectric Dam, whose planned construction would flood a historically rich part of the Daugava River valley and would likely have unfavorable ecological consequences. Protests by prominent scientists and the Latvian press, never welcomed by Moscow, were the immediate result. The dam project, however, continued unimpeded and was largely completed by 1965.

The intraparty struggle ended after Khrushchev's visit to Riga in June 1959, following which Pelše replaced Jānis Kalnbērziņš as first secretary of the LCP. A massive purge of Latvia's "national communists" soon followed that echoed the Estonian purge of 1950 and with a similar result: from 1949 to 1961 some 2,000 members of the Party were expelled for being sympathetic to "national communism." In this case, however, unlike the purge of the Communist Party of Estonia (ECP) a decade earlier, the victims were not murdered: Berklavs was exiled to Vladimir province in Russia, although he was not removed from the party, and Dzērve lost both his position and his membership in the Academy of Sciences. Under Pelše and his successors the LCP became the most uncompromisingly orthodox of the Baltic party organizations for the next three decades.[2] Meanwhile, the trend toward gradual nativization stalled as Russians and "Moscow Latvians" maintained their dominance within the party leadership. By the early 1960s, the proportion of Latvians in the LCP stabilized at around 35–40 percent; even after 45 years of Soviet rule, Latvians constituted only 39.7 percent of the republic's party members. Yet it should be noted that many Latvians residing outside their republic, mostly in the Russian Republic (RSFSR) were members of the CPSU.

The nativization of the Estonian and Lithuanian parties proceeded with greater ease. By 1963 the percentage of ethnic Estonians in the

ECP exceeded 50 percent for the first time while the proportion of Lithuanians in their section of the CPSU was 61.5 percent in 1965 (up from 38 percent in 1953) as natives became more proportionately represented in the party's leading bodies, the Politburo and the Secretariat.[3] With the influence of nontitular cadres diminishing during the 1960s, the Estonian and Lithuanian parties were left largely in the hands of individuals who had authentic roots in the republics.

Meanwhile, the ranks of the Baltic sections of the CPSU continued to swell. In Latvia party membership increased from 42,000 in 1953 to 107,000 in 1967 to 182,000 members and candidates in 1988. By the Khrushchev era many ordinary people had come to accept not only the permanence of Soviet power, but also the legitimacy of the Communist Party as a means for achieving career goals. Despite the oppression that was a prime feature of Soviet rule, career opportunities that before the war had not been available to the poorer strata—factory and farm workers—opened up as the prospect of acquiring an education and becoming a party member increased. As membership in the party was no longer an indication of one's ideological engagement, even intellectuals who were privately skeptical about Marxism-Leninism increasingly took the view that joining it would allow them to exercise at least some influence on life in their republic. But even if most people did not choose to become party members, it seems clear that the peoples of the Baltic republics were increasingly opting to work within the system rather than against it. At no time, however, were the local party institutions in complete control of the Baltic republics: Moscow always had the final word.

The relative stability of the Estonian and Lithuanian parties in the post-Stalin decades may be demonstrated by the continuity of the top party leaders: Johannes (Ivan) Käbin remained in charge of the ECP for nearly three decades (1950–1978). His successor, Karl Vaino (b. 1923), a Russian-born Estonian, headed the party from 1978 to 1988, even though he never mastered his ancestral language. Lithuania's Antanas Sniečkus enjoyed an exceptionally long tenure, as he loyally served Stalin, Khrushchev, and finally Leonid Brezhnev (1906–1982), who came to power in a 1964 coup that sent his predecessor into retirement. After Sniečkus's death in 1974 the top post in Lithuania went to Petras Griškevičius, who retained it until his own demise in 1987.

In Latvia the party leadership stabilized once the purges ended in 1961 under the supervision of the reliably pro-Moscow Arvīds Pelše. In 1966, following Pelše's promotion to Moscow to head the Party Control Committee (he was also made a full Politburo member, where until 1983 he was one of the few non-Slavs to participate in the deliberations of the Party's leading body), Augusts Voss (1919–1994), another "Moscow Latvian," took the post of first secretary, in which capacity he continued his predecessor's Russophile policy until 1984.

Although the longtime leaders of the Baltic communist parties were unswervingly loyal to Moscow, each exemplified that brand of Soviet republican leader, especially common during the Brezhnev era, who was able to negotiate the treacherous waters of Kremlin politics while providing limited protection to the residents of their respective republics. Yet from Estonia to Kyrgyzstan no top leader of any republican communist party regarded himself as a mouthpiece of his people. Indeed, Sniečkus was no Lithuanian nationalist, and Käbin fell well short of being an Estonian patriot. Nevertheless, each had made peace with the local cultural establishment and each tolerated some nonthreatening manifestations of local national feeling.

CULTURE AND RELIGION

Not even during the relatively liberal post-Stalin years were national cultures allowed to flourish without guidance from Moscow, although the ideological restraints that remained in place during the Khrushchev years were considerably less severe than the restrictions that had been imposed upon art, literature, and other aspects of local culture during the first Soviet occupation in 1940–1941.

The ideological controls on art during the Stalin era may be illustrated by a document received by the Latvian Soviet Socialist Republic's (SSR's) Administration of Art Affairs in January 1941, which listed 120 themes to which Soviet artists were expected to pay particular attention, including:

- "Theme No. 27: The 1905 Revolution in Russia. A rally. The orator is held high on the workers' hands. Red flags."
- "Theme No. 120: The RK(b)P CC Politburo inspects a large new construction."[4]

No doubt similar directives were again issued after the war. Indeed, the darkest era for national cultures in the region was 1947 to 1953—Stalin's last years. While many of the most talented writers, intellectuals, and other cultural figures of the independence era had fled to the West rather than face persecution at the hands of Soviet authorities, those who remained behind risked punishment for sins such as "deviationism," "formalism," and "bourgeois nationalism." The official Soviet aesthetic, "socialist realism," which required writers and artists to glorify the working class and its struggle for emancipation, was imposed once again on the occupied territories. Thus only politically reliable authors could hope to see their works in print, since in order to publish one usually had to be a party member and a member of the republic branch of the guardian of literary orthodoxy, the Union of Writers. Likewise, artists and musicians also found their creative lives regulated by the Union of Artists and the Union of Composers.

On the other hand, conformist writer and artists were given a guaranteed material existence. Thus, although the occupation was unpleasant for the creative intelligentsia of the Baltic republics, as it was for society as a whole, the system provided material security for those who went along. And, as Latvian curator and art critic Hēlena Demakova (and minister of culture 2006–2009) reminded her readers, "those that did go along formed the majority."[5]

Since the early decades of the 20th century literature in the form of poems, novels, and short stories had been one of the most important means of cultural expression among the Estonians, Latvians, and Lithuanians, who by 1940 had already created their own pantheons of hallowed national writers (see chapter 5). However, during the period between the annexation of the Baltic states and Khrushchev's thaw in the mid-1950s, few literary works of high quality were published in the Baltic republics, or elsewhere in the USSR. Indeed, for at least a decade after the war, émigré writers living in the United States, Canada, Australia, and elsewhere were more productive than the writers who remained in their home countries, where they faced Soviet restrictions on artistic expression. However, by the late 1950s, with the return of many writers who had been expelled from the Estonian, Latvian, and Lithuanian writers' unions in the 1940s, local writers began to publish in greater quantity and quality as the captive mind began, within limits, to be emancipated. It was during the thaw that the Baltic peoples were also allowed to recover some of their literary past, as thousands of previously banned publications from the pre-1940 period were allowed back into print.

A significant event in the recovery of Estonian literary life was the publication of Rudolf Sirge's (1904–1970) *The Land and the People* (1956), a novel, also published in Russian, that depicted the trauma of 1940–1941 in the Estonian countryside. In 1958, Jaan Kross (1920–2007) debuted with a poetry collection, *The Coal Concentrator,* on his way to becoming Estonia's internationally best-known and most-translated writer. Among his most acclaimed works is *The Tsar's Madman* (1978), a novel that focused on the relationship between Estonians and Baltic Germans during the 19th century but has typically been interpreted as a metaphor for Soviet colonization in the 20th century.

Among the best-known Lithuanian writers during the post-Stalin decades was Justinas Marcinkevičius (1930–2011), a party member whose epic poem *Twentieth Spring* (1956) explored the postwar experience of dislocation and made him one of the most famous literary figures in the country.[6] In the 1960s Marcinkevičius turned to writing plays about Lithuanian national history, and later he would be regarded as one of the most prominent members of *Sajūdis*, the reform movement that led the struggle for Lithuanian independence. Among Marcinkevičius's most significant works was the play *Mindaugas* (1968), which examined the founding of the medieval Lithuanian state and its first king and consolidated its author's reputation, in the words of a later scholar, "as a national poet capable of evoking and consolidating the myths needed to ensure the nation's survival."[7]

One of the most beloved and best-translated Latvian writers during Soviet times was Vilis Lācis. However, as noted in chapter 6, as a Soviet official during the 1940s and 1950s, Lācis also bore some personal responsibility for the arrests and deportations of that tragic era. Although some Latvian writers were able during the mid-1950s to publish works that were somewhat critical of the Soviet experience, after the party purge in 1959–1961, Latvian cultural life stagnated. By the time Latvian intellectual life began to recover in the late 1960s Alberts Bels (b. 1938) had emerged as one of its leading lights. His short novel *The Investigator* (1967) evoked the Latvian national experience during the Stalin era, while *The Cage* (1972) used the metaphor of a person trapped in a cage to explore the fate of the individual in a standardized society. While audacious authors like Bels pushed against the boundaries of the permissible, their influence is difficult to assess. It seems safe to say that in the Baltic republics, as in the Soviet Union in general (and everywhere), less serious genres such as detective novels generally had greater popular appeal than the works of nonconformist writers.

Yet thousands of Estonians, Latvians, and Lithuanians (and Russians, too) continued to participate in the local folksong festivals, which remained one of the most visible displays of national culture in the Baltic republics. A Latvian folksong festival held in Daugavpils in July 1959 involved 5,000 singers and attracted an audience of 70,000. Still larger festivals were held in Estonian cities in 1965 and 1969. These were opportunities for local peoples to express national pride in ways acceptable, and sometimes unacceptable, to Moscow. The latter was the case at the 1965 festival in Estonia, when an audience of 120,000 demanded a repeat performance of the song "My Homeland is My Love," an unofficial anthem of the Estonian people. Long after the hymns to Stalin disappeared, song festivals were expected to make a clear display of the local inhabitants' allegiance to the USSR, for the song festivals were not merely exhibitions of pride in one's national culture, but they were also intended to be demonstrations of Soviet unity, as Russian songs and songs and dances from other Union republics were a regular feature of the Baltic song festivals into the late 1980s.

Still, Moscow allowed the titular nations of each Soviet republic some latitude in developing and expressing national culture. Thus, as noted earlier, each of the Baltic republics had its own creative unions for writers, composers, and artists and each had its own newspapers that appeared in the local language. These, of course, were complimented by a wide variety of Russian-language periodicals, for Russian remained the *lingua franca* of all the republics. While Estonians, Latvians, and Lithuanians all had their own schools where they were taught in their own language (as did the Baltic Russians), Russian was taught virtually everywhere. Among the non-Russian minorities in the Baltic states, the only one to acquire cultural rights during the Soviet era was the Polish minority in Lithuania, which had its own Polish-language schools as well as the only Polish newspaper in the entire USSR.[8]

In the religious sphere a brief relaxation of Soviet policy after Stalin's death was followed by further repression. The return home in the mid-1950s of a number of those priests who managed to survive the earlier deportations contributed to a recovery of religious life, but this was offset by the inauguration of an antireligious campaign 1957 that resulted in the closing of numerous churches throughout the USSR. Although the impact of the Soviet antireligious measures on personal belief is difficult to measure, it is evident that external manifestations of religiosity, such as participation in church ceremonies, declined during the 1960s. This was especially true of Estonians and Latvians, who endured a deficit of functioning churches, Protestant pastors, and bibles. Lithuanians, whose national identity was closely tied to Catholicism, were better able to train young men for the priesthood and perpetuate their religious traditions.

Of course, for the new "Soviet man," religion was little more than outdated superstition—a relic of the past to be discarded. An individual's Soviet identity as an enlightened worker and a defender of communism was to supersede his religious and national identity. One instrument commonly used for the creation of a Soviet identity was sport. When the Soviet Union participated in international athletic competitions, such as the Olympics beginning in 1956, athletes competed as members of Soviet national teams; thus individual successes by Baltic athletes were seen as successes for the Soviet system.

Although the Estonian, Latvian, and Lithuanian republics could not field their own teams for the Olympics or for most other international competitions, republic teams did sometimes compete against the national teams of Soviet bloc countries such as Czechoslovakia or East Germany. A Latvian basketball team, the Army Sports Club (ASK) Riga, even won the 1958 European Cup.

SOCIOECONOMIC DEVELOPMENTS

From the Stalin era onward, the Baltic republics were the most modernized and industrialized of the 15 Soviet republics and were thoroughly enmeshed in a highly centralized economic network. While the goal of eliminating the private sector completely was beyond the power of even the Communist Party—a shadow economy continued to provide services that remained a low priority for the USSR State Planning Commission (Gosplan) in Moscow—the subjection of the local economies to the interests of the center took place quickly and decisively after the war as the Five Year Plan was extended to Moscow's newest satrapies. If Gosplan controlled Soviet planning as a whole, local planning was in the hands of the State Planning Commissions of the Estonian, Latvian, and Lithuanian SSRs, whose authority was limited to the development of those sectors that were under the jurisdiction of each republic's Council of Ministers. While the indigenous Baltic elites controlled only the weaker and smaller economic sectors, Russians and other Slavic immigrants built, managed, and staffed much of the more powerful all-Union sector of the economy, which benefited from its closer ties with Soviet authorities in Moscow.

In the late 1950s the establishment of regional economic councils (Rus. *sovnarkhozy*) heralded a shift toward limited economic decentralization. The new policy meant that planners in each republic would enjoy greater autonomy and less interference from Moscow. By 1962 however, Khrushchev's colleagues in the Presidium had grown weary of their boss's unpredictable schemes and the country soon reverted to centralized economic planning. Within a few years the *sovnarkhozy* were abolished and the power of the central ministries expanded once again, thereby disabusing the republics of any illusion that they might control their own resources or solve economic and workforce problems on their own.

Although production slowed somewhat during the 1960s, industry in the Baltic republics continued to develop more rapidly than in the rest of the USSR. Many enterprises focused on provisioning the military, which maintained a heavy presence in each of the Baltic republics. As the headquarters of the Baltic Military District since July 1945, Riga and the Latvian republic were especially important to the defense of the USSR. Airfields were located at Liepāja, Tukums, Jelgava, and Lielvārde, and a series of naval ports protected the Baltic coast. An arsenal of nuclear rockets was located at Zeltiņi in eastern Latvia, while an early warning system was installed at the Skrunda base in Courland to locate enemy rockets before they could reach the USSR. A virtual ghost town in the postwar years, Liepāja was once again used as a naval base and became home to a fleet of submarines. The Soviets also located a number of important military installations in Estonia and Lithuania through which hundreds of thousands of soldiers, sailors, pilots, and support personnel revolved. It should come as little surprise, then, that many enterprises in the Baltic republics that manufactured vehicles, electronics, and clothing were as important to the military as they were to Soviet consumers.

Local consumers benefited from Gosplan's emphasis on light industry and food processing in the Baltics. To the other republics they exported energy, machinery, industrial equipment, and some consumer goods and agricultural products. However, with few natural resources aside from oil shale (in Estonia), fertilizers, and timber, the Baltic republics were importers of necessary industrial raw materials such as coal, iron, and cotton. Despite this disadvantage, the Baltic republics were relatively productive: with only 2.8 percent of the total Soviet population, they were responsible for an estimated 3.6 percent of the Soviet gross domestic product by the end of the 1960s.[9] Commercial ports that had atrophied during the independence era experienced a revival during the Soviet era. Ventspils, for example, became the USSR's busiest Baltic port by the 1980s. As the terminus of an oil pipeline, the city became the main channel for Soviet petroleum exports to Western markets. Tallinn and Klaipēda experienced a similar revival as conduits for the Soviet Union's increasing trade with the outside world.

As a result of this increased productivity, Baltic wages and incomes, especially in Estonia and Latvia, exceeded the Soviet average. Tuuli Jaik, an ordinary Estonian woman born in 1910, recalled the post-Stalin years as a period of peace and security, when "People got hired more easily and without the long personal biography."

Soon I found a job as a night watchman, and after that worked in the Sangar sewing factory, doing all kinds of jobs; the last one was ironing denim trousers. This was demanding piecework, but the wages were higher than I had ever earned before. Poverty and misery were long since over. I retired from the sewing factory in 1965 at 55 years of age and began drawing a fairly large pension—52 roubles a month. Even as a factory worker I had enough money both to live on and save in the bank.[10]

Collective farmers also saw their lives improve during the 1960s and 1970s. Allowed to farm subsidiary private plots for their personal consumption and to sell their goods in local markets (the private plots produced a large proportion of the meat, eggs, potatoes, vegetables, berries, and fruit consumed in the Baltic republics), rural laborers enjoyed incomes that often exceeded those of urban industrial workers.

Although their relatively high incomes translated into superior living standards for Latvians and Estonians, living standards still remained well below those of Scandinavian and west European norms—and by some measures even below the levels enjoyed by the citizens of the Baltic republics in 1939. Indeed, even high per capita incomes did not necessarily translate into purchasing power in a Soviet economy that was deficit in the production of consumer goods. Still, consumers living in the Estonian, Latvian, and Lithuanian SSRs did not fare badly during the 1968–1975 period, which was the peak era of Soviet consumerism. Indeed, the prospect of acquiring a car, a summer cottage, a washing machine, quality furniture, or a trip abroad encouraged conformity and only reinforced the locals' outward acceptance of the existing system. As Tuuli Jaik recalled: "Life at the beginning of the Soviet era had been very hard. But the situation improved over time, unemployment diminished, and wages gradually increased. For anyone who was the least bit thrifty, it was easy to save money after everyday living expenses were met, especially in the last decades."[11]

But the relative advantages enjoyed by the Baltic republics were not limited to the higher standard of living enjoyed by their citizens. Having been added in 1959 to the list of cities that foreigners could visit, Tallinn, Riga, and Vilnius frequently hosted foreign delegations and participated in cultural and scientific exchanges. By this time the Baltic republics had gained a reputation as the "Soviet West"—a place where leading members of the Soviet intelligentsia and others could travel "abroad" while never leaving the Soviet homeland. Performers from the Baltic republics toured foreign countries and their athletic teams began to appear in international competitions. It was not long before Estonians in the northern regions, already able listen to Finnish radio, could watch television programs broadcast from Helsinki (even if most Soviet programs watched by Estonians were in Russian), and after 1965 thousands were able to visit Finland via the ferry line from

Tallinn. No less than Tallinn and Riga, the Lithuanian capital Vilnius, which had been a neglected provincial town under Polish rule during the interwar period, became a conduit through which Western influences (forbidden literature, U.S. films, jazz) slipped into the USSR despite the surveillance of Soviet security forces (KGB).

As diligently as Moscow and the local communist parties worked to Sovietize the Baltic republics, in many respects they remained foreign to other Soviet visitors and distinctly "Western." Local attitudes and outlooks were hardly less Western than the architectural heritage of their cities. As eager consumers of Western entertainment and fashions, the peoples of the Baltic republics often found Western cultural imports more attractive than those from Russia. Indeed, as the most European parts of the Soviet Union, the Baltic republics were simply able to enjoy greater contacts with the West—which no doubt contributed to the locals' consciousness of the discrepancies between the quality of life in the West and in the Soviet Union. Even if the authorities invested in the rebuilding and modernization of the three republics, a brief trip abroad or a few minutes of foreign television would have been sufficient to convince anyone but the most deluded that the Soviet regime for all its promises of modernization and plenty had failed to surpass that which was taken for granted in "capitalist" countries. To take one of the most pressing examples, the deficit of housing didn't even begin to be addressed until the late 1950s, at which point the regime began the construction of monotonously uniform residential blocks—not only in the cities, but in the countryside for agricultural laborers as well—that were exactly like those located in Moscow, Novosibirsk, and Turkmenistan. Indeed, even if the peoples of the Baltic republics enjoyed a higher standard of living than most other Soviet citizens, their conditions were still demonstrably worse than those in the Western countries to which they frequently compared themselves. This was especially the case after economic stagnation set in during the mid-1970s and shortages and queues once again became a part of daily life.

Meanwhile, social trends in the Baltic republics reflected the perils of rapid modernization and urbanization, aggravated by factors particular to life under Soviet rule. Social indicators in Lithuania, like economic development, generally tended to follow the patterns prevailing in Estonia and Latvia. For example, Estonian and Latvian birthrates had always been among the lowest in the USSR, bottoming out in the mid-1960s. In defiantly Catholic Lithuania, which had earlier enjoyed higher birthrates, the decline began in the 1960s and steadily continued thereafter. In Estonia and Latvia, an old tradition of late marriage contributed to this trend, but significant roles were also played by inadequate housing, increasing divorce rates, and terminated pregnancies. In the absence of reliable alternatives, abortion (legalized in 1955) became the most common method of birth control in the USSR. That the numbers of registered abortions in each of the Baltic republics, as in the USSR more generally, well exceeded the numbers of live births remains one of the sadder facts about life under communism.

There were also other negative social indicators during these relatively prosperous decades. An increase in crime in the 1970s paralleled similar developments in the West, while rising alcohol consumption in the Baltic republics was part of a general Soviet trend and was arguably a consequence of the state's dependence on the revenues raised by the sale of alcohol. By 1970 Estonians, who preferred hard spirits to wine or beer, consumed 50 percent more alcohol per capita than residents of the RSFSR or the United States. Trends in Lithuania and Latvia were similar, with tragic results: in Latvia, alcohol was a factor in an alarming number of auto accidents and in the majority of drownings and crimes; alcohol was also surely a catalyst in the growing divorce rates and, toward the end of the Soviet era (and continuing into the 1990s), a catastrophic drop in male life expectancy.

RUSSIFICATION, NATIONALISM, AND DISSENT

Among the Soviet-era trends that most disturbed the locals was the continuing influx of Russians and other immigrants into the Baltic republics. Latvia in particular continued to attract immigrants, typically unskilled people fleeing the poverty of the Soviet collective farms to find work in construction or factories. By 1970 the Latvians' share of the republic's population had fallen below 57 percent, with Latvians accounting for less than half of all urban dwellers. Likewise, by 1970 natives accounted for just over 68 percent of the population of the Estonian republic, while the corresponding figure for Lithuanians was 80 percent, which held steady through the end of the Soviet era. It would appear that the arguments of longtime Lithuanian party boss Antanas Sniečkus for reduced immigration and for the planning of industrial projects in a way that was more consistent with the republic's resource profile were rather more successful than similar arguments by Latvian or Estonian leaders, assuming they were made at all. Yet Lithuania was never much of a magnet for Russians in the first place: since Lithuanian cities were less developed and had never had large Russian communities, they were less attractive to Slavic immigrants than cities such as Riga and Tartu, each of which had been Russian cultural centers during the tsarist era.

The cultural Russification of Baltic cities was further facilitated by the adoption of a new educational system throughout the USSR in 1959.[12] Henceforward, the Russian language became a "voluntary" subject in Baltic schools where it was not already the language of instruction. In practice this meant that non-Russians were pressured to become bilingual—practically unavoidable for those who aspired to higher study or professional careers—while immigrants could continue to speak Russian. The results of this policy were reflected in the Soviet census of 1970, which showed that while only 18 percent of ethnic Russians living in Latvia, the most heavily Russified of the Baltic republics, could speak the native tongue, nearly half of all Latvians could speak Russian. By 1989 this could be said of four out of every five Latvians, who enjoyed Russian-language television program and feature films and who had little choice but to use the Russian language in the workplaces, in the shops, and on the streets of Latvia's larger cities where Latvians now formed a minority.

Yet Soviet nationalities policies remained unclear and inconsistent during the era of "developed socialism." Khrushchev's successor Leonid Brezhnev, the top party leader from 1964 to 1982, attempted to clarify the Soviet Union's nationalities policy at the 24th Party Congress in March 1971 when he announced the emergence of a "new historical community of people—the Soviet people." Although, Brezhnev now declared, the party intended to foster "a spirit of profound respect for all nations and nationalities," he emphasized that it would work to promote the further "drawing-together" (Rus. *sblizhenie*) of nations.[13] Such pronouncements have been often been mistaken for an intent to completely assimilate the Baltic peoples into a larger "Soviet" nation. However, this conclusion must be temporized by Moscow's continued support for national cultures in the Soviet republics. As noted earlier, the traditional song festivals continued throughout the Soviet period (if modified by the inclusion of performances by representatives of other Soviet nations) and considerable resources were devoted to literature, film, art, and all manner of cultural expression in each of the Baltic republics as long as they were not overtly political or suggest an anti-Russian perspective.

An important arena for the "drawing-together" of the nationalities was the Soviet system of higher education. Students from each of the 15 Union republics were enrolled in more than 500 Soviet universities, academies, and institutes, and thousands of students from other Union republics attended higher schools in Estonia, Latvia, and Lithuania. Likewise, the number of Baltic students studying outside their republics, usually in the RSFSR, was comparable to the number of

Estonians, Latvians, and Lithuanians enrolled in native institutions. In 1974–1975, the Estonian SSR had 6 institutions of higher education, while Latvia and Lithuania had 10 and 12, respectively; most, however, were specialized institutes or academies rather than universities. In addition, each republic had its own Academy of Sciences, which served as the republics' main research centers.

Immigrants (primarily Russians) and natives often chose different educational and career paths. While immigrants tended to concentrate in technological fields such as engineering, local peoples were more likely to choose the educational, cultural, and artistic fields, in addition to the study of agriculture and economics. This is indicative of a more general bifurcation of the lives of natives and immigrants in the Baltic republics. As one Russian journalist observed in 1988: "The population was divided along linguistic lines. The Estonians had their own kindergartens, schools, enterprises, and regions. The Russians had theirs."[14] Indeed, in Latvia and Estonia, where the concentration of Russians was higher than in Lithuania, society was split between natives and immigrants, each with its own language, institutions, educational preferences, industrial specialization, and geographical concentration. Yet most of the immigrants were transient, leaving well before they could be integrated, taking up scarce housing, rarely mastering the local language, and remaining ignorant of the culture. Resentment was the inevitable result.

The Brezhnev regime's efforts to strengthen the unity of the country by promoting the "drawing-together" of its many nations and nationalities coincided with, and was a response to, growing manifestations of local nationalism throughout the Soviet Union. In the Baltic republics, as in Russia itself, such expressions of national feeling were mostly connected to a growing interest in folklore, culture, and local history. However, at least two Latvian underground organizations were uncovered in the early 1960s, and attempts to create an underground Estonian nationalist party resulted in a series of political trials in 1970. Rather than being indicative of a persistent pattern of anti-Soviet resistance, such activity was in reality episodic and limited to small groups and individuals. Political defiance was the exception rather than the rule. Yet as the Soviet state strove to attain international respectability it was no longer able to terrorize the population into submission as it did in Stalin's day. By the 1970s the old methods of shooting or deporting the unreliable had been replaced by imprisonment in psychiatric hospitals and, in some cases, exile abroad. Certainly this decline in the risk factor, combined with rising expectations, political information supplied by Western radio broadcasts, and an indelible memory of statehood and independence, contributed to the growth of nationalist and dissident movements in the Baltic republics in the 1970s.

Few events raised more questions about Moscow's imperial pretensions among Soviet dissidents and among communists abroad than the Soviet response to the Prague Spring of 1968. If the Czechs and Slovaks who tried to create "socialism with a human face" offered a more attractive alternative (to many) to Soviet socialism, Moscow saw the movement as a threat to its authority in the communist bloc and forcibly squelched the democratic-minded reforms recently embraced by the Czechoslovak leadership. Having displayed its will to its satellites in eastern Europe, the CPSU began a counteroffensive against "nationalist deviations" within the USSR, and in troublesome Lithuania in particular, where small-scale dissent took several forms in the late 1960s and 1970s. Some dissidents were defenders of the rights of the Catholic Church and of religious believers in general; some advanced the cause of human rights; still others demanded national rights and self-determination. Although each of these movements overlapped—indeed, to Lithuanians, Catholicism and nationality are closely related—rarely was dissent expressed through violence.

An exception was the two days of rioting and public demonstrations in Kaunas that followed the public self-immolation of 19-year-old Romas Kalanta on May 14, 1972. However, since most dissidents sought to force the regime to observe its own laws and international agreements, they usually emphasized legal and nonviolent methods of protest. *Samizdat'* (the Russian word for self-publishing) was a common form of dissident activity and it was used to great effect especially by Lithuanian religious activists, who in March 1972 began to publish *The Chronicle of the Lithuanian Catholic Church* in imitation of the Moscow human rights publication, *Chronicle of Current Events*. Other well-known Lithuanian dissident groups included the civil rights organizations Catholic Committee for the Defense of Human Rights and the Lithuanian Helsinki Watch Group. Meanwhile, the ideas of nationalist dissidents, focusing on the restoration of Lithuanian independence, were reflected in publications such as *Varpas* (The Bell), *Perspektyvos* (Perspectives), and *Aušra* (Dawn), which was named after a patriotic newspaper from the previous century's "national awakening" and whose stated aim was to awaken Lithuania from its "spiritual sleep."

For more than a decade official reaction to Lithuanian dissent vacillated between a relatively soft approach and a hardline one. Arrests were followed by trials rather than deportations or shootings. A KGB crackdown on dissident activity in the early 1980s stifled the voices of many critics who would have to wait until the Gorbachev era to be heard from again. Nevertheless, despite official repression, the

Lithuanian church, buoyed by the 1978 election of the Polish bishop Karol Wojtyła as Pope John Paul II, continued to defy the regime and to defend the rights of believers that were guaranteed by the Soviet constitution.

If dissent in Lithuania was more outspoken than in the other Baltic republics, this was due in part to the predominant role Catholicism played there. The completely subservient Lutheran church played almost no role in Estonian or Latvian dissident movements. Rather than having a national–religious orientation, the quieter Estonian movement, a reflection of the traditional cautiousness and stoicism of the Estonian people, is better characterized as national–democratic. As in Lithuania, however, the main weapons of Estonian dissidents were demonstrations and *samizdat'*. Another method was to draw the West's attention to their country's plight, as did the Estonian Democratic Movement and the Estonian National Front. Their joint appeal to the United Nations, issued in October 1972, listed the abuses of human and political rights and demanded the restoration of Estonian independence.

Led by communists who completely lacked national feeling, Latvia was the most repressed and most Russified of the Baltic republics and its dissident activity was the least conspicuous. The most noteworthy document of Latvian dissent was the "Letter of the Seventeen Communists" (1972), which called on the communist parties of Romania, Yugoslavia, France, Spain, and Austria to help Latvian communists correct the mistakes of the CPSU—foremost among which was the official policy of "Great Russian chauvinism." Yet even this act drew far less attention and caused far less embarrassment to the Kremlin than the defection of admired cultural figures such as Mikhail Baryshnikov, the Riga-born leading male dancer of the Kirov Ballet, whose flight in 1974 seems to have been motivated less by politics than by a desire for artistic growth.[15]

Solidarity among dissidents of the different Baltic republics was virtually absent during the Brezhnev era. However, the 40th anniversary of the Molotov–Ribbentrop Pact, on August 23, 1979, did not go unnoticed in the three republics. To commemorate the occasion, a group of local activists, mostly Lithuanians and a handful of Latvians and Estonians, addressed a public appeal to foreign governments, the USSR, and the secretary general of the United Nations. In the appeal they demanded the pact's publication along with an acknowledgement of its secret protocols on the division of eastern Europe. This would not be the last time that activists in the Baltics would demand an investigation into this notorious document.

At the conclusion of the Brezhnev era, a time that would later be remembered as a period of "stagnation" (Rus. *vremia zastoia*), there were few reasons to believe that the Baltic republics would achieve their independence anytime soon, if ever. By this time, a KGB crackdown on dissident activity throughout the USSR had, with few exceptions (notably Lithuanian Catholics), effectively stifled open expressions of nationalist or democratic thought. The presence of more than 150,000 Soviet officers and soldiers in the region further discouraged any misguided thoughts of independence. While Western countries in general and the United States in particular suffered from oil shortages, economic sluggishness, political scandals, and foreign policy setbacks, the USSR appeared strong enough to brook any challenges, even if it was already becoming apparent that the economy was slowing down. The Soviet Union had long ago achieved nuclear parity with the United States, and with the exception of troublesome Poland its control over its satellite states remained firm as socialist revolutions encouraged by Moscow brewed in numerous countries in Africa and Central America. The oil and natural gas that flowed from newly exploited deposits in Siberia contributed to the postponement of a reckoning with Soviet economic realities.[16]

Although popular enthusiasm for communist ideology by this time had grown shallow, Soviet leaders were never more confident of the USSR's global position and of the country's glorious future. With regional leaders maintaining order in what amounted to personal fiefdoms, the republics were relatively quiet. To some observers, the creation of a truly "Soviet" people was not a utopian dream but a certifiable fact: the new Soviet Man—little concerned with his national or religious identity, loyal to the Soviet state, and dedicated to building a communist society—was coming into being. Although his language and culture would be Russian, his worldview would be thoroughly Soviet. In this context, some observers placed the future of the Baltic peoples as distinct nationalities in doubt. For example, in 1979, the scholar Hélène Carrère d'Encausse proposed three possible destinies for the non-Russian nationalities of the USSR: (1) assimilation, (2) survival and development, or (3) weakness and possible extinction. According to this analysis, among the USSR's European peoples, Belarusians were in the first category, Ukrainians were in the second, and the Baltic peoples—the Estonians and Latvians in particular—were in the third.[17]

The demographic facts appeared to bear out this conclusion. In 1980, the combined total of Latvians, Estonians, and Lithuanians living in their native republics barely reached 5 million out of a total Soviet population of 262 million. Birthrates in the Baltic republics were among the lowest in the USSR, with most of the population growth

in the Baltic republics during the 1970s being the result of immigration. Nevertheless, d'Encausse's sad prediction underestimated the
vitality of the Baltic peoples. While certainly on the defensive, Baltic
national communities nevertheless managed to retain the use of
their native language and were in fact, countered political scientist
V. Stanley Vardys (himself a native of Lithuania), "strong, competi-
tive, and very self-conscious."[18] Moreover, the pace of Russian colonization could no longer be sustained, for Russians suffered from low
birthrates, too; "the seemingly inexhaustible reservoir of would-be
colonists was drying up," recalled the Estonia-born social scientist
Rein Taagepera.[19]

While Soviet terror had long ago given way to a more "normal"
life in the Baltic republics, most Estonians, Latvians, and Lithuanians
were resigned to economic stagnation and shortages, resigned to the
rising pressure of Russification, resigned, for the foreseeable future,
to communist and Soviet rule. Far from addressing the concerns of its
dissatisfied citizens, in the early 1980s the regime took strong police
measures to stifle any popular expressions of discontent in the Baltics
and throughout the USSR. The message was clear: Soviet policies were
made by the Communist Party alone.

GLASNOST' IN THE BALTICS

Yet the Communist Party was in fact composed of human beings,
and some of them eventually began to reassess the results of the great
Soviet experiment and found them wanting. This was particularly true
of Mikhail S. Gorbachev (b. 1931), a career servant of the party whose
appointment to the post of general secretary in April 1985 signified
a generational change at the top of the Soviet leadership that made
possible the revolutionary events that soon followed. In contrast to
the dull and frequently infirm leaders who came before him—Leonid
Brezhnev (1964–1982), Yuri Andropov (1982–1984) and Konstantin
Chernenko (1984–1985)—Gorbachev was relatively young, energetic,
and charismatic. That he would be the last Soviet ruler, the last CPSU
general secretary, or even the architect of a radical reform program,
was not at all evident in in the spring of 1985. Indeed, during the first
years of Gorbachev's leadership the USSR remained a heavily centralized and intolerant police state.

In an effort both to combat local corruption and consolidate his own
position, in his first year in power Gorbachev embarked on the biggest purge of the Communist Party elite since Stalin's day. Conservative Brezhnev-era officials were the first to go. While Lithuania's First

Secretary Petras Griškevičius and Estonia's Karl Vaino managed to avoid the initial sweep, the apparatuses of their parties were quickly overhauled. In Latvia, change at the top had preceded Gorbachev: in 1984, First Secretary Augusts Voss was promoted to the post of chairman of the USSR Supreme Soviet's Committee for Nationalities and was replaced in Riga by Boriss Pugo (1937–1991), a Russian Latvian who had headed the Latvian KGB since 1980.

Gorbachev's long-term plan was unclear during his first two years at the helm. *Perestroika* ("restructuring"), a Russian word that

Soviet leader Mikhail Gorbachev, left, converses with Algirdas Brazauskas, leader of the breakaway Communist Party of Lithuania, on January 13, 1990 in Vilnius. While Gorbachev was unable to stop the Baltics' drive toward independence, the popular Brazauskas later ended up serving as president of the democratic Republic of Lithuania. (AP Photo/Victor Yurchenko)

gained currency in 1987, aimed to reinvigorate the stagnant Soviet economy. Beyond that broad aim, however, the parameters of *perestroika* were ill-defined. Indeed, *perestroika* was a largely improvised policy that began as an attempt to unleash the energies and talents of the Soviet people but ultimately took on a life of its own. To overcome the bureaucratic resistance to restructuring, a policy of *glasnost'* ("openness") was articulated that aimed to encourage criticism of entrenched elites. *Glasnost'*, in its narrow conception, was the necessary corollary to *perestroika*; however, it was not long before *glasnost'* too exceeded the designs of its architect. As Anatol Lieven, a journalist of Baltic German extraction who was based in the Baltic republics in the early 1990s, observed: "Glasnost was inevitably going to bring a new honesty about the past; but since the entire Communist claim to leadership was based on lies, this honesty would sooner or later bring down the whole system."[20]

Russian nationalist intellectuals were the first to seize the opportunity provided by *glasnost'*, as they dominated public debate during much of the first two years of the Gorbachev era. At first their main concern was ecology—in particular Soviet plans to embark on a massive project to divert several northern and Siberian rivers to arid Central Asia, which was halted in August 1986 after a vigorous debate in the official Soviet press. This victory, occurring in the wake of the Chernobyl disaster the previous spring, encouraged the efforts of Latvians who were concerned about the possible environmental impact of a proposed hydroelectric complex, to be built at Daugavpils on Latvia's largest river, the Daugava. Popular protest in the form of letter writing, led by the Environmental Protection Club, successfully pressured the authorities to halt construction in November 1987. The plans of mayor Alfrēds Rubiks (b. 1935) to build an underground metro system in Riga, which would have required the importation of thousands of workers from the Soviet interior, were greeted with popular disapproval and were quickly scotched by the authorities.

Meanwhile, Estonian intellectuals discussed their concerns about the potential environmental impact of intensive phosphate excavation in Kabala-Toolse, a plan that would also require the immigration of tens of thousands of laborers. If the protests that took place at the University of Tartu in April 1987 were overlooked by the official press, Estonian media reports about the ecological impact of phosphate mining helped convince the Soviet leadership to abandon the project in October. In Lithuania, the environmental debate focused on the Ignalina Atomic Energy Station, a Chernobyl-type installation located only 80 miles from Vilnius. Opposition to its planned expansion was one of the first causes to mobilize Lithuanian activists in the spring of 1988. The Baltic peoples, and soon afterward other Soviet nationalities, were quick to grasp the potential for change in this new, more tolerant atmosphere as people learned to organize and to test the limits of the permissible.

Thus Gorbachev's attempt to produce guided reform from above had the unintended effect of inducing challenges to Soviet policies, which in the Baltic republics metamorphosed into national protests. Latvians were the first of the Baltic peoples to confront Soviet authorities openly. On June 14, 1987, a date that coincided with the Soviet occupation in June 1940 and the mass deportations of June 1941, thousands of Latvians took part in a demonstration near the Freedom Monument in Riga, organized by the tiny human rights group Helsinki-86. Following the success of this demonstration, others soon followed as Western broadcasts via Voice of America and Radio Free Europe increased local awareness of the political situation in the USSR and likely emboldened the dissenters, thousands of whom gathered in each of the Baltic capitals on August 23, 1987, to protest the Molotov–Ribbentrop Pact of 1939. These demonstrations, like the still larger rally that took place in Riga on November 18, the anniversary of Latvia's declaration of independence in 1918, were harbingers of the massive "calendar demonstrations" of 1988 and 1989.

At the heart of the Baltic challenges to Moscow was the matter of historical truth. While the official line (discussed in chapter 6) claimed that the Baltic republics voluntarily joined the USSR in 1940, many if not most of their inhabitants regarded their republics as occupied territories. The liberalized atmosphere ushered in by Gorbachev's policy of *glasnost'* made it possible for Baltic societies to address the darker aspects of Soviet rule in the region—the occupation and annexation of 1940, the deportations of 1941 and afterward, the drive for collectivization.

Intellectuals in the Latvian Writers' Union, an organization whose main purpose had been to censor and control Latvian writers before it become a haven for nonconformist intellectuals in the 1960s, were among the first to challenge the standard Soviet interpretation of the events of 1940. On June 1–2, 1988, the issue was debated at a union plenum, whose speeches were subsequently published for the reading public. Among the plenum's numerous resolutions were: Stalin forcibly annexed Latvia to the USSR; Latvian ought to be the state language of the republic; political and taxing authority should be devolved to the republican and local levels; and, most damning of all: the secret protocols of the Molotov–Ribbentrop Pact should be published.

Reformist Latvian writers were instrumental in the creation of the Popular Front of Latvia (PFL) in the weeks ahead, following the creation of analogous organizations—each ostensibly in favor of *perestroika*—in Estonia and Lithuania. Meanwhile, a group of former political prisoners, human rights advocates, and environmental and cultural activists announced their intention to create the Latvian National Independence Movement (LNIM), a more confrontational organization than the PFL. With the Communist Party maintaining its monopoly of power, Latvia did not by any means enjoy full political liberty; however, the activities of the PFL and the LNIM, and indeed the fact of their very existence, indicated that a Latvian "reawakening" was in full swing by mid-1988.

Although Gorbachev's restrained approach to *glasnost'* indicated that certain subjects were not open to debate, this did not deter Estonian reformers from challenging Soviet orthodoxy in the economic arena. In the fall of 1987 establishment reformers in Estonia, emboldened by their success in getting Soviet authorities to halt projects for new phosphate mines, published a plan for the republic's economic autonomy. Concerned with the impact that the hyper-centralization of the Soviet economy was having on Estonia, this group recommended that enterprises and resources presently managed by Soviet authorities be placed under Estonian jurisdiction and that market principles and prices be introduced in interrepublic and foreign trade. The idea was in effect to turn the Estonian republic into a "self-managing economic zone." Although rejected by the ECP, the proposal proved popular and anticipated the growth of a nationalist movement whose minimum goal was "republic sovereignty" (as guaranteed in the Soviet constitution) for Estonia. By the spring of 1988 the blue–black–white flag of the prewar Estonian state reappeared at demonstrations throughout the country.

Responding to Gorbachev's encouragement of the creation of "informal" groups for the support of *perestroika*, in April 1988 Estonian reformers, both establishment communists and independent intellectuals, created a "Popular Front for the Support of Restructuring in the USSR," which soon became the Popular Front of Estonia (PFE). Edgar Savisaar (b. 1950), a signatory of the economic plan introduced the previous fall (and later a prime minister of the independent Republic of Estonia), proposed the Popular Front's creation and emerged as its leader. Although the PFE's members were overwhelmingly ethnic

Estonians, membership was not based on nationality but rather on common goals, including economic sovereignty for Estonia, greater concern for the environment, and limits on immigration.

ECP First Secretary Karl Vaino soon fell victim to the changing mood in Estonia: on June 17, 1988, he was dismissed (over 100,000 people went out the next day to celebrate) and replaced by an Estonian, Vaino Väljas (b. 1931), a native Estonian and a moderate advocate of the PFE platform. Although Väljas hoped that the ECP and the PFE could work together to bring about the necessary changes in a controlled manner acceptable to Moscow, one of his first acts was to introduce the use of either Estonian or Russian at meetings of the ECP's leading body—a move that hardly endeared him to the activists of the Popular Front. Nevertheless, by the autumn of 1988 the entire leadership of the ECP was on the side of the reformers. But even if the Estonian section of the Communist Party was indeed transforming itself, it continually lagged behind the Popular Front, which by November was calling for an overhaul of the federal structure of the USSR with the goal of assigning greater rights to the republics. By this time other, more radical Estonian organizations, such as the Estonian Heritage Society, dedicated to restoring pre-Soviet monuments and led by future Estonian prime minister Mart Laar, as well as the Estonian National Independence Party, were making an even bolder demand: they wanted nothing less than the reestablishment of the Estonian state that existed before 1940.

SINGING REVOLUTION

While the Czechs call their struggle in 1989 to liberate their country from communist rule the "Velvet Revolution," in the Baltic states this period was stretched out over four years (1987–1991) and is remembered as the "Singing Revolution." Continuing a tradition begun during the national awakenings of the 19th century, the Baltic peoples used their traditional song festivals as a means of expressing their distinctiveness and national unity. Long since abandoned were old Soviet anthems such as "Latvians Sing Praise to Stalin" and "May the Land of Soviets Be Glorified," which Latvians were forced to sing at the festival in Riga in 1948. Forty years later at least 250,000 people, more than one in four Estonians, gathered at the Tallinn Song Festival Grounds where they participated in a stirring rendition of "My Native Land," the interwar national anthem that had been expressly forbidden by the Soviet regime.

The event, which took place in September 1988, marked the pinnacle of the Baltic republics' Singing Revolution, but the autumn brought further success. On November 16, the Estonian Supreme Soviet, an increasingly pro-Estonian body, declared by a vote of 258 to 1 the republic's sovereignty and its right to veto USSR laws that violated that sovereignty. Although far short of a full declaration of independence, the vote was to set the precedent for later sovereignty declarations in other parts of the Soviet empire. In historical retrospect the surprising thing about the declaration is that the body which passed it was a purely Soviet creation, for the Estonian Supreme Soviet had been "elected" in 1985 and contained numerous non-Estonians. Gorbachev was unmoved.

At this stage of the revolution Estonia was well out ahead of its more cautious Baltic neighbors: it had been the first of the republics to dump its Brezhnevite leadership, to brandish its prewar flag, and to declare the republic's sovereignty. In Lithuania, which was led by the Brezhnevite First Secretary Petras Griškevičius until his death in November 1987, and then for another year by the lifelong *apparatchik* Ringaudas Songaila (b. 1929), the situation stagnated until the birth on May 23, 1988, of a new mass organization called the Lithuanian Movement for Restructuring, later known simply as *Sąjūdis* (Movement). Before long this organization, a counterpart to the popular fronts in Latvia and Estonia, emerged as the most popular force for Lithuanian nationalism.

Initially *Sąjūdis* was a movement that united various strata of Lithuanian society, including nationalists from Kaunas, liberal intellectuals from Vilnius, and communist reformers. Independent of the Communist Party but at first not necessarily inimical to it, *Sąjūdis* quickly gained mass legitimacy as it called for a meaningful definition of "sovereignty," economic independence, and a discussion of Stalinism and the Molotov–Ribbentrop Pact. Still bolder demands were put forward by another Lithuanian nationalist movement, the Lithuanian Freedom League, which unlike the more cautious *Sąjūdis* sought outright independence from the USSR and was unwilling to cooperate in any way with the Communist Party.

At this stage the Lithuanian party leadership was not yet prepared to collaborate with the reform movements and instead attempted to contain undesirable manifestations of *glasnost'*. Unlike in Estonia, where the party leadership strove to accommodate the Popular Front, in Lithuania relations between the party and *Sąjūdis* grew tense, especially as nationalist demonstrations began to draw growing crowds in the summer of 1988. This policy of noncooperation cost the party dearly, as it appeared to be recalcitrant and unresponsive to popular feeling, and as a result the Communist Party of Lithuania found itself increasingly marginalized. Indeed, it was *Sąjūdis* that would define the republic's political agenda for the remainder of the Soviet era.

Leaders of the Lithuanian and Latvian communist parties soon realized that they could not depend on help from the Kremlin, where Gorbachev too was caught between orthodox communists who sought to roll back *perestroika* and radical reformists who urged him on. Despite the more liberal atmosphere of the time there was still considerable uncertainty about the future: one could not be certain that *perestroika* and *glasnost'* were not just the latest whim of the latest Soviet tsar. Nevertheless, Moscow tolerated and often even supported the popular fronts and *Sąjūdis* in the belief that they could be useful allies against hardliners within the CPSU.

In an attempt to clarify the present party line, in August 1988 Gorbachev sent his Politburo ally Alexander Yakovlev (1923–2005) to Lithuania and Latvia to deliver a message: the communist parties of the Baltic republics, Yakovlev suggested, should work with the reform movements in the republics in a common effort to implement the goals of *perestroika*. At the same time, the Kremlin also held firmly to the line that Baltic ideas about independence were simply senseless dreams: the USSR was a single interdependent economic system, not to be taken apart. Yakovlev's visit was followed by Moscow's efforts to co-opt the new mass movements while maintaining pressure on the Baltic communist parties. *Sąjūdis* was even given access to the official media, which increased its public visibility. Meanwhile, the hardline leaders of the Lithuanian section of the CPSU were made to understand that they had lost the support of Moscow. On October 20, First Secretary Ringaudas Songaila was pensioned off and replaced by the more flexible Algirdas Brazauskas (1932–2010), a popular figure who since June had been the party's liaison to *Sąjūdis*.

Similar changes took place in the party leaderships of the other Baltic republics. Unable to keep up with the Kremlin's shifting reformist line, Latvia's First Secretary Boriss Pugo was transferred to Moscow in early October to head the Party Control Commission and was replaced by a compromise candidate, Jānis Vagris (b. 1930), a native Latvian. Anatolijs Gorbunovs (b. 1942), by now one of the Latvian party's leading reformers, took the post of chairman of the Supreme Soviet of the Latvian SSR. Yet even if the leaders of the Baltic republics tried to follow Moscow's uncertain reformist line, they could not hope to keep up with the pace being set by the popular fronts, *Sąjūdis*, and other, often less compromising organizations.

By the time *Sąjūdis* and the other Baltic popular fronts held founding congresses in October 1988 they had eclipsed the republican communist parties as the leading political forces in their republics. As the fronts became disillusioned with the slow pace of *perestroika* and began to take more radical stances (including, eventually, independence for the Baltic republics), Moscow's support for them evaporated. Likewise, at the republic level, as the demands of the popular fronts grew more radical, the remaining Communist Party hardliners became less willing to cooperate with them. Some fell under the influence of new political organizations founded by the Russian-speaking populations of the Baltic republics, including the International Movement of Workers in the Estonian SSR (later called the Intermovement), formed in July 1988, and a Latvian counterpart called the Interfront, which was created in October. Russian-speakers in Lithuania founded *Edinstvo* (Unity) in November. Fearing that the rise of national movements in the Baltics would encroach upon Russian interests, these organizations called for "internationalism" (meaning Soviet rule and the privileging of the Russian language) and firm support from the CPSU in Moscow. In Estonia as many as one-third of the Russian-speakers were active participants in the Intermovement.

Indeed, the reawakening of local nationalism in the Baltic republics often asserted itself in ways that were threatening to non-native settlers. Initially one of the main concerns of the Russian-speaking population was the local push for declaring the indigenous languages the state languages of the Baltic republics—a focal point for nationalist groups throughout the Soviet periphery. This of course would jeopardize the traditional primacy of the Russian language, the only language most of the settlers knew. Lithuania passed a language law in November 1988, followed by Estonia in January 1989 and Latvia the following May. Vehemently opposing laws they took to be discriminatory and exclusionary, some of the leaders of the Russophone organizations took a "Great Russian chauvinist" stance: seeking safe harbor in the empire, they called for the restoration of Moscow's firm control over the republics. The battle cries of the Russian-speaking organizations grew ever more shrill as the popular fronts began to endorse the idea of independence. Convinced that if the Baltic republics seceded from the USSR then the Russians who lived there would suddenly find themselves a vulnerable minority in a hostile environment, the Interfront, Intermovement, and *Edinstvo* were natural allies of the hardline elements in the KGB and the CPSU. It should be noted, however, that these organizations probably did not represent the majority of Russians who lived in the Baltic republics—many of whom actually supported the goals of the popular fronts—but only the most conservative and frightened among them.

SOVEREIGNTY OR INDEPENDENCE?

A critical development that did much to advance the cause of the Baltic republics was the election in March 1989 of a new USSR Congress of People's Deputies (CPD). In creating the congress, Gorbachev's intention was to establish an institutional and semi-democratic counterweight to the undemocratic and unrepresentative CPSU. Although one-third of its 2,250 seats were reserved for public organizations such as the CPSU and its Youth League (*Komsomol*) in order to ensure the body's essential conservatism, the remainder went to representatives of the regions and districts, who were elected by popular vote.

While the Communist Party dominated the elections to the CPD (87.6 percent of the seats were awarded to members of the CPSU), the popular fronts and *Sąjūdis* heavily influenced the selection of Baltic representatives. To take the most extreme case, of the 42 elected Lithuanian deputies, 36 had been nominated by *Sąjūdis*. These deputies saw the CPD not only as a qualified triumph for the reform movement, but also as a televised medium through which they could articulate their demands for sovereignty and economic autonomy within the USSR. Deputies from the Baltic republics challenged the limits of *glasnost'* when they raised concerns about the history of the Baltic states' incorporation into the Soviet Union—the matter upon which the legitimacy of Soviet rule depended. Even Lithuania's party boss Algirdas Brazauskas, a moderate who was concerned that *Sąjūdis* was moving too quickly, could not avoid addressing the issue, stressing at one of the congress's early sessions (May 31, 1989) that the Soviet government's vagueness on the matter weakened his own party.[21]

Under pressure from the Baltic delegates, a commission under the CPSU Central Committee was created to study the question. By the time its report, which confirmed the existence of the Molotov–Ribbentrop pact's secret protocols, was adopted by the congress in December 1989, the Soviet government had developed a new line on this critical issue: even if the pact had been a violation of the sovereignty of the Baltic states, its argument ran, the incorporation of these countries into the USSR had been accomplished through the voluntary actions of their parliaments. The pact and the incorporation of the republics, the Kremlin now claimed, were two different matters. As Gorbachev said on September 19, there were "no grounds to question the decision by the Baltic republics to join the USSR and the choice made by their peoples."[22] Thus throughout 1989 the Soviet government in Moscow and the Baltic republics were increasingly working at cross-purposes: as the former struggled to strengthen a reformed union of sovereign socialist republics, the goal of nearly all indigenous Baltic organizations had become the restoration of unfettered independence.

Unlike the 1930s, when the Baltic states failed to cooperate with each other in any meaningful way, from 1989 onward Baltic activists saw cooperation as a vital component of their effort to break free of Soviet rule. They made contacts with the other republics of the Soviet empire, with the West, and with each other, thereby lessening the likelihood of a violent crackdown on their movements of national liberation. The Baltic Council of popular fronts, formed in July 1989, met on a regular basis to discuss and coordinate their activities. Most famously, the popular fronts organized the "Baltic Way" demonstration of August 23, 1989, in which up to two million people held hands to form a human chain running through Tallinn, Riga, and Vilnius. Perhaps more than any single act, this demonstration of solidarity drew the world's attention to the plight of the Baltic republics and their struggle for freedom. Moreover, demonstrations such as this, as well as the song festivals, induced a dramatic transformation of consciousness not only among the masses of the Baltic republics, but also among their leaders, many of whom now became aware of their own latent nationalist sentiments—or who were savvy enough to see which way the winds were blowing.

But the Baltics were not the only aggrieved Soviet satrapies, and their aspirations to national independence should be viewed within the context of the more general struggle of the republics against the dictates of the "center" (Moscow) that began to unfold at the end of the 1980s. In contrast to the relatively peaceful situation in the Baltics, in Alma-Ata, the capital of the Kazakh SSR, rioting occurred in December 1986 when its first secretary was replaced by a Russian; and in April 1989, a peaceful demonstration was suppressed by the Soviet army in Tblisi, Georgia, with more than 20 killed. Worse still was the civil war that threatened to break out between the Armenian and Azerbaijan republics over the disputed Nagorno-Karabakh region, an Armenian enclave in Azerbaijan. Challenges from the Belarusian, Moldovan, and Ukrainian republics followed. Meanwhile, beyond the USSR's western borders, by the end of 1989 a "velvet revolution" had swept through central and southeastern Europe, toppling communist regimes and obliterating the military and economic structures that linked the USSR to its former satellites. It was the latter route— the nonviolent one taken by Poland (exemplified by the nonviolent

tactics of the Solidarity movement), Hungary, and Czechoslovakia—
that Baltic leaders intended to take as they moved toward the goal of
independence.

Indeed, the successful revolutions in east central Europe emboldened the separatists in the Baltics and other Soviet republics to take
decisive action. Their efforts were further encouraged by the repeated
assertions of Gorbachev and other Politburo members throughout
1989 that Moscow would not use military force to resolve its disputes
with Baltic nationalists. However, in contrast to his magnanimous
treatment of the satellite regimes that comprised the USSR's "outer
empire," Gorbachev had trouble meeting the Baltic nationalists half-
way, believing that this would lead to the disintegration of the inner
empire.[23] The Union, the Soviet president insisted, must be preserved.
Thus, in the unfolding struggle of the Soviet "periphery" against the
"center," Gorbachev took a middle position, advocating both strong
republics *and* a strong center. This notion was captured by the CPSU's
draft program on "The Party's Nationalities Policy in Present-Day
Conditions," issued on August 17, 1989. "Without a strong union," the
draft said, "there cannot be strong republics. And without strong republics, there cannot be a strong union."[24]

For the Baltic republics such a formula was increasingly unacceptable. By the summer of 1989 the momentum toward independence,
reinforced by overlapping nationalist tides in east central Europe and
in the other Soviet republics, had become self-sustaining.[25] In November the Estonian Supreme Soviet annulled the 1940 vote to join the
USSR. Lithuania and Latvia did the same three months later. Amidst
these declarations by the Baltic legislatures, on Christmas Eve of 1989
the USSR Congress of People's Deputies condemned the Molotov–
Ribbentrop Pact and declared it legally invalid.

Following the lead of the popular fronts and other new movements,
the communist parties of the Estonian, Latvian, and Lithuanian SSRs
soon found themselves in the paradoxical position of endorsing independence for their republics, albeit in a gradual and controlled manner. They also found that if they did not distance themselves from the
CPSU, they ran the risk of appearing out of touch with the mood of
the people. Concerned about the prospect of losing in the local elections planned for early 1990—free, multiparty elections that would
determine who controlled the Lithuanian government—the Communist Party of Lithuania was the first to seek a divorce from the mother
organization. Brazauskas first informed Gorbachev of this plan on December 1, 1989, less than a week before the Lithuanian Supreme Soviet
voted to eliminate the Communist Party's monopoly on power. The

Lithuanian party's separation from the CPSU, Brazauskas reasoned, was the only way for his party to retain enough popular support to succeed in the elections. Sensitive to the charge that the Communist Party had not changed during *perestroika*, Gorbachev hoped that his Lithuanian comrades could be convinced to remain in the CPSU while a new program was prepared for the Party congress, scheduled for the following spring.

Despite Gorbachev's pleas, on December 20 the overwhelming majority voted for the independence of the Communist Party of Lithuania from the larger CPSU. The remainder, about 160 of the 1,033 delegates, decided to remain aligned with the CPSU, retaining the CPSU's program and forming their own central committee to rival that headed by Brazauskas. An analogous split in the ECP occurred in March 1990 and in the Communist Party of Latvia the following month. However, the majority of LCP members, who in fact were mostly non-Latvian, remained loyal to Moscow and elected Riga's mayor Alfrēds Rubiks to the post of first secretary. The example of Rubiks, once a supporter of Gorbachev's *perestroika* but now eager to apply the brakes, provides an interesting counterpart to Lithuania's Brazauskas, another career *apparatchik* who moved in the opposite direction as circumstances evolved. Later Rubiks would be the only communist leader to serve time in prison for backing the hardline coup against Gorbachev in 1991, while Brazauskas would end up being the first president of post-Soviet Lithuania (see chapter 8).

Still convinced that the breach in the party could be healed and that most ordinary Lithuanians truly supported the Soviet system, Gorbachev rejected Brazauskas's argument and in January went to Vilnius (he was the first and only CPSU general secretary to do so) to plead his case. Addressing both wings of the Lithuanian party, he promised "big changes in the operation of the Party [CPSU]." The party, he haughtily declared, "will deliberate, work at its plenums and Congresses, decide on Union affairs, political questions, how perestroika should be developed, and meanwhile comrade Brazauskas will be reading newspapers to learn what we have decided and what the fate of Lithuania should be in this connection."[26] For Brazauskas, however, the withdrawal of the Lithuanian section from the mother party was irrevocable.

While in Vilnius, Gorbachev also took his case to the Lithuanian people. Speaking with factory workers, Gorbachev emphasized the political, economic, and defense ties that bound together all the Union republics and warned Lithuanians of the dangers of ethnic strife and even bloodshed should they continue their secessionist course. "At present," he insisted, "no republic can live without the other republics . . . We're all tied together now." Despite his assurances that progress was being made toward the creation of "a full-fledged federation with sovereign republics and a unified CPSU as a mighty integrating political force under conditions of democratization and decentralization," Lithuanians refused to accept his argument.[27] Contrary to Gorbachev's intentions, his visit to Lithuania exposed the vast gulf that had emerged between his way of thinking and that of ordinary Lithuanians, who increasingly sided with the pro-independence movement headed by *Sąjūdis*.

Indeed, it was a radicalized *Sąjūdis,* then approaching the height of its popularity, that dominated the local elections of early March 1990. *Sąjūdis*-supported candidates won 98 of 141 seats in the parliament, while most of the rest went to members of the independent Communist Party of Lithuania.[28] The chairman of the new Lithuanian Supreme Soviet (the Russian word "Soviet" was quickly replaced by "Council") and head of state was Vytautas Landsbergis (b. 1932), a musicologist and a leader of *Sąjūdis* since November 1988. Landsbergis was convinced that there was no time to waste: Lithuania must declare its independence immediately, before Gorbachev accrued additional powers as president (a post to which he was elected by the CPD on March 14) that would allow him to prevent the secession of the republics. Thus on the same day as Landsbergis's election, March 11, 1990, the legislature declared the Republic of Lithuania's exit from the USSR. Although the right to secede was guaranteed in the existing Soviet constitution, officials in Moscow insisted that the Lithuanian government had violated the constitution and thereby perpetrated an illegal act.

As in Lithuania, legislative elections were held in Latvia and Estonia in February and March of 1990. Candidates who supported both the popular front platform and independence easily carried the day in Latvia, with the result that hardliners in the LCP were effectively excluded from power. Estonians, split between radicals (independence now) and moderates (independence later), considered it necessary to compromise. Thus on March 30 the Estonian parliament, renamed the Supreme Council of the Republic of Estonia in early May, confirmed Estonia's status as an occupied country and declared the republic to be "in a transition phase toward independence." Likewise, on May 4 the Latvian Supreme Soviet endorsed the goal of restoring the independence of the Republic of Latvia, following a transitional period. While Gorbachev pronounced the decisions null and void, the Baltic republics began to dismantle the symbols of Soviet domination.

By May 1990 all three Baltic republics had formally declared their intention to achieve independence from the USSR, but with one important difference between them: whereas at this stage Estonia and Latvia still approached independence as a matter to be negotiated with Moscow, Lithuania treated its independence as an accomplished, irrevocable fact.

STALEMATE

To many ordinary Lithuanians he was an arrogant academic, in contrast to the "man of the people" image cultivated by the communist leader Algirdas Brazauskas. But in the eyes of the Lithuanian intelligentsia Vytautas Landsbergis was untainted. As journalist Anatol Lieven wrote, "Much of the Lithuanian intelligentsia identifies passionately with a national cultural vision of Lithuania. They love Landsbergis because he is the perfect symbol of that identification."[29] One ancestor had fought the Russian Empire during the 1830–1831 rebellion; his grandfather, a writer, had played a role in the founding of the modern Lithuanian state; in 1941 his father, an architect who later helped reconstruct a Lithuanian Vilnius after World War II, had been appointed a minister in a Lithuanian Provisional Government composed of anti-Soviet rebels. Standing up to Moscow as his ancestors had before him, Vytautas Landsbergis was, in the spring of 1990, the living embodiment of Lithuanian patriotism.

Landsbergis and the Communist Party had been on a collision course ever since November 20, 1988, when upon becoming president of *Sąjūdis* he declared that "Only Lithuania can decide and execute its own laws."[30] Three months later he called for the full restoration of Lithuanian sovereignty—a first step toward the country's independence. In response to a warning from the CPSU, Landsbergis declared "We're not extremist and we are not violent, but we are determined."[31] This was August 1989, as the Soviet Union's "outer empire" in east central Europe began to crumble. Little more than six months later the Supreme Council of the Republic of Lithuania, which he now chaired, declared its full independence from the USSR. The decision was based partly on the mistaken belief, encouraged by émigré contacts in the United States, that President George H. W. Bush (1989–1993) would provide the country with diplomatic recognition.[32] Although many deputies were uncomfortable with a declaration of immediate secession, the principle of independence had already won out in Lithuania; few were willing to vote against it.

The Vilnius declaration provoked a strong reaction from Gorbachev, who immediately called it "invalid and illegal." Some observers, including Brazauskas, believed that the Soviet president's denunciation was only for public consumption, and that his private views regarding Lithuania's eventual independence were somewhat more flexible. Gorbachev's foreign policy advisor Anatoly Chernyaev, who was in a position to know, was convinced that the Soviet president

> sincerely didn't believe that the people of those three republics really wanted to break with the Union. He thought that they were being misled, just as he thought world opinion was too. And he wasn't lying when he said that he was ready to settle the issue "constitutionally," that is through a referendum and a "legal divorce." He was against keeping the Baltic countries in by force, but would use any other method to prevent their secession. And thus he inadvertently joined those who were ready, for the sake of the same goal, to go all the way.[33]

Now grasping more fully both the precariousness of his own political position and the potential domino effect on the other republics about which his hardline colleagues had been warning him for months, Gorbachev saw that first Lithuania would leave, then Estonia and Latvia. Not only would the extensive Soviet military deployments along the Baltic be lost, thereby compromising the USSR's ability either to defend itself or project its forces into Europe, but the precedent set by the Baltics would ultimately trigger the collapse of the entire empire. Lithuania, Gorbachev concluded, had to be stopped.

To force Landsbergis to rescind the declaration of independence, the Soviet president applied steady pressure on Lithuania. Soviet military planes and helicopters began unscheduled maneuvers over the republic; buildings were seized from the independent Communist Party of Lithuania by Interior Ministry troops and handed over to the pro-Moscow loyalists. Meanwhile, a new law on secession began to be worked out in the USSR Congress of People's Deputies and was passed on April 7, 1990. According to this plan, Lithuania, like any other Soviet republic, would have to jump a series of legal hurdles before it could attain its independence: first there would have to be a referendum on the matter, to be followed by a five-year waiting period for sorting out the details.

Despite Gorbachev's maneuvers, Landsbergis maintained his conviction that Soviet law did not apply to Lithuania, an illegally occupied country. Thus in mid-April, an exasperated Gorbachev resorted to imposing a partial embargo on the vulnerable republic, thereby cutting off much of its energy supply. Although Landsbergis refused to rescind the declaration of independence, at the end of June he and the Supreme Council agreed to suspend its implementation for 100 days while Vilnius and Moscow worked to negotiate a settlement. With the Lithuanian parliament approving of the moratorium, Gorbachev agreed to lift the sanctions. By this time, however, Gorbachev had to deal with another, potentially more threatening crisis: on June 8, 1990, the RSFSR Supreme Soviet, chaired by Boris Yeltsin (1931–2007), declared Russia's sovereignty and gave its laws precedence over the laws of the USSR, thereby setting into motion a "parade of sovereignties" in the other Union republics. In the process, Yeltsin, embroiled in a bitter political and personal rivalry with Gorbachev, had agreed that his government would cooperate with Lithuania. The enemy of my enemy, the wily Yeltsin (elected president of the RSFSR in June 1991) surely reasoned, may prove to be a valuable friend.

As Yeltsin cultivated allies in the Baltics, establishing bilateral relations between the RSFSR and each of the Baltic republics and personally meeting with Baltic leaders in August 1990, negotiations between Moscow (Gorbachev) and the Lithuanian government went nowhere. The same was true of the Soviet government's negotiations with the other Baltic republics: each side repeatedly set out its positions but proved unable to find common ground with the others. The struggle between the republics and the "center" had reached an impasse.

Meanwhile, the Baltic rebellion had spread to the military. The spring draft was a disaster in the Baltics and in other rebellious regions such as the Caucasus republics and western Ukraine. With the active help of pro-independence parties, Baltic soldiers had even begun deserting. With the Soviet army falling apart—the vast majority of conscription-age men from the Baltics failed to show up during the annual call-up—and the Union threatening to fracture along national lines, Gorbachev was facing intense pressure from his hardline colleagues to take control of the situation. Thus in the fall of 1990, Gorbachev's ruling style took a sharp authoritarian turn. In November, the Soviet president acquired new emergency powers and placed known reactionaries at the head of the ministries of interior and defense. The Soviet program for accelerated economic reform, called the Shatalin (or "500 Days") Plan, was dropped, as goods disappeared from the store shelves and the queues for basic staples like sugar appeared.

As for the Lithuanian problem, Gorbachev would work with the republic's Soviet loyalists rather than with Landsbergis and Brazauskas. Still, to this point Gorbachev had refused to allow the matter to be settled by means of force, as the hardliners who surrounded him sometimes urged him to do. Although the Soviet army had been used to quell demonstrations in Tblisi, the capital of the Georgian SSR, in April 1989, and to stop ethnic fighting in Azerbaijan's capital, Baku, in January 1990, Gorbachev was averse to the application of brute force. Moreover, the Soviet leader was keenly aware that a crackdown on Lithuania would provoke a backlash in Washington, which in turn would jeopardize his entire reform program—and his political survival. As Soviet Minister of Defense Dmitri Yazov told a U.S. official in the spring of 1990: "If one republic secedes, Gorbachev is through. And if he has to use force to prevent one from leaving, he's out too."[34]

THE COLLAPSE

While Gorbachev had long been under pressure from his colleagues in the Politburo to do something about the situation in the Baltics, it was the Moscow loyalists in the rump Communist Party of Lithuania who finally convinced him that a show of force was necessary. In early January 1991, as the pro-empire *Edinstvo* group led a series of demonstrations against the nationalist government in Vilnius, Soviet troops began to occupy strategic buildings. The Lithuanian government's dispute with Moscow over prices only aggravated the tense situation in the streets. Taking advantage of the political disarray in Lithuania as the government resigned on January 10, pro-empire forces quickly went into action.

The situation turned violent during the night of January 12–13 when a mysterious "National Salvation Committee" claimed to have seized power in Lithuania. At the same time, Soviet paratroopers and members of the KGB Alpha unit attacked the Vilnius television tower, then surrounded by thousands of mostly young Lithuanians. Fifteen were killed and hundreds were injured. Convinced that this was a prelude to an attack on the parliament, Landsbergis called upon Lithuanians to gather at Independence Square to defend their government; they would greet any assault with passive resistance. Despite the fact that international attention was otherwise focused on the conflict in the Persian Gulf, television viewers around the world witnessed scenes of brutality and heroic resistance in Vilnius. Indeed, it was likely this factor—world opinion, along with the presence of Western journalists—that prevented Moscow from launching a final, lethal assault.

Meanwhile, in Riga, where a similar attack appeared imminent, thousands gathered in the streets, surrounding key public buildings with hastily constructed barricades. Five Latvians were killed on

January 20 when Soviet special forces attacked buildings belonging to the Ministry of Internal Affairs. As in Lithuania, a "National Salvation Committee" appeared during the crackdown, led by Party First Secretary Alfrēds Rubiks and supported by the Latvian Interfront. Russian democrats, fearing that the RSFSR was next, organized demonstrations in Moscow and demanded the Soviet president's resignation.

Not wanting to tarnish the liberal image he had carefully cultivated for Western consumption, Gorbachev denied responsibility for both the attack in Vilnius and the deaths in Riga. Meanwhile, on January 13, immediately after the Vilnius incidents, Boris Yeltsin, then conducting his own struggle against the Soviet "center" (and in this sense realizing that his fate was entwined with that of the Baltic leaders), flew to Tallinn to offer his support as the head of the RSFSR government. While the immediate crisis passed, for several months afterward the Kremlin continued to conduct a policy of low-level harassment in both Latvia and Lithuania.

None of the three Baltic republics was dissuaded from pursuing its course. With Landsbergis at the height of his popularity, on February 9 a referendum was held in Lithuania on the matter of independence: 90 percent of voters were in favor. Likewise, on March 3, referenda were held in Estonia and Latvia, where 78 percent and 74 percent voted "yes," including many Russian-speakers.[35] Planning to conduct referenda of its own in mid-March, the Soviet leadership refused to acknowledge the legitimacy of those held in the Baltic republics.

By this time Gorbachev had shifted tactics once again, abandoning the hardliners, who no longer trusted him, to pursue a more flexible position that was more favorable to republican sovereignty. On March 17, the Soviet president held a Union-wide referendum on the question of voluntarily preserving the USSR "as a renewed federation of equal sovereign republics," but the Baltic republics, having conducted their own referenda and now regarding themselves as independent states, refused to participate. Throughout the spring of 1991 Moscow negotiated the terms of a new Union Treaty with the leaders of the republics, but the three Baltic republics—as well as Georgia, Armenia, and Moldova—refused to participate.

Having reached agreement with the governments of the nine participating republics, a new Union Treaty was set to be signed on August 20, 1991. On August 4, Gorbachev left Moscow for his annual vacation on the Crimean shore. Two weeks later a group of Soviet hardliners—his own appointees—arrived at his vacation house, where they tried to persuade the president to endorse their plans for the introduction of a state of emergency. There would be no new Union Treaty, they told Gorbachev. Refusing to go along with their plot, Gorbachev was confined to house arrest in Foros while the self-proclaimed State Committee on the State of Emergency—a coalition of forces from the KGB, military, Ministry of the Interior, and the party apparatus—announced its takeover early on the morning of August 19. They expected no serious opposition.

Yeltsin's heroic resistance in Moscow marked the summit of his stunning career as an anticommunist rebel after decades of loyal service in Russia's Sverdlovsk region. Inexplicably managing to evade arrest, he declared the takeover an illegal *coup d'état* and galvanized popular resistance to it. While the commander of the Baltic Military District announced that it was taking control of Estonia, Latvia, and Lithuania, the three Baltic governments threw their support to Yeltsin and called for a general strike. As the coup collapsed—it seems the putschists had no stomach for the large-scale violence that would have been required to pull it off—Estonia and Latvia declared their full independence, on August 20 and 21, respectively. Despite a few casualties in Lithuania, which had regarded itself as independent since March 1990, Soviet military units quickly retreated to their barracks.

Throughout the USSR the bungled coup attempt completely destroyed whatever popular legitimacy the Communist Party had still enjoyed prior to August 19. When Gorbachev returned to Moscow on August 21, he was the president of a state that for all practical purposes no longer existed and the head of a party from which he immediately resigned and that was soon to be outlawed. Power had irrevocably passed from the Party to the state, and from the Kremlin to the republics.

This much was clear to Latvian authorities, who on August 24 banned the KGB from operating within the territory of Latvia. That evening removal crews set about the arduous task of dismantling the Lenin statue that stood on Riga's main boulevard—formerly Lenin Street, now once again Liberty Avenue. The same task had just been completed the previous day in Tallinn. Tartu's Lenin statue been dismantled sometime earlier and was reportedly driven through the city with a noose around its neck.[36] Meanwhile, images of the removal of Vilnius's Lenin monument on August 22, 1991, were disseminated worldwide as the bronze statue, cut off at the knees and hanging from a crane, became an international symbol for the death of Soviet communism.[37] The reassembled statue now sits in Grūtas Park outside Vilnius, where it joined statues of Stalin, Marx, and other discarded icons of a dream whose failure brought misery to millions.

A statue of Vladimir Lenin was erected in 1950 at Brīvības bulvaris (then known as Lenin Avenue) in Riga to commemorate the 10th anniversary of Soviet Latvia. On August 27, 1991, the statue was dismantled, signifying the independent Latvian state's rejection of communism. (AP Photo/Imant Predelis)

As the remaining Soviet republics declared their independence one by one, on September 6, 1991, a rudderless USSR formally recognized the independence of Estonia, Latvia, and Lithuania. Eleven days later the Baltic states were admitted to the United Nations. While in the formal sense the empire lingered on for several more months, Boris Yeltsin and the intoxicated leaders of Ukraine and Belarus decided officially to end the Soviet Union on December 31 and create in its place a looser Commonwealth of Independent States (CIS). The Baltic states, now completely independent and recognized as such by the international community, opted not to join. Their destiny, they concurred, was not with Russia but with the other sovereign nation-states of Europe.

NOTES

1. Daina Bleiere, et al., *History of Latvia: The 20th Century,* 2nd ed. (Riga: Jumava, 2006), 378–79.

2. Bleiere, 399–405; William Prigge, "The Latvian Purges of 1959: A Revisionist Study," *Journal of Baltic Studies* 35, no. 3 (Fall 2004): 211–30. Berklavs later returned and became actively involved in the Latvian independence movement at the end of the 1980s.

3. Romuald Misiunas and Rein Taagepera, *The Baltic States: Years of Dependence 1940–1990,* expanded and updated edition (Berkeley and Los Angeles: University of California Press, 1993), 359–60.

4. Helēna Demakova, *Different Conversations. Writings on Art and Culture* (Riga: Visual Communications Department of the Latvian Academy of Art, 2002), 205–207. See the National Film Centre of Latvia, "Decades of Latvia in Newsreels: 1940s," http://nfc.balticuniverse.com/en/films/decades-of-latvia-in-newsreels-1940s (accessed July 7, 2014).

5. Ibid., 207.

6. Violeta Davoliūtė, *The Making and Breaking of Soviet Lithuania* (London and New York: Routledge, 2013), 95–97.

7. Donata Mitaitė, "Latvian Literature in 1968," in *Baltic Memory: Processes of Modernisation in Lithuanian, Latvian and Estonian Literature of the Soviet Period,* ed. Elena Baliutytė and Donata Mitaitė (Vilnius: Institute of Lithuanian Literature and Folklore, 2011), 41.

8. Dovile Budryte, *Taming Nationalism? Political Community Building in the Post-Soviet Baltic States* (Burlington, VT: Ashgate, 2005), 54.

9. Misiunas and Taagepera, 184.

10. Tiina Kirss, ed. and trans., *Estonian Life Stories* (Budapest and New York: Central European University Press, 2009), 69–70.

11. Ibid., 71.

12. Baltic republics retained an 11-year educational program, whereas the Soviet norm was 10 years.

13. Bohdan Nahaylo and Victor Swoboda, *Soviet Disunion: A History of the Nationalities Problem in the USSR* (New York: The Free Press, 1990), 172–73.

14. Gershon Shafir, *Immigrants and Nationalists: Ethnic Conflict and Accommodation in Catalonia, the Basque Country, Latvia, and Estonia* (Albany: State University of New York Press, 1995), 157, 159.

15. David Caute, *The Dancer Defects: The Struggle for Cultural Supremacy during the Cold War* (New York: Oxford University Press, 2003), 496–97.

16. See Stephen Kotkin, *Armageddon Averted: The Soviet Collapse, 1970–2000* (New York: Oxford University Press, 2001).

17. Hélène Carrère d'Encausse, *Decline of an Empire* (New York: Newsweek Books, 1979), 267.

18. V. Stanley Vardys, "The Baltic States in the Soviet Union," in *The Soviet Union and the Challenge of the Future. Volume 3: Ideology, Culture and Nationality,* ed. Alexander Shtromas and Morton A. Kaplan (New York: Paragon House, 1989), 440, 451.

19. Rein Taagepera, *Estonia: Return to Independence* (Boulder, CO: Westview Press, 1993), 108.

20. Anatol Lieven, *The Baltic Revolution: Estonia, Latvia, Lithuania and the Path to Independence* (New Haven, CT: Yale University Press, 1993), 222.

21. Rolf H. W. Theen, ed., *The U.S.S.R. First Congress of People's Deputies, Vol. 1* (New York: Paragon House, 1991), 244.

22. Walter C. Clemens, *Baltic Independence and Russian Empire* (New York: St. Martin's Press, 1991), 235.

23. Anatoly Chernyaev, *My Six Years with Gorbachev* (University Park: Pennsylvania State University Press, 2000), 189–90.

24. Ibid., 232.

25. See Mark R. Beissinger, *Nationalist Mobilization and the Collapse of the Soviet State* (New York: Cambridge University Press, 2002).

26. TASS, January 14, 1990.

27. *The Current Digest of the Soviet Press,* Vol. 42, no. 2, February 14, 1990, 3.

28. Two bodies were elected in each republic: first the new Congress of People's Deputies (CPD) and then the existing legislatures, called Supreme Soviets. Unlike the larger lower houses, the Supreme Soviets of the Estonian, Latvian and Lithuanian SSRs were standing bodies able to pass legislation.

29. Lieven, 25.

30. Richard J. Krickus, *Showdown: The Lithuanian Rebellion and the Breakup of the Soviet Empire* (Washington and London: Brassey's, 1997), 64.

31. Clemens, 126, 195.

32. Providing Lithuania with diplomatic recognition, Washington believed, would result in Gorbachev's ouster, which would be a setback to reform in the USSR and the improved international climate. Moreover, the State Department claimed that it had recognized the Lithuanian state in 1922 and had never withdrawn that recognition.

33. Chernyaev, 329–30.

34. Michael R. Beschloss and Strobe Talbott, *At the Highest Levels* (Boston: Little, Brown, 1993), 195.

35. A poll taken in December 1990 in Latvia found that 47 percent of non-Latvians supported independence (including 59 percent of those nonnatives who had been born in Lithuania). Perhaps 30 percent of non-Estonians voted in favor of independence in the March referendum.

Shafir, 183; Richard C. M. Mole, *The Baltic States from the Soviet Union to the European Union* (London and New York: Routledge, 2012), 79.

36. In 1997, the Tartu town council put the 3.5-meter statue up for auction, but it drew no bidders.

37. In 2012, a statue of John Lennon with the word "Imagine" emblazoned on its pedestal was unveiled in Vilnius on the exact spot where the Lenin statue had stood since 1952 and where the leaders of the anti-Russian revolt of 1863–1864 were executed.

Return to Europe

The implosion of the Union of Soviet Socialist Republics (during the final months of 1991) brought an end to Moscow's political domination of the non-Russian Soviet republics. Despite the initial caution of President George H.W. Bush, who was concerned that Western encouragement of local nationalisms in the USSR might undermine Soviet leader Mikhail Gorbachev, for nearly three years Bush's negotiating partner in the Kremlin, the United States and other countries quickly recognized the Baltic states' independence when they became the first of the Soviet republics to exit the USSR. Freed from the foreign domination they had endured for five decades, the Baltic states would follow the trail blazed in 1989 by Poland, Hungary, and the other former people's republics—a path that led away from Moscow and toward the West.

Like the new leaders of the former satellites, the men and women who took power in Vilnius, Riga, and Tallinn tended to be nationalists who conceived of their countries' "return to Europe" as a hedge against the resurgence of Russian imperialism, for only membership in Western institutions could provide them with the security they would need to maintain their independence and markets to replace what they had lost with the demise of the integrated Soviet social-ist economy. Thus one of the challenges facing all three Baltic states during the post-Soviet years was to balance their commitment to na-tional sovereignty with the practical need for cooperation with their European neighbors (and with each other) within the framework of international institutions.

The achievements of the past quarter century have been remark-able. All three Baltic states have become members of the North Atlan-tic Treaty Organization (NATO) and the European Union (EU) and all three have maintained an unequivocal commitment to democratic pro-cedures, even if their national minorities have justifiably complained about discrimination and exclusion. Presidents, prime ministers, and political parties have come and gone since the tumultuous 1990s, but as of this writing in late 2014 the Baltic states remain politically inde-pendent (if economically tethered to the policies of the EU) and their commitment to free markets and political liberty has proven resilient. But these successes have been accompanied by domestic political dis-sension, ethnic confrontation, and economic uncertainty.

Whatever the differences among and within them, Estonian, Latvian, and Lithuanian societies have chosen to reject Moscow's grip and have instead elected to return to Europe, and with that to accept European norms where political freedom, human rights, and the rule of law are concerned. If Moscow still tends to view the Baltic states—like it does Georgia, Kazakhstan, and Ukraine—as being within the Russian sphere of influence, the leaders of the Baltic states have made it clear that their countries are and always have been fundamentally European, even if they are first and foremost Estonian, Latvian, and Lithuanian.

POLITICS AND GOVERNMENT

The Baltics did not resume their lives as independent states with clean slates, for each had to decide what must be created anew, what must be discarded as unusable, and what could be recycled as part of that country's "usable past." It was to this usable past that Baltic leaders appealed when making their case for independence in 1989–1991, as activists in all three republics claimed that their goal was not to secede from the Soviet Union but rather to restore the republics whose inde-pendence was quashed in 1940. Framing the pursuit of independence in terms of maintaining legal continuity with the interwar republics—statehood was not something to be achieved but to be restored—Baltic nationalists tended to view the Soviet period as an unfortunate paren-thesis in the Baltic grand narrative.

Stressing the legal continuity between the post-Soviet and the prewar republics, the leaders of Latvia and Estonia elected to make their interwar constitutions the legal basis of the restored republics. Latvia made its choice on August 21, 1991, four months before the Soviet Union was formally dissolved by the leaders of Russia, Ukraine, and Belarus. As the coup by Soviet hardliners unraveled that summer day in Moscow, in Riga Latvia's Supreme Council seized the moment and declared the constitution of February 15, 1922, to be the law of the land, with no revisions or amendments. The political system of the restored Latvian state was to be based on that which existed before Soviet annexation in June 1940: the parliament (*Saeima*) would consist of 100 representatives elected for three-year terms by all citizens aged 18 or over on the basis of proportional representation (selected from party lists). Initially the president was to be elected by the *Saeima* for a term of three years, but in 1997 terms for representatives and the president were extended to four years. While the post is largely ceremonial, the Latvian president's responsibilities include the appointment of a prime minister, who in turn nominates other cabinet ministers. Few actions by Latvia's new political elite made more clear their concern with maintaining continuity with the prewar republic than the *Saeima*'s selection of Guntis Ulmanis (b. 1939), a grandnephew of Kārlis Ulmanis (prewar Latvia's last president), to be the country's first post-Soviet president. He served in that capacity from July 1993 to July 1999, when he was succeeded by the vigorously pro-European Vaira Vīķe-Freiberga (b. 1937), a former university professor in Canada and Latvia's first female president (1999–2007).

Estonia's leaders debated a new constitution for nearly a year before a new governing document came into force in July 1992. The resulting text was firmly based on the principles of the 1920 constitution, whose emphases included democratic freedoms and protection for ethnic minorities. Among the most important differences, however, were the new constitution's provisions for a clear separation of powers as well as its adoption of a presidency, elected by a unicameral legislature (*Riigikogu*) consisting of 101 members, in place of a State Elder as the country's ceremonial leader. While members of the *Riigikogu* are elected on the basis of proportional representation and serve four-year terms, the president's term of office is five years. Estonia's first post-Soviet president, Lennart Meri (1929–2006), spent nearly a decade in office (1992–2001), during which time he worked to enhance executive power while taking an active role in both domestic and foreign affairs. Meri's negotiations with Russia's president Yeltsin in 1994 were critical in achieving one of Estonia's (and all three

Baltic states') top foreign policy priorities: the final withdrawal of Russian forces.

After briefly resurrecting its prewar constitution, Lithuania's leaders rejected it as too authoritarian and elected to create a new document that would reflect the experiences of democratic countries such as the United States, France, and postwar Germany while retaining some elements of Soviet-style government—including the combining of some legislative and executive functions and provisions for social rights such as free medical care. After two years of debate in Lithuania's Supreme Council, the new constitution was approved by a voter referendum on October 25, 1992. As during the prewar period, the legislature is the *Seimas*, a popularly elected body consisting of 141 members, 70 of whom are chosen on the basis of proportional representation, with the remainder elected from single-member districts on the first-past-the-post principle. The executive branch consists of a popularly elected president, who serves a five-year term, and a prime minister, who is chosen by the president with the approval of the *Seimas*. As in Estonia and Latvia, the Lithuanian president's role is largely ceremonial and consultative with regard to domestic affairs, but the office has considerable power to shape foreign policy.

In reestablishing the democratic basis of their resurrected states, the Baltic republics rejected the single-party system of authoritarian rule that had guided and punished them during the Soviet era and returned to the uncertain world of political pluralism. In some cases the leaders who rose to the top during the struggle for independence— notably former *Sajūdis* leader Vytautas Landsbergis, who chaired the Lithuanian *Seimas* from 1996 to 2000 while heading the conservative Homeland Union coalition—maintained their prominence through the 1990s and beyond. Yet the political arena was now open to those who had experienced repression or exile during the Soviet era and who had not been well known during the years of the Singing Revolution. Indeed, the presidents of the post-Soviet Baltic states have thus far included one whose family had been sent to Siberia during the Stalin era (Lennart Meri, who was earlier known for making ethnographic films about the Finno-Ugrian peoples), two whose families had fled to the West during World War II (Vaira Vīķe-Freiberga and Valdus Adamkus, a civil servant in the United States before serving as president of Lithuania, 1998–2003 and 2004–2009), and another who was born in Sweden (Toomas Hendrik Ilves, elected president of Estonia in 2006). Such people have competed in the same arena as former Soviet *apparatchiks* such as Estonia's Arnold Rüütel (president 2001–2006) and Lithuania's Algirdas Brazauskas (president 1993–1998 and prime minister 2001–2006). The post-Soviet political scene was varied, colorful, and combative in all three Baltic states during the 1990s, but it was not long before the new systems stabilized and their leaders charted a sometimes controversial course for Europe.

While ethnic Estonian, Latvian, and Lithuanians were empowered by the return to independence, the Baltic political arena was explicitly discriminatory from the outset. All three Baltic governments barred former Soviet security (KGB) agents from standing for parliament and obtaining high positions in the state administration, but it was in Latvia that the approach to past "collaborators" was the most confrontational. If the winners in the struggles of 1988–1991 were suspicious of the losers, their insecurities were not unfounded, not least because 40 years of Soviet migration patterns had turned Latvia's cities into Russian colonies. At the end of the Soviet era Latvians comprised only a bare majority of the population of the republic that bore their name and were a minority in Riga and Daugavpils, the republic's first and second largest cities. Adding to the insecurities of Latvia's new rulers were the activities of the Communist Party of Latvia during the 1991 coup, for which its former first secretary Alfrēds Rubiks was sentenced to eight years in prison. Yet even if it was clear enough that the party's first loyalty was to Moscow rather than Latvia, the *Saeima* rejected a proposal to forbid former Communist Party officials and members from running for parliamentary seats.

As in Latvia, the Estonian government made every effort to remove the Soviet/Russian elites during the country's first years of independence. Top civil servants from the communist past were dismissed and replaced by a cadre of unusually young officials who were well educated but had no experience in governing. The purge and the laws on citizenship and language (discussed in greater detail below) also ensured that the government remained under the confident control of Estonian nationalists for years to come, which naturally fed the resentments of Soviet-era immigrants whose sense of insecurity was further heightened by the loss of a direct connection to Moscow as well as the factory closures and layoffs that accompanied the country's economic reforms. It was the lack of protection from Moscow that made possible the adoption of restrictive citizenship laws by the governments of Estonia and Latvia in the early 1990s. These laws, which were arguably the most significant measures enacted in the Baltic states to limit nonnative influence, effectively prevented hundreds of thousands of Soviet-era immigrants from voting in the parliamentary elections of 1992 and 1993.

Yet even if the way democracy was practiced (and limited) during the first post-Soviet years mirrored some of the ethnic and social divisions of the interwar era, the postcommunist states have weathered the various political, economic, and social crises of the 1990s and early 2000s with considerable resiliency. Governance is often messy in the Baltic states, but the commitment to democratic procedures has been firm for more than two decades. Moderate parties of the right-center (Estonia and Latvia) and the left-center (Lithuania) tend to gather the most popular support and continue to be voted into and out of power, which they share with coalition partners whose agendas may differ considerably from their own. These are systems that encourage compromise and cooperation, yet they are also systems in which political power is firmly in the hands of the titular nationality. While minorities have sometimes suffered from exclusion and disenfranchisement, nowhere in the Baltic states have they been silenced or repressed.

Perhaps the main difficulty the outsider encounters in trying to make sense of politics in the post-Soviet Baltic states has been the sheer number of parties and coalitions that compete for power. Many of the political groups that mushroomed in the early 1990s have changed their names, been subsumed into other parties, or, having failed time and again to garner enough votes to gain parliamentary representation, simply disappeared. While many political parties exist at the margins of national politics, are local in nature, or are merely single-issue parties, observers who are more familiar with the politics of larger countries (or, as in the case of the United States, political systems dominated by only two mass parties) may be confounded not only by the number of political parties that are active in the Baltic states but also by how few people even the largest parties represent. Few are mass-based organizations with broad memberships; some are financed by private businesses. For all the dozens of parties that have registered to compete in local and national elections in the Baltic states, it must be remembered that Lithuania in 2015 is a country of only three million people, Latvia two million, and Estonia a mere 1.3 million.

Of the 897,000 who voted in Estonia's 2007 parliamentary election—the first election in the world to use electronic voting (although few chose to vote this way)—Estonians could choose among 11 political parties. As coalition government is the norm in all three Baltic states, every voter in Estonia is aware that it is extremely unlikely that any one party will win a majority and govern alone. The winner of the 2011 election, with 27.8 percent of the vote, was the Reform Party, a pro-free market party that has participated in the government of Estonia for nearly its entire history since its founding in 1994 by Siim Kallas, then the president of the Bank of Estonia (hence its original nickname, the Party of Bankers). Its primary competitor over the past two decades has been the right-center Pro Patria Union (*Isamaaliit*, or "Fatherland Union"), whose history can tell us much about the complexity and fluidity of politics in Estonia, where minute differences on policy can cause a party to splinter just as easily as political expediency can encourage parties to merge or form alliances.

A party of national conservatism and Christian democracy whose main slogan was "A clean break with the past," the Pro Patria Union was born at the end of 1995 on the basis of a merger between the Estonian National Independence Party (a creation of the late Soviet era) and the National Coalition Party Pro Patria.[1] The fact that several political organizations were vying for the support of Estonia's conservative voters led to another merger in 2006 that brought about the union of Pro Patria Union and Res Publica, another party that identified itself as conservative. While the merged party, known as PPRP and chaired by Mart Laar (b. 1960), only placed third in both the 2007 and 2011 elections to the *Riigikogu*, the merger ensured that Estonia's conservatives would be able to compete more effectively against the more cohesive if less popular political left.

The consolidation of political forces that took place in the early 2000s weeded out some of the single-issue parties and ensured a certain balance in Estonian politics between the parties of the right, center, and left. While the Estonian Centre Party, which was formed on the basis of the Soviet-era Popular Front and continues to be chaired by Edgar Savisaar, is Estonia's leading centrist party, the Social Democratic Party (SDE), known between 1996 and 2004 as the Moderate People's Party, is the most popular party on the left. Upholding the social market economy and the welfare state while remaining committed to a Nordic identity for Estonia, the SDE has even produced a president, Toomas Hendrik Ilves (b. 1953). However, it typically underperforms in parliamentary elections—in Estonia it is difficult to garner popular support for policies necessitating a large public sector—and is usually in the opposition both in the national government and in most major cities.

If the first elections in the restored Republic of Estonia in 1992 yielded a *Riigikogu* that provided representation for no fewer than nine parties (and none for the Communist Party of Estonia's successor party, the Estonian Democratic Labour Party, later renamed the Estonian Left Party), only four parties earned seats in the 2011 elections and only two (the Reform Party and the Centre Party) entered the government. A similar trend toward consolidation can be seen in Latvia, where eight parties were awarded seats in the 1993 elections to the *Saeima*, compared to five in the 2010 and 2011 elections. Both countries have also seen increased political participation by (and representation for) their Russian-speaking communities as more Soviet-era migrants become naturalized citizens.

Of the Baltic states Lithuania has been the most ideologically diverse and politically fragmented. In the parliamentary election of October 2012 no Lithuanian party earned more than 19.82 percent of the vote, and that went to the Democratic Labour Party, which emerged from the reformist Lithuanian section of the Communist Party of the Soviet Union (CPSU) and even today is sometimes thought to be under the influence of the Kremlin. Close on its heels was the Social Democratic Party of Lithuania (18.37 percent), a Marxist party of the left. Together they formed a coalition with two other parties, including one that represented the country's Poles.

Despite frequent allegations of corruption, social democracy has had greater sway in post-Soviet Lithuania than in either Latvia or Estonia, countries where left-wing parties tend to be aligned with the interests of the Russophone minorities. That many Lithuanians missed some aspects of the Soviet welfare state was apparent in the October 1992 elections, when the Democratic Labour Party (44 percent) and the Social Democratic Party (6 percent) together earned half the vote in what was clearly a rebuke of the conservative–nationalist *Sajūdis* movement. Voters blamed *Sajūdis,* which had been created during the last years of the USSR as an opposition movement before taking the reins of government, for failing to deal effectively with the negative effects of the economic collapse, including runaway inflation, a decline in living standards, and unemployment. With *Sajūdis*'s defeat and the return of the Democratic Labour Party, Lithuania became the first transition country where a former communist party regained power in free elections—a pattern that would soon be repeated in Poland and Hungary.[2]

While the Lithuanian left has maintained its seat at the table and has participated in several parliamentary coalitions, its main competitor on the right since 1993 has been the *Sajūdis* offshoot Homeland Union, a conservative–nationalist party whose electoral fortunes have oscillated between political dominance (it held 70 seats in the *Seimas* following the 1996 elections) and marginalization (it earned only nine seats in the 2000 elections, with a plurality of 42 going to the Democratic Labour Party). Mergers with the Lithuanian Nationalist Union and the Lithuanian Christian Democrats in 2008 briefly made Homeland Union–Lithuanian Christian Democrats (TS-LKD) into Lithuania's largest party, but its popularity plummeted in the wake of the 2008–2010 economic crisis, following which it was excluded from government.

Latvian voters also have a wide array of parties from which to choose, with no fewer than 13 parties competing in the parliamentary election of September 2011. In Latvia's first post-Soviet elections, held in July 1993, the leading vote-getter was Latvia's Way, a right-of-center party of ethnic Latvians, which earned 32.4 percent of the vote. Despite declining electoral support, Latvia's Way remained a powerful force in Latvian politics and was part of every coalition government (and produced most of the country's prime ministers) until November 2002, when it garnered just under the 5 percent of the popular vote that is needed for representation. The early popularity of Latvia's Way was supplanted by the rise of New Era, which first competed in elections to the *Saeima* in 2002, when it campaigned on its promises to combat corruption and tax evasion. As is the case with many political parties in the Baltic states, New Era reacted to its subsequent decline in popularity by merging with two other parties to form Unity, a center-right party that serves as a counterweight to the left-wing Harmony Centre Alliance. As in Estonia, the Latvian right has been dominant but at the same time it has suffered from political fragmentation, divided between Unity, the People's Party, For Fatherland and Freedom/LNNK, and Latvia's First Party/Latvian Way.

Perhaps the most remarkable story in Latvian politics during the past decade has been the rise of Harmony Centre (*Saskaņas Centrs*), a social-democratic alliance whose members include the Socialist Party of Latvia and the Social Democratic Party "Harmony," which itself emerged from a merger of several left-wing parties. All tend to favor increased social spending and are guarded about Europe, but what unites them is their concern with minority rights, for the Harmony Centre Alliance is above all the party of Latvia's ethnic Russians. From its founding in 2005 the alliance has been headed by the former journalist Nils Ušakovs (b. 1976), who in 2009 became the first mayor of Riga of Russian descent since Latvia attained its independence in 1991. Harmony Centre's broad appeal to Latvia's Russophone community and its support for strengthening ties with Russia are also the reasons it has never participated in government, which has always been dominated by parties composed of (and appealing to) ethnic Latvians. Yet Harmony Centre's stronghold is Riga, where the population of Russians and Latvians is more or less evenly balanced, and where for a time Ušakovs's personal popularity seemed to transcend the ethnic divide. The alliance even gained the support of some Latvians, whose frustration with a government they accuse of catering to the country's wealthy businessmen (oligarchs) caused many to seek an alternative to the usual parties.

Overall, there are several conclusions one may draw about the political environment in the postcommunist Baltic states: (1) they have generally been dominated by members of the titular nationality, although the political participation of non-Latvians and non-Estonians has increased over the years; (2) most political parties tend to be short-lived, with numerous parties failing to last for more than one or two election cycles; (3) the restrictive citizenship laws enacted by Estonia and Latvia hurt the left by diminishing the electoral base for parties representing the interests of labor; (4) the fact that citizens of the Baltic states tend to vote more on the basis of personality or their feelings on a single issue rather than on the basis of party identification has hindered (but not prevented) the consolidation of political forces in these countries; and (5) until recent years governments tend to be very short-lived.

The last point merits some elaboration. Between 1992 and 2003 Estonia had eight governments, but only four governments between April 2003 and 2014. Latvia had eleven governments between 1993 and 2004, but only seven in the decade that followed. Between 1992 and 2001 Lithuania had eleven governments, but only five governments from July 2001 through the end of 2014. Despite the volatility of the Baltic governments during the postcommunist years, the domestic and foreign policies of Estonia, Latvia, and Lithuania have been fairly consistent since the 1990s. No matter which government is in power, the policies adopted in all three Baltic states have been shaped by a general consensus concerning the desire to be seen as a completely sovereign, liberal, democratic nation-state in an economically integrated Europe.

ECONOMIC DEVELOPMENT

By the time the Baltic states regained their independence in the summer of 1991, their economies were in free fall. In all three countries a catastrophic decline in production was coupled with hyperinflation that ate away at a living standard that had been the envy of other Soviet citizens since the 1950s. Once part of an integrated economic system geared largely toward Soviet needs rather than local ones, the Baltic states were now on their own: each had to reconstruct its banking network, substitute local currencies for the inconvertible Soviet ruble, replace the system of centralized planning with market mechanisms, privatize state-owned properties and enterprises, and reorient its foreign trade toward Europe while attracting Western investment.

Few questioned the conviction of most Baltic leaders that the old Soviet command economy had failed to keep pace with that of the capitalist West and must be reinvented. Thus the debate in the Baltic states, as in much of the former Soviet bloc, centered not on the desirability but the pace of the transition to a market-based economy. Advocates of what was called "shock therapy," a term that was used to describe the neoliberal reforms adopted in Poland beginning in 1989, argued for the most rapid economic reform possible in the belief that a semi-reformed system would simply perpetuate the distortions of the Soviet era and would deter investment. Moreover, supporters of shock therapy believed that the restoration of a market economy based on private property and the rule of law would facilitate the Baltic states' "return to Europe." Gradualists, who quickly lost the debate in Estonia but whose views resonated more widely in Lithuania and Latvia, urged a more measured approach to the transition, arguing that the negative short-term effects of shock therapy would undermine political reform and cause unnecessary suffering.

Eager to join Western institutions such as NATO and the EU, which many believed would ensure their future security and economic well-being, the Baltic states followed the advice of the International Monetary Fund (IMF), upon which all three depended for economic aid, and adopted the liberal economic path of rapid reform. While the Democratic Labour Party government (1992–1996) in Lithuania was initially reluctant to pursue this approach, it too succumbed to Western pressure to embrace the economics of shock therapy.

The early years of transition, especially 1992 and 1993, were the most excruciating for many, for this was an era of decay and uncertainty as well as one of creation and reinvention. As unemployment steadily rose, inflation in all three countries approached or exceeded 1,000 percent in 1992, destroying whatever savings people had managed to accumulate while making even the most basic foodstuffs, as well as rent and services, prohibitively expensive. Meanwhile, the decay of the Soviet military–industrial complex caused great hardship in the manufacturing sector throughout the former USSR. Factory workers in struggling enterprises—in the Baltics such people tended to be disproportionately Russian—saw their future prospects vanish as privatized factories shed employees or folded.

During the early years of this transition Baltic governments could do little to mitigate the ill effects of unemployment, unmet material needs, and general hopelessness. Adopting tight monetary policies, they were consequently unable to provide much of a cushion for those who were worst affected. Pensioners, whose numbers in the Baltic countries were then proportionally twice as large as in western Europe, found government austerity measures especially painful.

Moreover, with state subsidies for research, education, and cultural activities sharply reduced, Baltic universities and institutes, orchestras and theaters, and journals and libraries had to slash their budgets while searching for alternate sources of income.

Only after the introduction of local currencies in 1992 (Latvia and Estonia) and 1993 (Lithuania) was it possible for the Baltic governments to combat the greatest scourge facing local consumers—runaway inflation—which fell to the double digits in 1993–1994 and the single digits by 1997. By this time, the economies of all three states had turned the corner. Having contracted by as much as one third in 1992 alone, in 1994 the growth in the gross domestic product (GDP) for all three Baltic countries was positive for the first time since 1989. If the early phase of the transition produced misery and hardship in all three Baltic countries, the reforms began to bear fruit by the end of the 1990s. An economic boom that lasted from 2000 until 2007 earned them the nickname "Baltic tigers," for the Baltics enjoyed some of the fastest growth rates in Europe during the early years of this century. Yet even this stunning growth, more than 10 percent per annum at the height of the boom, did not necessarily improve conditions for people at the bottom of the economic ladder. Poverty remained a feature of rural life in all three Baltic states as the gap between the worst off and those in the middle and upper classes grew.

Estonia carried out its economic reforms first and most resolutely, with the aid of massive investment from Scandinavian countries. Adopting a tight monetary policy, Estonia limited government subsidies and expenditures, including pensions for the elderly, while cutting excessive taxation. If at first Latvia and Lithuania moved less decisively than Estonia, by the mid-1990s they too had developed the basic features of a market economy.

The key to economic reform in the Baltic states, as in the other former communist countries of eastern and central Europe, was the privatization of businesses and property that during Soviet times had been owned and run by the state. The idea was not only to right a historic wrong, but also to reestablish an ownership society on the basis of private property. In all three countries, small enterprises and farms were privatized first, while medium-size and larger enterprises were privatized afterward, generally after 1994. In Latvia and Lithuania, political opposition arising from public concerns about corruption and insider dealing, compounded by the sheer complexity of the process, discouraged the sort of rapid privatization that was achieved in Estonia; the result was a slower and more tortured transition to private ownership in these countries.

There were two main methods of privatization: cash sales of enterprises to core investors, which many saw as the most efficient way of restoring economic viability, and voucher systems, whereby residents received shares in enterprises based on certain criteria, such as (as in the Estonian system) their years of active employment and service in the economy. The system adopted by Latvia, however, illustrates one of the problems of voucher-based privatization: launched in May 1993, the Latvian plan called for all residents to receive 1 certificate for each year of residence in Latvia, plus 15 additional certificates if they could prove Latvian citizenship prior to June 1940. While the vouchers were freely tradable and the system ensured widespread participation in the privatization process, the country's Soviet-era immigrants saw the process as inherently discriminatory.

Indeed, in all three countries, the privatization process brought forth charges of discrimination, favoritism, and collusion. A common allegation during the early stage of privatization, and one that was often true, was that managers and former senior Communist Party officials were able to purchase shares at a discount and thereby retain control of the firms they had run during the Soviet period. Moreover, with privatization came the pain of streamlining and rising unemployment as well as the psychological difficulties of adjusting to the "risk and reward" mentality of the private sector. Many firms drifted under the new conditions, with the managers often expecting that losses would be smoothed over with government subsidies, as was common during Soviet days. More successful was the transfer to private owners of smaller enterprises such as restaurants, small shops, and services, where the smaller scales of operation facilitated innovative approaches to management. By the first decade of the 21st century however, the process of privatization was nearly complete in all three Baltic states and most of the largest enterprises had been sold off even if the state still holds sizable stakes in certain enterprises, such as the Latvian government's ownership of its national airline.

The issue of land reform posed no less a challenge to the new governments, each of which prioritized the return of farmlands to their pre-collectivization owners from the moment they secured their independence. As the old collective farms began to disintegrate, much of the land was transferred to private hands. However, the transition was far from smooth, as claims exceeded the acreage available and the plots transferred to private owners were often too small to be economically viable. Meanwhile, competing claims to the same properties and the lack of proper official documentation in many cases held the process up for several years.

Agriculture's share in the Baltic economies declined dramatically after 1991, and the proportion of the population employed in the agricultural sector dropped commensurately as the amount of fallow land increased. For example, in Lithuania, whose economy was the most dependent on agriculture during the Soviet era, the proportion of the population employed in agriculture dropped from 19.2 percent in 1998 to 7.9 percent in 2008. By the latter date agriculture comprised only 4.4 percent of the country's total GDP, half of what it had been a decade earlier. Meanwhile, employment in Lithuania's financial sector doubled while the industrial sector held more or less steady, employing around one-fifth the country's work force and producing about one-quarter of its GDP.

The economic profiles of Latvia and Estonia are similar. Agriculture produces only about 5 percent of Latvia's GDP and 4 percent of Estonia's. With the disappearance of Estonia's collective farms, employment in agriculture declined by a whopping 80 percent since the end of the Soviet era, with most of the displaced workers finding employment in other sectors of the economy. Industry is responsible for 30 percent of Estonia's economy and about one-quarter that of Latvia. In all three countries services account for the bulk—60 to 70 percent—of GDP.[3]

By most measures, these are modern economies that have retained few vestiges of the old Soviet system. Estonia in particular has made its mark in the technology sector, with the free communications service Skype (which was bought by Microsoft for $8.5 billion in 2011) as its best-known start-up. Yet even Estonia's burgeoning technology sector has its roots in the Soviet era: in its early years Skype, whose software was created by Estonians, was housed in the Institute of Cybernetics, founded in 1960 as an institute of the Estonian Academy of Sciences. While some have claimed that it was the radicalism of Estonia's post-Soviet leaders that was responsible for the country's early economic successes, it could also be argued that Estonia hit the ground running as the communist system collapsed; after all, the republic had been a laboratory for Soviet economic experiments since the 1960s and it inherited certain structural advantages that were lacking in the other republics, such as the prevalence of light industry and its greater economic decentralization.[4]

Still, being severed from the USSR's integrated economic system meant that the Baltic states would have to reorient their economies away from Russia (while reaping the benefits of Russia's transit trade with the West) and toward Western markets. The transition took place with stunning speed: while in 1991 the republics of the Soviet Union absorbed 94 percent of Estonia's exports and provided 84 percent of its imports, within a year these figures had dropped to 35 percent and 40 percent.[5] A similar pattern could be seen in Latvia and Lithuania, and in all three countries the transition accelerated after the collapse of the Russian ruble in August 1998 and continued after the Baltic states joined the EU in 2004.

Today the states of the EU, especially the northern ones, are the biggest trade partners of all three Baltic countries. In 2011, 61 percent of Lithuania's exports (led by refined petroleum, dairy and wood products, fertilizers, and chemical products) were delivered to EU members, and 16 percent of Lithuanian exports went to Russia.[6] In 2012, the main destinations for Estonia's exports (machinery and electrical equipment, followed by oil shale and electricity) were Sweden (16 percent), Finland (15 percent), and Russia (12 percent).[7] Latvia's main exports include wood products, base metals, machinery, and electrical equipment. And while Russia is the destination of 11 percent of Latvia's exports, the bulk go to EU countries (70 percent), mainly Lithuania (16 percent), Estonia (13 percent), and Germany (8 percent).[8] While all three remain dependent on Russia for oil and natural gas, Lithuania has the Baltic states' only petroleum refinery, Mažeikiai Nafta, in the Baltics. Privatized in 1999 (when it was bought by the U.S.-based Williams Companies, which then sold it to the Russian oil company Yukos—a transaction that prompted Prime Minister Rolandas Paksas to resign in protest) and subsequently upgraded, the majority of Mažeikiai is currently owned by the Polish company PKN Orlen. Processing oil that mostly comes from Russia, Mažeikiai exports the majority of its products to EU states and the United States.

The banking systems created in the Baltic states in the 1990s illustrate some of the costs and benefits of economic reform in the region. While the transition to market-based economies would not have been possible without the construction of banking networks in each of the Baltic countries, the frequent scandals associated with the financial sector have frequently undermined public and investor confidence. The most notorious case during the early years of the transition was the collapse of Latvia's largest commercial bank, Baltija Bank, in May 1995, which caused thousands of depositors to lose their savings and nearly brought down the entire Latvian banking system. Likewise, at the end of the year, two of Lithuania's largest banks were declared insolvent and Prime Minister Adolfas Šleževičius, who was reported to have used inside information to withdraw his savings before the suspension of operation, was ousted by the *Seimas*. Banks were also a factor in the 2008–2010 financial crisis as international investors began to withdraw their assets in the wake of the burst real estate bubble. As a result of the crisis, the government of Latvia acquired a 51 percent stake in the troubled Parex Bank, the country's largest, which in turn forced the government to take out a loan from the IMF and the European Commission. The Lithuanian government was likewise forced to nationalize the commercial bank Snoras in late 2011 following a public uproar about the 3.4 million litas (about one billion euros) that disappeared from its accounts.

Just as their residual dependence on Russia in the 1990s caused the Baltic countries to suffer in the wake of the Russian financial crisis of August 1998, the vulnerabilities of the Baltic economies were once again revealed during the worldwide financial crisis that struck a decade later, for by 2008 the Baltic states were deeply embedded in the world financial system and were dependent on the foreign credit that dried up following Lehman Brothers' bankruptcy in September of that year. If Latvia, whose economy grew by 12.2 percent in 2006, was the leader of the "Baltic tigers" during a period of dynamic economic growth, it quickly became a poster child for the global recession: in 2009 alone the Latvian economy contracted by nearly 18 percent—its worst performance since the early 1990s. As unemployment soared past 20 percent, 130,000 Latvians (and twice as many Lithuanians), mostly young and male, left their places of birth to seek employment opportunities in the EU, the United Kingdom, the United States, and elsewhere between 2009 and 2012.

If Lithuania and Estonia suffered less from the crisis than did Latvia, it was mostly a matter of degree, for all three Baltic economies had grown with extraordinary speed only to experience the sharpest reversal of fortune in all Europe. All three experienced a "housing bubble" (i.e., an overheated property market) that radically inflated real estate prices in the region's largest cities before bursting. The cost of purchasing an apartment in Tallinn and Vilnius nearly doubled between 2004 and 2007; in Riga the cost of an apartment, measured in price per square meter, rose by 267 percent. As real estate prices began to be corrected in late 2007, the Baltic economies decelerated; by 2008 the Baltic tigers had fallen into a recession as global liquidity evaporated, unemployment skyrocketed, and gross wages declined. In December it was announced that Latvia, the country that was hit worst by the crisis, would be the target of an IMF stabilization program amounting to $10.5 billion (7.5 billion euros)—more than one-third of the country's GDP.[9] While Lithuania and Estonia avoided the IMF, all three Baltic governments introduced severe deficit-cutting measures (cutting pensions, slashing the wages of state employees, increasing income and excise taxes) and all three intervened in the affairs of their troubled banks. "Education, health care, central administration: hardly any public sector category was spared by [Latvia's] reforms," one observer noted.[10]

The austerity measures were pushed through the Baltic parliaments virtually without debate, which in Latvia simply reinforced public perception about the relationship between the business oligarchs and the country's political elites. The reforms created widespread hardship, inspired public protests in Vilnius and Riga in January 2009, and caused some political instability in Lithuania and especially Latvia, where the government of Prime Minister Ivars Godmanis had to fend off a vote of no confidence by the *Saeima* (it was replaced in February by a more free-market right-center government under Valdis Dombrovskis). Yet even if the Baltic states suffered a cumulative GDP contraction of 18 percent in 2008–2009—among the worst performances in Europe—they were spared the widespread social unrest that plague Greece and Spain. Despite popular anger at corruption in Latvia and Lithuania even the radical left failed to make political headway.

While the fiscally conservative policies adopted by the Baltic states were inarguably painful to many, their defenders can claim that they also quickly paid off as the Baltic states began to claw their way out of the recession. By 2011 the Baltic economies were recording some of the highest growth rates (8.3 percent in Estonia, 5.5 percent in Latvia, and 5.9 percent in Lithuania) in Europe. Unemployment, which in early 2010 reached 20 percent in Latvia, 19 percent in Estonia, and 17 percent in Lithuania (the EU average peaked at 9.6 percent), remained a major problem for years afterward in Latvia and Lithuania, whereas in Estonia it had fallen to 6.9 percent by the second quarter of 2014 thanks in part to the country's ageing labor force.

RUSSIA AND THE BALTIC RUSSIANS

The Early 1990s: Negotiating with Russia

One of the most pressing domestic issues in the contemporary Baltic states concerns the integration of the region's Russian-speaking minorities. When the Soviet Union collapsed in 1991, nearly two million Russian-speakers resided in the Baltic states, their future status uncertain. This was a concern not only to the Baltic governments, but also to Russia, the Soviet Union's legal successor, for the Russian government now took on the role of "protector" of the more than 20 million Russian-speakers who were stranded in the former Soviet republics. If in 1990 Boris Yeltsin, then speaker of the Supreme Soviet of the Russian

Soviet Federative Socialist Republic (RSFSR), said that if the Baltic states opted for independence Russia would be the first to sign treaties with them, then as president of the Russian Federation (1991–1999) he soon began to change his tune, putting pressure on the Baltic states to observe the "human rights" of the region's Russian-speakers.

Despite the Russian president's rough warnings, Moscow's role in the region was generally passive in the 1990s, and it was during the Yeltsin years that the Baltic states and Russia managed to negotiate the Russian army's exit from the Baltic states. This did not come easily, as the Russian foreign ministry demands included: temporary bases in the Baltics; guarantees of Russia's military transit rights to Kaliningrad, its last remaining military outpost on the Baltic Sea (this condition affected Lithuania above all); financial compensation for the vacated bases; and guarantees for the social and political rights of Russian-speaking residents and of retired Soviet officers.[11] With the Baltic governments rejecting these stipulations, negotiations dragged on for several years.

Most of Russia's complaints were directed at Latvia and Estonia, whose treatment of their Russian-speaking minorities was a major impediment to negotiations. Lithuania's more accommodating stance did not go unnoticed in Moscow, which agreed to a timetable for withdrawal by August 31, 1993. With the encouragement of the U.S. government, on April 30, 1994, Latvia reached a compromise agreement with Russia over Skrunda, the location of a Soviet-built missile attack early warning system that Russia had hoped to keep.[12] On the same day the Russian and Latvian presidents and prime ministers signed an accord stipulating that Russian troops would withdraw from Latvia by August 31, 1994. Latvia also agreed, reluctantly, to provide residence permits for members of the Soviet military who retired there.

Estonia's difficult negotiations with Russia required the diplomatic skills of President Lennart Meri, who demanded that Yeltsin provide him with a specific date by which the nuclear submarine base at Paldiski, located 45 kilometers west of Tallinn, would be shut down. Like his Latvian counterpart Guntis Ulmanis, Meri ultimately agreed to grant retired military personnel and their families residence permits, but only after the two sides had reached an agreement about Paldiski. Although accounts of the negotiations in Moscow suggest that they were facilitated by Yeltsin's growing inebriation, the result was a treaty that guaranteed the withdrawal of Russia's military presence by August 31, 1994.[13]

The agreements that resulted in Russia's complete military withdrawal from the region were facilitated by a shared desire on behalf of the governments of Russia, Estonia, and Latvia to improve their relations with the West. The Baltic states hoped to clear the path for eventual admission to the EU and NATO, while Russia sought Western aid and investment as it reformed its economy. Early negotiations over the Estonian-Russian and Latvian-Russian borders were less successful, as Russia refused to even consider Estonian and Latvian demands to nullify the border changes that were made at the end of World War II (see chapter 6). As many central European countries shared frontiers that were imposed upon them after World War II, European leaders were reluctant to set a precedent by condoning Estonian and Latvian demands that the Russian Federation recognize their interwar borders. Estonian foreign minister Jüri Luik summed up Estonia's dilemma this way: "Nobody would like to have us in the [EU] if we have unresolved border issues. Estonia's eastern border would become the EU eastern border and the unresolved border disagreement or conflict would become a conflict for the EU."[14]

It was not until 2005 that Estonia and Russia signed the treaties that delineated their land and sea borders (these were ratified by the *Riigikogu* but not by the Russian Duma). Latvia and Russia came to a quiet agreement about their mutual border the following year. By this time the three Baltic states constituted the easternmost boundaries of both the NATO alliance and the EU, while a resurgent Russia, now enjoying a period of spectacular economic growth buoyed by rising energy prices, was under the leadership of Vladimir Putin (b. 1952), a highly disciplined former KGB officer who was determined to restore vertical power at home and Russia's great power status abroad.

Citizens and Noncitizens

The Baltics' relationship with Russia is nearly inseparable from Moscow's expressed concerns about the Russian-speaking minorities who constitute about one-quarter of the population of Estonia and Latvia and less than one-tenth of Lithuania's more homogeneous population. While Lithuanians have felt less threatened by their national minorities, many Latvians and Estonians see their Russian-speaking communities as an unwanted legacy of the Soviet era, when waves of colonizers arrived to work as administrators, party functionaries, and industrial laborers, while tens of thousands of Balts were relocated, at first forcibly and later voluntarily, to the other Soviet republics.

How the situation looked after nearly five decades of Soviet rule can be seen in the figures produced by the Soviet census of 1989, which showed that only 52 percent of Latvia's population consisted of ethnic Latvians, with most of the rest being ethnic Russians or

Russian-speakers. Ethnic Estonians comprised a mere 61.5 percent of Estonia's population in 1989, with nearly all the remainder comprising Russophones, most of whom were unable to speak the totally unrelated (and difficult to learn) Estonian language. Only Lithuania exited communism with its titular population relatively unthreatened: ethnic Lithuanians continued to comprise about 80 percent (and rising) of the population of their own republic, while the rest were mostly Poles and Russians. Now masters in their own homes, Estonian and Latvian leaders were committed to ensuring the survival of their nations, even if this meant that their states would consist of two unequal communities.

Even today hundreds of thousands of Russian-speakers in Estonia and Latvia do not identify with their host state and feel as if they have been marginalized and disenfranchised. Although large numbers of them voted for independence in 1991, most Russian-speakers were disappointed at the resulting nation-state, for they now found themselves to be unequal members of an ethnic minority living in a vaguely foreign land that was suffering from the ill effects of a post-imperial hangover and whose leaders remained wary of its ethnic minorities. The events of the late 1980s and early 1990s destroyed forever Moscow's pretense that there was a united "Soviet people" bound together in eternal friendship under the benevolent guardianship of the Russians. If there remained multiple ethnic communities in the Baltic states, there were now only two legal communities: citizens and noncitizens—those with rights and constitutional protections, and those without.

Alone among the Baltic states, Lithuania adopted the so-called "zero option," which based citizenship on territory rather than ethnicity and set neither language nor residence requirements for those living in the republic prior to the enactment of the citizenship law in November 1989. A second law published in December 1991 set the conditions for acquiring citizenship by means of naturalization: anyone who lived in Lithuania for 10 years could apply for Lithuanian citizenship provided they could speak Lithuanian and were willing to take a loyalty oath.

By early 1993 more than half of Lithuania's ethnic Russian, Polish, Belarusian, and Ukrainian inhabitants had received citizenship, and by the end of the millennium 99 percent of all residents of Lithuania had citizenship. Forty thousand others, however, chose to emigrate, thus reducing Lithuania's Russian population to just over 300,000. If the remaining Russians (5.8 percent of the population in 2011) and Poles (6.6 percent) who are concentrated in the poorer eastern part of the country have found Lithuania to be more hospitable to non-Lithuanians than Estonia or Latvia is to its Russian-speaking minorities, this is in part because of the Lithuanian government's more liberal and inclusive approach to its national minorities. Nevertheless, despite the international agreements that protect the right of Poles to use Polish in eastern Lithuania, tensions between representatives of the central government and local non-Lithuanian officials have flared on occasion, and Polish activists have frequently complained about unfairness with regard to education (they have demanded a "Polish" university), cultural rights, and access to public-sector employment.[15]

Citizenship policies in Latvia and Estonia were far tougher on their national minorities, in particular the Soviet-era immigrants, who were not granted automatic citizenship but were instead made to go through the naturalization process. Thus while the citizens of the preoccupation republics and their descendants were automatically declared citizens, the remainder—those who had come to the republic after June 1940, as well as their descendants—would have had to choose among four options: (1) apply for naturalization on the basis of specific language and residency criteria; (2) opt for Russian citizenship while remaining in Estonia or Latvia; (3) leave; or (4) remain "stateless," without the basic social and political rights accorded to citizens. Such policies disenfranchised the bulk of their Russian-speaking inhabitants. It was Estonia's dramatically reduced electorate—nearly one-third of the country consisted of "aliens" without Estonian citizenship—that in 1992 produced a *Riigikogu* that lacked even a single Russian-speaker. Latvia's first postcommunist elections produced a 100-member *Saeima* with seven ethnic Russians.

During this period of uncertainty many Estonians and Latvians wished that the Russian immigrants would simply "go back to Russia," a voluntary program for which the Latvian government even offered financial assistance in the hopes of avoiding an entrenched conflict between the majority and minority communities.[16] In the summer of 1993 the Estonian *Riigikogu* forced the issue by passing the Law on Aliens, which demanded that all noncitizens be registered and that they obtain new residence and work permits or face deportation. By this time tens of thousands of Russophones had left Estonia and Latvia for Russia and other former Soviet republics.

To many observers it seemed that by enacting strict naturalization requirements the governments of Estonia and Latvia were in effect discouraging the integration of their Russophone populations, for at the time of the USSR's breakup relatively few of the region's Russophones knew the Estonian or Latvian languages and many considered the language exams unreasonably difficult to pass. Nevertheless, under pressure from Moscow, the EU, and other international organizations, the citizenship laws of Estonia and Latvia were amended to simplify naturalization procedures and thus speed up the integration process. Although naturalization rates slowed after 1999, between 1992 and 2012 a total of 154,439 people gained Estonian citizenship and the number of stateless residents had fallen to 92,351—a number that is slightly exceeded by the number of residents of Estonia who were citizens of the Russian Federation (94,638). As of 2014 about half of Estonia's minority population lacked Estonian citizenship. Authors of a report on the issue concluded that "naturalisation has brought new members to the Estonian citizenry, made it ethnically more diverse and moved the country closer to full democratic participation."[17] At the same time, it may well also be the case that Estonia has managed to maintain a functioning political partly because of its willingness to allow Russian-speaking communities, concentrated in the northeast corner of the country, a large degree of cultural autonomy. It is possible that a policy of relative separation rather than integration may even have contributed to a growing acceptance of the Estonian state on the part of Russian-speakers.[18]

While Estonia's Russian-speaking minority is concentrated in Narva and Tallinn, Latvia's ethnic minorities are more broadly dispersed throughout the country; thus a policy of granting an ethnic enclave self-governance or cultural autonomy was less feasible there. Yet Latvia too has modified its policies since the early 1990s when, like Estonia, it adopted restrictive citizenship policies that granted automatic citizenship only to people who were citizens of Latvia in June 1940 and their descendants. Such a policy left some 28 percent of Latvia's residents—673,398 people—with undetermined status until the passage of a citizenship law in 1994, which required those who wished to become naturalized citizens to pass tests on the Latvian language and history.

Yet the goal of Latvia's citizenship law seemed to be aimed less at integrating the Russian community as quickly as possible than its opposite: the law's designers wished to ensure that Latvia would not be flooded by a rush of applicants, an outcome some Latvians believed would threaten their survival as a nation. But with the number of applicants turning out to be lower than expected—from 1995 to 1998 only 15,853 residents applied for naturalization—many Russians chose to remain stateless or take on citizenship in the Russian Federation.[19] The muddled policies of the Russian Federation in the 1990s facilitated this choice, as all former Soviet citizens qualified for natural-born Russian citizenship upon request. However, Russia's policy of allowing individuals living in the "near abroad" who opted for Russian citizenship to maintain citizenship in their country of residence was opposed by virtually all of Russia's neighbors, who suspected Moscow of implementing a strategy that would allow it to dominate the territories of the former USSR by creating millions of dual citizens.[20]

Responding to pressure from the EU and other Western institutions that Latvia wished to join, Latvia amended its citizenship law in 1998 to liberalize its requirements (the number of applicants nearly tripled in 1999), but language proficiency remains the main obstacle on the path to citizenship for most Russophones, a point that is reinforced by the fact that 41 percent of all applicants failed the language exam in 2011. A similar rate of failure was reported in Estonia earlier in the century. That in recent years only 2,000 to 3,000 residents of Latvia have bothered to apply for naturalization in any given year while 304,283 remained noncitizens as of October 2012 is revealing of Latvia's failures in that arena.[21]

In recent years the main concern of the Russophone minority in Latvia has been the legal status of the Russian language in a country where at the dawn of the millennium more people were fluent in Russian than in Latvian. As in Estonia, Latvian law considers Russian a foreign language (mirroring Soviet-era policies, the Latvian state now requires Russian children to study Latvian in elementary school), despite the fact that 37 percent of the population speak Russian at home. In an effort to force Latvia's publicly financed schools to use Latvian exclusively, in 2010 the National Alliance coalition, which united the conservative party For Fatherland and Freedom/LNNK and the ethno-nationalist party All For Latvia! for the 2010 parliamentary election, began collecting signatures to force a referendum on the issue.

Such expressions of Latvian nationalism in the political arena had the unintended effect of mobilizing the Russophone organizations, which in turn began to collect signatures in an effort to get their own referendum placed on the ballot that would make Russian Latvia's official second language and that would give Russian equal status to Latvian in government institutions. While the drive succeeded in collecting enough signatures to trigger a referendum in early 2012 (whereas the Latvian initiative failed), the results simply mirrored Latvia's ethnic divisions, with 25 percent voting in favor and the remainder rejecting the proposed amendment to the Latvian constitution.

If at first Latvia's president Andris Bērziņš (since 2011) hesitated to take sides, he nevertheless characterized the Russians' efforts to make Russian a second language in Latvia as "a deliberate incitement" before urging people to "go and protect the Latvian language."[22] A statement made at that time by Latvia's former president Valdis

Zatlers (2007–2011) that "Latvian has always been the only language in Latvia" may be taken as proof that Baltic politicians, like people everywhere, are not always comfortable with certain inconvenient truths.[23]

The Geopolitics of History in the Baltic States

In his annual address to the Federal Assembly in April 2005, Russian president Vladimir Putin offered an outline of Russia's recent history that has sometimes been mistaken as nostalgia for communism but in reality reflected a Russian imperial worldview that sharply contradicted the Baltic narrative of a "return to Europe." "Above all," Putin reminded his audience, "we should acknowledge that the collapse of the Soviet Union was a major geopolitical disaster of the century. As for the Russian nation, it became a genuine drama. Tens of millions of our co-citizens and compatriots found themselves outside Russian territory." This was Putin's inconvenient truth: Russians were traumatized by the loss of their empire; left unsaid was what should be done to heal the wounds of the Russian nation.

Two weeks later, on May 9, Putin played host to world leaders at the 60th anniversary of the Allied victory over Nazi Germany. On his way to Moscow, U.S. president George W. Bush *fils* stopped in Riga, where he delivered an address to Latvia's president Vaira Vīķe-Freiberga, Estonian president Arnold Rüütel, Lithuanian president Valdas Adamkus, and other dignitaries. "The Baltic countries have seen one of the most dramatic transformations in modern history, from captive nations to NATO allies and EU members in little more than a decade. The Latvian, Estonian, and Lithuanian people showed that the love of liberty is stronger than the will of an empire." Fully embracing the Baltic interpretation of postwar history, Bush continued: "The captivity of millions in Central and Eastern Europe will be remembered as one of the greatest wrongs of history." Never before had a U.S. president acknowledged what many Balts had long regarded as a shameful betrayal. It was an apology for which Estonians, Latvians, and Lithuanians had waited for nearly 60 years.

Despite the show of solidarity in Moscow, where the Russian and U.S. presidents stood side-by-side on the reviewing stand on Red Square to watch goose-stepping soldiers march past, these speeches were delivered at a difficult moment in Russian-Western relations and reflected their divergent views both of recent history and of Europe's future. In many important ways Russia and the West continued to be divided long after the fall of the Iron Curtain: while the West has promoted democracy, liberal economic reforms, and military cooperation in countries that once took their orders from Moscow, Russia's rulers continue to see the region between the Baltic and Black Seas as part of its own security perimeter. Millions of Russians and Russian-speakers from Estonia to Ukraine live in a zone whose past has been shaped by the bloody conflicts of the 20th century and whose present is influenced by a broadly shared desire for democracy and economic security that many associate with membership in Western institutions.

For such countries, the year 2004 was a turning point as a series of former Soviet satellites were invited to join an enlarged NATO, following an earlier round of NATO enlargement in 1999, and an expanded EU. That the Baltic states were admitted to these institutions was, in Putin's view, not only an insult to Russia but also a betrayal of an alleged promise made in 1990 by U.S. officials to then-Soviet leader Mikhail Gorbachev that NATO would not expand eastward. Having stomached NATO's admission of the Baltic states, Putin further suspected the West of intervening in neighboring Ukraine, where in November 2004 massive demonstrations broke out in response to irregularities in the recent presidential election. While Western leaders looked upon Ukraine's "Orange Revolution" with sympathy, the Russian president saw the West's support for democracy in Ukraine as an affront to Russia and a direct threat to Ukraine's Russian minority, which generally sought closer political and economic ties with Moscow rather than Europe. It was Putin's alleged concern for the rights of Russians in the territory of Ukraine that prompted Moscow's shocking seizure of Crimea in the spring of 2014—a unilateral border revision that triggered alarm bells in the Baltic states, which began to make preparations to deal with potential Russian aggression. If Russia could behave in such a manner in Ukraine, a neighbor that Russia accuses of persecuting its minority communities, might its leaders not be tempted to intervene in the Baltics where the Russian-speaking communities really do suffer from discrimination?

While irritation with the Baltic republics with regard to the rights of Russian speakers has been a consistent feature of Moscow's foreign policy for nearly a quarter century, the Kremlin's outrage is expressed most loudly when the Balts commemorate recent history in a manner that insults the Soviet-Russian memory of World War II. When geriatric former members of the Latvian Legion—a unit of the Waffen-SS created by the Nazis during World War II—gather at Riga's Freedom Monument every spring to commemorate their efforts to defend Latvia from the Soviets, they have always been met by counterdemonstrations attended by Russophones who accuse the Legion of having served the Nazis and who furthermore accuse sympathetic Latvian demonstrators of glorifying Nazism. Latvian nationalists who gather in support of the Legion, on the other hand, tend to see its members as anti-Soviet heroes who were unfairly maligned and punished during Soviet times. Latvian leaders have wisely distanced themselves from the Legionnaire Day celebrations: the government abandoned it as an official commemoration event in 2000 and Riga's mayor Nils Ušakovs tried to get the demonstrations banned. The annual event draws the attention of the international media and does little to heal relations between Latvia's estranged communities or between Latvia and Moscow.

While Legionnaires take center stage in Latvia every March 16, veterans of the Red Army gather every May 9 at Riga's Victory Park, created in the 1980s to commemorate the Soviet Union's defeat of the fascist invaders. In the absence of any Lenin monuments around which to rally, in the 1990s the imposing war monument at the center of Victory Park became a symbol for people who feel nostalgic about Soviet times and who harbor resentments against the Latvian state. For Latvian nationalists, on the other hand, the monument is a symbol of a Soviet occupation they regard as genocidal in intent, and hence of a great evil perpetrated by Russia's leaders for half a century. Like Legionnaire's Day, the May 9 celebrations do much to stir up tensions among the country's Latvians and Russian-speakers.[24]

The controversies surrounding the World War II commemorations are a reflection of the way Latvians and Russians remember the recent past. If most Latvians remember Soviet rule as being far worse than Nazi rule, for the Russian-speaking community the idea of Russia as an aggressor or that the Baltic states were "occupied" is completely alien; for Russians the main evil is "fascism"—a term that is often conflated with local (i.e., non-Russian) nationalism of any kind on the frontiers of the Russian state. Some members of the Russian-speaking community even take the questionable view that the Red Army saved Latvia's independence: if the Red Army hadn't defeated Hitler, said Boriss Cilevičs, a *Saeima* representative from the pro-Russian Harmony Centre and a native of the largely Russian city Daugavpils, there wouldn't be an independent Latvia today.

The way history is remembered and represented in the Baltic states today has fallen into predictable patterns—demonstrations that organize masses of people representing "we" (victims) against an insidious "they" (perpetrators) are met with criticism and counterdemonstrations, only to be repeated the following year—and it sometimes seems as if there is little common ground among people with opposing views. Two of the three Baltic presidents took a stand against the official Russian view of World War II, a view that is embraced by many Baltic Russians, by declining Putin's invitation to attend the V-E Day

60th anniversary summit in Moscow in May 2005. Only Vaira Vīķe-Freiberga attended, but in doing so the Latvian president felt compelled to write an editorial in which she lamented the impact of Russia's refusal to own up to its history of aggression against its neighbors:

> After the war, Germany made great efforts to atone for the unspeakable crimes committed under the Nazi regime. This process began with an honest evaluation of the country's Nazi-era history and continued with Germany's unequivocal renunciation of its totalitarian past. Russia would gain immensely by acting in a similar manner and by expressing its genuine regret for the crimes of the Soviet regime. Until Russia does so, it will continue to be haunted by the ghosts of its past, and its relations with its immediate neighbors will remain uneasy at best.[25]

Likewise, when asked about the future of Estonian-Russian relations in early 2006, Toomas Hendrik Ilves, Estonia's former foreign minister and soon-to-be president, replied:

> As long as Russia fails to come to terms with Estonian independence, or, on a greater scale, the "greatest tragedy of the 20th century," Mr. Putin's characterization of the collapse of the USSR, I doubt we will see much of a change. This has little to do with Estonia. We see Russia treat Poland, Ukraine, [and] Georgia in exactly the same neurotic way that has more to do with its own inability to deal with its past than anything Estonia has or has not done.[26]

Six months after he took office, President Ilves faced a major crisis in Estonian-Russian relations when the Estonian government decided to relocate a Soviet war memorial situated in the center of Tallinn.[27] Erected in 1947 by the Soviet regime, the Monument to the Liberators of Tallinn commemorated the Red Army soldiers who conquered the city at the end of World War II. The site's sacralized nature was reinforced in later years by the reburying of soldiers near the monument, to which an "eternal flame" was added in 1964. While the monument had survived the removal of Soviet-era monuments that took place in the Baltic states and in other former communist countries, Estonian authorities decided to rename it the Bronze Soldier and extinguish its eternal flame. For Estonians the statue symbolized their national tragedy; for Russians it was a symbol of shared suffering during the Great Patriotic War, the Russian name for World War II.

The decision by Estonian authorities to remove the polarizing statue was preceded by a series of incidents involving the erection

The Monument to the Liberators of Tallinn, popularly known as the Bronze Soldier, was erected in 1947 to commemorate the fallen soldiers of the Soviet Red Army during its struggle against Nazi Germany. Following a riot in April 2007, the polarizing monument was relocated to the outskirts of the city. (AFP/Getty Images)

of controversial war monuments and the desecration of others. Now it was decided to ban all displays of Soviet symbols, including those commemorating the Great Patriotic War. On the evening of April 26, 2007, a largely Russian-speaking crowd began protesting the exhumation of the soldiers buried underneath the Bronze Soldier that had begun that morning, but soon the protest turned into vandalism and looting while the surprised government held an emergency meeting at which it was decided to move the monument immediately in order to forestall even worse disturbances. What followed was a full-scale crisis in Tallinn, as the statue's removal prompted two nights of rioting and escalated tensions between the Estonian and Russian governments.

While the Kremlin denounced the move, state-controlled Russian media exacerbated the situation with its misrepresentations of the events surrounding the monument's relocation away from the city center. Over the following days and weeks Estonia fell victim to a cyber-attack that disabled the country's entire Internet structure (observers pointed to Russia, which denied the charges), while the Russian youth group *Nashi* ("Ours") blockaded the Estonian embassy in Moscow for a week. The incident also had economic repercussions, as a Russian boycott of Estonian goods was accompanied by a significant decline in Russian oil transit through Estonia—a threat not only to Estonia, but to other European countries dependent on Russian energy supplies. As the disturbances dissipated, the statue was reerected in a military cemetery on the outskirts of the city, where members of the Estonian government participated in a solemn opening ceremony on May 8, 2008.

The events surrounding the removal of the Bronze Soldier, like the controversial commemorative events in Latvia, demonstrate how far apart nationalists on both ends of the ethnic continuum remain in the Baltic states. Yet the recurrence of such incidents may also suggest that it is not only the independence of the Baltic states that Russia and many local Russian-speakers find so unnerving: it is the *Europeanization* of the former Soviet republics that is at the heart of the matter. Independence was one thing, but the integration of the Baltic states into NATO, the EU, and other Western institutions over which Russia exercised little influence was a slap at Russia's pretensions to "great power" status.

Russia's troubled relationships with the Baltic states can best be appreciated by considering its even more troubled relationships with certain other former Soviet republics, notably Georgia and Ukraine, where political disagreements that partly concern the ex-Soviet states' ties to the West have escalated to the point of armed conflict. During the presidency of the young, Western-educated, and mercurial Mikheil Sakaashvili (2004–2013), Georgia sought NATO membership as protection from Russia while Tbilisi acted to rein in the breakaway republics of Abkhazia and South Ossetia, both of which were cleansed of Georgians during the 1990s. Rejecting Georgia's push for NATO membership (an ambition that was tacitly encouraged by U.S. officials like Condoleezza Rice), Moscow supported the sovereignty of the breakaway republics with enormous financial subsidies and by issuing their residents Russian passports. After years of simmering, the situation in South Ossetia finally turned hostile in the summer of 2008. Insisting on Russia's right to protect Russians who live abroad, Russian president Dmitri Medvedev (2008–2012) approved the buildup of Russian forces that prompted Sakaashvili to launch a misguided preemptive attack on South Ossetia on the night of August 7–8. If Sakaashvili believed that the West could come to Georgia's defense, or that Russia would be intimidated by that possibility, he was mistaken, for Russia responded with force as the West looked on with caution.

With Georgian forces retreating from South Ossetia after only a few days of fighting, Russia's president ordered an end to military operations. In the aftermath of the conflict, Medvedev laid down five principles that would guide Russia's defense of its national interests. Among them: "[P]rotecting the lives and dignity of our citizens, wherever they may be, is an unquestionable priority for our country. Our foreign policy decisions will be based on this need."[28] Often seen as a liberal foil to former president Vladimir Putin, who was prime minister during the Medvedev presidency, Medvedev was no less committed to protecting Russia's interests in the "near abroad" than his predecessor (who was the same person as his successor).

Still more ominous for the Baltic states were the events that began to develop in Ukraine, another aspirant for membership in Western institutions, in late 2013 when demonstrators took to Kiev's Independence Square (*Maidan*) to protest a decision taken by President Viktor Yanukovych to end the negotiations that would bring about a closer political association between Ukraine and the EU. Unfolding amidst a worsening economic crisis that the Russian government intended to exploit to bind Kiev to Moscow—Russia offered $15 billion in loans to trump the EU's paltry offer of $838 million (€610 million)—the unrest resulted in Yanukovych's ouster in February 2014 by a rebellious Ukrainian parliament. Ignoring the chants of hundreds of thousands of Ukrainians at *Maidan*, the Kremlin insisted that the revolution was engineered by Western governments working in tandem with the "fascists" who had seized power Ukraine.

While enjoying the world's attention as it played host to the elaborately staged Winter Olympic Games in Sochi, Russia began to support "self-defense forces" in Crimea as a prelude to annexing the region to the Russian Federation, which was swiftly accomplished in March 2014. A strategically important peninsula located on the Black Sea, Crimea was, according to Ukraine's 2001 census, populated mostly by Russians (58.5 percent), Ukrainians (24.4 percent), and Crimean Tatars

(10.2 percent). The Russian actions in Crimea, ostensibly motivated by the need to protect ethnic Russians from abuse, prompted local forces in the eastern, mostly Russian, parts of Ukraine to announce on May 16 the formation of a separatist Donetsk People's Republic, which to date has been recognized only by the Russian-backed Republic of South Ossetia. Although Moscow denied aiding the rebels—just as it initially denied having anything to do with events in Crimea—there can be little doubt that the breakaway republic has benefited from Russian military and logistical support. The tremors in Crimea and eastern Ukraine were felt in Lithuania, Latvia, and Estonia, whose leaders were at one with the United States and the EU in declaring Russia to be the culprit.

While Putin, who returned to the presidency in May 2012, appeared to be wary of making a full-scale military commitment to protecting the Donetsk People's Republic, in the summer of 2014 Western countries tried to force the Kremlin to retreat from its Ukrainian adventures by imposing economic sanctions. Russia returned the favor by banning food imports from the United States, Australia, and the countries of the EU—a restriction that posed a greater challenge to the food-exporting countries of eastern European in particular. (As of 2014, Russia was the market for 19 percent of Estonia's food exports; it was also the destination for 22 percent of Lithuania's and 43 percent of Latvia's food exports.) However, the fact is that Europeans, already divided over how to respond to what is believed to be Russian aggression, are more dependent upon energy supplies from Russia than Russia is on food supplies from Europe. If energy is Russia's trump card, then few countries are more vulnerable to potential energy sanctions than the Baltic states, which are not connected to the gas pipelines of other EU states and have no means of accessing non-Russian gas. Estonia, with its tiny population and booming oil shale industry (the second largest after that of China), has some protection against a possible cutoff of Russian energy supplies; the other Baltic states, however, are almost entirely reliant on natural gas and oil from Russia and hence are more vulnerable to Russian sanctions.[29]

While nobody would argue that the Baltic states carry the same weight as Ukraine in the historical consciousness of Russia's political elites, the lesson is clear to all: Russia will protect its national interests and act as a guarantor for the rights of Russians living in the "near abroad." Short of an act of war against Estonia, Latvia, or Lithuania, it is hard to imagine anything else the Kremlin could have done to further cement the ties between the Baltic states and Europe than to snatch Crimea away from Ukraine, encourage a separatist movement in the eastern part of that troubled, divided country, and bellow about the threats to Russians living in neighboring countries while dangling the threat of withholding energy to its customers.

THE EUROPEAN UNION AND NATO

Integration into the economic and security institutions of the West was a goal of Baltic governments almost from the very moment they achieved their independence in the early 1990s. Simple pragmatism dictated that the Baltic states would also have to maintain amicable relations with Russia—after all, Russia, its enormous neighbor to the east, maintained troops and bases in all three Baltic states until 1994—but a consensus quickly emerged that the road to security and prosperity led westward: instead of joining the Commonwealth of Independent States (CIS) that formed after the collapse of the USSR, the Baltic states' new partners would be Poland, Scandinavia, and the countries of the European Union, a supranational organization that was formed on the basis of the existing European Community in November 1993.

Among the Baltic republics, Estonia had the closest relations with Western countries during the Soviet period and reached out to its neighbors with the least hesitation once Moscow reluctantly loosened its grip. A close cultural affinity to Finland and the ties that were cultivated during the Soviet era helped Estonia to attract significant Finnish foreign investment during the early years of independence. By the mid-1990s Swedish investment was even more substantial, while Finland soon emerged as Estonia's largest market and greatest source of imports. By cultivating such ties with its northern neighbors, Estonia sometimes portrayed itself more as a Scandinavian than Baltic country in an attempt to "sell" itself to the West—a tendency that at times irritated some Latvians and Lithuanians.

Nevertheless, Latvia and Lithuania followed a path similar to that of their northern neighbor in the belief that membership in international institutions, above all NATO and the EU, would mean greater stability and security. Even if many west European leaders believed that inviting the Baltic states to join the EU would be the morally correct thing to do, their concerns about the aspirants' domestic stability and economic preparedness meant that the Baltic states' quest for integration into Europe initially got a mixed reception. Moreover, Western countries were concerned about the possible influx of cheap labor from the east (i.e. "Polish plumbers"), which in turn might increase unemployment and depress wages within the EU. On the other hand, some European leaders believed that membership in the EU and other Western institutions might be the best way to ensure that the region would avoid political extremism, ethnic conflict, environmental catastrophes, or a reversion to communism.

Admission to Western institutions was not a given: these would have to be earned by meeting the strict criteria for membership in each of these organizations. European Commission President Jacques Delors warned in the early 1990s that it could take 15 to 20 years before the former communist countries would be ready for membership in the EU. Nevertheless, in June 1993 the European Council in Copenhagen declared the enlargement of the EU to include central and eastern European countries as an explicit goal. Qualified countries, however, would have to meet the "Copenhagen criteria": (1) they would possess stable institutions guaranteeing democracy, the rule of law, human rights, and protections for minorities; (2) they would have functioning market economies and the capacity to manage market competition within the EU; and (3) they must be willing and able to take on the "obligations of membership," which entailed harmonizing legislation, creating a single market, and forging common policies with other member states.[30]

While the Estonians, Latvians, and Lithuanians were now the rulers of their own countries, the external pressure to reform their legal and economic systems was considerable. It was the criticism coming from the West that forced Estonia and Latvia to tame their nationalism specifically by modifying their citizenship requirements. Following a series of visits by Max van der Stoel in 1993, the Conference on Security and Cooperation in Europe's High Commissioner on National Minorities, the Estonian government removed the language condition for certain sectors of the population such as the elderly and disabled people. Likewise, Latvia implemented some of Stoel's recommendations, such as the granting of citizenship to all children born in Latvia.[31] The easing of naturalization procedures for Soviet-era migrants resulted in a greater number of Russian-speakers obtaining citizenship, rendering them eligible to stand and vote in parliamentary elections. It seems unlikely that Latvia and Estonia would have adopted the more minority-friendly policies without European pressure. Russian criticism, on the other hand, counted for little; it was mostly the prospect of gaining membership in the EU that caused the governments to change their legislation.

A particular concern for Lithuania during its EU (and NATO) candidacy was Kaliningrad, a Russian exclave of 950,000 people, which for years after the Soviet collapse remained one of the Russian Federation's most highly militarized regions. In 2002, President Putin demanded that residents of Kaliningrad, which was cut off from the Russian mainland after 1991, be granted visa-free travel across Lithuania to the Russian proper. Lithuanian officials objected to what they saw as a violation of their country's sovereignty, for under this arrangement Lithuania would become a corridor through which Russia could move troops and equipment to and from the *oblast'*. At first the EU refused to make exceptions for those territories that did not belong to the future Schengen Area, comprising those European countries (now numbering 26) that abolished border controls at their common frontiers. In the end, however, Russia and the EU reached a compromise whereby special visas called Facilitated Transit Documents would be issued to those passing through the Schengen Area, including Lithuania, on their way from Kaliningrad to the Russian mainland (and vice-versa).

The populations of the Baltic states were sensitive to the loss of sovereignty that EU membership would entail. What would be the benefit, many asked, of exchanging Moscow's domination for that of Brussels? Euroskeptics were also anxious about higher prices and tax increases; they worried about the ability of local agriculture to compete with European producers. Estonians were particularly concerned about the potential for foreign interference in domestic affairs: in 2002 only 32 percent of the Estonian population favored joining the EU. Lithuanians seemed to be less anxious about the loss of sovereignty, with 48 percent of its citizens polling in favor of joining the EU. If Latvians shared the Estonians' initial skepticism, the promise of economic prosperity weighed more heavily as 67.5 percent of the voting population voted in favor in the referendum on EU membership that was conducted in September 2003.[32] Indeed, the more inevitable future membership in the EU appeared to be, the more the Baltic populations supported it. In Lithuania and Estonia, which conducted their referenda after the other candidate countries had obtained popular consent for EU membership, the results were, respectively, 69 percent and 90 percent in favor of joining.

Since their ascension to the EU on May 1, 2004 (along with Poland, Hungary, the Czech Republic, and four other countries), the Baltic states have been praised for having business-friendly climates and for their economic competitiveness. In 2014, the Heritage Organization's Index of Economic Freedom placed Estonia at number 13 (higher than the United Kingdom, Finland, Germany, Sweden, the Netherlands, and Taiwan), Lithuania at number 22, and Latvia at number 55 among the 177 countries that were ranked (Russia and Ukraine came in at 139 and 161, respectively).[33] Yet the Baltic states' entry into the EU did not happen without controversy and political turbulence, for states that adapt to the EU's regulations become the followers of rules imposed upon them from the outside. As one civil servant remarked of the rules on fisheries to which Lithuania was expected to adapt: "All the new items, such as control, fishing control, common organization of the market, structural issues, they were new to us. So, we had to implement them and we were not able to implement [them] ourselves without help."[34] One of most controversial examples of EU compliance in Lithuania concerned Ignalina, a Chernobyl-type nuclear power plant whose closing encountered fierce opposition from the Lithuanian populace who depended on it for energy and jobs. Unit One was shuttered at the end of 2004, while Unit Two, which continued to supply the majority of the country's electricity, was closed in December 2009. The decommissioning of the power plant, one of Lithuania's few domestic energy resources, also left Lithuania more dependent on Russian oil and natural gas.

Latvia's EU candidacy meant that it had to demonstrate progress in the struggle against the corruption that has blighted a country where successful business leaders called "oligarchs" (among them Aivars Lembergs, Andris Šķēle, and Ainārs Šlesers) parlayed their financial success into political influence while building extensive networks within the government, business, and media that turned a blind eye to their sometimes shady practices. To this end Latvia established the Corruption Prevention and Combatting Bureau (KNAB) in 2002, which investigated high-level graft and violations of campaign finance laws. When acting Prime Minister Aigars Kalvītis tried to dismiss KNAB's director, citizens rallied in central Riga in support of the agency, forcing the minister to resign at the end of 2007. As noted earlier, another antigovernment demonstration broke out in January 2009 in response to unpopular austerity measures and once again the focus of popular anger was the oligarchs who pulled the country's political and economic strings. The *Saeima*'s refusal to comply with a KNAB investigator's request to lift the parliamentary immunity of Ainārs Šlesers, the subject of a corruption investigation, sparked a full-scale crisis in 2011 that settled down only when President Zatlers dissolved the parliament prior to September's parliamentary elections, which saw the evisceration of the parties associated with the oligarchs. While it is possible that the Latvian government would have acted to tackle official corruption even without outside incentives—that is, to demonstrate its readiness for ascension into the EU—the reality is that corruption was generally seen as a given and it was only when the World Bank recommended that Latvia create an agency empowered to fight corruption that the government began to commit itself to meaningful reform.[35]

While EU requirements forced the Estonian, Latvian, and Lithuanian states to close down dangerous power plants, tackle high-level corruption, and enact reforms in a number of other areas as well, economic liberalization and integration into the EU also meant an influx of foreign investment that undermined local control over key sectors of the economy. In all three countries Scandinavian banks took over the financial sector: by 2006 some 60 percent of Latvia's financial sector was foreign owned; in Lithuania and Estonia it was more than 90 percent.[36] Optimistic about the impact of the Baltic states' integration into the EU, Scandinavian banks offered very low interest rates to the Baltic populations, which in turn fed a speculative housing market as private sector debt tripled in all three Baltic states between 2000 and 2008. As the Baltic states became attractive destinations for foreign investment, foreign money flooded the real estate market and inflated housing costs, profits, and wages, which in turn likely contributed to the severity of the financial crash's impact in the Baltic states.

Nevertheless, since 2011 the economies of Estonia, Latvia, and Lithuania have rebounded impressively and have been among Europe's most vigorous. Optimists may be able to convince themselves that this kind of growth is sustainable, yet a sober examination of the Baltic states' demographic trends—all three have ageing work forces and declining populations—makes it exceedingly difficult to imagine their economies continuing to grow at such rates. Meanwhile, all three have entered the Euro zone, with Estonia adopting the common currency on January 1, 2011, Latvia in 2014, and Lithuania in 2015, thereby completing a transition that has taken nearly a quarter century.

If entry into the economic institutions of the West initially encountered some skepticism among the Baltic populations, accession to NATO was almost universally hailed by the Baltic political classes (except Russian-speakers and those on the far left) as essential for their future security. Few outside Russia remember how controversial a proposition this was in the 1990s, when the former communist countries of east central Europe began to ready themselves for entry into an alliance that was founded as an explicitly anti-Soviet institution of collective security. Even the U.S. diplomat and historian George Kennan, who is credited with formulating the West's "containment" doctrine at the dawn of the Cold War, warned against an enlargement of NATO that, being neither "necessary nor desirable," was certain to provoke Moscow and likely to result, eventually, in a return to authoritarianism in Russia and a new cold war.[37]

If an irritated Kremlin reluctantly acquiesced to the admission of the central European states (Poland, Hungary, the Czech Republic) to

The presidents of the Baltic states (from left to right: Toomas Hendrik Ilves of Estonia, Andris Bērziņš of Latvia, and Dalia Grybauskaitė of Lithuania) meet with U.S. president Barack Obama on September 3, 2014, in Tallinn, Estonia, just prior to the NATO Summit in Wales, United Kingdom. (AP Photo/Charles Dharapak)

NATO, the Baltic states were a different story. The prospect of Lithuania joining the alliance caused Russian officials and generals to suggest that Russia might be forced to deploy tactical nuclear weapons in the neighboring Russian exclave Kaliningrad, which would then be surrounded by NATO states.[38] But Russia has never made the region into a nuclear threat; nor has there been a heavy redeployment of Russian troops to the region.

Aside from Russia's very serious objections and the lack of enthusiasm on the part of France and Germany, there were still other obstacles to the Baltic states' being admitted to NATO. One of them, the history of antagonism between Lithuania and Poland, was resolved with the signing of the Lithuanian-Polish Friendship Treaty in 1994. Still, questions remained. What would these small states bring to the alliance? Would the Baltic countries simply be consumers of security or would they be able to make substantial contributions to the defense of the alliance? Moreover, NATO countries spend on average about 2 percent of their GDP on defense: would the Baltic states be able to reach and maintain this standard?

During their campaign to gain acceptance for their states' entry into NATO, Baltic leaders insisted that they were dedicated to increasing and improving their defense capabilities. They had already demonstrated their commitment to regional cooperation—something they failed to do in the 1930s—by forming BALTBAT (1994), a combined infantry battalion, BALTRON (1997), a joint naval squadron, and BALTNET (1996), a coordinated Baltic air surveillance network. During this period the Baltic militaries worked to bring their forces in line with NATO standards while participating in the latter's Partnership for Peace program when it was launched in 1994. This allowed the Baltic states to participate in joint planning, training, and exercises with NATO military forces, including NATO peacekeeping operations in Bosnia and Kosovo. Such efforts were rewarded in November 2002 when it was announced at the Prague Summit that seven countries (Bulgaria, Estonia, Latvia, Lithuania, Romania, Slovakia, and Slovenia) had been invited to begin the negotiations that would lead to their accession to NATO. Sixteen months later, on May 1, 2004, the Baltic states became three of NATO's newest members—a development that prompted criticism from Russia and outpourings of relief and gratitude from Baltic politicians.

Although the current defense defending of Latvia (0.9 percent of GDP) and Lithuania (0.8 percent) falls short of the 2 percent prescribed by NATO, all three Baltic states have been active supporters of U.S. security efforts in Europe and elsewhere, contributing small forces to the U.S.-led wars in Iraq and Afghanistan. Baltic leaders likewise view the United States' presence in Europe as essential to the continent's security. While the U.S. commitment to Europe's defense is hardly in doubt, its military presence declined during the administration of Barack Obama, who took office in January 2009. Later that year the United States scrapped its plans to install missile-defense complexes in the Czech Republic and Poland, and in 2013 it withdrew its last remaining battle tanks from Germany. At a time when Washington was distracted by the ongoing turmoil in the Middle East, terrorism in North Africa, and uncertainty in Afghanistan, the Obama administration hoped to ease the growing tensions with Moscow by touting a "reset" of their relationship—a policy that was greeted with considerable skepticism by its domestic critics and those in the Baltic states.

However, in 2014 the Russian-Ukrainian conflict caused the Obama administration to once again reassess its relationship with Russia and consequently to strengthen its commitment to Europe. While at that time the United States maintained only a small fraction of the forces it had once stationed in Europe, Washington reassured states that felt threatened by potential Russian aggression by bolstering U.S. defense forces in east central Europe and rotating more ground and naval forces for training and exercises in Poland and the Baltic countries. Since 2004 NATO has carried out Baltic air patrols from a former Soviet base near Šiauliai in Lithuania. NATO's presence in the region further increased when the Estonian government agreed in the spring of 2014 to let it conduct its Baltic Air Policing patrols at Ämari Air Base near Tallinn. Latvian officials have been particularly vocal in calling for the establishment of permanent NATO bases in the Baltic states—a proposition that has caused some disagreement among the allies. Although Germany's president Angela Merkel, who did much to raise Germany's profile in international affairs during the early decades of the 21st century, has repeatedly reassured the Baltic governments that NATO is committed to their defense, she has opposed the establishment of NATO military bases or any long-term deployment of NATO troops in the eastern Baltic region. All would agree, however, with Latvian prime minister Laimdota Straujuma's assertion that Russia's actions in Ukraine had "fundamentally changed the security environment in Europe."[39]

The world has changed dramatically since the Baltic states were absorbed by the Soviet Union at the end of World War II. Few at that time could have imagined that half a century later Moscow's empire would disappear and that Germany, having been reduced to rubble and shamed before the entire world, would thoroughly rehabilitate its reputation as it peacefully took its place at the center of European political and economic life. Only the most optimistic Baltic patriots could have envisioned a free Estonia, a free Latvia, and a free Lithuania in the protective embrace of a united Western world. Perhaps least of all could one have imagined amidst the rubble of 1945—*Stunde Null* in Germany, the moment when Stalin was at the height of his powers and an Iron Curtain was soon to descend across the continent—a summit of Western leaders taking place in a Baltic capital, as happened in Riga in late November 2006. "As NATO allies," U.S. president George W. Bush told the assembled guests at the Grand Hall of the University of Latvia, "you will never again stand alone in defense of your freedom and you'll never be occupied by a foreign power."

As in all things, history will be the final judge.

NOTES

1. The National Coalition Party Pro Patria was founded in 1992 and led by the young historian Mart Laar, who served as the country's prime minister from 1992 to 1994 and again from 1999 to 2002.

2. Lithuania was the only one of the three Baltic states in which an ethnic minority party, the Union of Lithuanian Poles, was represented in the

parliament following the first post-Soviet elections. In general, however, ethno-national parties have had limited electoral success in Lithuania as Polish and Russian politicians have sought to cooperate with mainstream Lithuanian parties.

3. Central Intelligence Agency, *The World Factbook,* entries for Estonia, Latvia, and Lithuania, https://www.cia.gov/library/publications/the-world-factbook/ (accessed August 5, 2014); Ellus Saar and Marge Unt, "Falling High: Structure and Agency in Agriculture during the Transformation," *Journal of Baltic Studies* 41, no. 2 (June 2010): 220.

4. Dorothee Bohle and Béla Greskovits, *Capitalist Diversity on Europe's Periphery* (Ithaca, NY: Cornell University Press, 2012), 124–31.

5. Toivo U. Raun, *Estonia and the Estonians,* 2nd ed. (Stanford, CA: Hoover Institution Press, 2001), 255.

6. "External trade of Lithuania," Baltic Export, http://balticexport.com/?article=lietuvas-areja-tirdznieciba (accessed August 5, 2014).

7. "Last year exports of goods grew moderately," Statistics Estonia, February 11, 2013, http://www.stat.ee/65312 (accessed August 5, 2014).

8. "Foreign Trade Statistics," Investment and Development Agency of Latvia, http://www.liaa.gov.lv/trade-latvia/foreign-trade-statistics (accessed August 5, 2014).

9. Anders Åslund, *The Last Shall Be First: The East European Financial Crisis, 2008–10* (Washington, DC: Peterson Institute for International Economics, 2010), 35–38. The amount the Latvian government actually borrowed from the IMF was considerably smaller (€4.5 billion), and it was repaid by 2012.

10. Doug Bandow, "The Triumph of Good Economics: 'Austere' Baltic States Outgrow Their European Neighbors," *Forbes,* April 15, 2013, http://www.forbes.com/sites/dougbandow/2013/04/15/the-triumph-of-good-economics-austere-baltic-states-outgrow-their-european-neighbors/ (accessed August 20, 2014).

11. Richard C.M. Mole, *The Baltic States from the Soviet Union to the European Union* (London and New York: Routledge, 2012), 123.

12. The radar installation was blown up on the orders of Latvian authorities on May 4, 1995. The fascinating history of Skrunda is well told by Māris Goldmanis, whose blog *Latvian History,* written from a Latvian nationalist perspective, is a treasure trove for anyone interested in the modern history of that country. "Skrunda Soviet Radar Station," March 2, 2013, http://latvianhistory.com/2013/03/02/skrunda-soviet-radar-station/ (accessed August 19, 2014).

13. "Mart Laar: Meri and Yeltsin bargained over the treaties like at a bazaar in Bukhara," *Postimees,* July 25, 2014, http://news.postimees.ee/2868095/mart-laar-meri-and-yeltsin-bargained-over-the-treaties-like-at-a-bazaar-in-bukhara (accessed August 19, 2014).

14. Mole, 132.

15. Dovile Budryte, *Taming Nationalism? Political Community Building in the Post-Soviet Baltic States* (Burlington, VT: Ashgate, 2005), 161–70.

16. Mole, 83.

17. Priit Järve and Vadim Poleshchuk, "Country Report: Estonia," EUDO Citizen Observatory (January 2013), http://eudo-citizenship.eu/docs/CountryReports/Estonia.pdf (accessed August 6, 2014).

18. Budryte, 9.

19. Dual citizenship was forbidden to those who wish to become naturalized citizens in all three Baltic states, largely due to the fear that dual citizenship would allow Russia to take measures to "protect" its citizens in those countries. This prohibition forced Valdas Adamkus, who would serve as Lithuania's president from 1998 to 2003 and from 2004 to 2009, to renounce his U.S. citizenship in 1998 after a legal battle in Lithuania's courts. Lithuania changed its law in 2002 in such a manner that would allow ethnic Lithuanians residing in another state to retain their Lithuanian citizenship. Budryte, 152.

20. Igor Zevelev, *Russia and Its New Diasporas* (Washington, DC: United States Institute of Peace Press, 2001), 131–58.

21. Kristine Krūma, "Country Report: Latvia," EUDO Citizen Observatory (February 2013), http://eudo-citizenship.eu/docs/CountryReports/Latvia.pdf (accessed August 6, 2014).

22. "What's My Language?" *The Economist*, February 14, 2012, http://www.economist.com/blogs/easternapproaches/2012/02/latvias-referendum (accessed August 13, 2014).

23. "Vote on Russian Language in Latvia an 'Incitement'—Berzins," *RIA Novosti*, January 17, 2012, http://en.ria.ru/society/20120117/170808891.html (accessed August 19, 2014).

24. In June 1997, members of the radical Latvian nationalist organization *Pērkonkrusts*, a revival of an interwar organization of the same name, even tried (and failed) to blow up the monument at the center of Victory Park—an act of terrorism that justly prompted the condemnation of Latvia's Russophone community.

25. Vaira Vike-Freiberga, "Rights and Remembrance," *The Washington Post*, May 7, 2005, http://www.washingtonpost.com/wp-dyn/content/article/2005/05/06/AR2005050601217.html (accessed August 13, 2014).

26. "There is no such thing as a 'Baltic interest'," *The Baltic Times*, March 1, 2006.

27. Martin Ehala, "The Bronze Soldier: Identity Threat and Maintenance in Estonia," *Journal of Baltic Studies* 40, no. 1 (March 2009): 139–58; Marko Lehti, et al., "Never-Ending Second World War: Public Performances of National Dignity and the Drama of the Bronze Soldier," *Journal of Baltic Studies* 39, no. 4 (December 2008): 393–418. The contests over historical memory are also discussed in several chapters in the edited collection by Eiki Berg and Piret Ehin, *Identity and Foreign Policy: Baltic-Russian Relations and European Integration* (Burlington, VT: Ashgate, 2009).

28. "Interview given by Dmitry Medvedev to Television Channels Channel One, Rossia, NTV," President of Russia, August 31, 2008,

http://archive.kremlin.ru/eng/speeches/2008/08/31/1850_type829 12type82916_206003.shtml (accessed August 17, 2014).

29. The construction of Nord Stream, a natural gas pipeline that runs from Vyborg in Russia under the Baltic Sea to Germany, bypassing the Baltic states and eastern Europe, rendered the Baltic states still more vulnerable to Russian pressure, as it allows Moscow to threaten their energy supplies without affecting its west European markets.

30. John Van Oudenaren, "EU Enlargement: The Return to Europe." In *Europe Today: National Politics, European Integration, and European Security,* ed. Ronald Tiersky (Lanham, MD: Lexington Books, 2004), 125.

31. Mole, 91.

32. Ibid., 161–62.

33. "2014 Index of Economic Freedom." The Heritage Foundation, http://www.heritage.org/index/ranking (accessed August 20, 2014).

34. Jenny Svensson, "Governance through Mediation: EU Twinning in Lithuania." In *The European Union and the Baltic States: Changing Forms of Governance,* ed. Bengt Jacobsson (London and New York: Routledge, 2010), 68.

35. Gabriel Kuris, "Surmounting State Capture: Latvia's Anti-Corruption Agency Spurs Reform, 2002–2011," *Innovations for Successful Societies,* http://www.princeton.edu/successfulsocieties/content/data/policy_ note/PN_id215/Policy_Note_ID215.pdf (accessed August 20, 2014).

36. "The Baltic States in the EU: Yesterday, Today and Tomorrow," *Notre Europe,* http://www.notre-europe.eu/media/balticstateseu-grig askasekampmaslauskaitezorgenfreija-ne-jdi-july13.pdf?pdf=ok (accessed August 20, 2014).

37. Richard Ullman, "The US and the World: An Interview with George Kennan," *The New York Review of Books,* August 12, 1999, http://www.ny books.com/articles/archives/1999/aug/12/the-us-and-the-world-an-interview-with-george-kenn/ (accessed August 25, 2014).

38. Richard J. Krickus, *The Kaliningrad Question* (Lanham, MD: Rowman & Littlefield, 2002), 3.

39. "Merkel Pledges NATO Will Defend Baltic Member States," *The Baltic Times,* August 18, 2014.

Notable People in the History of the Baltic States

Adamkus, Valdas (b. 1926) President of Lithuania, 1998–2003 and 2004–2009.

Barons, Krišjānis (1835–1923) Hero of the Latvian national awakening and a revered collector of Latvian folk songs.

Basanavičius, Jonas (1851–1927) Priest, physician, and editor of *Aušra* (The Dawn); leader of the Lithuanian national awakening and a founder of the Republic of Lithuania in 1918.

Berklavs, Eduards (1914–2004) Communist official in Soviet Latvia who was purged from the leadership in 1959 for his opposition to unfavorable Soviet policies.

Brazauskas, Algirdas (1932–2010) Communist reformer during the *perestroika* era; President of Lithuania 1993–1998 and prime minister 2001–2006.

Buxhoevden, Albert von (c. 1165–1229) Third bishop of Livonia, founder of Riga, and a leader of the Baltic crusades.

Čakste, Jānis (1859–1927) Pre–World War I lawyer and activist and the first president of Latvia, 1922 to 1927.

Daukantas, Simon (1793–1864) Lithuanian writer and historian of the Romantic era.

Faehlmann, Friedrich Robert (1808–1850) Folklorist and founder of the Learned Estonian Society.

Gediminas (c. 1275–1341) Grand duke responsible for Lithuania's dramatic expansion during the 14th century.

Henry of Livonia (d. 1227) Catholic priest and author of an important medieval chronicle.

Herder, Johann Gottfried (1744–1803) Pastor and teacher at the Riga Dom School; promoted the idea of language as the basis of nationhood.

Hurt, Jakob (1839–1907) Collector of folk songs and ideologist of Estonia's national awakening.

Ilves, Toomas Hendrik (b. 1953) Pro-European president of Estonia since 2006.

Jannsen, Johann (1819–1890) Editor of the newspapers *Perno Postimees* (The Pärnu Courier) and *Eesti Postimees* (The Estonian Courier) during the Estonian national awakening.

Jogaila (1348–1434) Lithuanian grand duke (1386–1392) and king of Poland (1392–1434); his acceptance of Christianity in 1386 ended Lithuania's status as the only remaining non-Christian country in Europe.

Käbin, Johannes (1905–1999) Russian-born Estonian first secretary of the Estonian Communist Party from 1950 to 1978.

Kalnbērziņš, Jānis (1893–1986) First secretary of the Communist Party of Latvia from 1936 to 1959; victim of the 1959 purge that targeted "bourgeois nationalists."

Kettler, Gotthard (1517–1587) Last ruler of the Livonian Order and first Duke of Courland and Semigallia.

Kettler, Jacob (1610–1682) Duke of Courland and Semigallia and ruler of a small commercial empire that included colonies in Gambia and Tobago.

Koidula, Lydia (1843–1886) Poet, playwright, and newspaper editor during the Estonian national awakening.

Kreutzwald, Friedrich (1803–1882) Compiler of the Estonian national epic, *Kalevipoeg* (Son of Kalev).

Laar, Mart (b. 1960) Prime minister of Estonia 1992–1994 and 1999–2002; oversaw the privatization of Estonia's economy during the 1990s.

Landsbergis, Vytautas (b. 1932) Musicologist and head of *Sajūdis*, the movement which spearheaded the drive toward Lithuanian independence; chairman of the Supreme Council, 1990–1992; speaker of the *Seimas*, 1996–2000.

Meri, Lennart (1929–2006) President of the Republic of Estonia from 1992 to 2001.

Merkel, Garlieb (1796–1850) Baltic German writer whose works were among the first to draw attention to the plight of the Latvian and Estonian peasantry.

Mindaugas (d. 1263) Lithuanian monarch who unified the Lithuanian tribes during the Baltic crusades.

Päts, Konstantin (1874–1956) A founder of the first Estonian Republic; headed an authoritarian government from 1934 to 1940.

Plettenberg, Wolter von (c. 1450–1535) Master of the Livonian Order and ruler of the Livonian Confederation during a period of heightened religious and political conflict.

Pumpurs, Andrejs (1841–1902) Wrote *Lāčplēsis* (The Bear-Slayer), an epic poem drawn from Latvian mythology.

Rüütel, Arnold (b. 1928) Soviet-era politician who became the second post-Soviet president of Estonia (2001–2006).

Savisaar, Edgar (b. 1950) A founder of the Popular Front of Estonia; prime minister 1991–1992 and mayor of Tallinn since 2007.

Schiemann, Paul (1876–1944) Baltic German journalist and activist who promoted minority rights in interwar Latvia.

Smetona, Antanas (1874–1944) A founder of the Lithuanian Republic; head of an authoritarian government from 1926 to 1940.

Sniečkus, Antanas (1903–1974) First secretary of the Communist Party of Lithuania, 1927 to 1974.

Stender, Gotthard Friedrich (1714–1796) Baltic German whose works on Latvian grammar and language greatly influenced the development of Latvian literature.

Stučka, Pēteris (1865–1932) A leader of the Latvian Social Democratic Workers' Party and head of Latvia's Soviet government in 1918–1919.

Stulginskis, Aleksandras (1885–1969) President of the first Lithuanian Republic from 1920 to 1926.

Tõnisson, Jaan (1868–1941?) Editor of the first Estonian daily, *Postimees* (The Courier); a founder of the Estonian Republic and one of its outstanding political figures.

Ulmanis, Guntis (b. 1939) President of Latvia, 1993 to 1999.

Ulmanis, Kārlis (1877–1942) A founder of the Latvian Republic; headed a popular dictatorship from 1934 to 1940.

Valančius, Motiejus (1801–1875) Bishop of Samogitia and activist during the early years of the Lithuanian national awakening.

Valdemārs, Krišjānis (1825–1891) Economist and editor of *Pēterburgas avīzes* (St. Petersburg Newspaper) during the Latvian national awakening.

Vīķe-Freiberga, Vaira (b. 1937) Academic at the University of Montreal, 1965 to 1998; President of Latvia 1999–2007; the first woman president of any Baltic state.

Voldemaras, Augustinas (1883–1942) Nationalist leader who was a key figure in the establishment of an authoritarian government in Lithuania in 1926.

Voss, Augusts (1916–1994) Brezhnev-era first secretary of the Estonian Communist Party from 1966 to 1984.

Vytautas (1350–1430) Lithuanian grand duke (1392–1430) who defeated the Teutonic Knights in the Battle of Tannenberg (Grünwald).

Bibliographic Essay

Much has been written about Baltic history since the first edition of this book was published in 2003. Readers should begin with Andres Kasekamp's *A History of the Baltic States* (New York: Palgrave Macmillan, 2010) and Andrejs Plakans's *A Concise History of the Baltic States* (New York: Cambridge University Press, 2011). Written by two of the leading historians in the field, each offers a lively and informative overview of the region's general historical experience. Also of general interest is Matti Klinge's *The Baltic World* (Keuruu, Finland: Ostava, 1995).

Some of the best histories of the Baltic countries focus on the individual experiences of Estonia, Latvia, or Lithuania. The standard English-language work on Estonia has long been Toivo Raun's *Estonia and the Estonians* (Stanford, CA: Hoover Institution Press, 1987, 2001), which focuses primarily on the 20th century. The richly-illustrated *History of Estonia* (Tallinn: Avita, 2004), by a team of Estonian writers headed by Ain Mäesalu, is a lovely book that is well worth seeking out.

For Latvia the standard English-language work is Andrejs Plakans's *The Latvians: A Short History* (Stanford, CA: Hoover Institution Press, 1995). A detailed and unapologetically nationalist take on Latvia's modern history is *History of Latvia: The 20th Century,* 2nd ed.

(Riga: Jumava, 2006) by Daina Bleiere, Ilgvars Butulis, Inesis Feld-
manis, Aivars Stranga, and Antonijs Zunda. Certain older volumes on
Latvian history, namely *A History of Latvia* (Westport, CT: Greenwood
Press, 1951), by the Latvian statesman and scholar Alfred Bilmanis,
and *History of Latvia: An Outline* (Stockholm: M. Goppers, 1951) by
the Latvian historian Arnolds Spekke, remain engaging and still quite
useful, but neither makes any pretensions to objectivity. Also of interests is Tadeušs Puisāns's detailed book of more recent vintage, *The
Emerging Nation: The Path of Agonizing Development from Baltic Tribalism to Latvian Nationhood* (Riga: Centre of Baltic-Nordic History and
Political Studies, 1995), which focuses on the decades before Latvia
secured its independence in 1920.

Among the general works on Lithuanian history, Alfred Erich
Senn's classic *The Emergence of Modern Lithuania* (New York: Columbia University Press, 1959) holds up well, and the lengthier *Lithuania:
700 Years* (New York: Manyland Books, 1969), edited by Albertas
Gerutis, is useful if thoroughly anti-Soviet. Works by the late
V. Stanley Vardys also make significant contributions, including *Lithuania: The Rebel Nation* (Boulder, CO: Westview Press, 1997), coauthored
by Judith B. Sedaitis. A compelling account of Lithuania's early history
is S.C. Rowell's *Lithuania Ascending: A Pagan Empire within East-Central
Europe, 1295–1345* (New York: Cambridge University Press, 1994),
while Zigmantas Kiaupa's *The History of Lithuania before 1795* (Vilnius:
Lithuanian Institute of History, 2002) and Daniel Stone's *The Polish-
Lithuanian State, 1386–1795* (Seattle: University of Washington Press,
2001) take the reader up to the end of Lithuania's first era of statehood.
Among the more intriguing recent works is Tomas Balkelis's *The Making
of Modern Lithuania* (New York: Routledge, 2009), which concerns the
formation of the Lithuanian nation.

The literature on the Jewish experience in Lithuania is abundant.
Among the best general works are Masha Greenbaum's thorough
The Jews of Lithuania: A History of a Remarkable Community 1316–1945
(Jerusalem: Gefen, 1995) and Dov Levin's nicely illustrated volume,
The Litvaks: A Short History of the Jews in Lithuania (Jerusalem: Yad
Vashem, 2000).

For the earliest periods of Baltic history and prehistory, see Endre
Bojtár's *Foreword to the Past: A Cultural History of the Baltic People* (Budapest: Central European Press, 1999). Although some of the views
it expresses are dated, Marija Gimbutas's classic, *The Balts* (New
York: Frederick A. Praeger, 1963), remains noteworthy. On the German conquest of the Baltic region, see William Urban's *The Baltic
Crusade* (DeKalb, IL: Northern Illinois University Press, 1975), Eric

Christiansen's *The Northern Crusades: The Baltic and Catholic Frontier, 1100–1525* (New York: Penguin, 1997), and the outstanding collection of essays in Alan V. Murray, ed., *The Clash of Cultures on the Medieval Baltic Frontier* (London: Ashgate, 2009). Philippe Dollinger's *The German Hansa* (Stanford, CA: Stanford University Press, 1970) provides an overview of the region's economy during the Middle Ages.

Edward C. Thaden's *Russia's Western Borderlands, 1710–1870* (Princeton, NJ: Princeton University Press, 1984) is an excellent study of the Russian Empire's Baltic provinces. While another book edited by Thaden, *Russification in the Baltic Provinces and Finland, 1855–1914* (Princeton, NJ: Princeton University Press, 1981) features chapters by several top historians on the Baltic region, readers should also see Theodore Weeks's fine monograph *Nation and State in Late Imperial Russia: Nationalism and Russification on the Western Frontier, 1863–1914* (DeKalb, IL: Northern Illinois University Press, 1996).

On the establishment of the modern Baltic states Stanley Page's *The Formation of the Baltic States* (Cambridge, MA: Harvard University Press, 1959) remains a standard work. However, the English-language literature on the Baltic states during their first period of independence remains limited. The volume by Georg von Rauch, a Baltic German, titled *The Baltic States: The Years of Independence. Estonia, Latvia, Lithuania, 1917–1940* (Berkeley and Los Angeles: University of California Press, 1974), is still a leading account. Also see the edited collection by V. Stanley Vardys and Romuald J. Misiunas, *The Baltic States in Peace and War, 1917–1945* (University Park and London: The Pennsylvania State University Press, 1978). John Hiden's and Patrick Salmon's *The Baltic Nations and Europe: Estonia, Latvia, and Lithuania in the Twentieth Century* (London and New York: Longman, 1991) is an informative guide to the Baltic region's position in European diplomacy during the interwar period. With regard to interwar Lithuania see the collection edited by Alfonsas Eidintas, Vytautas Žalys, and Alfred Erich Senn, *Lithuania in European Politics: The Years of the First Republic, 1918–1940* (New York: St. Martin's Press, 1988).

Valdis O. Lumans's *Latvia in World War II* (New York: Fordham University Press, 2006) offers a thorough analysis of Latvia's experience during World War II. Memoirs of the war and the subsequent flight from the Soviet occupation have in recent years become something of a cottage industry, with Latvian authors producing many of the volumes that have appeared in English. These include *Walking since Daybreak: A Story of Eastern Europe, World War II, and the Heart of Our Century* (New York: Mariner Books, 1999) by Modris Eksteins, *The Amber Coast: A Latvian Family's Journey* (Taramac, FL: Llumis Press,

2010) by Ilse Zandstra, and Jane E. Cunningham's *The Rings of My Tree: A Latvian Woman's Journey* (Taramac, FL: Llumis Press, 2004). Readers of the brief autobiographies compiled in *Estonian Life Stories* (Budapest and New York: Central European University Press, 2009) will come away with much greater insight into the Estonian experience during the mid-20th century.

A number of memoirs of the Holocaust years are also available. Among the most compelling are Solly Ganor, *Light One Candle: A Survivor's Tale: From Lithuania to Jerusalem* (New York: Kodansha America, 1995), Harry Gordon, *The Shadow of Death: The Holocaust in Lithuania* (Lexington: The University Press of Kentucky, 1992), Bernhard Press, *The Murder of the Jews in Latvia, 1941–1945* (Evanston, IL: Northwestern University Press, 2000), and Edwin Anders, *Amidst Latvians during the Holocaust* (Riga: Occupation Museum of Latvia, 2011). Herman Kruk's diary, published as *The Last Days of the Jerusalem of Lithuania: Chronicles from the Vilna Ghetto and the Camps, 1939–44* (New Haven, CT: Yale University Press), is deservedly considered a classic of Holocaust literature.

While academic studies on the Holocaust in the Baltic states were rare before the 1990s, a number of important books have appeared in recent years. These include Andrew Ezergailis, *The Holocaust in Latvia, 1941–1944: The Missing Center* (Riga: The Historical Institute of Latvia, 1996), Andrej Angrick and Peter Klein, *The "Final Solution" in Riga: Exploitation and Annihilation, 1941–44* (New York: Berghahn Books, 2012), Anton Weiss-Wendt, *Murder without Hatred: Estonians and the Holocaust* (Syracuse, NY: Syracuse University Press, 2009), and Karen Sutton, *The Massacre of the Jews of Lithuania* (Jerusalem and New York: Gefen, 2008).

For the Soviet period, *The Baltic States: Years of Dependence 1940–1990* (Berkeley and Los Angeles: University of California Press, 1993), by Romuald Misiunas and Rein Taagepera, is likely to remain the standard work for many years. Useful companion volumes are Tonu Pärming's and Elmar Järvesoo's edited collection, *A Case Study of a Soviet Republic: The Estonian SSR* (Boulder, CO: Westview Press, 1978) and V. Stanley Vardys's *Lithuania Under the Soviets: Portrait of a Nation, 1940–65* (New York: Frederick A. Praeger, 1965). Anu Mai Kõll's *The Village and the Class War: The Anti-Kulak Campaign in Estonia* (New York: Central European University Press, 2013) is a case study in the exercise of Soviet control over the rural population, while Olaf Mertelsmann's *Everyday Life in Stalinist Estonia* (Frankfurt am Main: Peter Lang, 2012) takes a wider view of Stalinist oppression in Estonia. Both the Nazi and Soviet occupations are the topics covered in Andrejs Plakans's edited collection, *Experiencing Totalitarianism: The Invasion and Occupation of Latvia by the USSR and Nazi Germany 1939–1991* (Bloomington, IN: AuthorHouse, 2007).

Anatol Lieven's *The Baltic Revolution: Estonia, Latvia, Lithuania and the Path to Independence* (New Haven, CT: Yale University Press, 1993), is a lively account of the struggle for independence that also contains several interesting and enlightening chapters on the early history of the Baltic peoples. For individual country studies of the independence movements, see Rein Taagepera's *Estonia: Return to Independence* (Boulder, CO: Westview Press, 1993) and Richard J. Krickus's highly readable *Showdown: The Lithuanian Rebellion and the Breakup of the Soviet Empire* (Washington and London: Brassey's, 1997). Vytautas Landbergis's memoir, *Lithuania: Independent Again* (Seattle: University of Washington Press, 2000) is also of interest.

Those interested in more recent developments in the Baltic states will benefit from reading Alvis Purs's *Baltic Facades: Estonia, Latvia and Lithuania since 1945* (London: Reaktion, 2013). Purs, along with David Smith, Artis Pabriks, and Thomas Lane, was also a contributor to the combined volume *The Baltic States: Estonia, Latvia and Lithuania* (New York: Routledge, 2002), which focuses on the 20th century. *Imagining the Nation: History, Modernity, and Revolution in Latvia* (University Park: Pennsylvania State University Press, 2002) by Daina Stukuls Eglitis examines Latvia's postcommunist transition, while Dovile Budryte's *Taming Nationalism? Political Community Building in the Post-Soviet Baltic States* (Burlington, VT: Ashgate, 2005) explores the relationship between the Baltic states and their national minorities since the early 1990s in a broader European context. On the Baltic states' troubled relationship with Russia, see the essays collected in Eiki Berg and Piret Ehin, eds., *Identity and Foreign Policy: Baltic-Russian Relations and European Integration* (Burlington, VT: Ashgate, 2009).

For other topics of historical and contemporary interest, see the quarterly *Journal of Baltic Studies* and the weekly newspaper *The Baltic Times*.

Index

About the Author

KEVIN C. O'CONNOR is Associate Professor of history at Gonzaga University, Spokane, Washington. His published works include Greenwood's *Culture and Customs of the Baltic States* as well as *Intellectuals and Apparatchiks: Russian Nationalism and the Gorbachev Revolution*.

DATE			